MW01028059

iblical
erspectives 15

THE CHRISTIAN
and
ROCK MUSIC

A STUDY ON
BIBLICAL PRINCIPLES
OF MUSIC

Editor
Samuele Bacchiocchi

CONTRIBUTORS
**Samuele Bacchiocchi, Calvin M. Johansson,
Brian Neumann, Eurydice V. Osterman,
Güenter Preuss, Tore Sognefest,
Wolfgang H. M. Stefani**

iblical
erspectives

4990 Appian Way
Berrien Springs
Michigan 49103, USA

TABLE
OF
CONTENTS

Chapter 1
AN OVERVIEW OF
THE MUSIC DEBATE
by
Samuele Bacchiocchi

"To rock or not to rock," this is the critical question rocking many Christian churches today, including an increasing number of Seventh-day Adventist churches. A generation ago there was almost universal agreement that rock music, in whatever version, was inappropriate for personal and church use. At that time, young people who wanted to listen to the "worldly music" had to look for a hiding place, away from the hearing of their parents, teachers, and even some of their friends. Today, if a Christian teenager wants to listen to the same "worldly music"—and in many cases much worse—he can do so with the *encouragement* of his family, church, Christian school, and friends. It is not uncommon to hear rock music blaring out of dormitory rooms in Adventist academies and colleges.

Frankly, I must confess that it was *only* during 1999 that I became aware of the increasing popularity of "Christian" rock in Adventist churches. Some may quip that I must have been living on the moon. Perhaps it is true. I have been so absorbed with my research, writing, and lecturing that I have failed to observe the new musical development in my own Adventist church. This may be partly due also to the fact that until 1999 in my itinerant ministry around the world, I had not been confronted with actual rock bands playing in Adventist churches before I preach. By rock band I mean half a dozen youths playing the standard instruments: amplified electrical guitars, electrical bass, drum set, and keyboard instruments like synthesizers. For the first time I witnessed such bands playing before my preaching during my 1999 speaking engagements in North America and overseas.

At an Adventist youth rally overseas, I witnessed one night for the first time a band of hippie-looking-young people blasting high-decibel, heavy-beat, rock music with pulsating lights, smoke effects, and all the trimmings typical a night club. Nobody could tell what they were singing about because the excessive volume drowned out the words. Truly, it was a shocking experience for me. I felt that I had landed in a night club and not at a place of worship.

A few weeks later I had some similar experiences in Adventist churches in North America. When I shared these experiences with the 7,000-plus subscribers to my "Endtime Issues Newsletter," I received hundreds of email messages from different parts of the world. They all expressed the same concern about rock bands playing inappropriate music in their churches, schools, or youth rallies. Incidentally, to receive the free biweekly newsletter, simply email me your request at: <sbacchiocchi@qtm.net>

The reports coming in from many countries made me forcefully aware of the gravity of the situation. It became evident to me that the adoption of rock types of music is no longer an isolated problem, but a worldwide trend that is gaining momentum in Adventist churches, as in the rest of the Christian world. Many readers of my newsletters encouraged me to address the issue in a book. Initially I was reluctant to do so because I am no authority on music.

Surprisingly, a dozen professional musicians from different parts of the world offered to contribute chapters to this symposium. I took this as a sign that I should move ahead with this project. I decided that I could address the question of rock music from biblical, historical, and ethical perspectives, while competent musicians would examine more directly the musical aspects of rock. The project took off, and by God's grace it was completed in a record time of about six months.

A Needed Clarification. Before proceeding to explain the objectives, procedures, and overall content of this book, it is important to clear the air of possible misconceptions. The aim of this symposium is not to dismiss all contemporary music as "rock." I believe that I speak not only for myself but also for the contributors to this project when I say that there are many contemporary songs with music and words suitable for divine worship.

During the past ten years I have preached in many Adventist churches where small groups lead out in the "Praise Service," using hymns and contemporary songs, which are usually projected on a screen. Some of the songs are trivial and shallow in both tunes and words, but the same is true of some hymns. I can bear a few trivial choruses that repeat the same word ad nauseam, as long as they are not the only repertoire of the church service.

Some of the contemporary songs, however, breathe genuine devotion such as "As the deer pants after the water, so my soul longs for Thee." Both the tune and the words of this song fittingly express the spiritual longing of a sincere soul. So, it would be unfair to label all contemporary songs as "rock." Incidentally, my youngest son, Gianluca, informs me that the song "Welcome Home Children," which we used a few years ago for a special video-recording entitled "Sabbath in Songs," is a contemporary song. This goes to show that I have used contemporary songs in my ministry without even realizing it.

For me, the criterion is not whether a song is old or contemporary but whether its music, words, and manner of singing conform to the biblical principle of worship music. Contrary to prevailing misconceptions, the Bible clearly differentiates between the music used for social entertainment and the music worthy of the worship of God. This vital distinction is brought out in Chapter 7, "Biblical Principles of Music," which is the longest and, most likely, the most important chapter of this book.

Some readers of Chapter 7 will be surprised to discover that in Bible times, the music and instruments associated with social entertainment (which was mostly of a religious nature) were not allowed in the worship service of the Temple, synagogue, and early church. There is no question that God's people in Bible times clearly distinguished between sacred music used for divine worship and secular music employed for social entertainment. Those who deny this fact need to do some homework.

Some contemporary songs conform to the biblical principle of worship music. For example, the song mentioned earlier, "Welcome Home Children," has both a tune and words that speak to my heart when sung reverentially. Listen to the words:

> A great day is coming
> heaven's gates will open wide,
> and all who love the Lord will enter in.
> Joined with our loved ones
> who in Jesus Christ have died
> our eternal life together we'll begin.

It is hard not to be moved by the music and message of this contemporary song. These personal experiences and comments are designed to reassure readers that this book is not written by a "bunch of fanatics" determined to bash all contemporary music as "satanic rock." Our goal is to be constructive and not destructive. We want to help sincere Christians of all persuasions to better understand the biblical principles that should guide us in the choice of music suitable for personal and church use.

Objectives of This Book. This study has two major objectives. The first is to help people understand what makes rock music so different from any other form of music. Why is it that rock music has been the greatest propagator of moral, social, and aesthetic values during the past fifty years? What is it that makes rock music so attractive and irresistible to so many people worldwide, in spite of its revolutionary anti-Christian and countercultural values? Is there something unique in the structure of rock music itself that makes it substantially different and more addictive than any other forms of music? What are the problems in transforming rock music into a medium for Christian worship and evangelism? These important questions are examined in several chapters, as explained below.

The second objective of this study is to ascertain the major biblical principles of music. These principles are formulated in Chapters 6 and 7. The former considers how the unique Seventh-day Adventist beliefs of the Sabbath, Sanctuary, and Second Advent should impact the worship service, including the music. The latter examines the overall teachings of Scripture regarding music. Other chapters contribute in different ways to define biblical principles for making good musical choices.

The introduction is divided in two parts. The first defines the phrases "rock music" and "Contemporary Christian Music (CCM)." Since these two phrases are frequently used throughout this study, we want the reader to know what we mean by them. This section includes also the acknowledgments and an explanation about procedure and style. The second part gives an overview of the major issues we are addressing in this book. This section helps the readers to understand what are some of the important issues of the music controversy.

Part 1
DEFINING THE TERMS

Rock Music. Defining "rock music" is a most difficult task because, as Güenter Preuss explains in Chapter 11 of this book, "during its half-century of existence, it has generated a whole tribe of children and grandchildren. The old 'Stones' are still 'Rolling,' and they have become the literal grandfathers of the newest techno and rap freaks. The old man, called 'Rock 'n' Roll,' married all kinds of famous women who have given birth to milk-and-coffee babies, such as jazz-rock, classic-rock, latin-rock, polit-rock and others.

"No drug has been left untouched leading to psychedelic, acid rock and ecstasy-punched rave parties. Techno freaks claim that 'their' music is a world of its own, not just another 'rock' style. . . . The basic musical elements of rock, including 'Christian' rock, are volume, repetition and beat. It is a music designed not to be heard, but to be felt, to be drowned in. 'Turn on, dive in and drop out,' this is the motto and the effect searched for. . . . The lyrics are secondary to the music. Scientists speak about 'signal listening,' which means that the mention of a word or a short phrase suffices to evoke the topic and to stir up the listener's emotions. Each one of the hundreds of different youth culture groups have their own 'signal vocabulary.'"[1]

Preuss's definition of "rock music" applies specifically to secular rock. In this symposium, however, the phrase "rock music" is often used with a broader meaning. It includes all the music, whether secular or religious, where the rhythm, text, performers, and performance practices imitate rock music and musicians by stimulating people physically rather than elevating them spiritually. In other words, the phrase "rock music" is used in this book with the broad meaning of popular music used today for entertainment, often referred to as "pop music." In fact, in Chapters 9 and 10, Prof. Calvin Johanssen uses the phrase "pop music" as an all-inclusive term for the various versions of secular and religious rock music.

To illustrate my broader definition of "rock music," let me share an experience. I was invited to speak at a church where a rock band of four young men led out in the singing. Something surprising happened when they led out in the singing of "Amazing Grace." It was not long before the whole congregation was in a swinging mood. Some even stepped out of the pews and started dancing on the aisles. It was evident that the way the band was playing the hymn with the typical rock beat had caused the people to forget the words of the hymn, which are not an invitation to dance but to reflect on the amazing grace of God "that saved a wretch like me."

This example serves to illustrate the point that rock music is all pervasive. Sometimes it finds its way even in the singing of traditional hymns. Its impact is *musical* rather than *lyrical*. Many people love to sing even traditional hymns with a rock beat, because such music stimulates them physically. We live today in an entertainment oriented society where people seek for physical gratification everywhere, including the school and the church.

After 35 years of teaching, I can testify that teaching college freshmen is far more challenging today than it was 25 years ago. Young people have become so conditioned by the entertainment world, especially rock music, that if I do not make my lecture "fun," "physically stimulating," about one-third of the class falls asleep right in front of me. There is no satisfaction in teaching a sleeping class. The same is true in the church. The music and the sermon must be entertaining, otherwise members go to worship somewhere else. We shall return to this point shortly.

Contemporary Christian Music. To define "Contemporary Christian Music" (CCM) is just as problematic as defining "rock music" because it comes in a variety of species. We noted earlier that not all CCM is rock music, although the two are often confounded. It is estimated that between 80 to 90 percent of CCM comes in a wide variety of rock styles.[2]

In Chapter 11 Preuss explains: "The multicolored spectrum of this industry reaches out from the 'pastel' of folk, youth choir music, country, chanson, ballad, gospel, to the 'brighter tones' of folk rock, country rock, gospel rock, and finally the incredible 'blinding colors' of Christian hard core, heavy metal and techno. Between these extremes is the 'glitter' of rap, hip-hop, latin, reggae, all 'sanctified' through 'Christian' lyrics and an ever-increasing audience of believers and unbelievers."[3]

"Christian" rock is becoming more and more the only music to be found in Christian bookstores. A humorous experience by my former music professor Bjorn Keyn illustrates this point. In an essay Keyn prepared for this symposium, (but which I was unable to use because of duplication with the content of other chapters) he wrote: "Some years ago

I visited one of the largest Christian bookstores in California hoping to find a special recording of Handel's oratorio, 'The Messiah.' This store was well-known for its large stock of religious records. When I asked for the record, the lady behind the counter answered me politely but somewhat condescendingly that they didn't carry 'that kind of music,' because, as she said, 'We carry only Christian music here' (sic!). As I examined the enormous supply of recordings I found only rhythmically based music (beat music), like rock, gospel, blues, jazz, country, and related forms. This is what today is called 'Contemporary Christian Music' or 'Christian Rock.'"[4]

Major Christian bookstores usually carry a large selection of CCM classified under the major headings of secular rock such as metal, rap, techno-drive, punk, ska, retro, industrial, etc. These records are supposed to offer a "Christian" version of their secular counterpart. To help young people make the selections, Christian magazines provide charts listing in one column the secular rock bands and in another column the corresponding 'Christian' bands that play the same music, but with difference words.

It came as a total surprise to find a similar chart on the January 13, 1996, issue of *Insight*, the official Seventh-day Adventist magazine for teenagers. The article is entitled "Make the Switch," and lists thirty-two "Christian" artists who sound like their corresponsing secular counterpart. The deception is self-evident. Christians addicted to the secular rock band can satisfy their craving for rock just by listening to a "Christian" version. They can still get the same physical stimulation, since the music is the same.[5]

The same issue of *Insight* carries an interview with Roger Record, "Contemporary Christian Music: Is It Better than Secular Music?" Record is an Adventist Academy Bible teacher who sings with a band called "Imagination." In response to the question, "What is wrong with rock music and MTV?" Record said: "First, I don't believe that the *form* of music is wrong. But I believe that many *people* who use it—pop, rock, rap, or whatever—have been indirectly or directly influenced by the devil."[6] The solution that Record proposes to young people in his seminars is to switch from secular rock to CCM, because he said: "I would say any form of Christian music can be enjoyed."[7] The fundamental problem with Record's view, which is shared by many youth leaders and pastors today, is the failure to recognize that rock makes its impact *musically,* not *lyrically.* Changing the words does not alter the effects of rock on the mind, muscles, and hormone productions. This fact has been established by numerous scientific studies reported in both Chapters 5 and 9.

"Related to CCM and dependent upon it, is Contemporary Worship Music (CWM). Many of the same artists involved in CCM are also active in CWM, often recording in the same secular corporations. The significant difference is in the lyrics, which are more biblically based. An example is the song 'How Majestic Is Your Name' by Michael W. Smith. It mostly represents a type of soft rock. Two major problems with CWM is that it generally incorporates rock rhythms with a heavy bass line and it is very repetitious. Jesus warned against using vain repetitions in worship (Matt 6:7). This type of music is adopted by more and more Adventist young people who are organizing bands[8] and in some cases achieving professional status."[9]

Summing up, the distinction between secular rock music and much of CCM is in most cases relative, because the music is the same, only the words are different. And the words do not neutralize the harmful effects of rock music. For this reason, the phrase "rock music" is used in this book in its broader meaning, inclusive of all versions of rock, whether secular or religious. Sometimes the phrase "pop music" is used with the same inclusive meaning. When the term "Christian" is used to qualify rock, usually it is placed between quotations marks, simply because in our view to speak of "Christian rock" is an oxymoron, that is, a contradiction of terms.

Acknowledgments. It is most difficult for me to acknowledge my indebtedness to the many persons who have contributed to the realization of this symposium. First of all, I am indebted to the six scholars (musicians) who have contributed chapters to this book. Each one of them has gone beyond the call of duty by preparing an enlightening study on vital aspects of the rock-music debate.

Each contributor is introduced twice. First, some information about each contributor is given in this chapter in conjunction with their contribution to the discussion of rock music. Second, the basic biographical information is given at the beginning of the chapter each one has authored.

It is significant that the seven contributors (including this writer) represent six different nationalities. Prof. Calvin M. Johansson is an American, Musician Brian Neumann is South African, Dr. Eurydice V.

Osterman is Afro-American, Musician Güenter Preuss is German, Dr. Wolfgang H. M. Stefani is Australian, Lecturer Tore Sognefest is Norwegian, and I, the writer, am an Italian. Our different cultural and national backgrounds bring to this symposium a broader perspective.

A special acknowledgment must be given to five scholars who prepared essays that I was unable to include in this symposium. In some instances the essays were very profound and technical, above the comprehension of the average reader. In other instances, much of the material presented duplicated the content of other chapters. I wish to express my sincere apologies to these people for being unable to include their essays in this symposium. There is no question that I have personally benefited from their writings.

A special word of thanks goes to Joyce Jones and Deborah Everhart from Andrews University for correcting and improving the style of the manuscript. Jarrod Williamson from La Sierra University deserves special mention for taking time to correct and react to the manuscript. His comments have been most helpful.

My sincere gratitude goes to Donald J. Wood for designing a most attractive cover. Currently Wood is a student in the School of Journalism at Indiana University. In his busy schedule he took time to design this cover and to modify it several times on the basis of valuable comments received. Last but not least, I express my special thanks to my wife who has been my constant source of encouragement and inspiration during the past thirty-eight years of our married life. We saw little of one another while I was researching and writing this book. The same has been true while writing the previous fourteen books. Yet, without her love, patience, and encouragement, it would have been most difficult for me to complete this project in such a relatively short period of time.

Method and Style. This symposium is written from a biblical perspective. To my knowledge, each contributor accepts the Bible as normative for defining Christian beliefs and practices. Because the words of the Bible contain a divine message written by human authors who lived in specific historical situations, every effort must be made to understand their meaning in their historical context. This conviction is reflected in the methodology followed in the analysis of the biblical texts related to singing, musical instruments, and dancing.

As one would expect with seven contributors, the style of the book
is not uniform. You will soon discover that some chapters are easier to read
than others. To facilitate the reading, I took the liberty as editor to divide
each chapter into major parts and to subdivide the text under appropriate
headings. This gives some consistency to the layout of the book. Unless
otherwise specified, all Bible texts are quoted from the Revised Standard
Version, copyright 1946 and 1952.

Authors' Hope. It would be presumptuous to hope that this book
will change everyone's minds, especially those that are already made up.
But many people are confused, yet open. They are sincere but sincerely
wrong in what they believe. Several examples are given below in the
second part of this chapter.

A pastor told me: "I used to be known as 'Tambourine Pastor'
because I used it all the time to accompany the church music. But after I
read in your newsletter that the tambourine and other instruments associated with entertainment music were not allowed in the Temple, synagogue,
or early church, I decided that I would never again bring the tambourine
to church." These are the kind of people we hope to help with this book.

Many pastors, Bible teachers, youth leaders, lay members, and
young people have a limited understanding of the threat rock music poses
the Christian faith, and of the biblical teachings regarding music. They
assume that music is all a matter of taste and culture and the Bible gives
us no directives in the area of music. I shared the same view until I became
involved in this research.

Digging up all the information has been very time consuming. For
the past six months I have spent an average of 12-15 hours a day on this
project, as my wife can testify. It is obvious that busy pastors or lay people
can hardly find time to undertake a research of this nature. Those of us who
have the time and the skill to investigate new truths, have the obligation
to share them. This is what Christianity is all about. It is with this spirit that
each contributor presents his/her findings in this book.

Part 2
AN OVERVIEW OF THE ISSUES

Out of consideration toward those who appreciate an overview of
the major controversial issues examined in this symposium, I briefly list

the eight major issues, together with a summary of the response provided by each contributor in their respective chapters. Hopefully, this overview will wet the appetite for reading the rest of the book.

(1) The Morality of Music

Defenders of the use of "Christian" rock music for worship and evangelism maintain that music is void of moral qualities for either good or bad. Consequently, nothing is wrong in adopting rock music by changing its lyrics, because the message is not in the music but in the words. This view is emphatically stated in what is known as the *Christian Rocker's Creed* published in the popular *CCM Magazine*: "We hold these truths to be self-evident, that all music was created equal, that no instrument or style of music is in itself evil—that the diversity of musical expression which flows from man is but one evidence of the boundless creativity of our Heavenly Father."[10]

Similar statements could be multiplied as they abound in evangelical literature.[11] A couple of samples from Adventist literature suffice to show that this view is becoming popular in Adventist circles. In an article "Contemporary Music Is *Christian* Music," which appeared in *Ministry* (September 1996), Michael Tomlinson states: "I believe music itself is without moral qualities, either for good or evil. The question has more to do with what the music is employed to say or to do than with the music per se"[12] He goes so far as to say: "Do some church leaders denounce Christian 'rock' because they do not understand it or perhaps because they are blinded by the generational prejudice or personal preference?"[13] Tomlinson's view is clear. Music is morally neutral. Those church leaders who denounce "Christian" rock are either ignorant about it or prejudiced against it. Is this true? We shall soon find out.

Harold B. Hannum, a well-known and respected Adventist musician, expresses the same view, saying that "moral matters have to do with human actions and relations to others, not with the notes of a composition."[14] Later in the same book Hannum affirms: "Moral and religious values should be kept separate from purely aesthetic ones."[15]

The Response. The major response to the alleged moral neutrality of music is found in Chapter 13, "Music and Morality," authored by Wolfgang H. M. Stefani, an Australian musician, scholar, pastor, who has earned graduate degrees in music, and a Ph. D. in Religious Education at Andrews University in 1993. His dissertation was on "The Concept of God and Sacred Music Style." He taught music for nine years at the undergraduate and graduate level, including at the Andrews University SDA Theological Seminary.

I must confess that when I first read Stefani's essay, I was worried that it might be too deep for the average reader. He is a brilliant scholar whom I highly respect, but his writings tend to be above the comprehension of the average reader. A trusted friend encouraged me to include Stefani's essay in this symposium because some of the readers are well-educated and will appreciate his scholarly and compelling response to the alleged moral neutrality of music.

Simply stated, Stefani presents four major arguments. The first argument is historical. For the past two and half millennia, music has been considered to be such a potent and influential force in society that leading philosophers and politicians advocated its control by the nation's constitution. Thus, historically, music and morality have been intimately connected.

The second argument is theological. In a sin-infested world, every human creation reflects a degree of moral involvement. The notion that creative arts, like music, were not touched by the Fall was developed during the Middle Ages when the Catholic Church controlled artistic productions.

When the church lost its hold and society became secular, the notion that aesthetic arts are not subject to moral accountability continued. The result has been that "rock, rap, thrash metal, classical, jazz, Country and Western, soul, and a host of other musics, each with their own individual aesthetic standards, have inevitably become acceptable forms of musical expression, even in worship contexts."[16]

Stefani notes that this popular view ignores the radical distortion that sin has wrought in every field of human endeavor, including music. Christians are called to examine music, not only to determine if it is beautiful, but also to establish if it is morally compatible with biblical teachings.

The third argument is based on the scientific research of the past several decades which has shown that music "dictates feelings." "For example, incorporating music on a film soundtrack takes for granted that music impacts all people similarly. Indeed, if this were not the case a music soundtrack would be pointless."[17]   "A body of research now exists that demonstrates that music does communicate meaningfully in a way that can and ought to be evaluated for appropriateness, and even rightness or wrongness in a given context."[18]

The fourth argument is philosophical and yet very practically stated: "What rules the heart, forms the art." Stefani shows with compelling logic that musical styles are not neutral, but value-laden. "They are veritable embodiment of beliefs." In his dissertation he traces with compelling clarity the correlation between the evolution in the understanding of God and the development of new musical styles during the course of Christian history.

This is an important concept that I have explored in Chapter 2, because it shows that ultimately the battle over music styles is a theological battle over our understanding of God. Rock music today, both in its secular and "Christian" version, reflects an immanent "God within us" perception. This view of God promotes a strong physical and emotionally stimulating music by means of repetitive rhythms in order to achieve a direct contact with or experience of the divine.

Ultimately, what is at stake in the battle over music is the understanding of the very nature of God being worshipped. The question is: Does the church music serve to worship the holy and transcendent God of biblical revelation or a casual, personal-lover type of Being created by human imagination? The debate over this question is intense and will not go away because, intuitively, people sense that their music stands for the God whom they want to worship.

The non-neutrality of music is clearly recognized by musicians themselves. For example, Howard Hanson, famous composer and former head of the Eastman School of Music in Rochester, New York, said: "Music is made up of many ingredients and, according to the proportion of these components, it can be soothing or invigorating, ennobling or vulgarizing, philosophical or orgiastic. It has power for evil as well as good."[19]

Rock star Jimi Hendrix states the same view most emphatically: "You can hypnotize people with the music and when they get at their weakest point you can preach into their subconscious minds what you want to say"[20]

The truth of Hendrix's words have been known to the business world for long time. Businesses know that certain kinds of music can increase sales while other kinds of music can actually reduce sales. The Musak Corporation, which distributes music for businesses, advertises its services saying: "The science of stimulus progression employs the inherent power of music in a controlled pattern to achieve predetermined psychological and physiological effects on people. Leading companies and commercial establishments now employ the Musak concept to improve environment, attitudes, and performance."

The Bible itself discredits the notion of the neutrality of music through the story of David, who was called to soothe King Saul whenever troubled by an evil spirit. "Whenever the evil spirit from God was upon Saul, David took the lyre and played it with his hands; so Saul was refreshed, and was well, and the evil spirit departed from him" (1 Sam 16:23). Note that Saul was affected physically, emotionally, and spiritually, not by the singing of David, but purely by the instrumental music.

The notion that music is neutral apart from its words is discredited by Scripture, science, and common sense. Yet it still remains a popular deception used to justify the acceptance in Christian homes and churches of the pop music that stimulates people physically rather than elevating them spiritually.

(2) Rock Music Is Not Immoral

Closely related to the alleged moral neutrality of music is the popular assumption that the various types of rock music are just another musical genre that people may like or dislike, depending on their musical preferences or culture. Thus, nothing is immoral with rock music per se. It is only its improper use that is morally wrong. By changing its lyrics, Christians can legitimately use rock music to worship God and proclaim the Gospel.

This view, popular among many evangelical churches, is gaining credence in the Adventist church as well. For example, Steve Case, a veteran Adventist youth pastor and president of Piece of the Pie Ministries for youth, often answers questions about "Christian rock" in *Insight,* the official Adventist magazine for teenagers. To the question: "Is there really any such thing as 'Christian rock'? Would God listen to it or approve it?" Case replies: "I used to answer this question by saying that Christian rock is the devil's attempt to sneak into the church. . . . Now I answer questions on 'Christian rock' by asking, What is your bias about 'Christian rock'? Do you already think it's OK or not OK?"[21]

For Case, the private or church use of "Christian rock" is a matter of personal bias. He wrote in another article: "Musical preferences are personal. Which also means that musical tastes/preferences can change."[22] The advice that Case gives to teenagers about listening to "Christian rock" is as follows: "Does your music increase your faith in God and love for Him? If so, keep listening to it? If not, be willing to make good changes or turn it off."[23]

A similar view is expressed in the symposium *Shall We Dance,* which is sponsored by several Adventist organizations, including the North American Division of SDA. For the sake of accuracy, it must be stated that the opening statement of the introduction makes this disclaimer: "This book is *not* an official statement of the Seventh-day Adventist Church regarding standards and values."[24] It is comforting to know that the book, though sponsored by major Adventists institutions, *does not* reflect the church standards and values.

Regarding the use of "Christian rock," the symposium suggests that its use is a matter of personal taste and experience. "Some have experienced the [spiritual] impact through the loud, rhythmic demands of rock. Many more are learning the wider joys of an eclectic musical taste, accepting the impact of a variety of styles on a variety of moods and needs. Each of us must give our own answer to the question of the music itself. If its physical and emotional impact is in harmony with the spiritual song I want to sing, then I can judge it to be acceptable. If that impact battles against my spiritual sense, then I must conclude that music is wrong for me."[25]

The Response. Is the personal taste or preference of teenagers a valid criterion for determining whether or not they should listen to "Christian rock"? Can we expect teenagers to understand the ethical, social, and religious values communicated by rock music in any form? Can we blame young people for listening to rock music if we do not help them to see the dangers posed by such music?

It would appear to me that part of the problem of the increasing number of Adventist youth becoming addicted to various forms of rock music is the lack of strong leadership in the home, church, and school. A contributing factor is a lack of understanding of the intrinsic nature of rock music. Unfortunately, most people fail to realize that there is more to rock music that meets the eye or ear. I must confess that I myself was ignorant on this matter until I became involved in this research. Truly I can say that this research has been an eye-opening experience for me and I can only hope that the results of our labors will benefit many people.

The many months of painstaking investigation into the philosophical, ethical, social, and religious aspects of rock have convinced me that this music is a revolutionary "religious" countercultural and anti-Christian movement which uses its rhythm, melodies, and lyrics to promote, among other things, a pantheistic/hedonistic worldview, sexual perversion, civil disobedience, violence, satanism, occultism, homosexuality, masochism, and an open rejection of the Christian faith and values.

My analysis of rock music is in Chapters 2, 3, 4, 5. Briefly stated, this is what I learned. In Chapter 2 on "The Worldview of Rock Music," I found that rock music reflects a pantheistic conception of God as an immanent, impersonal, supernatural power which the individual can experience through the hypnotic rhythm of rock music and drugs. The pantheistic conception of God has facilitated the acceptance of rock music among Christians and secularly minded people, since both groups seek to fulfill the inner urge for a pleasurable experience of the supernatural through the hypnotic effects of rock music.

In Chapter 3 on "Rock Music from a Historical Perspective," I learned that rock music has gone through an easily discernible hardening process from rock 'n' roll to hard rock, acid rock, heavy metal rock, rap rock, thrash rock, etc. New types of more perverted forms of rock music are constantly appearing because rock addicts constantly demand something stronger and stronger to meet their craving.

In Chapter 4 on "The Rock and Roll Religion," I found that the pantheistic worldview promoted by rock music has eventually led to the rejection of the Christian faith and to the acceptance of a new kind of religious experience. The latter involves the use of rock music, sex, drugs, and dance to transcend the limitation of time and space and to connect with the supernatural.

In Chapter 5 on "The Rock Rhythm and a Christian Response," I discovered that rock music differs from all other forms of music because of its driving, loud, relentless beat. Scientific studies have shown that the rock beat can alter the mind and cause several physical reactions, including sexual arousal. The latter are discussed more fully in Chapter 8 on "The Effects of Rock Music," authored by Tore Sognefest, A Norwegian musician and author of the book *The Power of Music.*

The factual information gathered about the nature of rock music during the course of this investigation makes it abundantly clear that such music cannot be legitimately transformed into Christian music by changing its lyrics. In whatever version, rock music is and remains a music that embodies a spirit of rebellion against God and the moral principles he has revealed for our lives.

By stimulating the physical, sensual aspect of the human nature, rock music throws out of balance the order of the Christian life. It makes the gratification of the carnal nature more important than the cultivation of the spiritual aspect of our life.

Christians should respond to rock music by choosing instead good music that respects the proper balance among melody, harmony, and rhythm. The proper balance among these three reflects and fosters the order and balance in our Christian life among the spiritual, mental, and physical components of our being. Good and balanced music can and will contribute to keep our "spirit and soul and body . . . sound and blameless at the coming of our Lord Jesus Christ" (1 Thess 5:23).

(3) Rock Music and Evangelism

The debate over whether "to rock or not to rock" in evangelism is taking place across denominational lines. The defenders of the use of rock in evangelism appeal to practical considerations. They argue that rock is part of today's culture and thus it is needed to penetrate the rock generation.

A recent cover article in *Christianity Today* (July 17, 1999), entitled "The Triumph of Praise Songs—How Guitars Beat Out the Organ in the Worship Wars," captures vividly how pop music is replacing traditional music in many churches today. The author of the article, Michael S. Hamilton, reports that praise bands and worship teams are fast replacing organs and choirs. The baby-boomers' taste for rock music that has reshaped our society is now ruling the worship service as well.[26]

"Since the 1950s, denominational divisions have steadily become less important in American church life. We have the baby-boom generation to thank for much of this. But at bottom we are all still sectarians; we still prefer to congregate with the like-minded. Our new sectarianism is a sectarianism of worship style. The new sectarian creeds are the dogmas of music."[27]

This new "sectarianism of worship style" is characterized by the adoption of religious rock, which reflects the baby-boomers' taste, sound, and identity. The rock beat has become so much a part of their lives that they inevitably want to hear it in their church music as well. If the church wants to attract the rock-and-roll generation, then it had better offer them the music to which they are addicted—or else.

This popular view is embraced by increasing numbers of Adventists. In the article "Worship and Praise: One Model for Change in the Worship Hour," which appeared in *Ministry* (February 2000), John A. Solomon argues that if we want to reach the Baby Boomer generation, the church must offer them the kind of music they are accustomed to.[28]

Citing recent research, Solomon writes: "Baby Boomers have been heavily influenced by music with a beat. Only six percent listed classical music as music of their choice, with a bias against organ music. Overheads have replaced hymn books; synthesizers have replaced organs; and drums and guitars have taken their place in the repertoire of church music instrumentation."[29]

To justify the adoption of pop music for worship and evangelism, Solomon appeals to Moses, Miriam, and David who used "exuberant" music. "David and others who wrote the Psalms composed some of the greatest songs and lyrics in literature, and when they sang accompanied by tambourines and cymbals and the trumpet, ecstasy filled the air (Ps 145-150). The point is that God used this music, these instruments, and actions to bring glory to Himself. If He did it then, it may certainly be done in a variety of ways now."[30] Later we show that none of the "exuberant" music mentioned above was ever used in the worship of God in the Temple, synagogue, or early church.

The notion that the Bible sanctions rhythmic, "exuberant" music for divine worship is encouraging the adoption of CCM in Adventist worship and evangelism, besides giving rise to numerous bands. The article "Making Waves," which appeared in *Adventist Review* (July 17, 1997), reports on eight successful Adventist bands. "These artists see their style of music not as rebellion against the system, but as a ministry tool to rescue a new generation from rampant secularism and show them the saving grace of Jesus."[31]

The Response. The major response to the use of rock music in evangelism is found in Chapters 10 and 11. Chapter 10, "Pop Music and the Gospel," is authored by Calvin A. Johansson, D. M. A., Professor of Church Music at Evangel University and author of two major books, *Music and Ministry: A Biblical Counterpoint* and *Discipling Music Ministry: Twenty-first Century Directions.* Prof. Johansson is a leading authority on church music and is frequently quoted by authors dealing with this subject. I feel greatly honored by his willingness to contribute two chapters to this symposium.

In Chapter 10, Prof. Johansson compares and contrasts the values of pop music with those of the Gospel in eight specific areas. He concludes that "Pop characteristics are antipathetic to gospel characteristics. It seems obvious that a music (pop) which is so unlike the thing it is supposed to represent (the gospel) is unable to embody the gospel in its medium of witness (music). Hence, pop is useless in spiritual endeavor. If it is used, it does the cause of Christ much harm by painting an untrue picture of what the Christian life is."[32]

Chapter 11, "Christian Rock and Evangelism," is written by Güenter Preuss, a German Adventist musician, who for the past 15 years has served, first as Chairman of the Music Department of the Adventist College and Theological Seminary at Collonges-sous-Salève in France (1985-1995), and currently as Music Director of the SDA Baden-Wuerttemberg Conference in Germany (1995-2000).

Preuss has been deeply involved in the Adventist rock scene in Germany, endeavoring to help young people overcome their addiction to rock music. He is currently working on his doctoral dissertation on reformed hymnody between 1700 and 1870 at the Sorbonne University, in Paris. He submitted to me a manuscript of almost 100 pages loaded with documentation and argumentation. He convinced me immediately that he is a *true German scholar,* eager to be comprehensive and thorough. Let me assure you that it was not an easy task for me to reduce his essay to one fourth of its original length. I hope that someday he can publish his unabridged research.

Preuss commends the search for effective ways to reach secular-minded people with the Gospel, but questions the legitimacy of using rock music, partly because he has witnessed the impact of rock music on Adventist youth in Germany. He wrote: "Rock music in evangelism works on imagination, on thought associations, as any music. But rock music misrepresents the claims of the Gospel by encouraging worldly values. It makes people believe that they are all right, when in reality they desperately need a radical change in their lives—a conversion experience."[33]

Preuss finds that the idiom of rock music is unsuitable to communicate the Gospel because *the medium affects the message*. The medium used to win the youth determines the nature of the message to which they are won. If the church uses an entertainment type of rock music, which is associated with sex, drugs, and violence, it obviously is not able to challenge the youth with the moral claims of the Gospel.

The New Testament summons us to present clearly and compellingly the holiness of God's character, the desperate human plight, and the amazing grace of the Gospel. These are issues of life and death which cannot be presented with the frivolity and flippancy of pop music.

Listeners to religious rock will never be humbled by the majesty of God, nor will they be convicted of God's moral claims upon their lives. The relentless rock rhythm, the movements, the lights, and the demeanor of pop singers contain so much that is sensual and sexually suggestive that they can hardly communicate the holiness and purity of the Kingdom of God.

If we adopt a worldly appearance to attract the crowd, how can we paint in vivid colors the contrast between the kingdom of this world and the Kingdom of God? Paul recognized that the Gospel cannot be proclaimed through deceptive, worldly gimmicks. Thus he told the Corinthians: "My speech and my message were not in plausible words of wisdom [or we might say "with the exciting sounds of Greek songs"], but in demonstration of the Spirit and of power, that your faith might not rest in the wisdom of men [or we might say "in worldly excitements"] but in the power of God" (1 Cor 2:4-5).[34]

"God's proven method of evangelism is the 'foolishness of preaching' (1 Cor 1:21). He has committed to us the message of reconciliation (2 Cor 5:18). Our responsibility is not to contaminate this message with worldly idioms, like rock music. There is no need for the manipulation and stimulation of rock music to save people. Evangelism has been and is greatly aided by Christlike music presented by Christlike performers, but ultimately, it is the proclamation of the Word of God, accompanied by the convicting power of the Holy Spirit, that brings people into a saving relationship with Jesus Christ."[35]

(4) Rock Music and Black Heritage

In the Black community there is a prevailing assumption that rock music is part of the African-American heritage and, consequently, is a legitimate form of expression. Each culture defines its music according to its own criteria, and rock music allegedly reflects the roots of the African-American culture which can be traced back to West African slave culture. To deny to the Blacks the right to play rock music in their churches means to deprive them of their cultural heritage.

The Response. This important issue is examined in Chapter 12, "Rock Music and Culture," by a highly respected Afro-American musician, Eurydice V. Osterman, D. M. A., Professor of Music at Oakwood College, composer, and author of several publications, including the book *What God Says About Music.*

Dr. Osterman points out that "the prevailing assumption that rock music is a legitimate expression of African-American heritage ignores the significant differences that exist between the two. African-American heritage music is predominantly melodic and is based upon the rhythm of the dialect. Rock music, on the other hand, is based upon and is driven by a beat that overshadows and dominates all other musical elements. . . . While heritage music preserves and fosters unity, rock music creates division and influences rebellious attitudes toward moral values and a disrespect for authority."[36]

"The roots of the rock beat are to be found not in the religious music of the African-American heritage, but in secular and often irreligious music known as 'Rhythm and Blues.' This music became the expression of those Blacks who strayed away from or rejected the Christian faith. They wanted to become respected entertainers by playing a secular music. The mood of the Blues is one of sadness, punctuated by a regular, heavy beat. The emphasis is on the pleasures of this world, especially the enjoyment of illicit sex before or outside marriage."[37]

"The distinction that we find in African-American music between the religious Negro Spiritual and the secular, irreligious Rock and Roll reminds us of the simple fact that in all cultures we can expect to find some music which is pro-Christian and some which is anti-Christian in its values. This is the result of the fall of humankind which is present in every age, country, and culture. 'All have sinned and fall short of the glory of God' (Rom 3:23)."[38]

(5) Rock Music and the Bible

Perhaps the most significance aspect of the defense of "Christian" rock, is the appeal to certain Bible texts to defend the use of such music for church worship and evangelism. The prevailing assumption is that the Bible sanctions the use of rhythmic, dancing music and percussion instruments for divine worship.

In his book *The Contemporary Christian Music Debate*, Steve Miller writes: "The most striking observation of biblical worship is its wealth of variety and few restrictions on form."[39] He continues listing the variety of instruments, volumes and sounds, worshippers, manner, locations, occasions, times of the day, postures, and moods mentioned in the Bible. He concludes his survey saying: "Several implications concerning the present controversy can be noted. First, our creative Lord has allowed His creatures to exercise great creativity in worship. And God's Word does not even restrict us to the array of forms listed in the Bible."[40] Surprisingly, Miller is unaware that the Bible is very restrictive of the music and instruments to be used for divine worship.

The same view is found in Adventist literature. In her article "Sing the Song of Gladness," which appeared in *Ministry* (September 1996), Anita J. Strawn de Ojeda argues that, like us today, people in Bible time worshipped the Lord by praising Him with "timbrels, stringed instruments, organs, harps, cymbals, lyres, trumpets, and psalters. . . . First Chronicles 13:8 tells us that David and the Israelites played before God with all their might. . . . If my foot taps or my hands clap during a song, I am singing with 'all my might.' That is, my whole being is involved."[41]

"If David had been writing today, would he have said, 'Praise Him with drums and clapping; praise Him with guitars, and banjos, and synthesizers; praise Him with loud drums; praise Him upon the electric guitar" (see Ps 150:3-5)? Putting it all into context, he may well have said something similar to this."[42] Is this really what David would say today regarding the praise of God during the divine service? A close look at the ministry of music established by David shows otherwise.

The Response. This popular argument is examined especially in Chapter 7 "Biblical Principles of Music," where I survey the biblical teachings regarding music. Those who appeal to biblical injunctions to praise the Lord with a variety of instruments and volume to justify the use of rock music today ignore two important points.

First, in most cases the language of praise is figurative and hardly allows for a literal application to the divine service in God's House. For example, Psalm 149:5 encourages people to praise the Lord on the "couches." In verse 6 the praising is to be done with "two-edged swords in the hands." In verses 7 and 8 the Lord is to be praised for punishing the heathen with the sword, binding kings in chain and putting nobles in fetters. It is evident that the language is figurative because God would hardly expect people to praise Him during a divine service by standing or jumping on couches or while swinging a two-edged sword.

The same is true of Psalm 150 which speaks of praising the Lord "for his mighty deeds" (v. 2) in every possible *place* and with every available musical *instrument*. The *place* in which to praise the Lord is "his sanctuary," and "his mighty firmament." The *instruments* include eight familiar instruments.

This psalm makes sense only if we take the language to be highly figurative. For example, there is no way in which God's people on earth can praise the Lord "in his mighty firmament." The purpose of the psalm is not to specify the *location* and the *instruments* to be used for praise during the divine service, but rather to invite *everything* that breathes or makes sound to praise the Lord *everywhere.* The psalmist is describing with highly figurative language the attitude of praise that should characterize the believer at all times and in all places. To interpret this psalm as a license to dance, or to play drums in the church, is to misinterpret its intent.

A second important point ignored by those who believe that the Bible authorizes them to play any instrument and music in church is the biblical distinction between secular music produced for entertainment and sacred music performed in God's House. As shown in Chapters 6 and 7, the music and instruments used to praise the Lord outside the Temple during festival celebrations were different from the music played inside the Temple. Instruments like timbrels, flutes, pipes, and dulcimers could not be used in the Temple because of their association with secular entertainment. The same principle was respected also in the synagogue and early church, where no instruments of any kind were allowed.

Had the instruments and the music associated with social (religious) entertainment been used in God's House, the Israelites would have been tempted to turn their place of worship into a place of entertainment, as sometimes happens in some churches today. To prevent this thing from happening, instruments and music associated with entertainment were

excluded from the Temple, synagogue, and early church. It is the ignorance of these facts that leads people to believe that the Bible sanctions the
use of rock music for worship and evangelism. The lesson of Scripture and
history is evident. Music, like rock, which is associated with secular
entertainment is out of place in God's House in which we gather to worship
and not to be entertained.

(6) The Role of Luther

A popular argument used to defend the adoption of rock tunes for
church music today is the alleged borrowing of secular music by Christian
songwriters in the past. Anita J. Strawn de Ojeda wrote in *Ministry*:
"History shows that Christian songwriters borrowed elements from secular music."[43] She refers specifically to the early Christians and Luther. The
reasoning is that if Christians in the past adopted and adapted secular music
for church use, we can do the same today.

The example of Luther is often cited because of his enormous
influence in introducing congregational singing at the time of the Reformation. Steve Miller wrote: "The models for his [Luther's] lyrics were the
popular ballads of his day. The tunes were borrowed from German folk
songs, the music of the masses, and even a hymn to Mary. Luther was not
concerned with the association or origin of the tunes as he was with their
ability to communicate truth."[44]

In a similar vein, Michael Tomlinson wrote in *Ministry*: "Eliminating the secular roots of Christian music would mean to say good-bye to the
hymns of Martin Luther, whose music was borrowed from secular German
folk tunes."[45]

The Response. In view of the popularity of this argument, I took
time in Chapter 2 to investigate if it is true that Luther borrowed from the
secular, popular tunes of his day to compose his chorales. What I found
is that this argument is just as misleading and inaccurate as the previous
ones mentioned so far. Let me mention here only three facts, since the rest
of the information is available in Chapter 2.

First, of the thirty-seven chorales composed by Luther, only *one*
tune came directly from a secular folk song. Fifteen were composed by
Luther himself, thirteen came from Latin hymns or service music, two had
originally been religious pilgrims' songs, four were derived from German

religious folk songs, and two are of unknown origin.[46] What most people ignore is that even the one tune borrowed from a folk song, which "appeared in Luther's hymnal of 1535, was later replaced by another melody in the 1539 song book. Historians believe that Luther discarded it because people associated it with its previous secular text."[47]

Second, Luther changed the melodic and rhythmic structure of the tunes he borrowed from secular sources in order to eliminate any possible worldly influence. In his scholarly book, *Martin Luther, His Music, His Message,* Robert Harrell explains: "The most effective way of [negating] worldly influence would be to 'de-rhythm' the music. By avoiding dance tunes and 'de-rhythming' other songs, Luther achieved a chorale with a marked rhythm, but without the devices that would remind the people of the secular world. So successful was the work done by Luther and other Lutheran musicians that scholars were often unable to detect the secular origins of chorales. The other way in which Luther sought to remove secular associations from the mind of the congregation was through the use of Scripture and scriptural allusions in the texts. By filling his chorales with the written Word, Luther sought to direct the thoughts of his people toward the Living Word."[48]

Harrell concludes his well-documented study, saying: "A study of Luther's chorales reveals two important facts about Luther's use of secular elements in his sacred music: (1) Although there was much popular music available to him, from drinking songs to dance tunes to religious folk songs and carols, Luther chose only those tunes which best lend themselves to sacred themes and avoided the vulgar, 'rollicking drinking songs' and dance tunes. (2) No material which Luther used for a chorale remained unchanged, except for the one case noted previously. Rather, 'he carefully tested the melodies he considered, and when necessary molded them into suitability. . . . Alteration were freely made.'"[49]

Third, Luther arranged music for young people of his time in a way to lead them *away* from the attraction of worldly music. This cannot be said of "Christian" rock music today which retains the melody and rhythm of secular rock. Luther explained why he changed the musical arrangements of his songs: "These songs were arranged in four parts for no other reason than that I wanted to attract the youth (who should and must be trained in music and other fine arts) away from love songs and carnal pieces and to give them something wholesome to learn instead, so that they can enter with pleasure into what is good, as befitting to youth."[50]

In the light of these facts, anyone who uses Luther's statement "Why should the Devil have all the good tunes?" to defend the use of rock music in the church, ought to know that the argument is clearly negated by what Luther himself said and did. Luther's use of secular music teaches us not to sanitize rock music which promotes sex, drugs, and violence, but to choose instead the best music of our culture and make it a fitting vehicle to communicate the Word of God. What a marvellous example we have in Martin Luther! And how grossly distorted Luther's example has been by those who wish to legitimize the use of rock for worship and evangelism!

(7) Church Music and Adventist Theology

The ongoing debate over the use of contemporary music in Adventist worship is largely based on subjective tastes or popular trends. But the music and worship style of the Adventist church should reflect its unique message and prophetic mission. Adventists should not accept uncritically the worship style of other denominations. In his book *And Worship Him,* Norval Pease, my former professor of worship at the Andrews University Seventh-day Adventist Theological Seminary, states: "We are Adventists, and we must approach worship as Adventists. A worship service that meets the needs of Methodists, Episcopalians, or Presbyterians may be unsatisfactory for us."[51]

The answer to the Adventist worship renewal is not found in the adoption of "Christian" rock, but in a re-examination of how our distinctive Adventist beliefs should impact the various parts of the church service, including music. Such an ambitious undertaking is beyond the scope of this book. What I have attempted to do is to submit in Chapter 6 some preliminary reflections on "An Adventist Theology of Church Music."

The chapter attempts to define how the three distinctive Seventh-day Adventist beliefs of the Sabbath, Christ's ministry in the heavenly sanctuary, and the Second Advent should impact on the choice and the performance of music during the divine service. Briefly stated these are the conclusions.

The Sabbath teaches us to respect the distinction between the *sacred* and the *secular,* not only in time, but also in such areas as church music and worship. To use secular music for the church service on the Sabbath is to treat the Sabbath as a secular day and the church as a secular place.

The study of the music of the Jerusalem Temple, as well as the heavenly sanctuary, reveals that instruments and music associated with entertainment were not allowed in the Temple services, nor are they used in the liturgy of the heavenly sanctuary. The lesson from the sanctuary is that church music must express great reverence and respect for God.

Belief in the certainty and soon-appearance of the Rock of Ages, with the greatest musical band of angels this world has ever seen, can fire up the imagination of musicians today to compose new songs, and inspire Advent believers to joyfully sing about the hope that burns without their hearts.

(8) Rock Music and the Endtime Deception

Seventh-day Adventists believe that we live today in the final countdown to the great controversy between true and false worship, as described in book of Revelation through the imagery of a beast that promotes the false worship of Babylon. This apocalyptic prophecy envisions the antitypical Babylon leading all the nations into the false worship of God (Rev 13:16; 14:8; 18:3).

It is important to remember that the apocalyptic imagery of the false worship promoted by Babylon in Revelation derives from the historical chapter of Daniel 3, which describes an event of prophetic endtime significance. On the Plain of Dura, all the inhabitants of the Babylonian empire were called to worship the golden image of king Nebuchadnezzar. A fiery furnace was prepared for those who refused to do homage to the golden image. Daniel informs us that "every kind of music" (Dan 3:7, 10) was used to cause all classes of people from all the provinces of the empire to corporately worship the golden image (Dan 3:10).

Twice in Daniel 3 there is a long list of the different musical instruments used to produce "every kind of music" (Dan 3:7,10). This eclectic music was played to induce people to worship the golden image. Could it be that, as in ancient Babylon, Satan is using today "every kind of music" to lead the world into the endtime false worship of the "beast and its image" (Rev 14:9)? Could it be that a Satanic stroke of genius will write Gospel songs that will have the marking of every taste of music: folk music, jazz, rock, disco, country-western, rap, calypso? Could it be that many Christians will come to love this kind of Gospel songs because they sound very much like the music of Babylon?

Rock Music and Endtime False Worship. Historically, Adventists have identified Babylon with the power of the papacy that will lead the world into perverted forms of worship. While acknowledging the prophetic role that the papacy has played in leading many people to believe in the intercessory role of Mary and the saints, one wonders if rock music also will play a vital role in promoting the end-time false worship!

This would not be the first time in Scripture that music is connected to false worship. At the foot of Mount Sinai music and dancing were involved in the worship of the golden calf (Ex 32:19). In the plains of Moab, on the borders to the Promised Land, the Israelites were *"beguiled with music and dancing"*[52] into a terrible apostasy (Num 25:1-2). They were lured through music to participate in heathen worship—something which they may have resisted under other circumstances.

The universal and revolutionary impact of rock music upon humanity at large is recognized by many social analysts. In his book *Rock Music,* sociologist William Schafer acknowledges that rock music has become a worldwide "tool for altering consciouness."[53] When Bob Geldorf organized his "Live-Aid" program to raise money for the Ethiopian famine victims, popular rock bands joined in from different parts of the world. Linked via satellite, the program generated such a worldwide interest that sociologists began to explore music as a phenomenon for "the formation of an international youth culture . . . based on common, worldwide tastes and values."[54]

No other music today transcends cultural and national bounderies like rock. From Minneapolis to Moscow and from Stockholm to Johannesburg, the rock beat reigns supreme. The global impact of rock music, its open rejection of the Christian faith, and its promotion of a new religious experience characterized by rhythmic music, sex, drugs, and dance, could well prove to be the most effective medium for leading mankind into the final apocalyptic false worship.

In their thought-provoking book, *Music in the Balance*, Frank Garlock and Kurt Woetzel acknowledge that "A large segment of the Christian community has enthusiastically embraced this music of the world, the associated antics, and the philosophy. All three have been implanted into the life of the church. Not only have many Christians accepted the music as suitable for praise and worship, but an atmosphere pervades the contemporary Christian concerts not unlike the early concerts of the Elvis era. Believers have made idols of their own rock and roll singers and continue to worship at their feet with devotion and their pocket books."[55]

Wolfgang Stefani perceptively asks: "Could it be that by fostering a homogenized global musical style—a style that is increasingly visible in the Christian music culture—the stage is set for a global, religious identity response? A response that will allow people of all nations, all religious backgrounds to say, 'Yes, this is my music, this is who I am: this is my music for being happy and religious and I am part of it; I am right at home now.'"[56]

The summon of the Three Angels Messages to come out of spiritual Babylon by rejecting its false worship could well include also the rejection of the rock music of Babylon. Soon the whole world will be gathered for the final showdown in the antitypical, apocalyptic Plain of Dura and "every kind of music" will be played to lead the inhabitants of the earth to "worship the beast and its image" (Rev 14:9). It is noteworthy that in Revelation the outcome of the showdown involves the silencing of the music of Babylon: "So shall Babylon the great city be thrown with violence, and shall be found no more; and the sound of harpers and minstrels, of flute players and trumpeters, shall be heard in thee no more" (Rev 18:21-22).

Those who reason that there is nothing wrong with the music of Babylon may be conditioning themselves to accept the false worship promoted by Babylon. Satan has his own songs to promote the endtime false worship. Could it be that by adopting the music of Babylon, some will miss the chance to sing the New Song of Moses and of the Lamb? May this question resonate in our consciousness and challenge us to stand for truth like the three Hebrew worthies.

ENDNOTES

1. Güenter Preuss, "Rock Music and Evangelism," Chapter 11 of this symposium, pp. 304-305.

2. David W. Gould, *Contemporary Christian Music Under the Spotlight* (Oak Harbor, WA, 1998), p. 16.

3. Güenter Preuss (note 1), p. 305.

4. Bjorn Keyn, "A Look at Contemporary Christian Music," private essay prepared for this symposium, p. 1. Regretfully I was unable to use this excellent essay because much of the same material is covered in other chapters.

5. "Making the Switch!" *Insight* (January 13, 1996), p. 13.

6. Roger Record "Contemporary Christian Music: Is It Better than Secular Music?" *Insight* (January 13, 1996), p. 8.

7. Ibid., p. 11.

8. See, Jeff Trubey, "Making Waves," *Adventist Review* (July 17, 1997), p. 8-13.

9. Güenter Preuss (note 1), p. 306.

10. "Christian Rocker's Creed," *CCM Magazine* (November 1988), p. 12.

11. For a listing of about 20 statements from evangelical leaders who believe in the neutrality of music, see David W. Gould (note 2), pp. 19-21.

12. Michael Tomlinson, "Contemporary Christian Music is *Christian* Music," *Ministry* (September 1966), p. 26.

13. Ibid.

14. Harold Byron Hannum, *Christian Search for Beauty* (Nashville, TN, 1975), p. 51.

15. Ibid., p. 112.

16. Wolfgang H. M. Stefani, "Music and Morality," Chapter 13 of this symposium, p. 350.

17. Ibid., p. 352.

18. Ibid., p. 354.

19. Howard Hanson as quoted in the *American Journal of Psychiatry* 90 (1943), p. 317.

20. Jimi Hendrix, interviewed in *Life* (October 3, 1969), p. 4.

21. Steve Case, "Pastor Steve Answers," *Insight* (August 16, 1997), p. 6.

22. Steve Case, "What About Christian Rock?" *Insight* (March 20, 1999), p. 7.

23. Ibid.

24. Steve Case, ed., *Shall We Dance: Rediscovering Christ-Centered Standards* (Riverside, CA, 1996), p. 15.

25. Ibid., p. 134.

26. Michael S. Hamilton, "The Triumph of Praise Songs," *Christianity Today* (July 17, 1999), p. 29.

27. Ibid.

28. John A. Solomon, "Worship and Praise: One Model for Change in the Worship Hour," *Ministry* (February 2000), p. 16.

29. Ibid., p. 17.

30. Ibid.

31. Jeff Trubey, "Making Waves," *Adventist Review* (July 17, 1997), p. 9.

32. Calvin M. Johansson, "Pop Music and the Gospel," Chapter 10 of this symposium, p. 296.

33. Güenter Preuss (note 1), p. 316.

34. Ibid.

35. Ibid., P. 317.

36. Eurydice V. Osterman, "Rock Music and Culture," Chapter 12 of this symposium, pp. 326-327.

37. Ibid., p. 327.

38. Ibid.

39. Steve Miller, *The Contemporary Christian Music Debate. Worldly Compromise or Agent of Renewal* (Wheaton, IL, 1993), p. 78.

40. Ibid., pp. 78-81.

41. Anita J. Strawn de Ojeda, "Sing the Song of Gladness," *Ministry* (September 1996), p. 5.

42. Ibid., p. 6.

43. Ibid.

44. Steve Miller (note 39), p. 113.

45. Michael Tomlison (note 12), p. 27.

46. The data is compiled from different sources and is quoted in Robert Harrell, *Martin Luther, His Music, His Message* (Greenville, SC, 1980), p. 18.

47. Ulrich S. Leupold, "Learning from Luther? Some Observations on Luther's Hymns," *Journal of Church Music* 8 (1966), p. 5.

48. Robert Harrell (note 43), p. 21.

49. Ibid., pp. 21-22.

50. Luther's foreword to Johann Walter's collection as quoted by Friedrich Blume, *Protestant Church Music: A History* (New York, 1974), p. 78.

51. Norval Peace, *And Worship Him* (Nashville, 1967), p. 8.

52. Ellen G. White, *The Story of Patriarchs and Prophets* (Mountain View, CA, 1958), p. 454. Italics added.

53. William J. Shafer, *Rock Music* (Minneapolis, MN, 1972), p. 62.

54. Deanna Campbell Robinson and others, *Music at the Margins: Popular Music and Global Cultural Diversity* (London, 1991), p. xi.

55. Frank Garlock and Kurt Woetzel, *Music in the Balance* (Greenville, SC, 1992), pp. 82-83.

56. Wolfgang H. M. Stefani, "Endnotes: Music as Ecumenical Force," *Journal of the Adventist Theological Society* 5/1 (1994), pp. 221-222.

Chapter 2
THE WORLDVIEW
OF ROCK MUSIC
by
Samuele Bacchiocchi

Rock music is the most popular cultural phenomenon of the second half of the twentieth century and the single greatest propagator of the moral, social, and religious values of our society. Social analysts concur that rock music has become a primary force in shaping the thinking and lifestyle of this generation.

In his book *Rock Music*, sociologist William Schafer describes rock music "as one of the principal dialects in the language of culture.... A strong counter culture has built itself around a musical sensibility, with music as a basic mode of communication and aesthetic expression."[1] Schafer is not opposed to rock music. He simply acknowledges that rock has become a "tool for altering consciousness."[2]

It is unquestionable that rock, in its various styles, is the most popular form of music influencing the world today. People listen to rock not only in the privacy of their cars or homes, but in the work place, the shopping mall, bars, clubs, health clubs, recreational places, and in an increasing number of churches.

In the fifty years since its emergence, rock music has come to dominate the musical taste of many people in various parts of the world. In 1976, two social scientists at Temple University wanted to investigate the physical and emotional impact of rock music on students. They easily found 56 rock enthusiasts for their study; but when they tried to form a control group, "a significant sample could not be found that disliked hard rock music."[3]

The Revolutionary Nature of Rock. In his essay "Rock and Roll, Religion and the Deconstruction of American Values," sociologist Charles Pressler notes that "rock and roll music and its messages ushered in a new view of the world and a new mode of interpersonal relationships—and by nearly any definition, the social effects of rock music can be described as 'revolutionary.'"[4] The revolution started by rock music has distinct religious connotations that are examined in Chapter 4. In his book *You Say You Want a Revolution*, sociologist Robert Pielke argues compellingly that the rock revolution which began in the 1950s has created a religious transformation of the American culture. Our concern is to ascertain whether the nature of this religious transformation is a bane or blessing for the Christian faith.

The revolutionary nature of rock music is succinctly described by sociologist William Schafer: "Rock has acted as a catalyst, a force uniting and amplifying ideas and feelings. It is a medium, a means of communicating emotions . . . the medium is the message. Associated with rock, for instance, is a cult of irrationality, a reverence for the instinctual, the visceral—and a distrust of reason and logic; this form of anti-intellectualism can be highly dangerous, can lead to totalitarian modes of thought and action. Linked with this anti-intellectualism is an interest in the occult: magic, superstition, exotic religious thought, anything contrary to the main current of Western thought. Also directly connected is an obsession with the unconscious mind; the force of drug culture has been its promise to reveal the hidden, instinctual man, to free the individual from restrictions and limitations of his conscious mind and his gross physical body."[5]

More will be said during the course of our study on the philosophical presuppositions of rock music. At this point it suffices to note that the conflict of values stirred up by the message of rock music has pitted the youth of the rock generation against their rocking elders. The conflict has extended to many Christian churches where sanitized forms of rock music have been adopted. In fact, the introduction of "Christian" rock music during church services has become one of the most emotive and divisive issues that is splitting congregations in different denominations, including my own Seventh-day Adventist Church.

In this study the term "Christian" is consistently placed between quotation marks when used to designate the religious version of rock music. The reason is simple. Our research indicates that rock music embodies ethical, philosophical, social, and religious beliefs which are antithetical to Christian beliefs and values.

The Presuppositions of Rock Music. Some Christians consider "Christian" rock music an outrageous worldly compromise, while others think of it as a providential agent of renewal and evangelistic outreach. Unfortunately, much of the discussion about the pros and cons of "Christian" rock music has been superficial, especially among those who believe that Christians should reject the "secular" version of rock music, but accept the "Christian" version. The discussion centers primarily on the rhythm, the lyrics, the physiological and psychological impact of rock music, the graphics of the music's packaging, and the lifestyles of the artists. These are important factors which are considered in the next chapters, but what is even more important is an understanding of the philosophical and theological presuppositions espoused by rock music.

Human activities are shaped by the presuppositions of individuals and nations. Taken together, these presuppositions form what we call a worldview which affects everything we are and do. This means that our understanding of God and of His revelation gives meaning to our life and shapes our activities, including the production of musical art forms. The changing styles of church music usually reflect a change in the worldview of the time, as interpreted by contemporary composers.

An evaluation of rock music, whether it be its secular or "Christian" versions, necessitates an understanding of the worldview (theological presuppositions) that gave rise to such music. What are some of the fundamental beliefs that rock music contains and proclaims, and why is the rock "creed" so widely accepted today? An understanding of the worldview of rock music provides a basis for determining whether or not rock music can be legitimately sanitized and made into a medium to worship the Lord in the beauty of holiness and to evangelize the unconverted.

For the sake of clarity, let me state at the outset the findings of this investigation. Rock music embodies and promotes a humanistic/pantheistic worldview which stems both from its Western African roots and secular humanism. This worldview openly rejects God and His revealed moral principles, promoting instead hedonism, individualism, materialism, amoralism, atheism, sex, drugs, violence, the occult, and other forms of human perversion.

Our study shows that by shifting the locus of faith from God to self, rock music knocks the props out of the Christian faith by making God a commodity used for personal gratification. Any attempt to sanitize and convert rock music into a medium to worship God and proclaim the Gospel ultimately prostitutes the Christian faith, weakening its witness to the world today.

Objective of This Chapter. This chapter seeks to understand the worldview of rock music by following what may appear to some as a tortuous procedure. The reasons for this procedure will become evident by the time the reader reaches the latter part of the chapter.

The first and broad objective is to examine how the production of music during the history of Western Christian thought has been influenced by the evolution in the understanding of God. The historical shift from the transcendental understanding of "God beyond us" during the medieval period, to the immanental conception of "God for us" during the sixteenth century Reformation, and to "God within us" perception from the seventeenth-century to our times helps us understand the gradual evolution of church music from the medieval chant, to the Lutheran chorale, and to today's "Christian" rock.

The second and narrower objective is to consider some significant ideologies that account for the origin and worldwide popularity of rock music today. We focus on three significant areas. First, we look at how the modern manifestation of a strong immanental "God within us" conception has caused people to seek an immediate emotional experience of God through the stimulus of loud, rhythmic music. Second, we discuss how the pantheistic/immanent orientation of Western African music has influenced the worldview and style of rock music. Lastly, we examine how the influence of humanistic ideas has shaped much of Western thought, especially during the past two centuries. We shall see that the convergence of these developments in our time has facilitated the adoption of rock music, both in the secular and Christian world.

Two Significant Studies. Two major studies have helped me to understand the relationship between the development of new religious music styles and the evolution of concepts of God. The first study is the doctoral dissertation of Wolfgang Stefani on "The Concept of God and the Sacred Music Style" presented at Andrews University on October 1993.

Stefani presents compelling documentation showing that "music styles are religious-value laden—they are veritable embodiments of beliefs about reality. . . . The issues surrounding sacred music style discussions extends far deeper than petty likes and dislikes. At the bottom line, the clash over sacred music styles may well be a clash of underlying beliefs about the nature of ultimate reality, not of inconsequential aesthetic preferences."[6]

In terms of our present study, Stefani's research suggests that the current debate over the use of "Christian" rock in church worship is ultimately a theological debate about our understanding of God, and not merely a controversy about aesthetic music preferences. This is a most important observation that provides the key to understanding why the use rock music, both in its secular and "Christian" versions, threatens the very theological foundation of the Christian faith. Those who argue that the use of "Christian" rock in church worship is simply a matter of cultural or personal preferences ignore the fact that church music embodies and expresses our theological beliefs. Both the style and content of church music reflect our understanding of God, His revelation, and our relationship with Him.

The second significant study is by Calvin M. Johansson, who is Professor of Music at Evangel College in Springfield, Missouri. He has written several books on church music, including a doctoral dissertation.[7] He has contributed two insightful chapters to this symposium. In his book *Discipling Music Ministry: Twenty-first Century Directions*, Johansson shows how "tracing the history of Western worldviews gives us a clear picture of culture's steady drift toward human autonomy. That move, unrelenting in its press for influence and control, has deeply affected the Christian church. Evangelism, teaching, and worship, as well as daily Christian living, have all been changed, albeit subtly, by the humanistic influence to make individuals and their desire supreme. Church music has been part of that change."[8]

Johansson notes that the change in church music brought about by contemporary humanistic influences can be seen in the relentless preoccupation with pleasuring self. He finds that "a survey of Contemporary Christian Music (CCM), the most popular genre of religious music, shows many songs transparently, even heretically, oriented around the satisfaction of people. . . . But when the preoccupation is with the self . . . then worship is convoluted, reflecting culture's elevation of people over God."[9]

Part 1
THE EVOLUTION OF THE CONCEPT OF GOD
AND OF MUSIC STYLES
IN WESTERN CHRISTIAN THOUGHT

The music used in Christian worship reflects a church's under-standing of God and of His revelation contained in Scripture. The problem is that there is an inherent paradox in the biblical revelation of God. On one hand, God is revealed as a transcendent Being, "the high and lofty One who inhabits eternity, whose name is Holy" (Is 57:15). On the other hand, God is revealed as an immanent Being, who dwells "with him who is of a contrite and humble spirit" (Is 57:15).

Paul W. Hoon perceptively explains that "Christian worship rests on a paradox, that God is both like and unlike man; He is personal, but He is more than personal. When the former aspect is exaggerated . . . God becomes a kind of divine pal, worship becomes chatty intimacy, devoid of reverence and evoking the more infantile elements in human personality. When the latter aspect is exaggerated, worship loses its concreteness and reality, and tends to evaporate into vague states of mystical piety."[10]

This apparent contradictory transcendent/immanent view of God has historically impacted Christian worship. Worship styles have swung from one extreme to another, depending on the Christian understanding of God. The lesson of history is that it is essential to maintain a balance between a transcendent and an immanent view of God in order to ensure a healthy Christian life and worship, including church music.

The swing from a predominantly transcendence-oriented, other-worldly worship and artistic expression, to an immanence-oriented, this-worldly worship and artistic style, can be traced in the history of Western Christian culture. Wolfgang Stefani offers a simple and useful categori-zation of this development under the following three headings: "(1) God beyond us, (2) God for us, and (3) God beside us/within us."[11] These three categories serve as a basis for our historical survey which shows how each of these views of God has affected Christian life and worship during the course of Christian history.

1. The "God Beyond Us" Orientation

Early Church. The transcendental conception of "God beyond us" prevailed, though in different forms, during the first fifteen centuries of Christianity. The early Christians strongly rejected the prevailing immanental orientation of pagan religions, where the gods were present and interacted with people. This was especially true of the mystery religions with orgiastic rituals designed to lead people into direct contact with the divinity. Music played an important role in these rituals and exerted an irresistible attraction for the masses.

Alfred Sendrey notes that the pagan mystery religions brought to Rome "a great number of foreign musicians and dancers. Their instruments and concert music gained little by little a firm foothold in the theater, and were later copiously employed in the entertainment music of the Romans."[12]

In some ways, the ecstatic rites of the pagan mystery religions which intoxicated the masses resemble the frenzy excitement caused today by rock concerts. Christians who believed in a holy transcendent God strongly rejected the musical extravaganza of pagan cults.[13] As Hanoch Avenary observes: "Jingling, banging, and rattling accompanied heathen cults, and the frenzying shawms of a dozen ecstatic rites intoxicated the masses. Amid this euphoric farewell feast of a dying civilization, the voices of non-conformists were emerging from places of Jewish and early Christian worship."[14]

Defenders of "Christian" rock music argue that they follow the tradition of Christians who in the past have adopted secular music and artistic forms to communicate the Christian message. This argument can not be supported by the witness of early Christians who refused to participate in, or adopt, those secular forms of entertainment which were antithetical to the Christian message and moral values.

In chapter 7 we shall see that Christians followed the tradition of the synagogue in prohibiting the use of musical instruments in their church services because of their pagan association. The popular view that rock music can be adopted and adapted to reach the secular society, because the church in the past has adopted secular music to reach the masses, is based on plain ignorance of the historical reality. The truth of the matter is that the early Christians distanced themselves, not only from secular songs, but also from the musical instruments used for secular entertainment and pagan worship. We return to this point in Chapter 7.

Rejection of Secular Entertainment. A second-century document known as the *Octavius,* written by Minicius Felix, contains a dialogue between a pagan, Caecilius, and a Christian, Octavius. Pagan

Caecilius charges his Christian friend, Octavius, of abstention from social life, saying: "You are abstaining from respectable enjoyments. You do not visit exhibitions; you have no concern in public display; you reject the public banquets, and you abhor the sacred contests."[15] Octavious acknowledges the truth of this charge and explains the motives that prompted this abstention, namely, the violence and immorality promoted by such shows were contrary to Christian values.

"For in the chariot races who does not shudder at the madness of the crowd brawling amongst itself? Or at the teaching of murder in the gladiatorial combats? In the theater also the madness is not less, but the debauchery is more prolonged: for now a mimic either expounds or shows forth adulteries; now a nerveless player, while he feigns lust, suggests it; the same actor disgraces your gods by attributing to them adulteries, sighs, hatred."[16]

The early Christians survived and became a transforming force in the Roman empire, not by sanitizing the pagan forms of entertainment in order to use them to communicate the Christian message, but by rejecting the secular, immoral shows and values promoted by the Hollywood stars of their time. They refused to attend their shows, even if it meant being ridiculed and rejected as "misanthropists,"—a term often used to denote their non-conformist lifestyle. Imagine what would happen today in America, or in any Christian country, if all professing Christians would follow the example of the early Christians by refusing to watch or participate in any form of entertainment that promotes violence or immorality! The entertainment industry would soon have to clean up their programs if they wanted to remain in business.

Music in the Early Church. In the early church, the music was largely inspired by the vision of a majestic, transcendent God and Savior to be approached with awe and reverence. We find a glimpse of such music in the "Christ-centered" hymns of the New Testament, especially in the book of Revelation (Rev 4:8,11; 5:9; Eph 5:14; 1 Tim 3:16; Col 1:15-20).

In discussing how the transcendent vision of the divinity moulded the musical styles of both early Christianity and Islam, Lois Ibsen Al Faruqi offers this informative desription: "Religious music avoided the emotive, the frivolous, the unfettered responses either to great joy or great sorrow. The limited range and contiguity of notes in Gregorian and Quranic chant, the prevalence of stepwise progression, the avoidance of large melodic leaps—all these contributed to this demand. The relaxed tempos, the calm and continuous movement, the rejection of strong accents and changes of intensity or volume were likewise conducive to an attitude of contemplation and departure from worldly involvement. The use of regularly repeated metric units would have tended to arouse associations, kinaesthetic movements and emotions incompatible with the notion of religiosity among Muslims and early Christians. These were therefore avoided. . . . Music contributed little or nothing to dramatic/ programmatic content or tone painting imitating the objects, events, ideas or feelings of this world. Hence abstract quality has been a marked feature. . . . Formal characteristics accorded with this tendency, making elements of unity and change dependent upon correspondence with poetic units rather than with narrative or descriptive factors."[17]

She continues explaining that not only the structure of the music, but also the way it was performed was influenced by the lofty conception of God and the avoidance of secular associations: "Performance practice, relying on the human voice, has avoided the secular associations which instruments might bring, as well as the chordal harmonies which could be suggestive of emotional or dramatic effects. Even the use of the human voice or voices . . . has avoided the sensual and imitative in order to enhance the spiritual effect on the listener."[18]

The solemn, awe-inspiring music of the early church was driven by a lofty view of God. Its avoidance of the secular associations that musical instruments might bring is particularly relevant to the current debate over the use of music and instruments associated with the rock scene. The lesson to be learned from the witness of the early church is that the worship of a holy, majestic God calls for sacred music which avoids secular associations.

The Middle Ages. The imperial recognition and protection granted to Christianity in the fourth century did not significantly change the transcendent "God beyond us" view of the Godhead. Christians adapted the artistic formulas used to extol the glory of the monarch to represent their conception of the omnipotence and transcendence of God. The development of sacerdotalism and sacramentalism distanced God even further from the direct experience of the worshippers, whose participation in worship was minimized. In fact, the singing was performed mostly by the clergy, and not by the congregation. Lay members were spectators rather than participants in the church services.

The conception of "God beyond us" was reflected in the music of the time, where, as Paul Lang points out, "the subject and aim of Christian cult music was and remained . . . the glorification of God and the edification of man."[19] The focus of church music, as Wolfgang Stefani notes, "was the transcendent God, and humankind was to be taught about Him and raised to His realm. Contemplation, rather than involvement was the emphasis; idealism, not realism; instruction, not pleasure; spiritual meaning, not psycho-physiological power were the objectives. These ideals can be traced in most Christian artistic expressions over a period of a thousand years."[20]

The societal consciousness of God as the transcendent and omnipotent Ruler of mankind, that existed during the Middle Ages, has never been equalled. As Calvin Johansson points out, "There were no 'sacred' and 'secular' categories. Art, music, and drama had but one end—the praise of God. No cost was too much, no effort too great to bring to pass that which brought glory to the Creator. Hence, art was full of ecclesiastical symbolism. In music, triple meter had religious significance because it was thought to symbolize the three persons of the Trinity. The musical interval of an augmented fourth was avoided because its lack of consonance was thought to represent the *diabolus in musica*, the devil in music."[21]

For most of the Middle Ages sacred music was limited to the monophony of chant, which consisted of one note sung at a time without harmony or accompaniment. Around the turn of the millennium, medieval composers introduced polyphony— two, three, or four parts sung simultaneously. This was an incredible innovation. Before polyphony, all singing consisted of one melodic line, known as chant. There was no harmony, no chords, no pianos, no orchestras.

Those who argue that the church in the past borrowed secular melodies to compose sacred music ignore the fact that medieval music was very homogeneous, and there was "no distinction between the sacred and the profane until the beginning of the Baroque Era."[22] "The differences between plainsong, troubadour and folk styles were less important than their melodic interpenetration and their common relationship to a timeless universal deity."[23]

Though battered by barbarian invasions and influences, the medieval society remained oriented toward God and the church. People lived to serve God with their work and church. They perceived God as a transcendent Being "beyond us" and their church music reveals their concern to honor the infinite and omnipotent Ruler of the universe, rather than to seek personal enjoyment.

2. The "God For Us" Orientation

The medieval transcendental orientation of "God beyond us" was gradually replaced, beginning in the sixteenth-century, with an immanent conception of "God for us." The Protestant Reformation played a major role in shortening the "distance" between God and the believer. By stripping away the mediatorial role of priests and saints and by emphasizing the priesthood of all believers who have direct access to God, the Reformation helped people to see God as a "kind" Being, "for us" and close to us, more than "above us."

The medieval vision of God as an exacting, unapproachable Judge was replaced by that of a loving God eager to save all those who accept the reconciliation provided through the atoning sacrifice of His Son. Though God was still recognized as above and beyond, the shift in focus was on the loving Savior whom the believers could approach directly and personally.

The Role of Luther. The new vision of the nearness and accessibility of God encouraged the production of a music that was more expressive of everyday life. Luther played a leading role in producing music expressive of the new understanding of God and salvation, and in promoting congregational singing in the common language of the people. Contrary to Luther, Calvin and Zwingli censured the singing of lyrics not found in the Scripture, allowing only the Psalms to be sung in worship.

In Luther's day, congregations were not allowed to sing in the Catholic church service. Thus, the "musical training" of most people consisted mainly of popular tunes picked up on the street. As Friedrich Blume points out, "people accustomed to singing only in a secular surrounding and to remaining silent in the traditional church . . . now they had to learn how to sing in the church."[24]

Luther developed a unique style of church music, known as chorale, by borrowing some familiar, singable tunes, to which he added Christian text. Defenders of "Christian" rock argue that since Luther borrowed tunes from barroom songs of the day and added Christian texts to them (known as *contrafacta*), we can also borrow tunes from the rock music of our day and add to them Christian lyrics.

Larry Norman, a well-known CCM leader, wrote the song "Why Should the Devil Have All the Good Music." The title of the song is drawn from a statement which originated with Luther. Norman felt that if Luther could use melodies that were sung in pubs, contemporary musicians could do the same. Poor Luther! He would be shocked to know how his words have been twisted to say something totally different from what they were intended to mean.

Luther and Secular Music. The appeal to Luther is frequent in pro "Christian" rock literature. For example, in his book *The Contemporary Christian Music Debate,* Steve Miller wrote: "The models for his [Luther's] lyrics were the popular ballads of his day. The tunes were borrowed from German folk songs, the music of the masses, and even a hymn to Mary. Luther was not concerned with the association or origin of the tunes as he was with their ability to communicate truth."[25]

In a similar vein, Michael Tomlinson, an Adventist pastor, wrote in *Ministry*: "Eliminating the secular roots of Christian music would mean to say good-bye to the hymns of Martin Luther, whose music was borrowed from secular German folk tunes."[26] In the same issue of *Ministry* (September 1996), Lillianne Doukhan, Professor of Church Music at the Seventh-day Adventist Theological Seminary at Andrews University, wrote: "Martin Luther used melodies and rhythms familiar to the people for his chorales. Contrary to Calvin, Luther did not perceive the church as separate from society; in his philosophy, secular elements could be transformed according to a new understanding."[27]

The argument that we can borrow popular rock tunes, because Luther borrowed secular, popular tunes of his day, is misleading and inaccurate, for at least five reasons.

First, Luther used what may be called the "classical" music of his day, and not a sacrilegious type of music like most secular rock music today. Luther did not adopt the sensual, erotic music of the day. On the contrary, he warned against the use of "erotic ranting" as being the devil's means to corrupt human nature.[28]

The tunes adopted by Luther, writes Ulrich Leopold, "were folky, but never vulgar. Rollicking drinking songs were available in the sixteenth century too. Luther steered clear of them. He never considered music a mere tool that could be employed regardless of its original association . . . but was careful to match text and tune, so that each text would have its proper tune and so that both would complement each other."[29]

Second, of the thirty-seven chorales composed by Luther, only *one* tune came directly from a secular folk song. Fifteen were composed by Luther himself, thirteen came from Latin hymns or service music, two had originally been religious pilgrim songs, four were derived from German religious folk songs, and two are of unknown origin.[30] What most people ignore is the fact that the one tune borrowed from a folk song, which "appeared in Luther's hymnal of 1535, was later replaced by another melody in the 1539 song book. Historians believe that Luther discarded it because people associated it with its previous secular text."[31]

These facts discredit the popular assumption that Luther borrowed the majority of his songs from secular sources. In fact, he derived very little from secular sources. Luther's favorite composer was Josquin de Prez, who is regarded as the most competent composer of that century.[32]

Luther Sought to Remove Worldly Connotations. Third, Luther changed the melodic and rhythmic structure of the tunes he borrowed from secular sources in order to eliminate any possible worldly influence. In his scholarly book, *Martin Luther: His Music, His Message*, Robert Harrell explains: "The most effective way of [negating] worldly influence would be to 'de-rhythm' the music. By avoiding dance tunes and 'de-rhythming' other songs, Luther achieved a chorale with a marked rhythm, but without the devices that would remind the people of the secular world. So successful was the work done by Luther and other Lutheran musicians that scholars were often unable to detect the secular origins of chorales. The other way in which Luther sought to remove secular associations from the mind of the congregation was through the use of Scripture and scriptural allusions in the texts. By filling his chorales with the written Word, Luther sought to direct the thoughts of his people toward the Living Word."[33]

Harrell concludes his well-documented study, saying: "A study of Luther's chorales reveals two important facts about Luther's use of secular elements in his sacred music: (1) Although there was much popular music available to him, from drinking songs to dance tunes to religious folk songs and carols, Luther chose only those tunes which best lent themselves to sacred themes and avoided the vulgar, 'rollicking drinking songs' and dance tunes. (2) No material which Luther used for a chorale remained unchanged, except for the one case noted previously. Rather, 'he carefully tested the melodies he considered, and when necessary molded them into suitability. . . . Alterations were freely made.'"[34]

Fourth, it is important to note that Luther lived in the "Age of Faith," and not in the "Age of Skepticism" like ours. The culture of Luther's time was influenced by religious faith and moral values. The major universities and the fine arts were controlled or sponsored by the church. The distinction between secular and religious music was relative.

Friedrich Blume explains: "Protestantism preserved the medieval classification of the world, with secular art subjected to an intellectual discipline characterized by piety and churchliness. Under these conditions the disparity between sacred and secular music could at first hardly become a problem."[35] In the light of this fact, "to say that Luther borrowed from secular sources is to admit that he relied on, at the worst, a religion-based culture."[36]

There is a world of difference between the secular culture of Luther's time and that of our times. The secular music of Luther's day was largely inspired by a religious faith, while most secular rock music today openly rejects and defies the Christian faith and moral values.

Fifth, Luther arranged music for young people of his time in a way to lead them *away* from the attraction of worldly music. This can not be said of "Christian" rock music today which retains the melody and rhythm of secular rock. Luther explained why he changed the musical arrangements of his songs: "These songs were arranged in four parts for no other reason than that I wanted to attract the youth (who should and must be trained in music and other fine arts) away from love songs and carnal pieces and to give them something wholesome to learn instead, so that they can enter with pleasure into what is good, as befitting to youth."[37]

In the light of these facts, anyone who uses Luther's statement "Why should the Devil have all the good tunes?" to defend the use of rock music in the church ought to know that the argument is clearly negated by what Luther said and did. Luther's use of secular music teaches us not to sanitize rock music which promotes sex, drugs, and violence, but to choose instead the best music of our culture and make it a fitting vehicle to communicate the Word of God. What a marvellous example we have in Martin Luther!

3. The "God Beside Us/Within Us" Orientation

The immanent concept of "God for us," promoted by the sixteenth-century Reformation, progressively moved more and more toward a subjective understanding and experience of God. This development from "God beside us" to "God within us" began in the seventeenth century and has continued to our time.

The immanent aspect of the immediate and intimate experience of God has been increasingly emphasized. The personal and internal experience of the divine became the hallmark of Pietism, Methodism, Evangelicalism, American revivalism, the Holiness movement, and Pentecostalism. Rock music, as we shall see, follows a similar orientation in offering to its fans the means to plug in to a "supernatural" power.

Wolfgang Stefani notes two different streams among these movements—streams which have been gradually merging together in the late twentieth century. "The first category—'God besides us'— included Pietism (in its initial seventeenth- and eighteenth-century phase), Methodism, and Evangelicalism. The second category—'God within us'—included nineteenth-century American Revivalism, the Holiness Movement, and Pentecostalism. The first stream stressed daily, cooperative relationship with the Holy Spirit, while the second placed emphasis on the abandonment to the Spirit's control. While both highlighted the closeness of the Divine, the former adopted a more reasoned posture, whereas the latter favored a more unrestrained, intuitive approach."[38]

A common characteristic of these movements was the adoption of tunes for evangelical hymn books derived from the music of the opera house and concert halls. Church music became very self-oriented, emotional, sentimental, and appealing to the senses. This was especially true in the rapidly developing Charismatic movement. The goal of music was to cause people to experience an ecstatic encounter with God at the emotional level.

Self-Orientation in Music. A good example of the self-orientation in music is the "Gospel song movement of the nineteenth century," which, as Calvin Johanssen explains, "gave new meaning to the concept of religious self-interest. Songs such as 'Will There Be Any Stars in My Crown?' and 'A Sinner Like Me' were typical of the 'me-centrism' of culture's progress. Coupled with melodramatic nostalgia, they joined the trend toward complete subjectivity. Gospels songs such as 'My Mother's Prayer,' ('As I wondered 'round the homestead, Many a dear familiar spot Bro't within my recollection Scenes I'd seemingly forgot'), as well as 'I am Coming, Dear Saviour,' were typical of the genre's selfish orientation."[39]

This self-orientation characterizes much of secular and "Christian" rock music, which speaks far more of "I" and "me," than of Christ and God. Even the recently knighted Sir Elton John, author of the popular song "Candle in the Wind," does not hesitate to sing about his solution to boredom:

> I'm getting bored
> being part of mankind,
> think I'll buy a forty-four
> and give 'em all a sunrise.
> Yea, think I'm gonna kill myself,
> cause a little suicide.[40]

What a tragic way to find a solution to boredom! Yet, this solution is hardly surprising when "self" displaces God in a person's life. The same self-orientation is present in many "Christian" rock songs, as we shall see in the next chapter. An example can be found in the words of the song "Beheaded," which is sung by the popular "Christian" band known as "Vengeance."

> I want (my) head chopped off
> You'll see (my) body rot
> But then (I'll) reign with Christ
> And then you will fry.[41]

This outrageous "Christian" song, which ends with the screams of tortured sinners, reveals a clear direction in rock music, namely, to focus on the human dilemmas, rather than on God's provision for the salvation of every human being.

Charlie Peacock, an awarding-winning artist, songwriter, and producer of Contemporary Christian Music (CCM), in his book *At the Crossroad: An Insider's Look at the Past, Present, and Future of Contemporary Christian Music*, acknowledges the shift from God to self that has occurred in CCM, partly due to charismatic influence. He writes: "By emphasizing the work and gifts of the Holy Spirit, especially spontaneous revelational prophesying and speaking in tongues, the focus shifted from knowing God through His Word to knowing God through experience. This in turn shifted the focus from thinking to feeling, wherein for many believers their experience became as much the measure of truth as the sure Word of Truth. . . . For some Christians, the desire for charismatic experiences gradually eclipsed their desire to learn of God through the Bible."[42]

Pentecostal "God Within Us" Experience. The present search for a charismatic experience through music can be traced to the early Pentecostal music of the nineteenth century, which usually took up to two-thirds of the worship service.[43] The music was characterized by hand clapping, foot stomping, and dancing in the spirit.[44]

"The intense singing was commonly accompanied by the strum of guitars, the rhythmic beat of tambourines and drums, and the blare of brass as new converts brought their instruments from now-forsaken dance bands into the house of worship."[45] Repetitious choruses with tunes of secular origin, together with drama and mime, were all used to generate emotional excitement rather than intellectual comprehension.[46]

George P. Jackson, a specialist on North American folk hymnody, provides a colorful eyewitness account of how music functioned in the service of a Church of God in Cleveland, Tennessee, in 1929. The music began at the high point of the service, known as "the altar service." "Then the songs' function, as a rhythmic, tom-tom-like noise for inducing the desired ecstacy, became apparent. For from that time on there was no let-up. The spirit moved some to dance, others to speak in the unknown tongue, to shout, to jerk, or to fall in a dead trance. Mourners in ever-increasing numbers fell on their knees, elbows in a folding chair, at the altar, while the exhorters clapped hands to the time of the music. . . . After half an hour of this, the singing came to an end. Also the instrument strummers, worn out, dropped out one by one, leaving only the piano player and a tambourine whacker whom I could not see, to carry on the steady, and almost terrifying rhythmic noise."[47]

Indiana Adventist Campmeeting. The use of loud, rhythmic music, to cause an immediate emotional "high" experience of God, was not foreign to early Adventism, as Ronald Graybill has documented.[48] An unusual manifestation of such an experience occurred at a campmeeting, held in Muncie, Indiana, on September 13-23, 1900. Stephen Haskell, an Adventist church leader and author, describes what he saw in a letter he wrote to Ellen White, on September 25, 1900: "It is beyond description. . . . There is a great power that goes with the movement that is on foot there . . . because of the music that is brought to play in the ceremony. They have an organ, one bass viol, three fiddles, two flutes, three tambourines, three horns, and a big bass drum, and perhaps other instruments which I have not mentioned . . . . When they get on a high key, you cannot hear a word from the congregation in their singing, nor hear anything, unless it be shrieks by those who are half insane. I do not think I overdraw it at all. I never saw such a confusion in my life. I have been through scenes of fanaticism, but I never saw anything like this."[49]

Ella Robinson, a granddaughter of Ellen White, offers us a similar description of such religious gatherings: "They were led to seek an experience of physical demonstration. The bass drum and the tambourines aided in this. It was expected that one, possibly more, of their number would fall prostrate to the floor. He would then be carried to the platform, where a dozen or more people would gather around and shout 'Glory to God' while others prayed and sang."[50]

It is noteworthy that the bedlam of noise of the Indiana Campmeeting and similar religious gatherings was inspired by the "Holy Flesh Doctrine," which was widely accepted by the Indiana Conference workers, including its president, R. S. Donnell.[51] According to their teachings, Christians can receive an incorruptible flesh now and be alive when Jesus returned. It should be noted that loud instrumental, rhythmic music played at their religious gatherings was designed to facilitate this physical experience of the divine transforming power. In many ways the "Holy Flesh Doctrine" represents another example of the "God within us" conception of the Divine that we have traced historically and of the attempt to experience God's power through loud and rhythmic music.

Ellen White took a strong stand against the "Holy Flesh Doctrine" and the music used to promote it. She wrote: "The Holy Spirit never reveals itself in such methods, in such a bedlam of noise. This is an invention of Satan to cover up his ingenious methods for making of none effect the pure, sincere, elevating, ennobling, sanctifying truth for this time. Better never have the worship of God blended with music than to use musical instruments to do the work which last January was represented to me would be brought into our campmeetings. . . . A bedlam of noise shocks the senses and perverts that which if conducted aright might be a blessing. . . . Those things which have been in the past will be in the future. Satan will make music a snare by *the way it is conducted*."[52]

Ellen White's warning had its intended effect. Loud and rhythmic instrumental music was discontinued in Adventist churches. It is only in recent times that loud, syncopated, rocky music has begun making its appearance again at Adventist youth rallies and in an increasing number of churches. This development is not surprising, since with prophetic insight Ellen White predicted at the turn of the century that "Those things which have been in the past will be in the future. Satan will make music a snare by *the way it is conducted*."[53]

Ragtime Music. It is noteworthy that the acceptance of loud, rhythmic music at the turn of the century by Pentecostal and some Adventist churches concides with the time when "ragtime music" was sweeping across America and Europe. On August 1899 Scott Joplin, a Black man known as the King of Rag Music, published *The Maple Leaf Rag.* People soon learned to dance to the syncopated beat of rag music, which was popularized by white band leader William Krell and others.

Rag music, which is the forerunner of the blues and of rock music, seems to have influenced the adoption of loud, rhythmic music by some Christian churches at the turn of the century, in the same way that rock music is influencing some Christian churches today. History is repeating itself. It is unfortunate, that all too often, Chrstian churches have been slow in learning the lesson of history.

From God-centered to Self-centered Music. The use of music to induce an ecstatic spiritual "high" is a manifestation of a strong immanental "God within us" conception, which causes people to seek an immediate emotional experience of God through the stimulus of rhythmic, loud music. The historical evolution we have briefly traced from the transcendental understanding of "God beyond us" during the medieval period, to the immanental conception of "God for us" during the sixteenth century Reformation, and to "God within us" perception from the seventeenth-century to our times, helps us understand the gradual evolution of church music from the chant to the chorale, and to today's "Christian" rock.

The popular attraction of "Christian" rock music today, as a means to induce an emotional "high," must be seen as the natural outcome of the gradual evolution in the understanding of God during Christian history. The shift from a predominantly transcendent view of "God beyond us" to an unmistakably immanent conception of "God within us" has encouraged the production of music which has gradually become more self-centered and less God-centered.

The historical evolution of church music traced above teaches us the importance of maintaining a correct understanding of God and His revelation. In Scripture, God has revealed Himself as being both transcendent and immanent, beyond us and within us. These two dimensions of God's self-revelation must be kept in proper balance to ensure a healthy religious experience and church music. Chapters 6 and 7 examine more closely how our theology must inform our religious experience, including the melody and rhythm of our music.

To understand why rock music has gained such an immense popularity in our society, and in many Christian churches, we need to briefly consider two significant concomitant developments. The first is the pantheistic/immanent orientation of the African music which is the root of rock music. The second is the influence of humanistic ideas which have shaped much of Western thought, especially during the past two centuries. Both of these developments, as we shall see, have facilitated the adoption of rock music in the secular and Christian world.

African Roots of Rock Music. In his penetrating analysis of rock music, published by Oxford University Press and entitled *The Triumph of Vulgarity: Rock Music in the Mirror of Romanticism*, Robert Pattison points out that rock music draws its inspiration not from the transcendental religions of Confucianism or Islam, but from its original home in Africa and India.[54] The reason for its presence in these cultures is a pantheistic/immanental conception of God—a Being not beyond, but within, the individual and the natural world. This conception is reflected especially in the structural features of the West African possession-trance type of music.

Pattison explains that the individual in these cultures "lives out a creed that swallows up history. His home is the eternal, primitive *now* from which rock traces its descent:

> Hail, hail, rock 'n' roll,
> Deliver me from days of old,
> Long live rock 'n' roll,
> The beat of the drums loud and bold,

sang Black guru Chuck Berry in the rock classic 'School Days.' . . . Rock is drawn to primitive cultures that promises release from a history that seems to promise the death of the imagination."[55]

The African roots of rock music explains why, according to Pattison, that "the Delta is the root and the Mississipi the stem for the flowering of African music in America. . . . Sam Philipps had the ideal credentials to be instigator of the rock revolution. He was born in Alabama and reared among the cotton fields. He grew up with a passion for the Black music that was an integral part of the agricultural life in the Delta and for the people that made it."[56]

"The secret of Philipps' success was not his devotion to black genius but his appreciation for the white taste. . . . He is the source of the most famous remark ever made about rock, made before there was rock:

'If I could find a white boy who could sing like a nigger, I could make a million dollars' . . . . Phillips found his white boy in Elvis Presley. Nineteen-year-old Elvis cut his first professional record for Phillips on July 6, 1954, a date that will live forever as the day on which rock began. . . . What belief in the incarnation is to a Christian, devotion to this myth of black origins is to the rocker."[57] It is unfortunate that Sam Philipps, who grasped the market potential of black music, identifies his own race with an offensive and unnecessary term.

The pantheistic/immanent focus of rock music resembles the this-worldly orientation of our humanistic culture, as well as "the God within us" orientation of many Christians today. The convergence of these three factors helps us to understand why rock music, both in its secular and "Christian" versions, has become the most popular genre of music today. Simply stated, Afro-American, humanists, and many Christians have been attracted to rock music because they find in it the medium that helps them to express and experience their similar pantheistic/immanent worldview. Each group experiences through rock music, though in different ways, the feeling of being plugged in to something greater than themselves.

Revival Music and Afro-American Conversions. Further support for the commonality between the African music and the "God within us" orientation of much of Christianity today is provided by recent scholarly studies on the relationship between Christianity and the Afro-American experience. The research indicates that prior to 1740, relatively few Afro-Americans were converted to Christianity in North America.[58] The situation changed dramatically with the advent of revival movements and campmeetings in the latter half of the eighteenth century, continuing into the nineteenth century. Conversions among Afro-Americans increased markedly, especially to Methodist, Baptist, and independent denominations.

Olly Wilson maintains that a significant factor often overlooked is "that several aspects of the common forms of worship used by the Protestant revivalist movement in the United States at that time were consonant with several traditional West African practices."[59]

On a similar vein, Melville Herskovits argues that Afro-Americans were attracted to the revival type of Christianity because "its ritualism most resembled the type of worship known to them."[60] Some of the common characteristics included "Loud emotional cries and groans throughout the service, worshippers leaping out of their seats, screaming, jerking, shouting, falling into convulsions, speaking in tongues, and engaging in dance; the use of music in creating an emotional atmosphere; the performance of hymns and spiritual songs in call-response format or verse-chorus structure where the congregations joined in on familiar choruses or repetitive lines; and the accepted exuberant and excited participation."[61]

Afro-Americans responded to this kind of revival music and programs, because in many ways they reflected their native African roots and cultural orientation. It was out of the same African roots that later rock and roll music was born. It is hard to believe, notes Pattison, "that the most prosperous civilization in the history of mankind should in the fulness of its power ascribe its popular music to the influence of an oppressed African minority atrophying among the farmland of its poorest economic sector."[62] Yet it happened. Why? The answer is to be found in the influence of humanism in Western societies—an ideological movement which, as we shall now see, shares a similar pantheistic, this-worldly orientation of rock music, and consequently found in such music a means to express the humanistic faith.

The Influence of Humanism. Humanism is an ideological movement that began in the sixteenth century with the cultural rebirth of the Renaissance and has gained increasing momentum until our time. We could sum up humanism as a shift in focus from divinity to humanity. The humanists largely repudiated the religious, other-worldly medieval culture, promoting instead self-centeredness, self-determination, self-pleasure, self-cultivation, and self-importance. During the succeeding centuries, humanism gave rise to such movements as the "Enlightenment," which emphasized the primacy of human reason, and "Romanticism," which idealized human passions and envisioned a fantasy world which could never be.

Arts, like music, came to fulfill the religious function vacated by traditional religion. This process was facilitated by the pantheistic orientation of Romanticism, an orientation which prevails today in our society. Pantheism rejects the existence of any transcendent being, identifying the divine with all natural processes. What this means is that pantheists seek to find God, not beyond them, but within them and in the things around them.

Pattison defines Pantheism as "a garbage-pail philosophy, indiscriminately mixing scraps of everything. Fine distinctions between right and wrong, high and low, true and false, the worthy and unworthy, disappear in pantheism's tolerant and eclectic philosophy."[63]

"Pantheistic ideas have gradually usurped the place of established opinion. Heretical pantheism is the orthodoxy of modern culture, a revolution in thought for which there is no precedent."[64] "Pantheism acknowledges . . . that we live in a universe of sensual experience of which I am the center and infinite circumference. By this admission, pantheism gains in honesty what it sheds in guilt."[65]

Rock music, according to Pattison, is the ritual of the pantheistic culture of our time, as "a means of approaching the infinite."[66] Through the ecstasy of rock music, the fan transcends the limitation of time and space and plugs into a surrealistic world of fantasy.

Many Christians are attracted to rock music and attempt to sanitize it for church use, because secular rock music provides what many describe as "a new kind of religious experience for young people."[67] In the next chapter we take a closer look at rock music as a religious phenomenon. For our immediate purpose, Evan Davies offers an adequate description of such an experience: "The rockmania behaviors manifest entrancement in the technical sense of being entirely possessed by the experience. . . . The regularity of the rhythm is enhanced by the overbalance of the bass and percussion. The output of excessively high volume creates a physiological sensory response which floods one's sensory modality. Reiteration of the thematic and verbal material also creates hypnotic effect."[68]

The capacity of rock music to create an hypnotic effect obviously attracts those Christians who are looking for an emotional "high" experience of God within them. Their theological understanding of God as a universal power present within them and around them, and their eagerness to connect to such a power, predisposes them toward rock music. Why? Simply because rock, through its relentless beat, loudness, and ritual dance, creates the false perception of plugging into the supernatural.

By adopting modified versions of rock music, Christians are susceptible to adopt the self-centered, hedonistic worldview of the rock scene and become citizens of the "City of Self." As Pattison explains, "In rock, the universe is composed of two cities. The City of the World is peopled by the zombies who have succumbed to cash. These zombies believe in transcendent values, traditional class antagonism, and politics as usual. This is a noncity, a city of negatives, of stifled creativity, of withering selfhood. Alongside the City of the World is the City of Self. The City of Self is peopled by rockers who acknowledge only one vulgar order of primitive feeling. Though it overlaps the City of the World, this City of Self is growing, creative, and potentially infinite."[69]

For the Christian, the alternative is between the City "whose builder and maker is God" (Heb 11:10), where "nothing unclean shall enter in it" (Rev 21:27), and the City of Self, where all forms of evil are welcomed. By choosing the music played in the City of Self, Christians run the risk of failing to enter into the City of God.

CONCLUSION

Four major conclusions emerge from the foregoing investigation. First, the production of music in Christian history has been largely influenced by the evolution of the understanding of God. The historical shift from the transcendental understanding of "God beyond us" during the medieval period, to the immanental conception of "God for us" during the sixteenth-century Reformation, and to "God within us" perception from the seventeenth century to our times, helps us understand the gradual evolution of church music from the medieval chant, to the Lutheran chorale, to today's "Christian" rock.

Second, the convergence that has occurred in our time among (1) the immanent conception of "God within us" popular among Evangelicals; (2) the humanistic/pantheistic view of God as a natural process, pervasive in our secular society; and (3) the pantheistic/immanent focus of rock music, derived from its African roots, each in its own way has facilitated the acceptance of rock music among Christians and secularly minded people. Since both groups are seeking to fulfill the inner urge for a pleasurable experience of the supernatural, rock music provides an attractive medium to approach the infinite through its hypnotic effects.

Third, rock music poses an insidious and subtle threat to the Christian faith by shifting the focus of faith from God to self and undermining the Christian claim to divine revelation. Pattison expresses this threat concisely and eloquently: "Rock knocks the props from under religion, first, by shifting the locus of faith from God to self, and secondly, by depriving sects and churches of their claim to exclusive revelation. By forcing churches to compete on the basis of their ability to titillate the instincts of their worshippers, vulgar pantheism compels the champions of organized religions to abandon their pretension to superior truth and turns them into entrepreneurs of emotional stimulation. Once God has become a commodity used for self-gratification, his fortunes depend on the vagaries of the emotional marketplace, and his claim to command allegiance on the basis of omnipotence or omniscience vanishes in a blaze of solipsism [self is the only reality] as his priests and shamans pander to the feeling, not the faith, of their customers."[70]

Fourth, the worldview of rock music is inimical and antithetical to the Christian faith. By rejecting the transcendent/immanent God of biblical revelation and promoting instead a pantheistic view of the supernatural that can be experienced through its rhythmic sounds, rock music is gradually undermining the *raison d'être* of Christianity. The use of rock music in worship is dangerous because it turns the church service into a make-believe fantasy world in which self-satisfaction is more important than the adoration of a holy God.

A suitable closing statement for this chapter is provided by Pattison's prediction: "In the short run, rock and religion are complementary and will remain so until pantheism shall have made the traditional denominations as precarious as the passing California cults."[71]

ENDNOTES

1. William J. Schafer, *Rock Music* (Minneapolis, MN, 1972), pp. 13, 99.

2. Ibid., p. 62.

3. Clair V. Wilson and Leona S. Aiken, "The Effect of Intensity Levels upon Physiological and Subjective Affective Response to Rock Music," *Journal of Musical Therapy* 14:2 (1977), p. 62.

4. Charles A. Pressler, "Rock and Roll, Religion and the Deconstruction of American Values," in *All Music: Essays on the Hermeneutics of Music,* ed. Fabio B. Dasilva and David L. Brunsma (Avebury, England, 1996), p. 133.

5. William J. Schafer (note 1), p. 76.

6. Wolfgang H. M. Stefani, "The Concept of God and the Sacred Music Style: An Intercultural Exploration of Divine Transcendence/ Immanence as a Stylistic Determinant for Worship Music with Paradigmatic Implications for the Contemporary Christian Context," Ph.D. dissertation, Andrews University (Berrien Springs, MI 1993), pp. 278-279.

7. Calvin M. Johansson, "Some Theological Considerations Foundational to a Philosophy of Church Music," DMA dissertation, Southwestern Baptist Theological Seminary (Fort Worth, TX, 1974); *Music and Ministry: A Biblical Counterpoint* (Peabody, MA, 1998).

8. Calvin M. Johansson, *Discipling Music Ministry: Twenty-First Century Directions* (Peabody, MA, 1992), p. 45.

9. Ibid., p. 49.

10. Paul W. Hoon, "The Relation of Theology and Music in Worship," *Union Seminary Quarterly Review* 11 (January 1956), p. 36.

11. Wolfgang H. M. Stefani (note 6), p. 225.

12. Alfred Sendrey, *Music in the Social and Religious Life of Antiquity* (Rutherford, England, 1974), p. 383.

13. For a discussion of the Christian rejection of the growing musical extravaganza in secular life, see Johannes Quasten, *Music and Worship in Pagan and Christian Antiquity* (Washington, DC 1983), p. 125.

14. Hanoch Avenary, "The Emergence of Synagogue Song," *Encyclopedia Judaica* (1971), vol. 12, p. 566.

15. *The Octavious of Minucius Felix* 12, *The Ante-Nicene Fathers*, eds. Alexander Roberts and James Donaldson (Grand Rapids, MI,1972), vol. 4, p. 179.

16. *The Octavius of Minucius Felix* 37, p. 196.

17. Lois Ibsen Al Faruqi, "What Makes 'Religious Music' Religious?" in *Sacred Sound: Music in Religious Thought and Practice*, ed. Joyce Irwin, *Journal of the American Academy of Religion Thematic Studies*, vol. 50, (Chico, CA, Scholars Press, 1983), p. 28.

18. Ibid.

19. Paul Henry Lang, *Music in Western Christianity* (New York, 1969), p. 58.

20. Wolfgang H. M. Stefani (note 6), p. 228.

21. Calvin M. Johansson (note 8), p. 36.

22. F. Joseph Smith, "Church Music and Tradition," in *Cantors at the Crossroad: Essays on Church Music in Honor of Walter Buszin*, ed. Johannes Riedel (St. Louis, MO, 1967), pp. 9-10.

23. Christopher Ballantine, *Music and Its Social Meaning* (New York, 1984), p. 92.

24. Friedrich Blume, *Protestant Church Music: A History* (New York, 1974), p.65.

25. Steve Miller, *The Contemporary Christian Music Debate. Worldly Compromise or Agent of Renewal* (Wheaton, IL, 1993), p. 113.

26. Michael Tomlison, "Contemporary Christian Music Is *Christian* Music," *Ministry* (September 1966), p. 27.

27. Lillianne Doukhan, "Historical Perspectives on Change in Worship Music," *Ministry* (September 1966), p. 7.

28. Friedrich Blume (note 24), p. 10.

29. Ulrich S. Leupold, "Learning from Luther? Some Observation on Luther's Hymns," *Journal of Church Music* 8 (1966), p. 5.

30. The data is compiled from different sources and is quoted in Robert Harrell, *Martin Luther, His Music, His Message* (Greenville, SC, 1980), p. 18.

31. Ulrich S. Leupold (note 29), p. 5.

32. Friedrich Blume (note 24), p. 8.

33. Robert Harrell (note 30), p. 21.

34. Ibid., pp. 21-22.

35. Friedrich Blume (note 24), p. 29.

36. Tim Fisher, *The Battle for Church Music* (Greenville, SC, 1992), p. 165.

37. Luther's foreword to Johann Walter's collection as quoted by Friedrich Blume (note 24), p. 78.

38. Wolfgang H. M. Stefani (note 6), p. 234.

39. Calvin M. Johansson (note 8), p. 48.

40. Cited in Steve Peters and Mark Littleton, *Truth About Rock* (Minneapolis, MN, 1998), p. 26.

41. Cited in Jeff Godwin, *What's Wrong With Christian Rock?* (Chico, CA, 1990), pp. 230-231.

42. Charlie Peacock, *At the Crossroad: An Insider's Look at the Past, Present, and Future of Contemporary Christian Music* (Nashville, TN, 1999), p. 44.

43. Larry T. Duncan, "Music Among Early Pentecostals," *The Hymn* 38 (January 1987), p. 14.

44. Ibid.

45. Ibid.

46. Delton L. Alford, "Pentecostal and Charismatic Music," *Dictionary of Pentecostal and Charismatic Movements*, ed. Stanley M. Burgess and Gary B. McGee (Grand Rapids, MI, 1988), pp. 693-694.

47. George Pullen Jackson, *White Spirituals in the Southern Uplands: The Story of the Fasola Folk, Their Songs, Singings, and "Buckwheat Notes,"* (Chapel Hill, NC, 1933), p.153.

48. See Ronald Graybill, *Singing and Society: The Hymns of the Saturday-keeping Adventists, 1849-1863* (Berrien Springs, MI, n. d.), p. 25.

49. Stephen N. Haskell, Letter to Ellen White, September 25, 1900. Ellen G. White Research Center.

50. See Ella Robinson, *S. N. Haskell: Man of Action (Washington,* DC, 1967), p. 169.

51. Ibid., pp. 169-170.

52. Ellen G. White, *Selected Messages* (Washington, DC, 1958), vol. 2, pp. 36-37, emphasis supplied.

53. Ibid, emphasis supplied.

54. Robert Pattison, *The Triumph of Vulgarity: Rock Music in the Mirror of Romanticism* (New York, 1987), p. 70.

55. Ibid., pp. 31-32.

56. Ibid., p. 32.

57. Ibid., pp. 32-33.

58. Olly Wilson, "The Association of Movement and Music as a Manifestation of a Black Conceptual Approach to Music-Making," in *More than Dancing: Essays on Afro-American Music and Musicians*, ed. Irene V. Jackson (Westport, CT, 1985), p. 13.

59. Ibid.

60. Melville J. Herskovits, *The Myth of the Negro Past* (Boston,MA, 1958), p. 233.

61. Wolfgang H. M. Stefani (note 6), p. 259. The source of the information is Portia Katrenia Maultsby, "The Use and Performance of Hymnody, Spirituals and Gospels in the Black Church," *The Western Journal of Black Studies* 7 (1983), p. 163.

62. Robert Pattison (note 54), p. 36.

63. Ibid., p. 23.

64. Ibid., p. 20.

65. Ibid., p. 27.

66. Ibid., p. 29.

67. Edward F. Heenan and H. Rosanne Falkenstein, "Religious Rock: What It Is Saying," *Popular Music and Society* 2 (Summer 1973), p. 311.

68. Evan Davies, "Psychological Characteristics of Beatle Mania," *Journal of the History of Ideas* 30 (January-March 1969), p. 279.

69. Robert Pattison (note 54), p. 159.

70. Ibid., pp. 186-187.

71. Ibid., p. 187.

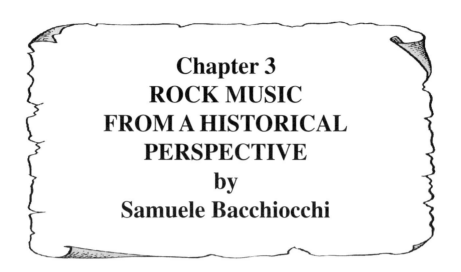

Chapter 3
ROCK MUSIC
FROM A HISTORICAL
PERSPECTIVE
by
Samuele Bacchiocchi

In his best-selling *The Closing of the American Mind,* University of Chicago Professor Allan Bloom examines some of the factors which in recent years have negatively impacted the intellectual, cultural, and moral development of American young people. The book stayed on the best-seller list of *The New York Times* for over six months, selling over a million copies. It is evident that many people appreciate the insightful analysis Bloom provides on what he calls "the closing of the American mind."

In the chapter entitled "Music," Bloom describes rock music as "junk food for the soul" which gives vent to the "rawest passions" and against which there is "no intellectual resistance."[1] We could also add that there is no significant resistance against rock music on the part of many Christian churches which have adopted a sanitized version of such music for their worship service and evangelistic outreach.

Bloom bases his conclusion on the observation of his students during the past thirty years. He notes that in the previous generation, when his students were raised on classical music, they had a greater interest for higher learning about truth, justice, beauty, friendship, etc. By contrast, the students of this generation, who are raised on rock music, show less interest for higher learning, being more interested instead in business and immediate pleasures.[2]

Classical music, according to Bloom, is essentially harmonic, while rock music is rhythmic. Harmonic music appeals more to the mind and makes its listeners more contemplative. Rhythmic music appeals more to the emotions and makes its listeners more passionate. The effect on the brain of prolonged exposure to electrical amplification of rhythmic music is "similar to that of drugs."[3] Bloom's thesis is supported by scientific studies cited by Tore Sognefest, a Norwegian musician and author who contributed Chapter 8 to this symposium. One study reported by the Scripps Howard News Service states that "exposure to rock music causes abnormal neuron structures in the region of the brain associated with learning and memory."[4]

In an interview, Bloom said that he agrees with Plato that "music expresses the dark chaotic forces of the soul and the kind of music on which people are raised determines the balance of their souls. The influence of rock music on kids today reasserts a central role of music that had fallen into disuse for almost a hundred years. Once we recognize this new centrality, however, we have to discuss which passions are aroused, how they are expressed, and the role this plays in the life of society."[5]

In recent years there has been considerable discussion on the revolutionary impact of rock music on the mental, moral, spiritual, and social behavior of people. Yet there are still significant questions that remain unanswered.

What is there about rock music that has attracted so many people worldwide and has made it such a revolutionary social phenomenon? Why is it that jazz or the blues, for example, did not have the same revolutionary impact on society? Is rock music just a musical style like many others, or does it embody certain "religious" beliefs, almost hypnotic powers, and value systems that are countercultural and anti-Christian?

Objective of This Chapter. This chapter seeks to answer the above questions by examining the historical and ideological evolution of rock music. The purpose of this survey is not merely to inform the reader about the history of rock music. Such information is readily available in far more comprehensive studies. Rather, our concern is to help the reader understand the real nature of rock music by tracing its ideological evolution and by focusing on the values that have emerged during the course of its history. This analysis continues in the following chapter which examines more closely the nature of rock music.

This study shows that rock music has gone through an easily discernible hardening process. What began in the fifties as plain rock has gradually become mellow rock, folk rock, soul rock, funk rock, psychedelic rock, disco, hard rock, heavy metal rock, punk rock, thrash metal rock, rave rock, and rap rock. New types of rock music are constantly appearing, while the old ones are still acclaimed.

A popular assumption is that these various types of rock music are just another musical genre that people may like or dislike, depending on their musical preferences or culture. Thus, nothing is immoral about rock music per se. It is only its improper use that is morally wrong. So, by changing its lyrics, Christians can legitimately use rock music to worship God and proclaim the Gospel.

This study invites readers to take a closer look at the intrinsic nature of rock music. Unfortunately, most people fail to realize that there is more to rock music than meets the eye. Our investigation indicates that rock music is a revolutionary "religious" countercultural and anti-Christian movement which uses its rhythm, melodies, and lyrics to promote, among other things, a pantheistic/hedonistic worldview, an open rejection of the Christian faith and values, sexual perversion, civil disobedience, violence, satanism, occultism, homosexuality, and masochism.

These characteristics of rock music become more evident as we trace its historical development and ideological characteristics in this and the following chapters. The findings of this study give us reason to conclude that rock music is not an amoral musical style, but a music of rebellion which defies God, rejects accepted morality, and promotes all sorts of perverted behavior. No other music has ever appeared during the past twenty centuries which so blatantly rejects the moral values and beliefs that Christianity represents. This conclusion becomes increasingly evident during the course of our historical survey of rock music.

We pose a probing question at crucial points of our investigation into the historical evolution of rock. Can rock music be legitimately transformed into a fitting medium to worship God and proclaim the Gospel's message? In answering this question, we keep in mind that *the medium affects the message.* The answer to this question becomes self-evident during the course of this investigation as we uncover the ethical and religious values promoted by rock.

For the sake of clarity this chapter is divided into four parts. The first part traces the roots of rock music to the African rhythmic music, which was adopted in various forms by Negro Spirituals, the Rhythm and Blues, and later by Rock and Roll. Special consideration is given to the role of Elvis Presley in the promotion of rock music and of its values.

The second part considers the development of rock music during the sixties, focusing especially on the influence of the Beatles. Through their music, these "fantastic four" young Englishmen played a major role in promoting the use of drugs and the rejection of Christianity.

The third part looks at music during the seventies. During this decade several factors contributed to the rise of superstitious and satanic types of rock music, which promoted various forms of satanic worship and occult activities. This alarming aspect of rock music is obviously ignored by those who see nothing wrong in the intrinsic nature of rock music.

The last part focuses on the hardening process of rock music which has occurred since 1980. During this period new types of rock music appeared which superseded the previous ones in loudness of beat, vulgarity, and profanity. The information gathered in this historical survey provides the basis for addressing the fundamental probing question of whether or not rock music can legitimately be transformed into a fitting medium to worship God and proclaim the Gospel.

PART I
THE BEGINNINGS OF ROCK MUSIC

In Chapter 2, we noted that rock music draws its inspiration from its original home in Western Africa where religious worship is often a bodily celebration of the supernatural through rhythmic music. As Michael Ventura points out, "The metaphysical goal of the African way is to experience the intense meeting of the human world and the spirit world. Spurred by the holy drums, deep in the meditation of the dance, one is literally entered by a god or goddess. Goddesses may enter men, and gods may enter women. The body literally becomes the crossroads, human and divine are united within it—and it can happen to anyone.

"In Abomey, Africa, these deities that speak through humans are called *vodun.* The word means 'mysteries.' From their *vodun* comes our *Voodoo,* and it is to Voodoos that we must look for the roots of our music. . . . Voodoo is not so much Africa in the New World as it is Africa meeting the New World, absorbing it and being absorbed by it, and reforming the ancient metaphysics according to what it now had to face."[6]

The popular acceptance of African rhythmic music has been facilitated by the convergence in our time between the immanent conception of "God within us" prevailing among Evangelicals, and the humanistic/pantheistic view of God pervasive in our society. We noted in Chapter 2 that since both groups are seeking to fulfill their inner urge for a pleasurable experience of the supernatural, African rhythmic music through its hypnotic rhythm, provides an attractive medium to approach the infinite.

A unique characteristic of African music is its rhythm, which to the Africans is the spice of life. English musicologist A. M. Jones explains that "He [the African] is intoxicated by this rhythmic harmony or rhythmic polyphony, just as we react to chordal harmony. It is this remarkable interplay of main beats that causes him irresistibly, when he hears the drums, to start moving his feet, his arms, his whole body. This to him is real music."[7] The beat is indeed the defining characteristic of rock music. We shall see that its unique rhythm, which impacts directly on the body, distinguishes rock music from all other forms of music.

A popular assumption is that the music rhythm of the African Voodoo is associated with Devil worship. This is not necessarily true. African culture sees supernatural beings as being inherently neither good or evil, but capable of going either way, depending on the skills of those musicians who practice their arts for good or evil. The presence of the occult and satanism in some types of rock music discussed later in this chapter, does not represent the original intent of the Voodoo beat, which was to communicate with the supernatural, whether good or evil.

Negro Spirituals. The roots of rock music are generally traced to the Negro Spirituals which developed in the deep South of the United States. These simple songs deserve our respect because they express the sufferings and oppressions of the American Negro. Though rhythmic in music, the Spirituals always contained a message of hope to be found in God's deliverance of His people. The sufferer finds the solution and ultimate hope in God, who exchanges tattered clothing for a white robe and delivers from death through a fiery chariot. The theology of the Spirituals may not always be accurate, but the great faith and trust in God is unmistakable.

In time, those Blacks who rejected the message of hope of the Negro Spirituals developed another musical form to express their suffering and despair. Their music, known as "Rhythm and Blues," became the expression of those who rejected any divine solution to their plight. The mood of the Blues is one of sadness and despair punctuated by a regular, heavy beat.

Hubert Spence observes: "The 'Blues' feeling was strongly evident but there was a clear rejection of any solution outside of man. Its message described man either drowning in his suffering, taking his life in the suffering, or partaking of some pleasurable act (such as fornication); through these actions the 'blues' were relieved. And by the 1930s in the fields and shanties of the delta country, there mutated this earthly, hard-driving style of music. It was played by blacks for the blacks (at that time called Negroes). Cured in misery, it was a lonesome, soul-sad music, full of cries and punctuated by a heavy regular beat."[8]

The Birth of Rock Music. After World War II, the beat of the Blues became intensified with electric guitars, bass, and drums. The first recordings were made by Chuck Berry, Bo Diddley, and John Lee Hooker. These "race" records, as they were then known in the recording industry, were played in 1952 by disc jockey Alan Freed on his late afternoon *Moondog Matinee* radio program in Cleveland. Borrowing a phrase occurring in several Rhythm-and-Blues songs, Freed dubbed the style "rock and roll." This phrase was used in the ghetto as an euphemism for promiscuous sexual intercourse engaged in the back seat of a car. In this perspective, the designation "Christian rock" sounds strange indeed.

Freed went on to New York City to play his tunes on WABC, one of the largest radio stations at that time. The accented beat began to take hold of American youth. Freed's popularity was not to last. In 1959 a payola scandal caused Freed to resign. He had been taking kickbacks from the rock singers and groups that he promoted. He died five years later at the age of forty-two, drunk and broke. The man who named the rock-and-roll era was its first victim.

The scandals which rocked the rock music did not diminish any interest for it. Singers like Bill Haley, Chuck Berry, and Buddy Holly contributed to popularize rock music. Especially influential was a movie entitled *Blackboard Jungle,* which featured a song by Bill Haley and the Comets called "Rock Around the Clock."

The real breakthrough came when nineteen-year-old Elvis Presley began singing the "race" songs in the Black style. Presley cut his first professional record for Sam Philipps on July 6, 1954, a date which many see as the real birthday of rock music—that is, when rock music began to capture national and international attention. After his first hit "Heartbreak Hotel," Presley established himself as the "King of Rock and Roll."

Rock music in many ways was similar to what was popular before, since it was marked by guitars, pianos, trumpets, and other instruments. Yet, as Hubert Spence explains, "the sound was quite different: a constant drum beat permeated the music which made it very conducive to dancing. The back-beat or syncopation became the dominant characteristic in its rhythm."[9] This distinguishing characteristic of rock music deserves careful consideration because of its unique impact on the physical aspect of the body. We examine the rhythm of rock music in Chapter 4.

The Influence of Elvis Presley. The broad impact of Presley in shaping the rock movement is concisely stated in the *Dictionary of American Pop/Rock*: "Presley represented not only a new sound but a new look (sideburns and ducktail haircut), new dress (blue suede shoes), new sensibility (the sneer), new mores (a more sensual approach to love), new speech ('all shook up'), and new dances. His hysterical acceptance was the expression of a young generation in conflict with and in rebellion against the older generation."[10]

Presley's stage techniques were strongly visceral in movement and they drew out of his audiences not only adulation but also a salacious response. Every girl wanted Elvis for a boyfriend and lover. The lawless impact of his music soon became evident in the destructive behavior and riots of his fans during his rock concerts.

"The older generation woke up. This snortin', snarlin' stallion of a singer was changing the way young people looked at life. Suddenly the triumvirate of school, family, and church had lost meaning. All that mattered was looking, acting, listening to, and being like Elvis. Pastors, parents, and newspaper editors took notice and began preaching against the rebelliousness that Presley symbolized. Something had to be done."[11]

Unfortunately, not much could be done because Elvis had set in motion a movement that not even his death could stop. He died in August 1977. Apparently a combination of prescription drugs combined with a crash diet placed a high strain on his heart, causing a heart attack. His death became for his fans his apotheosis, that is, the deification of their idol. His Graceland estate has become a multimillion-dollar industry and a virtual shrine for the pilgrimage of many Elvis worshippers. This important "religious" dimension of rock music is examined in Chapter 4.

A paradoxical aspect of Presley's musical career is his obsession for religious fetishism. He spent hours reading the Bible aloud and forced the visitors to the converted church building in Graceland to sit and listen to his readings. Throughout his career, Presley had Gospel quartets backing up his music. In his younger years Presley attended a Black Baptist church in Memphis (East Trigg), Tennessee, where he studied the responses of the people to rhythmic music. The movement style he adopted onstage was reminiscent of the movements used by Black preachers of the Pentecostal churches he attended. Presley was steeped in the Gospel style of singing. He unsuccessfully auditioned to join the Blackwood Gospel Quartet. Rock and roll was born when Presley recorded Rhythm and Blues songs as a white country boy sounding like a Black Gospel singer.

Presley and the Charismatic Movement. Presley's interest in Gospel music suggests the possible influence of the latter in the production of his rock music. Hubert Spence perceptively asks: "Dare we state that the birth of today's rock music was in collaboration with the Neo-Pentecostal fleshly movements? Movements supposedly under the power of the Holy Spirit became wedded to the visceral part of man. Truly, the flesh and the 'Spirit' were made one in man's thinking. This was a union the Devil had been trying to deceptively bring about for many centuries in the church. We read of this dialectical desire in the Corinthian church. Today, the Charismatic Movement has come from the same visceral womb."[12]

The suggestion that the Charismatic Movement—which has its tentacles in practically all denominations, including some Adventist churches—comes from the same visceral womb of the rock music movement deserves serious consideration for two reasons. First, the popularity of "Christian" rock in charismatic churches points to a common origin. Second, the commitment of both movements to use the stimulus of loud rhythmic music to induce an ecstatic "spiritual high" suggests also a common origin. In Chapter 2 we noted that the search for an ecstatic "spiritual high" has been facilitated by the gradual shift in Christian history from a predominantly transcendent view of "God beyond us" to an unmistakably immanent conception of "God within us." The latter makes the personal and emotional experience of God more important than any intellectual apprehension of God through His revealed Word.

In his book *At the Cross Roads: An Insider's Look at the Past, Present, and Future of Contemporary Christian Music,* Charlie Peacock, an award-winning artist and producer of Contemporary Christian Music, acknowledges that the "Charismatic experience has come to be perceived as a more personal, tangible, and valuable encounter with God than the encounter which comes by reading and meditating over the Spirit-inspired Scriptures. The fallout from this view of life in the Spirit has been substantial."[13]

During the course of this study, we will have occasion to reflect on the extent of the fallout. We shall see that the Charismatics' attempt to experience a direct encounter with God by means of the artificial stimulation provided by the rhythm of "Christian" rock ultimately manipulates God Himself into an object for self-gratification.

In light of the facts we have just uncovered about the origin of rock music in the sixties, let us pose again our probing question: Can rock music, which traces its roots in Voodoo's beat as a means to experience direct contact with the spirit world, be legitimately transformed into a fitting medium to worship God and proclaim the Gospel's message? In answering this question, we need to remember that *the medium affects the message.*

PART 2
ROCK MUSIC IN THE 1960s

Several factors contributed to the popularization of rock music in the 1960s. This was one of the most tempestuous decades in modern American history. The carnage of the Vietmam War, the "God-is-dead" movement, the rise of the hippie movement, political assassinations, the spread of mind-altering drugs, the fear of nuclear war, the violent protests in many college campuses, suspicion of conventional institutions, and other factors made this a time of great disillusionment among young people.

The Jesus Music. The seedbed of turbulence of the sixties facilitated the rapid growth of secular rock music on one hand and of the Jesus movement on the other. Many young people who became disenchanted with the drug culture and the political establishment began seeking for something deeper. Since they had long abandoned the traditional churches of their parents, they began developing their religious study groups. It became cool for young people to "try Jesus" as previously they had tried drugs.

To support the new religious experience, the Jesus movement introduced the so-called "Jesus Music," which later became known as Contemporary Christian Music (CCM). This music was a sanitized version of secular rock to which Christian lyrics were added. Larry Norman is regarded as one of the first innovators. He formed the rock band called "People" and recorded his first album *Upon This Rock,* which is considered by many as the first recording of "Christian" rock music. Norman became controversial among Evangelicals because of his outspoken lyrics which do not speak well for the Christian faith. The so-called Christian rock music was largely inspired by secular rock, which at that time was successfully promoted, especially by the Beatles.

The Role of the Beatles. The Beatles are considered the major players to hit the rock scene during the sixties. They were four young Englishmen in high-heeled boots, undersized suits, and with bowl-shaped haircuts. When they appeared on the Ed Sullivan Show in February 1964, sixty-eight million people (one of the largest TV audiences in history) tuned in to watch their performance. Initially, they did not come across as vulgar and immoral as they had become known in England. Their songs like "Love Me Do," "She Loves You," and "I Want to Hold Your Hand," appeared innocuous enough. Parents felt that they could trust them with their daughters for all that they wanted to do was to hold their hands.

The Beatles were received overwhelmingly in America. Their songs had a lock on the charts both in America and England. All ages opened their hearts to the fabulous four who seemed to be an innocent, fun-loving rock group. But before long the Beatles revealed their true colors.

In the summer of 1966, John Lennon made his controversial statement: "Christianity will go; it will vanish and shrink, I need not argue about that; I am right and we will be proved right. We are more popular than Jesus right now."[14] From that time on, the Beatles became heavily involved in drugs and Eastern transcendentalism.

Lennon admitted that for a period of three years he was constantly on LSD. He believed that LSD could lead people to the utopia for which they were looking. The Beatles often would spend a whole night under the influence of drugs during their recording session. Out of these recording sessions came the album called *Sgt. Pepper's Lonely Hearts Club,* which made manifest the Beatles' commitment to drugs.

By the end of 1967, most rock musicians were on LSD, commonly referred to as "acid." The list included John Lennon, Paul McCartney, George Harrison, Mick Jagger, Keith Richards, Brian Jones, Pete Townsend, Steve Winwood, Brian Wilson, Donovan, Cat Stevens, Jim Morrison, Eric Clapton, and Jimi Hendrix.

In his history of rock music, *Hungry for Heaven: Rock and Roll Search for Redemption,* Steve Turner writes: "This [LSD] was the Damascus Road tablet. People started out on trips as hard-nosed materialists after a bit of fun, and emerged with their egos ripped and mauled, unsure at first whether they'd see God or whether they were god."[15]

The association between rock music and the drug culture was influenced especially by Harvard University Professor Timothy Leary, author of *The Psychedelic Reader* and *The Psychedelic Experience.* He was a close friend of the Beatles whom he called "The Four Evangelists." Leary interpreted the effects of LSD on himself as the "deepest religious experience" of his life and founded the League of Spiritual Discovery, which campaigned for the legal use of LSD as the "sacramental catalyst to the new consciousness." At a convention of psychologists in Philadelphia, he stated: "Drugs are the religion of the twenty-first century. Pursuing religion without drugs is like studying astronomy with the naked eye."[16]

The impact on the American public was astonishing. Suddenly marijuana, speed, and LSD were "cool," the "in" thing to do. Songs like *Lucy in the Sky of Diamonds*, allegedly an acronym for LSD, could best be listened to if a person was "zonked." Tripping on LSD became the passage way to the rock scene. The music of Jimi Hendrix, The Grateful Dead, and Cream resonated with LSD consciousness.

For some rock groups, LSD became more than a trip to a vague "psychedelic experience." It was "disarranging minds by hauling demons and monsters from what appeared to be the depths of the sub-conscious."[17] Eric Clapton recalls an hallucinating experience in San Francisco while playing on stage with the group Cream. He felt his "guitar apparently resonating with the spirit world."[18] Drugs and rhythm became a staple of the rock movement because they both function as stimulants to experience a "spiritual high."

Rejection of Christianity. The theological views of the Beatles became clearer during the last five years of their writing (1965-1970). When they returned from India in 1965, they behaved as if they had some sort of "conversion" experience. Their "conversion," however, took place not on Damascus road, but at the Ganges river. There they discovered that LSD allegedly reveals a truth hidden to people, namely, that the whole world is a massive, heavenly divinity and we are all potentially divine. This meant that monotheistic religions such as Christianity, Judaism, and Islam were out; instead, pantheistic religions like Hinduism, Buddism, and New Age were in.

"In the song 'I Found Out,' the lyrics are very bold: 'There ain't no Jesus gonna come from the sky. Now that I found out I know I can cry.' Throughout the song Lennon states that he has seen through religion 'from Jesus to Paul' and that religion was simply a form of drug. In the same song he declares, 'God is merely a concept by which we measure our pain.'

"In another song 'God,' Lennon declared that he did not believe in the Bible, Jesus, magic, Buddha, Yoga, or even the Beatles; 'I just believe in me, Yoko [his wife] and me, and that's reality.' In the closing lyrics of the song 'God,' he instructed his millions of listeners, 'And so dear friends, you just have to carry on, the dream is over.'"[19] It is evident that for Lennon Christianity is only a fanciful dream which offers no hope for the future. The truth is that his songs have no message of hope—only an invitation to experience the fleeting pleasures of the moment. At times Lennon was brutally blasphemous, openly attacking Christ, Christianity, and the clergy.

Paul McCartney, another member of the Beatles, publicly announced in 1965: "None of us believes in God." Their official press officer, Derek Taylor said: "It's incredible! Here are four boys from Liverpool. They're rude, they're profane, they're vulgar, and they've taken over the world. It's as if they'd founded a new religion. They're completely anti-Christ. I mean, I am anti-Christ as well, but they're so anti-Christ they shock *me,* which isn't an easy thing."[20]

When the rock people turned their back against Christianity, they swallowed Hindu teachings, especially those of the guru Maharishi Mahesh Yogi, the founder of the Spiritual Regeneration Movement. In Hindu teaching, rhythmic music releases souls trapped in the world of delusion, enabling them to experience a "god-consciousness." The rock group The Who, who adopted Hindu teachings, used their music as an allegorical description of a journey from spiritual darkness to "god-realization."

The attraction of the Indian gurus did not last long for rock musicians. The fabulous wealth of the gurus, the number of Rolls Royces, and their abusive treatment of women, all revealed that they were less than gods. This disillusionment may have contributed to the obsession with Satanism which became characteristic of the 1970s.

It is impossible to estimate the impact of the Beatles' music on western civilization. Their music and lyrics promoted philosophies characterized by atheism, nihilism, rebellion, mystical surrealism, instant gratification, and a life built on the ups and downs of drug culture.

An article in *Time* magazine rightly points out that there is more to the Beatles' music than meets the eyes: "The battle lines involved much more than their music. It involved a drug culture, an anti-God theme, an anti-America, pro-revolution stand. It involved recognizing that Lennon was more than a musician."[21] As in the case of Elvis Presley, Lennon became for the rock fans a superhuman icon, a demigod. The cult of rock heroes is a significant aspect of the rock scene to be considered in Chapter 4.

Drug Craze and Acid Rock. The phenomenon of the drug craze gained momentum in the latter part of the sixties and has continued to our times. From 1966 to 1970, the drug scene and the hippies influenced the driving, hypnotic beat of rock music. A new form of rock music, known as Acid or Psychedelic Rock, began hitting the airwaves by 1967. The idea of this music was to recreate the illusion of the LSD (lysergic acid diethylamine) drug "trip" by means of music and the use of lights.

Acid rock was slower and more languid than hard rock, and it was used both to induce the "psychedelic trip" and to enhance such an experience for those taking drugs. The drug culture of the rock music of the time took its toll on victims. Drugs and alcohol largely account for the deaths of such famous rock stars as Elvis Presley, Jimi Hendrix, John Bonham, Jim Morrison, Sid Vicious, Janis Joplin, Bon Scott, Keith Moon, Bob Marley, and others.

The death of Jimi Hendrix on September 17, 1970, caused a worldwide outpouring of grief. For some rock fans, the death of Jimi was like the death of Jesus Himself. He was regarded as the most influential, dynamic, and musically competent player of the time. To gain the attention of the crowd, Hendrix would raise his guitar to his mouth, pluck the strings with his teeth, and then sensually fondle the guitar. He would pantomime an act of copulation by using the guitar as his sexual partner.

At the height of the performance, Hendrix would smash his guitar and amplifier, dousing them with lighter fluid. Amidst the smoke and flames he would walk off the stage. His stage manager carried spare amplifiers, guitars, and speakers, because Hendrix would destroy at least two speakers at every show.

Hendrix was especially known for his drug-oriented lifestyle expressed in such songs as "Purple Haze." He was arrested on narcotics charges on numerous occasions. The use of rock music and drugs was for Hendrix a kind of spiritual experience—a way to plug into a fake spiritual world. The drugs that he glorified eventually took his life. He had just performed at a huge Isle of Wight concert in Great Britain. On the night of September 17, 1970, he stayed in the flat of a German girl, Monika. They smoked grass together until 3:00 a.m. when they went to bed together. At 10:20 a.m., Monika found Henrix face down, suffocated in his own vomit from a drug overdose.

The lesson from the death of rock stars such as Presley and Hendrix is plain. The wealth and fame heaped upon the superstars of the rock culture do not provide inner peace and purpose in life. Inner peace and harmony are to be found not through magic drugs or exciting rock music, but through the Rock of Ages who invites us to come to Him and find rest in Him (Matt 11:28).

During this era, drugs became the means of bringing the rock culture into the realm of religion. Unfortunately, it was a godless religion, dominated by the Prince of Evil. The seeds sowed in the sixties bore fruit in the seventies, as satanic music was produced by numerous rock musicians.

In the light of the facts we have just uncovered about rock music in the sixties, let us pose again our probing question: Can rock music, which in the sixties rejected Christianity, glorified sexual perversion, and promoted drugs which claimed the lives of some of its heroes, be legitimately transformed into a fitting medium to worship God and proclaim the Gospel's message? In answering this question, it is important to remember that *the medium affects the message.* If the medium is associated with the rejection of Christianity, sexual perversion, and drugs, it cannot be legitimately used to communicate the moral claims of the Gospel.

PART 3
ROCK MUSIC IN THE 1970s

The open rejection of Christianity, the disillusionment of Hindu teachings, and the use of drugs to induce a "psychedelic experience" each in its own way contributed to the rise of a superstitious and satanic music which dominated the 1970s and has continued to our times.

The Decade of Satanic Music. In his book *Confronting Contemporary Christian Music,* Hubert Spence, Professor and President of the Foundations Schools, provides an informative list of the groups and titles of songs that came out during the 1970s and early 1980s with clear references to Hell and Satan. He writes: "First in the titles, there were 'Go to Hell' by Alice Cooper; 'Highway to Hell' by AC/DC; 'Hell Ain't a Bad Place to Be'; 'Good Day in Hell' by the Eagles. Some song titles concerned Satan, Lucifer, or the Devil: 'Their Satanic Majesty's Request'; 'Dancing with Mr. D'; 'Sympathy for the Devil'—all by the Rolling Stones. In this last song, 'Sympathy for the Devil,' Lucifer himself speaks and requests 'courtesy' and 'sympathy' from all who meet him. Other song titles indicate a theme of witches, wizards, and sorcerers, all of which are centered in the occult. Other songs included 'The Wizard' by Black Sabbath and 'Rhiannon' by Fleetwood Mac (dedicated to a Welsh witch of the same name). . . . Other songs deal with human sacrifice, such as the one by AC/DC entitled 'If You Want Blood, You've Got It.' It was again seen in Black Sabbath's song, 'Sabbath, Bloody Sabbath.'"[22]

Some of the rock music is directly addressed to Satan. Brian Johnson of AC/DC sings of Satan's pitiless killing of people in the song "Hell's Bells," saying: "I am a rolling thunder, pouring rain, I am coming like a hurricane; my lightning's flashing across the sky; you're only young but you're gonna die. I take no prisoners, won't spare no lives; nobody's putting up a fight. I've got my bell, gonna take you to hell; I'm gonna get you, yeah. Satan will get you, Hell's bells, yea, hell's bells."

Another AC/CD singer, Bon Scott, sings about Satan in the hit "Highway to Hell," saying: "Hey, Satan look at me, I'm on my way to the Promise land, I'm on a highway to hell." The song "Bohemian Rhapsody" recorded by the homosexual group "Queen" has a line which says: "Beelzebub has a devil set aside for me."

Chris De Burg mixes blasphemy with occultism in his songs. The cover of his album "Chris De Burgh Live S. A.," includes the Christian cross and the satanic symbol of the inverted cross. His song, "Spanish Train" ends with the words, "The devil still cheats and wins more souls. As for the Lord, well, he's just doing his best."

Iron Maiden has come under fire for making more satanic music than almost any other band. Most of his lyrics are obsessed with hellish imagery. The album, "The Number of the Beast," which is advertized as being forged in the fires of hell, includes a song called "666." The opening track of "Moonchild" is supposed to be sung by the devil.

Satanic Influence. As mentioned above, the group "Fleetwood Mac" had a hit called "Rhiannon," which is dedicated to a Welsh witch. Stevie Nicks, the lead singer, sometimes dedicated sons in a concert to "all the witches of the world." Their satanic leanings are evident in the closing lyrics of the song "Hail, great shadow of demon, great shadow of dragon."

The name of the group "Black Sabbath" refers to an occultic ritual which they have been known to introduce at some of their concerts. Their first album, "Black Sabbath," pictured a witch on the cover. Their albums include "We Sold Our Souls for Rock and Roll," with the cover featuring the satanic "S" and "Sabbath, Bloody Sabbath," with the cover showing a nude satanic ritual emblazoned with the number of the antichrist, 666.

Rock historian Steve Turner describes this period, by saying: "Like no rock group before them, the Rolling Stones invoked the devil, entitling an album 'Their Satanic Majesty's Request.' They even took on the person of Lucifer and, on many occasions, played on occult association. On a TV special Jagger ripped off his black shirt to reveal a tattoo of the devil on his chest."[23]

The rock music of this period that dealt also with occultic activities included conscious life after death in the Jefferson Starship's song "Your Mind Has Left Your Body," and Gary Wright's song "Dream Weaver." Sun worship is present in such songs like "Light the Sky on Fire" by the Jefferson Starship. A song called "God the Sun" was sung by the group America.

The Satanic influence of rock music can be seen also in those songs which encouraged suicide. For example, the song "Don't Fear the Reaper" was sung by Blue Oyster Cult; "Why Don't You Die Young and Stay Pretty" by Blondie; and "Homocide" by the Group 999 (the inverted 666).

Other songs promote the abuse or even the murdering of children. The Dead Kennedy, a punk rock band, recorded a song called "I Kill Children." Part of the lyrics say: "God told me to skin you alive, I kill children, I love to see them die. I kill children and make their mamas cry. Crush them under my car, I want to hear them scream; feed them poison candy, to spoil their Halloween." The same theme is found in the songs "Children of the Grave" by Black Sabbath and "Hell Is for Children" by Pat Benatar.

Perhaps one of the most disgusting satanic themes to be found in the rock music of this period is the idea of having sex with demons. "Many believed that a demon in female form had the powers of sexual union with men in their sleep. The 1978 hit 'Undercover Angel' dealt with this belief. Terry Gibb's 1980 hit 'Somebody's Knocking' promoted homosexual relationships with demons. And even Alice Cooper's song 'Cold Ethyl' promoted necrophilia or cohabitation with a corpse kept in the freezer."[24] Alice Cooper also sang a song called "I Love the Dead," in which a haunting melody openly and graphically speaks of engaging in sex with a dead body.

Satanic Symbols. The deep involvement of some rock stars in the occult and Satanic worship is reflected in their use of satanic symbols. As the Cross and water serve as symbols of Christianity, so Satan's worshippers have developed their own symbols which some rock stars use especially on the jacket of their albums. A perusal of all the Satanic symbols would take us beyond the limited scope of this chapter. Only a few are mentioned here.[25]

One of the prominent satanic symbols used by rock groups is the "S" depicted as a jagged lightening bolt. This symbol is derived from Luke 10:18, which says: "I saw Satan like lightning fall from heaven." The "S" printed like a jagged lightning bolt appears in the name of the rock group KISS and repeatedly on the album "We Sold our Soul to Rock 'n' Roll," produced by Black Sabbath. David Bowie is pictured on one of his album covers with the same jagged "S" painted on his face.

An inverted cross has been a symbol of satanism through the centuries. It is used as a background to some of the performances of Madonna and was a feature of the Rolling Stones' 1981 world tour. It has also appeared on the cover of a Duran Duran album.

Another satanic symbol is the *pentagram,* a five-pointed star-shaped figure symbolizing Satan worship. The rock group Rush uses this symbol extensively on their album covers. The satanic symbol "Winged Globes," which consists of a solar disk, is used by such rock groups as Aerosmith, Journey, REO Speedwagon, and New Riders of the Purple Sage. Other symbols include the serpent, the Egyptian pyramid, the goat's head, the skull, and the hexagram. The rock group Santana has an album *Abraxas* which is named after a powerful witchcraft demon. Another album, *Festival,* features a Hindo idol on the cover with two serpents on either side of the idol. The two serpents represent the duality of good and evil that can live in harmony with each other.

In her book *Numerology,* Sybil Leek, one of Britain's best-known witches, claims that "Many rock musicians cast spells and incancations upon their music, and then to demonstrate that they have made a pact with the devil they place occultic symbols on their record sleeves. Such symbols include crystal balls, goats' heads, upside down crosses, tarot card characters, pyramids, 2/4, palmistry signs of the Zodiac, the satanic ass, a five-pointed star in a circle, the extended tongue, and the 'Il Cornuto.'"[26] The latter is a traditional Sicilian sign consisting of the forefinger and the little finger extended, while the other fingers are curled into a fist. The sign is used by black arts practitioners to ward off "the evil eye." The Beatles appear to have been the first band to use this sign on the cover of their album "Yellow Submarine."

Satanic Involvement. The satanic symbols used by rock stars are reflective of their involvement in the occult and satanic worship. Some of them have expressed openly in interviews their involvement in occult activities. Hubert Spence reports some examples: "The lead singer for Meat Loaf stated: 'When I go on stage, I get possessed.' Their composer, Jim Steinman said, 'I've always been fascinated by the supernatural and always felt rock was the perfect medium for it.' The lead singer for Queen, Freddie Mercury, said, 'On the stage I am a devil. I think I may go mad in several years time.' David Bowie, who had drawings of pentagrams on his walls, said, 'Rock has always been the Devil's music because it lets in the baser elements.' Ozzie Osborne, formerly of Black Sabbath, is a professing devil worshipper. He said, 'I know that there is some supernatural force using me to bring forth my rock and roll.'"[27]

"The Rolling Stones outdid themselves in one concert years ago at Altamont, California. While they sang 'Sympathy for the Devil,' several members of Hell's Angels (a gang hired to be security force for the Stones) went to the front of the stage and beat a young black boy to death in front of thousands of screaming fans. Such actions inspired Don McLean to write his rock hit 'American Pie.' In the song he depicts the hideous scene of that concert: 'As I watched him [Mick Jaggar] on the stage, my hands were clenched in fists of rage. No angel born in hell could break that Satan spell. And as the flames climbed high into the night, to start the sacrificial rite, I saw Satan laughing with delight. The day the music died.'"[28]

Another example of the total disrespect for human life is provided by the rock group The Who. In 1979 they presented a concert in Cincinnati, Ohio, at the Riverfront Coliseum. At the opening of that concert, eleven people were trampled to death by the crowd fighting to get inside. What was the response of Townshend, the band leader, to these tragic deaths? Plain cynicism. In an interview published by *The Rolling Stone* magazine, he said: "We're a Rock and Roll band. You know, we don't ___ around, worrying about eleven people dying."[29] Such callous indifference toward the loss of eleven human lives can only be inspired by Satan himself, who, as Jesus said, "was a murderer from the beginning" (John 8:44).

In his book *Dancing with Demons*, Jeff Godwin gives startling evidence on a number of popular rock musicians who have studied the ancient beat of satanic worship. These rockers include Brian Jones (Rolling Stones), John Phillips (The Mamas and the Papas), and Paul McCartney (The Beatles).[30] These men have studied with satanic masters in order to learn how to use effectively the hypnotic power of the rock beat in their songs.

The presence of satanic influence in the rhythm and messages of many rock songs reminds us of Satan's objective to promote not only sin and confusion but also the *worship* of himself. This was true before he was cast out of heaven (Is14:12-16), it was true when he tempted Christ by offering Him all the kingdoms of the world in exchange for worship (Matt 4:8-9), and it is still true today. Satan knows that rock music is a most effective device that he can use effectively to lead millions to worship him rather than God. He wants worship, and this is exactly what he is receiving through the medium of rock music.

The manager of one of the biggest rock bands explains that rock has gone through four phases: sex, drugs, punk rock, and covenant with Satan. Speaking of the last phase he says: "Now we discovered the best motivation there is to buy a product. The best motivation in the world is religious commitment. No human being ever makes a deeper commitment than a religious commitment, so we decided that in the nineteen-eighties we are going to have religious services in our concerts. We are going to pronounce ourselves as Messiah. We are going to make intimate acquaintances and covenants with Satan . . . and we will be worshipped."[31] The statement is frightening because it speaks of deliberate association with Satan.

Summing up, the rock scene of the 1970s is truly a moral and social wasteland which defies description. It seems that the more depraved were the lyrics, the more albums were sold. Motley Crue sold two million copies of "Shout to the Devil" which says: "Out go the lights; in goes my knife; pull out his life; consider the bastard dead." The popularity of such outrageous rock music which blatantly promotes murder, violence, and satanic worship provides one of the most compelling evidences of the sacrilegious and depraved nature of rock music.

In light of the facts we have just uncovered about the rock music of the seventies, let us pose again our probing question: Can rock music, which promotes defiance against God, rejection of accepted moral values, and glorification of Satan be transformed into a fitting medium to worship God and proclaim the Gospel? In answering this question, it is important to remember that *the medium affects the message.* If the medium is associated with the rejection of the Christian faith, sex, drugs, and occultic practices, it cannot be used legitimately to communicate the moral claims of the Gospel.

PART 4
ROCK MUSIC SINCE THE 1980s

In tracing the history of rock music from its origin through the seventies, we have already detected an easily discernible hardening process. We shall now see that this hardening process continues through the eighties to our time. What began in the fifties as plain rock gradually became hard rock, heavy metal rock, punk rock, thrash metal rock, and rap rock, to name a few. New types of rock music are constantly appearing, superseding the previous ones in beat, loudness, vulgarity, and profanity.

David Marshall notes: "Rock, Hard Rock, and Heavy Metal contain lyrics. Kerrang, Thrash Metal, and Rave are just wild, iterative, mind-bursting loud noises with no obvious lyrics but, according to some sources, containing subliminal messages here and there."[32]

"Rock and Roll will never die," its devotees say. They are right. But if the past is any guide, the current rock music fads will be superseded by new types of rock music which will be more outrageous in glorifying sexual perversion, violence, drugs, and satanism. The reason is not difficult to find. Rock music is addictive like drugs, and those addicted to it are constantly seeking for stronger types of rock music in order to satisfy their craving. With this in mind, let us briefly look at some of the most significant developments in the rock scene since the 1980s.

The Sex Pistols. The 1980s brought sexuality and satanism to a new high in performances by The Sex Pistols and Madonna. The Sex Pistols is one of the basest rock bands for immorality of lyrics, music, and stage performance. They were catapulted into the rock limelight by the production of their song "Anarchy in the U. K." They were banned from Britain. Their music extolled homosexuality, bestiality, lesbianism, sodomy, masochism, transvestism, and other forms of perversion.

An indication of their depravity can be found in their album "God Save the Queen, She Ain't No Human Being." The song insults Queen Elizabeth as a nonhuman being at the very time of her Silver Jubilee anniversary celebration. Malcolm McLaren, the founder of this rock group, states their philosophy: "Rock and Roll is not just music. You're selling an attitude too. The kids need a sense of adventure and Rock and Roll needs to find a way to give it to them, wham out the hardest and cruelest lyrics and propaganda."[33]   A music that sells an attitude of open defiance against all accepted moral values should have no place in the Christian life and worship.

Madonna: The "PR" of Sexuality. Next to Michael Jackson, the most popular product of the rock culture of our times is undoubtedly Louise Ciccone, better known by her assumed name of Madonna. She was raised in a middle-class, Italian-American family in Bay City, Michigan. In view of her Catholic upbringing, it is incredible that she would take on the name of "Madonna" to parade her sexuality. After all, for Catholics the Madonna represents the virginity and purity of Jesus' mother.

By assuming a name that represents virginity and purity to promote her immoral sexual antics, Madonna revealed her determination to profane sacred symbols through her rock songs. A more appropriate biblical name she could have chosen for her seductive appeal is "Jezebel"— the woman who in biblical history became the symbol of seduction (Rev 2:20).

In some performances, Madonna uses a cross as a background for her sexual posing. In others she uses the inverted cross, which historically has been a symbol of satanism. When she sang her unbecoming songs, such as "Like a Virgin" and "Vogue," she wore a brass-spiked bra at her concerts, flaunting her sexuality and taunting the crowd with a smooth come-on. She has peddled pornography through the tens of millions of records sold.

In the *Rutherford Magazine,* John Whitehead states: "Madonna is trying to provoke us to re-examine the traditional definition of what is permissible and what is or not pornographic or erotic. . . . The only things left is hedonism. But it is not a hedonism anchored in 'secular humanism' or secularism. It is a hedonism anchored in a new form of paganism."[34]

In her book *Hole in Our Soul, The Loss of Beauty and Meaning in American Popular Music,* Martha Bayles, a television and art critic, notes that "Madonna is most at home in decadence. Her most convincing work, in terms of form expressing content, celebrates gay male life-style at its most hedonistic. For example, her video 'Vogue' sets a spare, Chic-influenced sound against a deadpan display of black-tie preening as practiced in gay clubs. More recently, 'Justify My Love' and some of the songs on the album *Erotica* use a whispery vocal and chicken-scratch beat to underline a deliberately vacuous celebration of sadomasochism. . . . 'Justify My Love' received a major sales and rental boost after being banned by MTV, and the X-rated book *Sex* was sold coyly shrink-wrapped in Mylar plastic."[35]

Madonna stands out for her ability to cynically manipulate religious imagery to promote her immoral agenda through her rock songs. The immense popularity that she enjoys is a sad commentary on the moral decadence of our society. Hubert Spence writes: "We as a country have gone so long without examples of true, honorable culture, we believe the glitter and extravaganza of a rock performance are the standard for the serious, artistic ability. And remember, she [Madonna] makes her money at peddling pornography as a cultural event."[36]

Madonna's sacrilegious attitude toward Christian symbols is shared by numerous rock musicians who, like her, interject religious elements in their names and performances. Some of them appeal to the public with such names as Jesus Jones, Faith No More, and MC 900 FT Jesus. In the album "Born Again" by the rock band Black Sabbath, one line says: "The only good Christian is a dead Christian." In another album called "Welcome to Hell," the rock group Venom, says: "We're possessed by all that is evil. The death of You, God, we demand."

The audacity of some rock musicians to call even for the death of God is indicative of the depth of their depravity communicated through their rock music. Let us pose again our probing question: Can rock music, some of which blatantly profanes and blasphemes God and the Christian faith, be transformed into a medium to worship God and to proclaim the Gospel's message? In answering this question, it is important to remember that *the medium affects the message.*

Michael Jackson: The Human Deified. The 1980s brought to the forefront the grown-up Michael Jackson, who first made a national debut in 1969 as a member of the Jackson Family. He stepped out as a single artist in the mid-1970s and was soaring in popularity by the 1980s. His two albums "Off the Wall" and "Thriller" made him an international celebrity.

The "Thriller," which has sold over forty million copies, reveals Jackson's fascination with the supernatural and the lurid. Both the album and the video deal with the occult, specifically the horror of living with corpses. To pacify the leaders of the Jehovah's Witness church, to which he belonged at that time, he placed a disclaimer at the beginning of the video, saying: "Due to my strong personal convictions, I wish to stress that this film in no way endorses a belief in the occult –Michael Jackson." The disclaimer does not detract from the fact that the album and video do definitely promote the occult.

In the videos "Bad" and "Dangerous," Michael Jackson lives up to the message of the titles. Again Martha Bayles, TV and art critic, notes that "After witnessing these videos, in which Jackson ceaselessly grabs his crotch, smashes car windows, and zips up his fly (in that rather unconvincing order), most people shake their heads and say he's out of touch."[37]

The truth of the matter is that Jackson is not merely out of touch, but sometimes out of control. The accusations of homosexual relationships with children, his strange marriage to Elvis Presley's daughter who soon left him, and the child he has fathered with another woman out of wedlock are all indications of his moral decadence. Yet "he has carefully staged himself throughout the world as an icon of deity. His videos regularly display him giving erotic gestures to the camera; his extravagantly rendered stage productions present strong implications of his godhood (manifested in his entrances and exits), lauding him as the savior of the world."[38] The sad reality is that Jackson desperately needs a Savior to cleanse him from all his sinful living reflected in his rock music.

Heavy Metal. The crave for more aggressive, noise-dominated, obscene, violent lyrics has contributed to the rise of harsher types of rock music, such as "Heavy Metal" and "Rap Music." We take a brief look at each of them here in closing our historical survey of rock music.

All observers, friend and foe, agree that Heavy Metal bands not only play one of the most strident forms of rock music but also create for its fans an imaginary world which glamorizes sex, drugs, and violence. Stephen Davis, the biographer of Led Zeppelin, the leading star of Heavy Metal, describes such music as "creating its own private universe for its fans. The music is only part of it. Something else is going on."[39]

The "something else" which goes on at metal rock concerts is mentioned by Tipper Gore, the wife of Vice-President Al Gore. She writes: "In [Metal Rock] concerts, the most strident bands not only play their music at the highest decibel levels, but perform what they describe as 'vaudeville acts' that glamorize explicit sex, alcohol and drug use, and bloody violence. Some depict the most extreme antisocial behavior imaginable."[40] We might say that metal rock bands not only scream, but they also provide reasons for screaming.

From its beginning in the seventies, Heavy Metal rock music has become increasingly more loud, vulgar, and sadistic. Martha Bayles describes this trend: "Good old promiscuity went the way of the dodo bird, as 'speed metal' and 'death metal' groups beefed up their act with bloody sadism. The mid-1980s were the heyday of rock videos depicting female victims chained, caged, beaten, and bound with barbed wire, all to wet the appetites of twelve-and-thirteen-year-olds for on-stage performances such as the famous one in which the group W. A. S. P. sang its hit song, 'F___ Like a Beast,' while pretending to batter a woman's skull and rape her with a chain saw."[41] "Metal rock stars brag about having intercourse during performances, recording sessions, and video tapings."[42]

Observers of the rock scene note that the young people most deeply involved in heavy metal are angry, troubled adolescents such as dropouts and runaways.[43] "These youngsters display a grotesque combination of vaunting ambition and drooping despair, based on the conviction that the only alternative to rock stardom is death in the gutter."[44] Nor do the stars provide much guidance. "They are just as nihilistic as their followers, only instead of getting punished for self-destructive behavior, they get rewarded."[45]

It is hard to believe that even Heavy Metal, known not only for its thundering beat but also for glamorizing sex, drugs, and violence, has been adopted by "Christian" bands to praise God and reach the unsaved. For example, "Christian" heavy metal bands like Stryper have shared the same concert stage with secular bands and have recorded their music on the same secular labels, which are sold in the same retail stores. The four members of Stryper look a lot like the members of the KISS band. They wear tight leather and spandex clothing, use a lot of makeup and chains, and have wild hair. The group wants to be known as "a metal band for Christ."[46]

Again we need to pose our probing question: Can Heavy Metal, which blatantly promotes some of the worse types of violent and destructive behavior, be transformed into a fitting medium to worship God and to proclaim the Gospel's message? Can the world of Metal Rock be legitimately and effectively infiltrated by sheep in wolves' clothing? In answering this question, it is important to remember that *the medium affects the message.*

Rap Music. Closely related to Heavy Metal is "Rap Music," which incorporates many of the sounds and styles of Heavy Metal rock. The term "Rap" refers to rhyming of words chanted or "rapped" according to a heavily rhythmic musical accompaniment known as hip-hop. In other words, Rap music consists of chanted rhyme backed by heavy rhythms. It is seen as part of the Afro-American tradition. It is produced on "a particular part of sound montage: Afro-American speech fitted to Afro-American rhythms, and addressing the problems of growing up black."[47]

Rap music is widely denounced by journalists, religious leaders, and Black opinion-makers for its shocking indecency, especially in promoting the abuse and exploitation of women. In his article on "The Corruption of Rock," British journalist Michael Medved points out that "the worst attitudes toward women are displayed by some of the Rap musicians. In Rap culture, terms like 'my bitch' or 'my whore' are habitually used to describe girlfriends. One of the worst offenders among the Rap musicians is NWA ."[48]

The album in which NWA is most abusive of women is called "Nasty as They Wanna Be." Its central theme is the mutilation of the genitals of female partners. In Florida a judge ruled this album too obscene for young people. In spite of its abusive and obscene language, the album sold 1.7 million copies.

In his article "How Rap's Hate Lyrics Harm Youngsters," Bob Demoss analyzes the same album where he found that in less than sixty minutes there were 226 uses of the "F" word, 163 uses of the word "bitch," 87 descriptions of oral sex, and 117 explicit references to male and female genitalia.[49] Numerous writers and church leaders have strongly condemned the violence promoted by cult rappers through their lyrics.

Hubert Spence notes that "Although crime and hate have been an ongoing side effect of the rock music, the Rap sound has mushroomed crime in the areas of the gang concept. Even small towns are now being affected, and Rap stars have become the teachers of these gangs. This type of music is one of the largest reasons for the recent upsurge of racial tension and fear in the streets. Such social fires are being fed by these rhythmic proclaimers of hatred and violence."[50]

The widespread denunciation of Rap music for its shocking indecency by many civil and religious leaders has not prevented Christian bands from adopting such music to praise God and reach the unsaved. Numerous "Christian Rap" bands advertise their services and offer their albums on the web. It is evident that no matter how shocking the new types of rock music are, there are Christians who are prepared to sanitize them by changing the lyrics.

CONCLUSION

The historical survey conducted in this chapter shows that rock music has undergone an easily discernible hardening process. What began in the fifties as plain rock, gradually became mellow rock, folk rock, soul rock, funk rock, psychedelic rock, disco, hard rock, heavy metal rock, punk rock, thrash metal rock, rave rock, and rap rock. Each new type of rock has proven to be more sexually explicit, violent, and vulgar than the previous ones.

Al Menconi, well known for his ministry designed to help Christian families evaluate the content of popular music, asks the question: "How did it happen?" His answer: "One song at a time." To illustrate how much perversion society is willing to accept, "if it comes in small bites," Menconi gives a sampling of eight rock songs, beginning from the 1964

Beatles' song "I Wanna Hold Your Hand" to the 1994 Nine Inch Nail's song "I Wanna F--- You Like an Animal" and the 1998 Janet Jackson's song "Tonight's The Night."[51]

The intensification of sexual explicitness and perversion is self-evident in these songs. In their song the Beatles "suggested that physical agressiveness was okay without an emotional commitment." The Nine Inch Nail's song is "rape-suggesting and aggressive." Janet Jackson's song "was the first popular song about lesbian sex." Al Menconi concludes: "Any song about any form of perversion is [today] considered acceptable. How did it happen? One song at a time."[52]

The time has now come to answer our introductory probing question which has been repeated several times during the course of our survey: Can rock music be legitimately transformed into a fitting medium to worship God and proclaim the Gospel's message?

By now the answer should be self-evident. The investigation of the worldview of rock music conducted in Chapter 2 and of its historical development in this chapter clearly reveals that any attempt to Christianize secular rock music by changing its lyrics ultimately results in the prostitution of the Christian faith and worship. Four major reasons support this conclusion.

(1) Rock Music Distorts the Message of the Bible. Rock music, in whatever forms, distorts the message of the Bible simply because the *medium affects the message.* The medium used to win the youth determines the nature of the message to which they are won. If the church uses a rock type of music, which is associated with sex, drugs, satanism, violence, and the rejection of the Christian faith, it obviously is not able to challenge the youth to live up to the moral claims of the Gospel.

The New Testament summons us to present clearly and compellingly the holiness of God's character, the desperate human plight, and the amazing grace of the Gospel. These issues of life and death cannot be presented with the frivolity and flippancy of rock music.

Listeners to religious rock may never be humbled by the majesty of God, nor be convicted of God's moral claims upon their lives. The relentless rock rhythm, the movements, the lights, and the demeanor of pop singers contain so much that is sensual and sexually suggestive that they hardly can communicate the holiness and purity of the Kingdom of God.

If we adopt a worldly appearance to attract the crowd, how can we paint in vivid colors the contrast between the kingdom of this world and the Kingdom of God? Paul recognized that the Gospel cannot be proclaimed through deceptive worldly gimmicks. Thus, he told the Corinthians: "My speech and my message were not in plausible words of wisdom [or we might say "with the exciting sounds of Greek songs"], but in demonstration of the Spirit and of power, that your faith might not rest in the wisdom of men [or we might say "in worldly excitements"], but in the power of God" (1 Cor 2:4-5).

The biblical call to "worship the Lord in the beauty of holiness" (Ps 96:9; 29:2; 1 Chron 16:20; 2 Chron 20:21) is compromised "by using combinations of sounds which are violent, mind-numbing, vulgar, raw, mesmerizing, rebellious, grossly repetitive, uncreative, undisciplined, and chaotic sounding. If listeners do not hear these things, it is because rock has dulled their aesthetic sensibilities."[53]

The casual dress and interactive behavior encouraged by the rock music played during the church service creates a social-club atmosphere, thus causing people to forget the solemnity of God's House. In my itinerant ministry around the world, I have been confronted with rock bands playing in Adventist churches and youth rallies. It is common in such settings for some members to dress casually as if they were attending a rock concert. Moreover, as soon as they hear the beat of the drum they start swinging. In one particular church, the swinging got out of control. The members filed out of the pews and started dancing in the aisles and some even on the platform.

Rock music, in whatever form, causes people to believe that the church is a place where they can have fun with God. The purpose of worship in the Bible is not self-centered excitement, but God-centered adoration (Ps 96:2; 57:9; 47:6; Rom 15:9; Acts 16:25).

(2) Rock Music Compromises the Church's Stand for Separation. The Christian mandate is not to conform to the world, but to confront the world with God's revealed truths (Rom 12:2). Scripture explicitly admonishes us to "take no part in the unfruitful works of darkness, but instead expose them" (Eph 5:11). John admonishes us not to "love the world or the things in the world" (1 John 2:15).

Paul understood the fundamental truth that the acceptance of the Gospel entails a separation from the world "by the renewal of your *mind*"

(Rom 12:2). Do the various varieties of religious rock music today invite young people to separate from the world through the renewal of their *minds*? Hardly so. Pop music appeals primarily to the body rather than the mind; it cultivates a taste for secular rock rather than for sacred music. It communicates a message of solidarity with the world rather than separation from it.

Larry Norman, a superstar in the CCM scene, acknowledges that "in order to decide whether Christian music has any weakness or strengths you have to decide what its purpose is. If it is for non-Christians—to convince them that Christ is an important alternative to seek in their life—then most Christian music is a failure because *it does not convincingly communicate that particular message.*"[54] Indeed, the message it communicates is one of conformity to the world rather than separation from it.

God's people have always been separated from the world by refusing to participate in the ungodly practices of the secular society. The early Christians turned the pagan world upside down, as we have seen in Chapter 2, not by sanitizing the pagan forms of entertainment (the circus, theater, music), but by abstaining from them altogether.

To preserve our Christian identity, we must understand our culture and refuse to accept what violates the moral principles God has revealed. "If we are blind to the spirit of our age, innocently sopping up the mores and cultural patterns of an unchristian society, our character and witness becomes weakened. Defences break down and before we realize it we are believing, saying, doing, understanding, and acting like the unregenerate."[55]

As Christians we cannot be the "children of the light," exposing the deeds of darkness, when we conform too closely to the world by adopting a music that embodies the very worldly spirit of rebellion. Such a close identification with the spirit of the world can only leave many confused as to the power of the Gospel to change the old nature into a brand new life.

(3) Rock Music Embodies the Spirit of Rebellion. Our historical survey has shown that rock music promotes, among other things, a pantheistic/hedonistic worldview, sexual perversion, civil disobedience, violence, satanism, occultism, homosexuality, masochism, and an open rejection of the Christian faith and values. No other music has appeared during the past twenty centuries which so blatantly rejects all the moral values and beliefs espoused by Christianity.

The spirit of rebellion of rock music is acknowledged even by the media. For example, *Newsweek* writes: "It is not just the earsplitting sound and relentless beat—kids at a heavy-metal concert don't sit in their seats, they stand on them and move—*it is the spirit of rebellion* .... The fans imitate the heavy-metal dress of their idols—sleeveless T-shirts, leather jackets, studded leather wrist bands—and in concert, they will shake their fists in unison above their heads as they scream the lyrics along with the band."[56]

As the embodiment of the spirit of rebellion of our times, rock music can hardly be adopted to express the spirit of Christian commitment to God. As Gary Erickson perceptively observes, "a sheep dressed in wolf's clothing is a strange way to approach the sinner or the saint. The whole scenario is confusing to the world and to the church."[57]

Our Christian commission is to communicate the Gospel not through confusing signals, but through a clear and direct message. Paul states this principle: "Even in the case of lifeless things that make sound, such as the flute or harp, how will anyone know what tune is being played unless there is a distinction in the notes? Again, if the trumpet does not sound a clear call, who will get ready for battle?" (1 Cor 14:7-8; NIV).

Rock music, even in its "Christian" version, does not give a clear call to "come out of her, my people, lest you take part in her sins" (Rev 18:4). Young people who watch Christian rock bands performing, whether in an open-air concert or in a youth rally at church, can easily fantasize that they are at a secular rock concert.

This is especially true when professional "Christian" rock bands mimic the secular rock scene with long hair, freakish dress, light effects, smoke, incessant drumming, vulgar gesticulations, and shrieking vocal sounds. With so much visual and auditory stimulation coming directly from the rock culture, young people can easily be led to believe that the music of Babylon must not be that bad after all. Ultimately, some are tempted to go back into the music of Babylon, rather than heeding God's summon to "come out of her my people."

(4) Rock Music Can Alter the Mind. Another important reason why rock music cannot be legitimately Christianized is that its hypnotic beat can alter the mind, weaken moral sensitivity and inhibitions, and cause people to write, see, and do the most hideous things. No other musical genre is known to have the same mind-altering capacities. This point becomes clearer in Chapters 4 and 8 where we examine significant scientific studies on the physiological and psychological effects of rock music.

At this juncture, it suffices to cite the testimony of Jimi Hendrix, who is regarded as the best rock guitarist who ever lived. He said: "Music is a spiritual thing of its own. We can hypnotize people with music, and when they are at their weakest point we can preach into their subconscience what we want them to say. That is why the name 'Electric Church' flashes in and out. The music flows from the air; and that is why I can connect with a spirit."[58]

Rock music can hypnotize people because it makes its impact *musically rather than lyrically.* As sociologist Simon Frith points out in his book *Sound Effects, Youth, Leisure, and the Politics of Rock 'n' Roll,* "A word-based approached is not helpful at getting at the meaning of rock . . . . The words, if they are noticed at all, are *absorbed after the music has made its mark."*[59]

The avalanche of decibels, especially of hard rock, is designed to blast the emotions and control the mind. Former rock star Bob Larson explains: "Rock, at least in its harsher forms, doesn't tickle your ears. It jams you in the skull like a freight train. You don't *listen* to loud rock; it baptizes you with a liturgy of sex, drugs, perversion, and the occult."[60]

To think that one can sanitize rock music just by changing its lyrics is like believing that poison can be made harmless just by administering it with love. Poison kills no matter how it is administered. By the same token, the rock beat alters the human mind, making it susceptible to wrong feelings and practices whether the lyrics are sacred or secular.

The capacity of rock music, in whatever version, to alter the human mind through its hypnotic beat, irrespective of its lyrics, makes the adoption of such music for Christian worship morally wrong. Christians must avoid any substance or medium that can alter their minds, because it is through the mind that we serve God (Rom 12:2) and are renewed into the image of God (Eph 4:23-24; Col 3:10).

Summing up, rock music cannot be legitimately transformed into Christian music simply by changing its lyrics. Such a split is not feasible because "Christian" rock, of whatever category, is still rock music—a music that embodies a spirit of rebellion against God and the moral principles He has revealed for our lives.

Much of the discussion about rock music focuses today on its effects on humans rather than on its offensiveness to God. The result is that many are more interested in defining what God might permit rather than what pleases Him. It is imperative to shift our focus from self to God and to listen to His call to holiness. This word is seldom used today, yet the Bible repeatedly calls us to be a holy people among a secular-minded and perverse generation (Ex 19:6; Deut 7:6; 14:2; Ps 1:1; Is 64:12; 1 Pet 2:9; 1 John 2:2-6). When we accept God's call to be a holy people and to come out of Babylon (Rev 18:4), then the rock music of Babylon will no longer be an attraction for us.

ENDNOTES

1. Allan Bloom, *The Closing of the American Mind* (New York, 1987), p. 73.

2. Ibid., pp. 70, 80.

3. Ibid., p. 80.

4. Robert L. Stone, ed., *Essays on the Closing of the American Mind* (Chicago, IL, 1989), p. 237.

5. Allan Bloom, "Too Much Tolerance," *Essays on the Closing of the American Mind*, ed. Robert L. Stone (Chicago, IL, 1989), p. 239.

6. Michael Ventura, "Hear that Long Snake Moan," *Whole Earth Review* (Spring 1987), pp. 28-33.

7. A. M. Jones, "African Music," quoted in Leonard B. Meyer, *Emotion and Meaning in Music* (Chicago, IL, 1990), p. 242.

8. Hubert T. Spence, *Confronting Contemporary Christian Music* (Dunn, NC, 1997), p. 62.

9. Ibid., p. 92.

10. Arnold Shaw, *Dictionary of American Pop/Rock* (New York, 1982), p. 287.

11. Steve Peters and Mark Littleton, *Truth about Rock* (Minneapolis, MN, 1998), p. 15.

12. Hubert T. Spence (note 8), p. 63.

13. Charlie Peacock, *At the Cross Roads: An Insider's Look at the Past, Present, and Future of Contemporary Christian Music* (Nashville,TN, 1999), p. 44.

14. As cited by Hubert T. Spence (note 8), pp. 79-80.

15. Steve Turner, *Hungry for Heaven: Rock and Roll Search for Redemption* (London, England, 1994), p. 49.

16. Quoted by David Marshall, *Occult Explosion* (Alma Park, Grentham, England), p. 42.

17. Steve Turner (note 15), p. 86.

18. Ibid.

19. As cited by Hubert T. Spence (note 8), p. 83.

20. Quoted by David Marshall (note 16), p. 84.

21. *Time* (September 22, 1967).

22. Hubert T. Spence (note 8), p. 98.

23. Steve Turner (note 15), p. 81.

24. Hubert T. Spence (note 8), p. 94.

25. For a description of the various satanic symbols used by rock bands, see Hubert T. Spence (note 8), pp. 96-97.

26. Sybil Leek, *Numerology* (London, England, 1976), p 42.

27. Hubert T. Spence (note 8), p. 98.

28. Ibid., p. 99.

29. *The Rolling Stone* (June 26, 1980), p. 3.

30. Jeff Godwin, *Dancing with Demons* (Chino, CA, 1988), pp. 126-128.

31. *Buzz* (April 1982), as quoted in John Blanchard, *Pop Goes the Gospel: Rock in the Church* (Durham, England, 1991), p. 49.

32. David Marshall (note 16), p. 56.

33. Quoted by Hubert T. Spence (note 8), p. 70.

34. *Rutherford Magazine* (January 1993), quoted by Hubert T. Spence (note 8), p. 70.

35. Martha Bayles, *Hole in Our Soul: The Loss of Beauty and Meaning in American Popular Music* (Chicago, IL, 1994), p. 334.

36. Hubert T. Spence (note 8), p. 71.

37. Martha Bayles (note 35), p. 332.

38. Hubert T. Spence (note 8), p. 72.

39. Stephen Davis, *Hammer of the Gods: The Led Zeppelin Saga* (New York, 1985), p. 116.

40. Tipper Gore, *Raising PG Kids in an X-Rated Society* (Nashville, TN, 1987), pp. 50-51.

41. Martha Bayles (note 35), p. 254.

42. See Tipper Gore (note 40), p. 94; also David Mandelman, "The Devil and Sam Kineson, *"Rolling Stones* (February 23, 1989), pp. 24-25.

43. See Lionel Trilling, "From the Notebooks of Lionel Trilling," selected by Christopher Zinn, *Partisan Review* 54 (January 1987), p. 17.

44. See Janet Maslin, "The Personal Side of Heavy Metal," *New York Times* (June 17, 1988), p. 7.

45. Martha Bayles (note 35), p. 261.

46. "A Christian 'Heavy Metal' Band Makes Its Mark on the Secular Industry," *Christianity Today* (February 15, 1985), p. 23.

47. Martha Bayles (note 35), p. 363.

48. Michael Medved, "The Corruption of Rock," London *The Sunday Times* (February 28, 1993), p. 6.

49. Bob Demoss, "How Rap's Hate Lyrics Harm Youngsters," *Reader's Digest* (August 1994), pp. 88-92.

50. Hubert T. Spence (note 8), p. 73.

51. Al Menconi, "Breaking Moral Barriers: One Song at a Time," *The American Family Association Journal* (January 2000), p. 18.

52. Ibid.

53. Calvin M. Johansson, *Discipling Music Ministry: Twenty-First Century Directions* (Peabody, MA, 1992), p. 29.

54. Larry Norman, *Solid Rock* (Carol Stream, IL,1992), p. 28.

55. Calvin M. Johansson (note 53), p. 29.

56. Cathleen McGuigan, "Not the Sound of Silence," *Newsweek* (November 14, 1983), p. 102. Emphasis supplied.

57. Gary Erickson, *Music on the Rocks?* (Shippensburg, PA, 1993), p. 74.

58. *Life* (October 3, 1969), p. 74.

59. Simon Frith, *Sound Effects, Youth, Leisure, and the Politics of Rock 'n' Roll* (New York, 1981), p. 14.

60. Bob Larson, *Rock and the Church* (Carol Stream, IL, 1972), p. 83.

Chapter 4
THE ROCK AND ROLL RELIGION
by
Samuele Bacchiocchi

For the past half a century rock music has exercised a revolutionary impact on our society, shaping the thinking and living of the younger generation. Other musical styles like rag, jazz, and blues have come and gone. After a short popularity, they have gradually faded almost into oblivion. In contrast, the cultural resonance of rock music still remains unabated. As noted in the previous chapter, rock music has gone through an easily discernible hardening process, from plain rock in the fifties to metal rock and rap rock in the nineties. New types of rock music are constantly appearing, while older ones are still acclaimed.

The impact of rock music is felt not only in the secular society, but also in many Christians churches which have adopted "sanitized" forms of rock music for their worship services and their evangelistic outreach. Christian rock stars and concerts look and sound very much like their secular counterparts. Analysts predict that rock music is here to stay, and its impact on the church and society will be felt even more deeply in years to come. We are told that "the future of rock and roll will be even more diverse, and more excessive than the present."[1]

The prospect of a continuously increasing demand for more excessive and violent styles of rock music is reason for concern, because, as noted in Chapters 2 and 3, this music promotes, among other things, a pantheistic/hedonistic worldview, open rejection of the Christian faith and values, sexual perversion, civil disobedience, violence, satanism, occultism, homosexuality, and masochism.

Some would disagree with this characterization of rock music, because the lyrics of some rock songs are not immoral and anti-Christian. On the contrary, they speak out against all manner of injustice, racism, hatred, and nuclear weapons. This important argument is examined at the end of this chapter. We shall see that the presence and mixture of good and evil lyrics in rock music may well represent an effective satanic strategy to use the good lyrics to lead some Christians to accept more readily the evil ones.

If all rock songs dealt only with sex, drugs, and violence, fewer Christians would be attracted to such music. But the fact that some rock songs address legitimate social concerns facilitates the acceptance of rock music as a whole, though much of it promotes anti-Christian values and lifestyles.

Objectives of This Chapter. This chapter seeks to account for the long-lasting and overwhelming popularity of rock music by continuing the investigation conducted in Chapters 2 and 3 into the worldview of rock music and its historical development. We found that rock music draws its inspiration from a pantheistic conception of God as an immanent, impersonal, supernatural power which the individual can experience through the hypnotic rhythm of rock music, often accompanied by drugs. This pantheistic worldview, promoted by rock music, has eventually led to the rejection of the Christian faith and values, and the acceptance instead of "a new kind of religious experience for young people."[2]

This chapter takes a closer look at rock and roll as a religious experience which involves the use of rock music, drugs, and dance to transcend the limitation of time and space and connect with the supernatural. The attempt to plug directly into the supernatural by means of strong stimulating repetitive rhythms represents an immanent understanding of the deity.

Musical styles are not neutral. They are value-laden, embodying deeply held beliefs about the ultimate reality. This means that rock music is not simply a musical style, but a social-religious phenomemon that reveals underlying beliefs about the ultimate nature of reality and the supernatural.

The book which has been most helpful for my understanding of rock and roll as a religious phenomenon is *The Triumph of Vulgarity: Rock Music in the Mirror of Romanticism* by Robert Pattison. Pattison is a professor of humanities at Long Island University. His book is highly literate and provides an insightful analysis of the ideological roots and social impact of rock and roll. The book is frequently cited by authors dealing with rock music.

The findings of this study are very important because they reveal that there is more to rock music than meets the eye. Contrary to what many Christians believe, rock music is not just another musical genre that can be sanitized to worship God and proclaim the Gospel. A closer look reveals that rock and roll embodies an endtime apostate religious movement of open rebellion against God and the moral principles revealed in His word. Thus, it is imperative for Christians to understand the broader implications of the rock and roll phenomenon.

PART 1
THE ROCK AND ROLL RELIGION

In his book *You Say You Want a Revolution,* sociologist Robert G. Pielke argues that rock and roll can best be understood as a religious movement which has brought about a religious transformation in American culture.[3] Pielke writes: "All cultural revolutions are, at their core, religious movements, and as such they are struggles and conflicts at the deepest level of our consciousness (personal and collective)."[4]

To characterize rock and roll as a religious movement may seem inaccurate because a religion presupposes the worship of a supernatural, transcendent Being. At first, this hardly seems the case with rock and roll, which is a style of music concerned with such worldly interests as sex, drugs, violence, rebellion, and social issues. However, a close look reveals that rock and roll is more than music. It involves a self-centered worldview, a commitment to a set of beliefs, and a lifestyle with its own system of fashion, language, and values. It promotes a pantheistic view of the supernatural, reflected in the worship of the rock stars as semi-gods, and in the use of rock music, drugs, and dance to transcend limitations of time and space and connect with the infinite.

An Experience of the Supernatural. If religion is defined as an experience of the supernatural which causes an individual to adopt a set of beliefs and practices, then rock and roll can be viewed as a religion. Observers of the rock scene acknowledge the religious nature of rock concerts. Referring to rock concerts, a newspaper reporter wrote: "They are the religious ceremonies of a nonreligious age."[5] In fact, they are religious ceremonies of a pantheistic age which reduces God to an infinite power present everywhere and experienced through the rock rituals.

In his classic book *The Idea of the Holy,* Rudolf Otto describes the goal of religion as the apprehension and appreciation of the "holy," which he defines as "mysterium tremendum," that is, the indescribable majesty of the supernatural.[6]

In the presence of the supernatural, believers are overwhelmed by a sense of self-abasement, awe, and nothingness. In many ways, rock fans have a similar experience, especially when attending a rock concert. As sociologist Charles Pressler points out, "It does not require a particularly difficult stretch of the imagination to compare this feeling with that of the acolyte [fan] attending a rock concert, the epitome of the rock and roll experience, at which one's sensibilities are overwhelmed by the power and demands of the music. I suspect it does not matter whether the concert features The Beatles, Megadeath, or the New Kids on the Block—they are merely representatives of different rock and roll denominations—the loss of self in the presence of some kind of overwhelming agency would be the same."[7]

Some argue that the intense feelings experienced by those who attend a rock concert are not different from the feelings experienced by those who attend a classical music concert. This argument ignores the fact that classical music does not involve, as does rock, "a lifestyle, a system of fashion, a set of values, etc.—only rock music conforms to the meaning of the term 'religion.'"[8]

Pressler notes that some of the characteristic feelings in Christian worship, such as awe, humility in the presence of divine majesty, attraction, and appropriation of divine power, "also describe the feelings of a person attending a rock and roll concert or its electronic equivalent. Therefore, there seems to be legitimacy to the argument that at least emotionally, in terms of one's experience of the phenomenon, rock and roll constitutes a religion."[9]

Pressler extends the comparison to the awareness of the supernatural as experienced by Christians at church and by rock and rollers at a concert. He writes: "The experience of the rock and roll acolyte [fan] at the rock concert involves the presentation, by the priests, the rock band, of the concept of rock and roll, the concept that discloses the values, power, and revolutionary passions of rock and roll music. . . . Prior to the concert, the mysterium tremendum [the sense of the supernatural] hovers behind the acolyte, as a kind of expected presence that never becomes fully present. As the concert or CD proceeds, the acolyte, and also the presenters, are swept into the maelstrom of energy issued by the numinous [supernatural power]."[10]

Feelings Rather than Reason. Unfortunately the energy released by rock music engages feelings rather than reason. Rationality is secondary to emotion. As the lyrics of the song "Oh, Me," of the band Meat Puppets puts it:

> I don't have to think,
> I only have to do it.
> The results are always perfect . . .
> I formulate infinity.

The rocker knows the world as a feeling and this feeling is by and large an optimistic pantheistic experience of the infinite power. The Beach Boys express this feeling in the song "Good Vibrations," which speaks of "Good good good good good vibrations." In the album "Surf's Up," the Beach Boys elaborate on the feeling of good vibrations: "Feel flows. Feel goes."

In their popular song "Love Is All Around Us," the Troggs express this central tenet of rock religion: "My mind's made up by the way that I feel." Instinct and not reason is the measure of the rockers' universe. We shall return in a moment to the rocker's pantheistic experience of the supernatural.

The rocker tends to act according to his passions, rather than according to clear moral directives. Here lies a fundamental difference between the Christian and the rock and roller experience of the supernatural. The Christian's encounter with God during worship results in a clarification and reaffirmation of moral directives already revealed in Scripture. By contrast, the rocker's experience of the supernatural leaves him without moral directives, only with inflamed passions to follow the excessive, violent, and immoral behavior of their rock stars.

A Movement Toward Excess. Lacking the moral directives of a transcendent God, rock and roll has given rise to what Pressler calls "the move toward excess." The hardening process which rock music has experienced during the past half century will continue into the twenty-first century. As Pressler puts it, "the future of rock and roll will be even more diverse, and more excessive than the present. Female nudity has already become commercially considered in music videos, and has been for some time. Violence has become more graphic, more extensive, and more gratuitous, to the point that Blackie Lawless, of WASP, describes the presentation, on stage, of the introduction of a nude woman into a meat grinder, whereupon the handle will be turned and raw hamburger will be sprayed over the audience."[11]

The movement toward excess promoted by the rock and roll religion will involve future experimentation with new instruments and louder electronic sound production in order to satisfy its adherents. In terms of moral behavior, "Youth will continue to press on toward new ways of expressing their *difference* and will continue to provoke their elders through the presentation of excess—the values themselves cannot change that much, because the elders are members of the rock and roll generation themselves. So the tendency will be to continue to push, to deny similarity, and the children of our heavy-metalheads will find their own way to torment their parents. The concept of the colossal [supernatural] will always be presented in the insistence of the backbeat . . . and the beat goes on."[12]

Worshipping Rock Stars. The religious nature of the rock and roll movement can also be seen in the commitment of rock fans to the music and lifestyle of their rock stars—a commitment which competes with that of nominal Christians to their Lord Jesus Christ. Robert Pattison notes that, "The rocker lives his music with an intensity few nominal Christians imitate in their devotion to the faith. He goes to concerts and listens to his music with the same fidelity with which the Christian of earlier generations attended church and read his Bible. One of the most frequently repeated mottos in rock lyrics is 'Rock 'n' roll will never die!'—a cry of belief. The stars of rock undergo literal apotheosis [deification]: 'Jim Morrison is God' is a graffito now perpetuated by a third generation of rockers."[13]

The apotheosis, that is, the deification of rock stars, is very important to the rock and roll religion, because it provides idols to be worshipped and imitated in real life. In an article entitled "Forever Elvis,"

Newsweek calls Presley "a saint" and a "Jesus-like" figure.[14] The article adds: "You were somehow caught up with this figure, you worshipped him."[15] The worship of any human being is plain idolatry and utter blasphemy against God. It is a clear violation of the First Commandment: "You shall have no other gods before me" (Ex 20:3).

The rock and roll religion promotes the worship of rock stars like Christianity teaches the worship of Christ. Such worship entails not only listening to the music of rock stars, but also imitating their lifestyles and visiting their shrines. This resembles the way Christians imitate Christ's life and visit the places associated with His life and death.

"Many Elvis impersonators continue to course the places of entertainment throughout the world. His antics are not only perpetuated by those who look and dress like him, but the whole mode of his style is preserved by hundreds of other entertainers throughout the music industry. His mannerism and techniques which made him a legend have not only pervaded popular secular music since his debut but are now imitated in much of the contemporary Christian music as well."[16]

The worship of Presley is indicated by the sale of "more than one billion records, tapes, and compact discs worldwide."[17] His Graceland estate has become a multimillion-dollar industry and a virtual religious shrine for the pilgrimage of many rock and rollers. The *Daily News* reported that "Graceland has been drawing 3,500 fee-paying visitors each day—or a total of 1.5 million [in five years] since it opened to the public in 1982. . . . it has become the most recognizable and most visited private home in America, second only to the White House."[18]

What is true of the deification of Presley is also true of other rock stars. For example, Michael Jackson, as Hubert Spence points out, "has carefully staged himself throughout the world as an icon of deity. His videos regularly display him giving erotic gestures to the camera; his extravagantly-rendered stage productions present strong implications of his godhood (manifested in his entrances and exits), lauding him as the savior of the world."[19]

John Denver, a popular rock star who was killed in a plane crash in 1997, said in an interview: "Someday I'll be so complete, I won't even be human. I'll be God."[20] Rock musicians aspire to become divine and want their followers to honor them, follow them, and worship them as the caretakers of a new world.

The worship of rock stars is also promoted through biographies that exalt their saint-like qualities. Robert Pattison points out that "The most successful books about rock itself are the hagiographies [biographies of saints] of its stars, like Jerry Hopkins and Danny Sugerman's life of Jim Morrison, *No One Here Gets Out Alive*."[21]

For some rockers, being in the presence of their rock stars is like a religious experience of the supernatural. In her book *I'm With the Band*, Pamela Des Barres, a rock groupie, says: "Something came over me in the presence of rock idols, something vile and despicable, something wondrous and holy."[22] She explains that being with rock stars is a cross between "pornography and heaven."[23] The crossing between the holy and the profane experienced in the presence of rock stars reflects the deceptive capacity of rock stars to make evil appear as good.

The Music of Babylon. The worship of rock stars has influenced an increasing number of Christian churches. In their thought-provoking book, *Music in the Balance*, Frank Garlock and Kurt Woetzel acknowledge that "A large segment of the Christian community has enthusiastically embraced this music of the world, the associated antics, and the philosophy. All three have been implanted into the life of the church. Not only have many Christians accepted the music as suitable for praise and worship, but an atmosphere pervades the contemporary Christian concerts not unlike the early concerts of the Elvis era. Believers have made idols of their own rock and roll singers and continue to worship at their feet with devotion and their pocket books."[24]

The imitation of rock stars and their music in church services and concerts reminds us of the apocalyptic description of the endtime false worship promoted by those who bid to "make an image for the beast" (Rev 13:14). In Revelation 14 the beast and its image (v. 9) are identified with the false worship promoted by Babylon (v.8). Could it be that Satan is using deceptive rock music to bring about the Endtime false worship, as he used in the Plain of Dura of ancient Babylon to lead all the people to worship the golden image (Dan 3:7, 10)? We take up this question again in the closing remarks.

A Pantheistic Religion. Another significant indication of the religious nature of rock and roll can be found in its pantheistic orientation. Robert Pattison offers an insightful analysis of the pantheistic beliefs present in rock music. He traces these beliefs to the pantheistic ideas of Romanticism, a popular nineteenth-century humanistic movement which is still very pervasive today.[25]

Pantheism rejects the existence of any transcendent personal being, identifying the divine with all the natural processes. What this means is that, for the rock and rollers, God is not a transcendent personal Being beyond them, but an infinite power present around them and within them. Incredible as it may seem, the goal of rock is to "subsume the universe and become God."[26] God is "obliterated in a pantheist's cosmic orgasm."[27] Rock music, according to Pattison, is the ritual of the pantheistic culture of our time, "a means of approaching the infinite."[28] Through the ecstasy of rock music, the rock and roller transcends the limitations of time and space, and plugs into the infinite.

The pantheistic rock and roller equates self with God and the world at large. His feelings, rather than reason, are the fundamental way of knowing. This pantheistic mentality is reflected in the popular song "We Are the World," which was composed as a campaign song to raise money for African famine victims. Pattison observes that "by simultaneously playing on rock's expansive pantheism and its sentimentality about the primitive, the makers of 'We Are the World' created a song that zoomed to the top of the singles charts in four weeks and shipped 'multi-platinum' with certified sales of four million records in one month."[29]

The same pantheistic sentiment is expressed in the famous Beatles' song "I am the Walrus": "I am he as you are he as you are me and as we are all together." "All variations of self—I, he, you, we, they—are interchangeable. All feelings and events are equally valid, equally present, equally meaningful. Every event is the center of the universe. There is no transcendent location for meaning. . . . In *Eureka* Poe had written: 'That God may be all in all, each must become God.'"[30]

The goal of the rock religion, to subsume the universe and to become God, reminds us of the temptation which led our foreparents to rebel against God, with all the resulting consequences. The deceiver assured Adam and Eve that by partaking of the forbidden fruit, they would have a magic experience: "You will be like God" (Gen 3:5). In many ways this is what rock music promises to its followers: "If you listen to it you will lose consciousness of your human limitations and enjoy a godlike experience."

Pantheism and the Imperative of Fun. By reducing God to the natural process of the universe which is also within ourselves, rock teaches people to forget about a transcendent God and to find meaning instead in the immediate pleasure offered by the material world which they can feel. This explains why the pantheistic orientation of rock and roll leads to a hedonistic lifestyle, that is, to the search for immediate pleasure.

Pattison gives several examples of rock musicians to illustrate this point. "Chuck Berry is the universally acclaimed black prophet of the rock era because his songs are relentlessly about fun: 'I'm keep on dancin' till I got my kicks!' Fun, the highest aestetic achievement of a rigorous pantheism like Whitman's or rock's, is the pleasure derived from a universe which is ourselves and which we cannot transcend because to know it is to be in it: 'Well if you feel it 'n' like it, Go get your lover, then reel it 'n' rock it.' Chuck Berry's is a universe that pivots on an untranscendent celebration of the energy I can extract from the present moment without recourse to anything but myself. 'Go, go' is the repeated imperative of his lyrics, the imperative of fun."[31]

Another example of pantheistic hedonism is popular rock star Bob Dylan, of whom Pattison says: "After the religious imagery of 'I Dreamed I Saw St. Augustine' and the mystic allegory of 'All Along the Watch-tower,' Dylan ended his *John Wesley Harding* album with the apparently incongruous country-rock ballad, 'I'll Be Your Baby Tonight':

Kick your shoes off,
Do not fear,
Bring that bottle over here,
I'll be your baby tonight.

The troubles of the world enumerated in the lyrics of *John Wesley Harding* vanish in the rocker's final commitment to the sensible present of tonight, and what Dylan tells his lover is what rock has to say to transcendental observers everywhere:

Close your eyes, close the door,
You do not have to worry anymore,
I'll be your baby tonight.

Dylan raises Chuck Berry's doctrine of fun to the highest of rock art."[32]

The substitution of fun for the joy that comes from the enjoyment of respectable forms of art reveals the depraved nature of rock music. Its goal is to lead people away from the enjoyment of beautiful, genuine art inspired by a transcendent God, into the immediate excitement generated by the abuse of God's good creation.

PART 2
THE RITUAL OF SEX, DRUGS, AND DANCE

Sex as Union with the Infinite. Sex plays a vital role in the pantheistic religion of rock and roll because it is seen as an important ritual to experience union with the infinite. Some of the lyrics of rock songs that glorify sex are too obscene to be included here.[33] Even the less obscene samples given below are offensive. To omit them altogether could be interpreted as a failure to substantiate that sex is a vital component of the rock and roll religion.

Tone Loc is very graphic in the song "Wild Thing," which reached number two on the charts:

Could not get her off my ____
She was like static cling.
That's what happens
When bodies start slappin'
From doing the wild thing.

In her song "Throb," Janet Jackson, Michael's younger sister, relies on sexual sights that "build to an orgasmic, S———." The song "Anytime, Anyplace" depicts public sex. Paula Abdul uses sensual and erotic lyrics in such songs as "Head Over Heels, "Get Your Groove On," and "Sexy Thoughts."

The rock religion worships the genitalia as the creative hub of the universe. "I am the creative hub of the universe, and the creative hub of me is my genitalia. Little Feat says: 'I have a rocket in my pocket.' The crotch is the launchpad for the conquest of the universe. Rock has restored the pantheistic adoration of the phallus to the West. The real rock star is a young male, horny, and well-hung. Jim Morrison and Iggy Pop are the most prominent of a series of rock stars who have exposed themselves for a grateful public. Other rock stars, intimidated by modesty or the law, have propitiated the ritual demands of their audience by padding their crotches or highlighting their endowments. David Lee Roth, formerly of Van Halen and one of rock's transient sex symbols, usually performs in tight outfits accented by a bulging red G-string. With minor variations, his is the costume of most hard-rock idols."[34]

The worship of sexual organs is evident even in some album covers. That of "Velvet Underground and Nico," by Velvet Underground, features a yellow banana that peels back to reveal pink banana-flesh beneath. The album "Sticky Fingers," by Rolling Stones, features the crotch of a bulging pair of jeans with the zipper down to reveal the underwear.

"The ideal rock star is sexuality incarnate. He is the focus of every possible taste. . . . In life, Mick Jagger has come closest to fulfilling rock's pansexual fantasy, and he has received equal sexual obeisance from gushing girls, butch boys, mid-life sadists, and aging discomanes. A cunning rock star nourishes the fantasy that he is sexually omnivorous."[35]

The sexual appetite extends to incestual acts. The Artist, formerly known as Prince, praises his incestual relationship with his sister in his "Purple Rain" album:

> My sister never made love
> to anyone but me.
> Incest is everything
> it's said to be.

Pattison concludes his analysis of sex in the rock scene with this arresting statement: "Nothing could more firmly distinguish rock from other forms of popular music than its insistent penis worship."[36] The worship of the genitalia is fundamental to the rock and roll religion, because they are seen as the creative hub of the universe and as a means to approach divinity.

A good example is the song "Closer," sung by the popular rock band Nine Inch Nails. The lyrics say: "I want to feel you from the inside, I want to f— you like an animal, my whole existence is flawed, you get me closer to god." This perverted notion of sex as a means to get closer to god reminds one of the fertility cults of the ancient pagan worship where sexual organs and sacred prostitution served as means of interaction with the gods.

The sexual perversion promoted by the rock movement and the entertainment industry reminds us of the sexual sins and moral depravity in the days of Noah and Lot. Jesus referred to those days to characterize the age preceding His return (Luke 17:27). Similarly, Paul predicted that "in the last days" many will be "without natural affection, . . . incontinent" (2 Tim 3:1-3; KJV). Today we are witnessing the unprecedented fulfillment of this endtime sign given by Christ and clarified by Paul.

Drugs to Experience the Infinite. Drugs, like sex, play a vital role in the rituals of the rock and roll religion, because they alter the mind in ways conducive to a deceptive consciousness of the infinite. The rocker, who is "bound on an expedition to infinity, demands constant infusion of cosmic energy."[37] Drugs allegedly provide such cosmic energy.

In the celebrated drug song, "White Rabbit," Jefferson Airplane mentions the potential of drugs:

> One pill makes you bigger,
> And one pill makes you small,
> And the pills that mother gives you don't do anything at all.

Mother's licit prescriptions are seen as worthless because they do not alter the consciousness by making a person feel bigger or smaller. Drugs like amphetamines and cocaine produce an euphoric state that makes the rocker believe he finds himself at the center of a universe of pure energy.

"Rock's speed-freak envisions a totality, comprised of what the Velvet Underground calls 'white light/white heat: 'White light, don't you know it lightens up my eyes, Don't you know it fills me with surprise.' The perfect self, of which uppers provide a fleeting apprehension, is identical with the pure energy of white heat. Speed and coke are traditional fare on the menus of rock precisely because they are comestables that expand the self to incandescent godhead."[38]

This is also the reason for the use of hallucinogenic drugs like LSD and mescaline. They provide a similar experience of the "white light/white heat." In the song "Lucy in the Sky with Diamonds," the Beatles describe a world seen through "kaleidoscopic eyes" which is alive with "tangerine trees and marmalade skies." Pattison explains that "the difference between speed and hallucinogenic visions is one of quality, not of kind. Both aim to provide the self with a godlike eminence from which to apprehend its embrace of totality."[39]

Drugs provide rock musicians the ecstatic inspiration needed to produce their music. In his book *Lennon Remembers,* Jann Wenner quotes John Lennon, saying: "'Help' was made on Pot. 'A Hard Day's Night' I was on pills. That's drugs, that's bigger drugs than Pot. . . . Since I became a musician I've always needed a drug to survive."[40]

The rockers' use of various kinds of drugs to obliterate consciousness and experience contact with the supernatural reveals their desperate effort to fill the emptiness of their lives by reaching out to the supernatural through the hypnotic power of the rock beat and drugs. The results of such efforts are often tragic. Some reports list over eighty rock stars who have died in recent years in drug-related incidents.[41]

The title of Steve Turner's book, *Hungry for Heaven: Rock and Roll Search for Redemption,* sums up well the rock religion: It is a search for redemption through rock music and drugs. Turner describes drugs as "the Damascus Road" experience for rockers. "People started out on trips as hard-nosed materialists after a bit of fun, and emerged with their egos ripped and mauled, unsure at first whether they'd see God or whether they were god."[42]

The Good News of the Gospel is that the "Damascus Road" experience is found not through the rock beat and mind-altering drugs, but through a Person—the Person of Jesus Christ who says: "Come to me . . . and I will give you rest" (Matt 11:28). The acceptance of Christ's provision of salvation fills life with peace and purpose—something that the rock beat and drug can never offer.

The Rock Dance. Dance is also an important aspect of the liturgy of rock and roll, because it offers to the rockers an opportunity to imitate and represent bodily everything that they feel about the supernatural. "The liturgy of rock repeatedly calls on the believer to 'dance dance dance,' to 'keep on dancing and a-prancin.' One of the central texts of rock is the introduction to the Contours' 1962 hit, 'Do You Love Me Now That I Can Dance?':

> You broke my heart and made me cry
> When you said I couldn't dance–
> But now I'm back to let you know
> That I can really make romance.

"The ability to dance is equivalent to the ability to feel. It is the ritual celebration of the sentient self-imitating the Dionysian infinity. . . . Dance is one of the sacraments of rock."[43] The importance of dance lies in that it enables the rocker to express bodily the experience of the supernatural induced by the beat and, often, by drugs.

Pattison explains that while in rock mythology the ritual of dancing is performed in the street, in real life it is done in discos and at parties. "If rock is a new religion, it is not the oriental paganism portrayed in its own mythology but a fairly decorous pantheism whose practice no more demands orgies than Christian ritual requires human sacrifice at the mass. The dancing of rock happens in discos and at parties, not in the streets. Rock is the liturgy of this pantheism, . . . But the pantheism behind the liturgy, though vulgar, is tolerant and pluralistic."[44]

The Eclectic and Deceptive Nature of Rock Music. The plural-istic and eclectic nature of rock music can be very deceptive for Christians, because some songs sound Christian and others Satanic. Pattison ex-plains: "Some rock, like the songs of Soft Cell, is overly Christian; other rock, like Feederz's 'Jesus Entering from the Rear,' is blasphemous; and still other rock, like the music of the Police, is arguably Christian and atheistic all at once. There is Vedic rock, Zen rock, Rastafarian rock, born-again rock, never-born rock, and thanks to Kinky Friedman and the Texas Jewboys, even Jewish rock, each distinguished by its vulgar treatment of the religious material. Rock's pantheism happily accommodates the varieties of religious experience, careless of whatever contradiction arises, and on the *Billboard* album charts a record by U2 that features lead singer Bono's adaptation of the Gloria from the mass appears next to Mötley Crüe's *Shout at the Devil.*"[45]

The eclectic and pantheistic nature of rock music makes it possible for rock's fans to adore Satan "in the disco by night and Christ in the cathedral by day. Rock merely continues the American democratic religious tolerance and diversity."[46] Undoubtedly, most rock fans will admit that they are not consciously adoring Satan. But whether Satan is worshipped consciously or unconsciouly, the end result is the same: he receives the worship due only to God.

Initially rock music treated Christianity with blasphemy and contempt. Such songs as "Sympathy for the Devil," "Satan Rock," "Mrs. Robinson," Arthur Brown's "Fire," and others were deliberately sacreligious. With the advent of "Jesus Rock," however, the anti-scriptural overtones have been obscured so that the uncritical listener can be deceived into thinking that rock has become more acceptable to Christian ears.

In his book *The Day the Music Died,* former rock star Bob Larson notes: "The religion and rock syndrome of today may contain such varied themes as George Harrison's Hindu metaphysical view of 'My Sweet Lord' and Judy Collin's rendering of the beloved gospel number 'Amazing Grace.' In the last few years we have learned that supposedly 'Jesus is a Soul Man,' a 'Spirit in the Sky,' and a 'Superstar.' Rock religious lyrics today come complete with both hallelujahs and Hare Krismas. So far has the trend gone that even the Rolling Stones included a Jesus rock song on their album 'Exile on Main Street.' Rock has indeed become a religion complete with its own distorted and warped liturgy."[47]

The mingling of sacred with sacrilegious in rock music may explain why some Christian musicians have so readily crossed over to secular rock. After all, the lyrics of some secular rock songs do speak about Christ and Christian themes. Robert Sweet of the crossover rock group Stryper admitted: "We are not religious fanatics who are trying to convert everybody we meet. We are not trying to shut down rock radio stations or make magazines go out of business. We honestly believe that Jesus Christ is the Savior, but we are about the most unreligious Christian band you could imagine. Religion is real for us, but so is rock and roll."[48]

One wonders how people can claim to believe and accept Jesus Christ as the Savior, and yet be "the most unreligious Christian band you could imagine." Can religion be truly "real" for a crossover rock band that boasts to be "the most unreligious Christian band you could imagine"? Such a claim ignores the fact that the Christian religion is not only a profession, but also a practice—not only creed but also deed. Scripture teaches us that "as the body apart from the spirit is dead, so faith apart from works is dead" (James 2:26).

The mingling of sacred with sacrilegious in rock music may explain also why some Christians see nothing wrong with such music. Several reviewers of the first draft of this manuscript, which went out to the 8,000-plus subscribers to my "Endtime Issues" Newsletter, alerted me to the fact that the lyrics of some rock songs are not anti-Christian. In fact, they speak out against all manner of injustice, racism, hatred, and nuclear weapons. Their contention is that rock music can be legitimately adopted for Christian worship, after altering its lyrics, because some of it promotes worthy causes.

This observation is correct, but the contention is wrong because it ignores three major considerations. First, rock music, as we see in Chapter 5, makes its impact *musically* rather than *lyrically*. As sociologist Simon Frith points out in his book *Sound Effects, Youth, Leisure, and the Politics of Rock 'n' Roll*, "A word-based approach is not helpful at getting at the meaning of rock.... The words, if they are noticed at all, are absorbed after the music has made its mark."[49] This means that the hypnotic beat of rock music typically neutralizes whatever positive message the lyrics may contain. *The medium affects the message.* This important point is considered more fully in the following chapter.

Second, good and evil are often mixed in the same song. Take Alanis Morissette, for example. Her songs are popular because of her passion and rage at many social problems. But her language contains obscenities and psychosexual matter. Even those songs which contain no obscene language offer no biblical answer to human dilemmas. For example, in her song "You Learn," she croons:

I recommend getting your heart
trampled on to anyone,
I recommend walking around naked
in your living room.
Swallow it down
(what a jagged little pill).
It feels so good
(swimming in your stomach),
Then wait until dust settles.
You live, you learn,
You love, you learn,
You cry, you learn,
You lose, you learn,
You bleed, you learn,
You scream, you learn.

This song speaks of learning from pain. It may echo what living for Christ is all about, but Morissette does not offer the right answer. The solution to the problem of pain is not found in swallowing a pill, but in trusting in God's overruling providence to sustain us through suffering.

Lastly, the mixture of good and evil lyrics in rock music, as noted earlier, may well represent an effective satanic strategy to use the good lyrics to lead some Christians to accept more readily the evil ones. If all rock songs dealt only with sex, drugs, and violence, fewer Christians would be attracted to such music. But the fact that some rock songs address legitimate social concerns facilitates the acceptance of those rock songs which promote anti-Christian values and lifestyles.

Throughout the course of its history, Christianity has been plagued by the mixing of truth with error. The result has been the rise of countless heretical movements. The religious and social revolution brought about by the rock-and-roll movement must be seen within this historical context.

The best Christian defense against all forms of deceptions, including that of rock music, is to be found in a clear understanding of their false teachings and practices. This is what this symposium is all about. So far we have examined in Chapter 2 the philosophical worldview of rock music, in Chapter 3 the discernible hardening process of rock music, and in this chapter the deceptive religious experience offered by rock. In the following chapter we take a closer look at the actual structure and values of rock music.

CONCLUSION

The cultural revolution brought about by rock music during the latter half of the twentieth century is at its roots a religious movement based on a pantheistic understanding of God. For the rock and rollers, God is not a transcendent personal Being beyond them, but a supernatural power present around them and within them. Rock music, sex, drugs, and dance are important rituals of the rock religion, because they are supposed to provide the means to transcend the limitation of time and space and experience the supernatural.

In many ways rock music promises to its followers what Satan promised Adam and Eve: You can become like God by partaking of the forbidden fruit. Like our foreparents at the beginning of human history, many today are succumbing to Satan's temptation in the hope of enjoying a godlike experience.

The investigation of this chapter on the religious, social, and moral implications of the rock-and-roll movement invite us to consider a timely question: Could it be that the worldwide popularity of rock music, which promotes the worship of self and human idols, is part of the mastermind strategy to promote the endtime false worship described in the Three Angels Message of Revelation 14?

It is important to remember that the apocalyptic imagery of the false worship promoted by Babylon in Revelation 13 and 14 is derived from the historical chapter of Daniel 3, which describes an event of prophetic endtime significance. On the Plain of Dura, all the inhabitants of the Babylonian empire were called to worship the golden image of King Nebuchadnezzar. A fiery furnace was prepared for those who refused to pay homage to the golden image. Daniel informs us that "every kind of music" (Dan 3:7, 10) was used to cause all classes of people from all the provinces of the empire to corporately worship the golden image (Dan 3:10).

Twice in Daniel 3 there is a long list of the different musical instruments used to produce "every kind of music" (Dan 3:7,10). This eclectic music was played to induce people to worship the golden image. Could it be that, as in ancient Babylon, Satan is using today "every kind of music" to lead the world into the Endtime false worship of the "beast and its image" (Rev 14:9)? Could it be that a Satanic stroke of genius will write Gospel songs that will have the marking of every taste of music: folk music, jazz, rock, disco, country-western, rap, calypso? Could it be that many Christians will come to love these Gospel songs, because they sound very much like the music of Babylon?

The summon of the Three Angels Message to come out of spiritual Babylon, by rejecting its false worship, could well include also the rejection of the rock music of Babylon. Soon the whole world will be gathered for the final showdown in the antitypical, apocalyptic Plain of Dura and "every kind of music" will be played to lead the inhabitants of the earth to "worship the beast and its image" (Rev 14:9). It is noteworthy that in Revelation the outcome of the showdown involves the silencing of the music of Babylon: "So shall Babylon the great city be thrown down with violence, and shall be found no more; and the sound of harpers and minstrels, of flute players and trumpeters, shall be heard in thee no more" (Rev 18:21-22).

Those who reason that there is nothing wrong with the music of Babylon may be conditioning themselves to accept the false worship it promotes. Satan has his own songs for the Endtime false worship. Could it be that, by adopting the music of Babylon, some will miss the chance to sing the New Song of Moses and of the Lamb? May this question resonate in our consciousness and challenge us to stand for truth like the three Hebrew worthies.

ENDNOTES

1.   Charles A. Pressler, "Rock and Roll, Religion and the Deconstruction of American Values," in *All Music: Essays on the Hermeneutics of Music,* ed. Fabio B. Dasilva and David L. Brunsma (Aldershot, England, 1996), p. 146.

2. Evan Davies, "Psychological Characteristics of Beatle Mania," *Journal of the History of Ideas* 30 (January-March 1969), p. 279.

3. Robert G. Pielke, *You Say You Want to Revolution* (Chicago, IL, 1986), pp. 133-136.

4. Ibid., p. 133.

5. Patrick Anderson, *The Milwaukee Journal Magazine* (October 12, 1975), p. 43.

6. Rudolf Otto, *The Idea of the Holy* (London, England,1923), p. 5.

7. Charles A. Pressler (note 1), p. 135.

8. Ibid., p. 136.

9. Ibid., p. 138.

10. Ibid., p. 140.

11. Ibid., p. 146.

12. Ibid.

13. Robert Pattison, *The Triumph of Vulgarity: Rock Music in the Mirror of Romanticism* (Oxford, England,1987), p. 184.

14. Jim Miller, "Forever Elvis," *Newsweek* (August 3, 1987), p. 54.

15. Ibid.

16.   Frank Garlock and Kurt Woetzel, *Music in the Balance* (Greenville, SC, 1992), pp. 81-82.

17. "The Big Business of Elvis," *New York Daily News* (August 9, 1987), p. C 28.

18. Ibid.

19. Hubert T. Spence, *Confronting Contemporary Christian Music* (Dunn, NC, 1997), p. 72.

20. Cited by Steve Peters, *Why Knock Music* (Minneapolis, MN, 1992), p. 110.

21. Robert Pattison (note 13), p. 90.

22. Cited by Steve Peters and Mark Littleton, *The Truth About Rock* (Minneapolis, MN,1998), p. 79.

23. Ibid.

24. Frank Garlock and Kurt Woetzel (note 16), pp. 82-83.

25. Robert Pattison (note 13), pp. 20-29.

26. Ibid., p. 108.

27. Ibid., p. 111.

28. Ibid., p. 29.

29. Ibid., p. 94.

30. Ibid., pp. 94-95.

31. Ibid., p. 197.

32. Ibid., p. 198.

32. For a selection of obscene sexual lyrics found in rock songs, see Steve Peters and Mark Littleton, *Truth About Rock: Shattering the Myth of Harmless Music* (Minneapolis, MN, 1998), pp. 30-33; also Robert Pattison (note 13), pp. 114-119.

34. Robert Pattison (note 13), p. 114.

35. Ibid., p. 117.

36. Ibid., p. 115.

37. Ibid., p. 120.

38. Ibid.

39. Ibid., p. 121.

40. Jann Wenner, *Lennon Remembers* (New York, 1971), p. 53.

41. For a list of names, see Richard Peck, *Rock: Making Musical Choices* (Greenville, SC, 1985), pp. 27-28.

42. Steve Turner, *Hungry for Heaven: Rock and Roll Search for Redemption* (London, England, 1994), p. 49.

43. Robert Pattison (note 13), pp. 184-185.

44. Ibid., pp. 185-186.

45. Ibid., p. 186.

46. Ibid.

47. Bob Larson, *The Day the Music Died* (Carol Stream, IL, 1972), p. 21.

48. *Hit Parade* (November 1986), p. 21.

49. Simon Frith, *Sound Effects, Youth, Leisure, and the Politics of Rock 'n' Roll* (New York, 1981), p. 14.

Chapter 5
THE ROCK RHYTHM
and
A CHRISTIAN RESPONSE
by
Samuele Bacchiocchi

Rock music is the most popular cultural phenomenon of the second half of the twentieth century, influencing our entire culture. It is the greatest propagator of the moral, social, and aesthetic revolution we are experiencing today. The sound and philosophy of rock music penetrates virtually every area of daily activity. Its insistent, pulsating beat can be heard in homes, offices, places of businesses, and even churches. Rock music has penetrated every aspect of life.

Rock music has become an effective way to communicate a new set of values and to produce a new religious experience to an emerging generation. Before rock music, the family as a whole enjoyed music as a wholesome form of entertainment. The old European music influenced the music of the first half of the twentieth century and was regarded as "good for the kids."

A radical change began in the 1950s with the introduction of rock music, which has created a rift between the older and younger generation. Nothing excites the passions of young people today as does rock music. As Allan Bloom of the University of Chicago points out, "Today, a very large proportion of young people between the ages of ten and twenty live for rock music. . . . When they are in school and with their family, they long to plug themselves back into their music. Nothing surrounding them— school, family, church—has anything to do with their music world."[1]

What is it that makes rock music so attractive, an irresistible addiction for many people, in spite of its revolutionary anti-Christian and countercultural nature? Why is it that even Christian churches are adopting more and more Christianized forms of rock music for their worship service and evangelistic outreach? Is there something unique in the structure of rock music and/or in its lyrics that makes this music substantially different from any other form of music? Quentin Schultze notes that "Musicologists have pondered the enigmas of rock's attraction and have generally gone away mystified, for rock hardly fits into the high-culture formalist definition of musical accomplishment."[2]

Objectives of This Chapter. It would be presumptuous to claim that this chapter resolves the enigma of rock's attraction by identifying all the factors contributing to its unprecedented popularity. Any attempt to be comprehensive in the analysis of such a complex social phenomenon risks the danger of being superficial.

This chapter seeks to understand what accounts for the long-lasting and overwhelming popularity of rock music by continuing the investigation conducted in the last three chapters into the nature of rock music. The underlying assumption of this symposium is that Christians and secular people are attracted to rock music because of what it offers them in terms of excitement, worldview, value system, and religious experience.

So far our investigation has focused on the worldview of rock music, its ideological development, and religious experience. In Chapter 2 we found that rock music reflects a pantheistic conception of God as an immanent impersonal supernatural power which the individual can experience through the hypnotic rhythm of rock music and drugs. This pantheistic conception of God has facilitated the acceptance of rock music among both Christians and secularly minded people, because both groups seek to fulfill the inner urge for a pleasurable experience of the supernatural through the hypnotic effects of rock music.

In Chapter 3 we traced the ideological evolution of rock music by focusing on the values that have emerged during the course of its history. We found that rock music has gone through an easily discernible hardening process from rock 'n' roll to hard rock, acid rock, heavy metal rock, rap rock, thrash rock, etc. New types of rock music are constantly appearing, because rock fans constantly demand something stronger and stronger to meet their craving.

In Chapter 4 we found that the pantheistic worldview promoted by rock music has eventually led to the rejection of the Christian faith and to the acceptance of a new kind of religious experience. The latter involves the use of rock music, sex, drugs, and dance to transcend the limitation of time and space and connect to the supernatural.

This chapter continues and completes the investigation into the nature of rock music by taking a closer look at its defining characteristics, namely, its rhythm. We refer to scientific studies which indicate that the rock beat affects the body in a way that is unlike any other type of music. It alters the mind and causes several physical reactions, including sexual arousal.

This closer look at the nature of rock music provides a basis for discussing the overriding question of this symposium—Can rock music be legitimately transformed into a fitting medium to worship God and proclaim the Gospel's message? This chapter is designed to help in formulating a final answer to this question by offering an understanding of the structure of rock music and its effects.

This chapter is divided into two parts. The first part examines the structure of rock music itself, especially its characteristic rhythm and beat. Special consideration will be given to the effects of rock music on the mind, muscles, and sexual arousal. The second part discusses how the church should respond to rock music by choosing instead music that respects the proper balance among melody, harmony, and rhythm. Such balance reflects and fosters order and balance in our Christian life among the spiritual, mental, and physical components of our beings. The chapter closes by offering some practical suggestions on how to revitalize the singing of traditional hymns and to introduce new hymns to the congregation.

PART 1
THE STRUCTURE OF ROCK MUSIC

The defining characteristic of good music is a balance among three basic elements: melody, harmony, and rhythm. Other elements such as form, dynamics, text, and performance practices could be listed, but for the purpose of our study, we limit our discussion to the three above-mentioned elements. Rock music inverts this order by making rhythm its dominant element, then harmony, and last melody.

Before looking at the role that rhythm plays in rock music and its effect on the human body, it might be helpful for those less versed in music, to explain how melody, harmony, and rhythm are integrated in good music.

The Melody. The melody is the most prominent part of the music. It is the "story line" of a piece of music and consists in the horizontal arrangement of notes which is recognized first when we sing a song like "All to Jesus I Surrender." Those who sing what is called the harmony, such as the alto, tenor or bass parts, are singing a melody that "harmonizes" with the other three parts.

Aaron Copland, who is regarded as the dean of American composers, makes this observation about a good melody: "Why a good melody should have the power to move us has thus far defied all analysis . . . Though we may not be able to define what a good melody is in advance, we certainly can make some generalizations about melodies that we already know to be good."[3]

According to Copland a good melody has the following general characteristics:

"It must have rise and fall (i.e., pitches going up and down). A melody that remains static (on the same pitch) can through repetition produce a hypnotic effect. . . .

"It must have satisfying proportions (i. e., a beginning, middle, and ending) and give a sense of completeness. The melody tells the story of the piece.

"It must at some point (usually near the end) come to a climax and then a resolution. All good art will have a climax.

"It will be written in such a way to elicit an emotional response by the listener."[4] Rock music, as we shall see, lacks several of these essential characteristics of good music.

The Harmony. The harmony is produced by the chords which match the key structure in which the melody is written. It is the sound that we hear when the various parts coincide. "As a melody provides the 'profile' for a piece of music, the harmony is its 'personality.'"[5]

"Chords can provide both rest (consonance) and unrest (dissonance) in music. Good music will have a balance of rest and unrest. Harmonic chords can also color our mood as listeners. For example, What if every song were written with the harmonization in a minor key? That would definitely affect our mood. This aspect of music may be difficult for a nonmusician to comprehend. You know it when you hear it, but you may not be sure how to define it."[6]

The Rhythm. The rhythm is what makes the music move. Without rhythm, music becomes one continuous, boring, and uninteresting sound. "Rhythm is the orderly movement of music through time. Just as the heartbeat is the life of the body, rhythm is the life of the music and provides its essential energy. Without rhythm, music is dead. Melody and harmony must unfold together, and rhythm makes this simultaneous unfolding possible."[7]

Everything in nature, including the human body, has rhythm. There is a rhythm to the heartbeat, respiration, and speech. Scientists have discovered that even the brain functions in rhythm.[8] Brain waves have frequencies that are influenced by physical and mental states.

The same is true in music where rhythm is organized into regular recurring beats, which make up what is known as "meter." Usually the group of beats come in patterns of two, three, or four. "Repetition of these patterns in music is divided by measures. In any good piece of music, the strongest beat in a pattern (measure) is the downbeat (the first beat in the pattern). If a pattern has four beats, the strongest beat is the first, and the second strongest beat is the third, as pictured in the measure that follows:
/ONE, two, THREE, four/."[9]

Rhythm in Rock Music. Rock music reverses the common order of the beat by placing the emphasis on what is known as the offbeat. In the offbeat, the main emphasis falls on beat four and the secondary beat is on beat two as pictured in the measure that follows:
/one, TWO, three, FOUR/

The fundamental problem with rock music is its relentless beat which dominates the music and produces an hypnotic effect. Bob Larson, whose career as a popular rock musician gave him a firsthand experience of the rock scene, points out that "the major issue for consideration from a moral and spiritual standpoint is the extent to which a pulsated or syncopated beat overrides the other musical elements in a song so that the level of communication is primarily sexual and physically arousing."[10]

In good music, as Tim Fisher explains, "the correct order is a good melody, supported by balanced harmony, undergirded with a firm and consistent rhythm. Concert music (i. e., a symphony or another instrumental piece of music) will sometimes vary from this order because of a desire to showcase the talents of the composer or the dexterity of the performer. However, our topic here is Christian music as it relates to communicating the spoken word. If you desire to communicate a text with music, the order is clear: melody, harmony, then rhythm."[11] It should be clarified that "a firm and consistent rhythm," does not mean an over-accentuated rhythm as found in rock music.

Rock music reverses the order of good music by making the rhythm the most important part of the sound. Larson explains: "Unlike other forms of music which may reveal melodic inventiveness, the focus of rock is usually on the beat. It is a drummer's holiday. . . . Jazz has a rhythmic swing. It flows with an exciting yet ultimately releasing feeling. But rock is built from a hard, straight-up-and-down pounding rhythm that produces frustrated energy. Some rock sounds emphasize alternating beats, while other rock tunes in part or whole hammer every beat home. Though he may add fills (short percussion outburst), it is the drummer's job to keep the force of rock moving with the incessant pulsating and syncopated beat."[12]

Driving Beat. The heavy emphasis on beat is what distinguishes rock from every other type of music. Quentin Schultze notes: "The heart of rock and roll is rhythm and beat—those twin forces give rock its energy and propel its intentional simple harmony and melody. The appeal does not lie in harmony, because most rock and roll music consists of no more than four or five very simple cords in a very clearly defined key. Nor does the attraction lie in melody, since the rock and roll vocalist does not so much sing as shout and wail."[13]

The first and most important defining and distinguishing characteristic of rock music is its driving, loud, relentless beat. In his book, *The Art of Rock and Roll*, Charles Brown discusses the various types of rock music that have evolved since the days of Elvis Presley. He finds that the common denominator of all the kinds of rock music is its beat: "Perhaps the most important defining quality of rock and roll is the beat, . . . Rock and roll is different from other music primarily because of the beat."[14]

It is vitally important to understand that *rock music is different from all other music because of its heavy emphasis on the relentless beat.* This fact is acknowledged by rock musicians. In his book *A Conceptual Approach to Rock Music,* Gene Grier says that "rhythm is the most important and basic element of rock music because of the way in which we relate to it."[15] He instructs readers on how to write a good rock song by following the following four steps:

"1. Decide on a time signature.
2. Decide on a chord progression . . . .
3. Write the melody.
4. Write the lyrics."[16]

This statement is abundantly clear. Rock inverts the correct order of the elements of normal music by making rhythm and harmony more important than melody and lyrics.

Bob Larson, who prior to his conversion was a successful rock performer on television shows and entertained capacity audiences in Convention Hall, Atlantic City, explains that the "pulsating beat and fast rhythm will unmistakably identify rock music. . . . Since rock is a hybrid sound of whole traditions of music (jazz, Negro spiritual, country and western, blues), it is hard to assign any one sound as typical. It has become a musical melting pot for many styles, *all centered in the relentless beat.*"[17]

The defining role of the relentless beat in rock music explains why its impact is *musically* rather than *lyrically.* As sociologist Simon Frith points out in his book *Sound Effects, Youth, Leisure, and the Politics of Rock 'n' Roll,* "A word-based approach is not helpful at getting at the meaning of rock. . . . The words, if they are noticed at all, are absorbed after the music has made its mark."[18]

In a major study on the *Neurophysiology of Rock,* research scientists Daniel and Bernadette Skubik emphasize with amazing clarity (for scientists!) the *musical* impact of the rock beat. "The conclusion of these studies is twofold. First, lyrics are of minor importance here. Whether the words are evil, innocuous, or based in Holy Scripture, the overall neurophysiological effects generated by rock music remain the same. There is simply no such thing as Christian rock that is substantively different in its impact. Second, short-term implications involve a decrease in receptivity in discursive communication, while long-term implications pose serious questions for rehabilitation of degraded left-hemisphere cognitive skills. In less technical jargon and in specific context, *we should expect that abilities to receive and deliver the gospel, to pray discursively, and to study Scripture are compromised [by rock music].*"[19]

This scientific fact "*there is simply no such thing as Christian rock that is substantively different in its impact*" is obviously ignored by those who argue that rock music can be legitimately adopted for Christian worship by changing its lyrics. The fact is that changing the lyrics does not affect the mental-physical impact of rock on the functioning of the mind, muscles, and hormone production, because the beat is still there.

A driving, gentler beat is also present in soft rock, where the beat is very subtle and less "unfriendly" to the nerves. But, whether soft or hard, ultimately an over-accentuated rhythm has the same effect.

The Effects of the Rock Beat. A wealth of scientific research exists on the various psychological, physiological, and social negative effects of the rock beat on humans and animals. Experts have examined rock music, not as a spiritual or religious experience, but as a social, psychological, and physiological phenomenon. Since Chapter 8 deals specifically with the effects of rock music, only a few studies are cited in this context.

An important reason why rock music affects the body in a way that is unlike any other type of music is the unique character of the rock beat, usually referred to as "offbeat." The offbeat of rock music consists, as noted earlier, of a weak-strong sequence. This offbeat stops at the end of each bar or measure, as if the music stops and then starts again. This causes the listener to subconsciously come to an halt at the end of each bar. This is the opposite of the so-called dactylic or waltz-like beat, which reflects the heartbeat and other rhythms of the body.

Psychiatrist Verle Bell offers a graphic explanation of how rock beat causes addiction: "One of the most powerful releases of the fight-or-flight adrenaline high is music which is discordant in its beats or chords. Good music follows exact mathematical rules, which causes the mind to feel comforted, encouraged, and 'safe.' Musicians have found that when they go against these rules, the listener experiences an addictive high.

"Like unscrupulous 'diet' doctors who addicted their clients to amphetamines to ensure their continued dependence, musicians know that discordant music sells and sells. As in all addictions, victims become tolerant. The same music that once created a pleasant tingle of excitement no longer satisfies. The music must become more jarring, louder, and more discordant. One starts with soft rock, then rock 'n' roll, then on up to heavy metal music."[20]

Neuroscientists Daniel and Bernadette Skubik provide a concise explanation of how the rock beat affects the muscles, the mind, and the hormone levels. "Rhythm for which drums provide or generate the basic beat, produces measurable responses in the body's muscular system, brainwave patterns and hormone levels. Briefly, (1) muscle coordination and control become synchronized with the basic beat; (2) brainwave activity itself aligns with the rhythm so generated; and (3) various hormones (specifically, opiates and sex hormones) are released as a result of electrophysiological synchronization with the rhythm. These results have been regularly documented by various researchers, and though individual subjects may vary in their response over narrow ranges of controlled input, all normal subjects have reacted as indicated when the rhythm exceeds 3-4 beats per second—roughly speaking a rhythm exceeding the rate of the average heartbeat."[21]

The Effect of the Rock Beat on Muscles. John Diamond is a respected physician who has conducted extensive research on the impact of music on the human body. His book *Your Body Doesn't Lie* contains a wealth of information on this subject. After a study of over 20,000 records, he found that the rock beat affects the body negatively in several ways. For example, he found that the stopped offbeat weakens the body because it goes against the normal rhythm of human physiology, thus affecting the heart and blood pressure. The rock beat sets in motion an automatic fight-and-flight response, which causes a secretion of the hormone, epinephrine.[22] The body reacts to the beat with muscle weakness, anxiety, and aggressive behavior.

Diamond relates the unexpected way in which he came to research the effects of the rock beat. "Several years ago my research on the effect of music took an unexpected turn. Shopping in the record department of a large New York store, I became weak and restless and generally ill at ease. The place was vibrating with rock music. Later I did the obvious thing—I tested the effect of this music. . . . Using hundreds of subjects, I found that listening to rock music frequently causes all the muscles in the body to go weak. The normal pressure required to overpower a strong deltoid muscle in an adult male is about 40 to 45 pounds. When rock music is played, only 10 to 15 pounds is needed."[23]

In his book *Tuning the Human Instrument,* Steven Halpern reports several studies on how the rock rhythm affects the mind and the body. One of them is similar to the study of Dr. Diamond. He wrote: "Dr. Sheldon Deal, a nationally known chiropractor and author, and by no means an old fuddy-duddy categorically putting down all of Rock and Roll per se, demonstrated the effect of the standard Rock 'n' Roll beat on muscle strength of the body. Using tests basic to kinesiology [that is, movement dependent on stimulation], he showed that the rhythm arrangement that we hear all the time in pop music has a definite weakening effect on the subject's strength. . . . This effect held true *whether the subject liked the style of music or not.* In other words, how one 'felt' about the music, tastewise, was irrelevant in terms of how the body 'felt' . . . a common denominator cutting through most subjective reactions is that of sexual arousal."[24]

Other scientific studies have produced similar results. "Researchers at Louisiana State University found that listening to hard-driving rock music increased the heart rates and lowered the quality of workouts in a group of twenty-four young adults. In contrast, easy-listening or softer music lowered heart rates and allowed for longer training sessions."[25] Similar experiments are reported in Chapter 8. One of them was conducted by the author of the chapter, Tore Sognefest, a Norwagian music professor and author of the book *The Power of Music.*

In another study on the effects of rock music, "Researchers at Temple University found that university students exposed to recordings by the Beatles, Jimi Hendrix, the Rolling Stones, Led Zeppelin, and other similar bands, breathed faster, showed reduced skin resistance to stimuli, and had an increased heart rate compared to those exposed to random background noise."[26]

Rock Rhythm and Sexual Response. One of the best known effects of the rock rhythm is sexual arousal. Rock musicians are well aware of this fact and exploit it to their advantage. Gene Simmons of the rock group KISS was asked on *Entertainment Tonight* if parents should be concerned about teens listening to their music. With candid frankness Simmons replied: "They should be concerned because we are into girls— that is what rock is all about—sex with a 100-megaton bomb, the beat."[27]

Here, without comment, are a few other testimonies of rock stars. Mick Jagger said: "You can feel the adrenalin flowing through the body.

It's sort of sexual. I entice my audience. What I do is very much the same as a girl's striptease dance."[28] Jim Morrison stated: "I feel spiritual up there. Think of us as erotic politicians."[29] Richard Oldham, manager of the Rolling Stones, said: "Rock music is sex and you have to hit them [teenagers] in the face with it."[30] John Taylor, bassist for Duran Duran, stated: "When the music works, the audience and the performer often feel like they're having an orgasm together."[31] These comments by rock stars make it abundantly clear that rock is designed to stimulate people sexually.

How does the rock beat stimulate sexual arousal? Daniel and Bernadette Skubik explain the process: "When the beat generates high levels of sensory excitation (that is, when due to the pace of the rhythm and loudness of the music the auditory impact nears maximal reception), the brain is put in a state of stress. This state of stress is measurable in 'driving' brainwave activity. This driving activity occurs in *all* people when highly stimulated; subjective evaluation of the input—such as whether one likes or dislikes the music—is not a factor. To force its activity levels down and to achieve homeostasis, the brain releases the body's natural opioids. These opioids are naturally produced opiates chemically similar to drugs like morphine. They are used to control the body's sensitivity to pain. . . .

"Considerable evidence confirms that rock music generates or enhances sexual arousal by way of this same process. That is, to high sensory stimulation the body responds with the release of gonadotrophins as well as opioids. The result is a strong connection forged between a stressed fight-or-flight drive state and the young person's developing sexual drive, which then invariably links arousal to aggression. . . . As rock music has moved farther away from its historical roots and medium (viz. folk music), *it both causes and expresses an increasing association of overt aggression linked to sexuality.*"[32]

A similar and yet simpler explanation is given by Anne Rosenfeld in her article "Music, The Beautiful Disturber," published in *Psychology Today.* She explains that music arouses "a range of agitated feelings—tense, excited, sometimes sexual—through pronounced and insistent rhythms . . . artfully used to heighten the sexual tension . . . drumming may produce these powerful effects by actually driving the brain's electrical rhythms."[33]

The secretion of hormones, caused by the abnormal stimulus of the rock beat, results in an overstimulation of the sex glands without a normal release. Bob Larson points out that this is "the prelude to the release that will occur in the parked car after the dance, and it is a direct cause of the bodily obscenity that occurs on the dance floor. I speak not only from medical counsel, but also from personal observation when I state that girls who erotically give their bodies to the frenzied gyrations accompanying rock rhythms may be undergoing a sexually climactic condition. . . . We must also realize that unconscious emotion, because of its nature, is influenced by many factors, one of which is vibrations (e. g., the deep bass sound found in rock music). . . . The sex-related emotions generated by the vibrations in the unconscious seek expression in conscious thought and activity. I have observed couples who actually undergo an imaginary sex act in their minds and bodies while dancing. This abnormal, musically induced, simulated orgasm is both psychologically and physiologically destructive. Neurosis is the direct result. It is also sin!"[34]

Pleasure-oriented Church Music. The capacity of the rock beat to cause a sexual response is a most important factor to be considered by those who wish to transform rock music into a fitting medium to Christian worship and evangelism. Changing the lyrics does not eliminate the effect of the rock beat because its impact is *physical,* bypassing the master brain. Ultimately the question is: *Should church music stimulate people physically or elevate them spiritually?*

The answer to this question is largely dependant upon one's understanding of the nature of God and the worship to be rendered to Him. Those who envision God as a special friend, a kind of a lover, with whom they can have fun, see no problem in worshipping him by means of physically stimulating music. On the other hand, those who perceive God as a majestic, holy, and almighty Being to be approached with awe and reverence will only use the music that elevates them spiritually.

We live in a pleasure-oriented society and many have come to expect a pleasurable, self-satisfying experience from church music. Calvin Johansson, an authority on church music who has contributed Chapters 9 and 10 to this symposium, correctly observes that "when the main criterion for choosing the music used in worship is pleasure, then the music specifically crafted for that purpose becomes the logical choice. In our culture, that means the music of pop, with its melody, rhythm, and harmony has but one goal, easy self-gratification. Whether it be rock 'n' roll, rock, country, contemporary Christian music, heavy metal, new wave, gospel, country rock, swing, or rap, pop is the preferred music of most people."[35]

As our culture has become increasingly preoccupied with fulfilling personal pleasurable desires, the church is seeking to supply the religious counterpart by providing Christianized forms of rock music. Johansson rightly warns that "the result of using religious rock in worship is dangerous: The church service becomes a make-believe fantasy-world used to satisfy the less noble traits of the adamic nature."[36]

Religious rock music, by whatever name, is hedonistic, and hedonistic music can hardly contribute to build a strong spirituality. "No matter how one might try, or what one believes, musical immaturity does not produce holistic Christian maturity."[37]

The Effects of Rock on the Mind. Rock music affects not only the physical but also the mental processes of the body. Before mentioning a few significant studies on the mental effects of the rock beat, let me share a personal experience. I was invited to speak at a church where a rock band led out in the singing of the beloved hymn "Amazing Grace" with a heavy rock beat. It was not long before the whole congregation was in a swinging, dancing mood. The rock beat had caused the people to forget that the original mood and message of the song invites us not to dance for fun, but to contemplate God's amazing grace: "I once was lost but now I am found, Was blind, but now I see."

The reason the people forgot the mood and message of the song is simply because the rock beat impacted upon their body, bypassing their mental processes. As Christians, we need to be aware of the fact that music is perceived through the portion of the brain that receives stimuli for sensations and feelings, *without being first screened by the brain centers involving reason and intelligence.*

This discovery, which was made over fifty years ago and has been confirmed since then by numerous scientists,[38] has contributed to the development of music therapy. "Music, which does not depend upon the master brain to gain entrance into the organism, can still arouse by way of the thalamus—the relay station of all emotions, sensations, and feeling. Once a stimulus has been able to reach the thalamus, the master brain is *automatically invaded.*"[39]

Two German scientists, G. Harrer and H. Harrer, conducted experiments to determine the effect of music on the body. They found that even when the attention of the listener was purposely drawn away from the music, a strong, emotional response was registered on instruments measuring changes in the pulse and breath rates, as well as in the psychogal-vanic (electrical) skin reflexes.[40]

Bob Larson, who studied medicine before becoming a popular rock musician, explains this point with considerable clarity: "The spoken word must pass through the master brain to be interpreted, translated, and screened for moral content. Not so with music—especially with rock music. Such pounding fury can bypass this protective screen and cause a person to make no value judgment whatsoever on what he is hearing."[41]

Joseph Crow, a researcher at the University of Seattle, conducted an interesting study of the rock culture and its music. He found that "Rock is a use of music based on mathematical formulae to condition the mind through calculated frequencies (vibrations), and it is used to modify the body chemistry to make the mind susceptible to modification and indoc-trination. Rock music can be (and is) employed for mindbending, reeducation, and re-organization."[42]

Several scientific studies have established the negative effects of rock music on the mind. In his study of "Behavioral Kinesiology" [that is, movement dependent on stimulation], Diamond found that the weak rock beat causes "switched" thinking in the brain. "Using the principles and techniques of Behavioral Kinesology, I have also demonstrated that when the weakening beat is played, the phenomenon called *switching* occurs—that is, symmetry between the two cerebral hemispheres is lost, introducing subtle perceptual difficulties and a host of other early manifes-tations of stress. *The entire body is thrown into a state of alarm.*"[43]

Diamond continues explaining more fully the effects of rock music on the mind. "The perceptual changes that occur may well manifest themselves in children as decreased performance in school, hyperactivity, and restlessness; in adults, as decreased work output, increased errors, general inefficiency, reduced decision-making capacity on the job, and a nagging feeling that things just are not right—in short, the loss of energy for no apparent reason. *This has been observed clinically hundreds of times.* In my practice I have found that the academic records of many school children improve considerable after they stop listening to rock music while studying."[44]

Similar conclusions have been reached by other scientific studies on the effects of rock music on the mind. Psychologist Jeffery Arnett found that young people who listened to metal rock "reported a higher rate of a wide range of reckless behaviors, including driving behavior, sexual behavior, and drug use. They were also less satisfied with their family relationships. Girls who liked heavy-metal music were more reckless in the areas of shoplifting, vandalism, sexual behavior, drug use, and reported lower self-esteem."[45]

In his book *Rock Music,* William Shafer, a scholar not opposed to rock music, acknowledges that "rock is a tool for altering consciousness. . . . Associated with rock, for instance, is a cult of irrationality, a reverence for the instinctual, the visceral—and a distrust of reason and logic; this form of anti-intellectualism can be highly dangerous, can lead to totalitarian modes of thought and action. Linked with this anti-intellectualism is an interest in the occult: magic, superstittion, exotic religious thought, anything contrary to the main currect of Western thought."[46]

Rock Music and Patty Hearst's Conversion. One of the most frightening examples of the awesome power of rock music to alter the mind is the conversion of Patty Hearst. In February 1974, Patty Hearst was kidnapped by the Symbionese Liberation Army. Shortly after the kidnapping, Patty was caught on video cameras helping the SLA robbing banks. You wonder how they converted her? William Sargant, one of Britain's foremost experts on brainwashing, examined Patty Hearst.

Sargant's alarming conclusions were reported by *Newsweek*: "She was an unwilling victim of a 'forced conversion' or brainwashing. According to Sargant, a person whose nervous system is under constant pressure can 'inhibit' and 'exhibit paradoxical brain activity—bad becomes good and vice versa.' And that, Sargant argues, is precisely what happened to Patty Hearst. Her nervous system was kept at maximum stress by the *continual playing of loud rock music*."[47]

The capacity of rock music to alter the thinking process of a person like Patty Hearst, making her "an unwilling victim of a forced conversion," exemplifies the danger of exposing oneself to such music. In his book *Tuning the Human Instrument,* Steven Halpern warns us of this danger with these arresting words: "Rock stars are juggling fissionable material that could blow up at any time."[48]

Rock musicians have long recognized the mind-altering power of their music. Timothy Leary, the Harvard psychologist who ended up serving a Californian jail sentence for possession of marijuana, makes this point in his song "Turn on, Tune in, Drop out," which became an anthem for millions. In his book, *Politics of Ecstasy,* Leary states: "Don't listen to the words, it's the music that has its own message. . . . I've been stoned on the music many times. . . . The music is what will get you going."[49]

In a similar fashion, Mick Jagger said: "We are moving after the minds and so are most of the new groups." [50] In *Melody Maker* he said: "Communication is the answer to the whole of the world's problems and music is the key to it all because the music opens the door to everybody's mind." [51] Graham Nash similarly stated: "Pop music is *the* mass medium for conditioning the way people think."[52]

Rock Music Is Felt, not Heard. Rock music has a unique mind-altering power because, as Bob Larson explains with enviable clarity, contrary to other forms of music, "it is written to be felt rather than heard. It is performed to dull the attention of the listener. It is not the melodic inventiveness or the chromatic arrangement of the chords that interests the average teenager. Rock performers try to produce a 'sound' with the dull, steady, heavy, throbbing, mid-deadening beat. And it is this beat that is captivating so many young people, making them easy prey for the lyrics. Other types of music could be found guilty or wrong also, but at present rock music is the most damaging to the young contingent of Americans who are preparing to take the leadership of the country in the years ahead."[53]

The subordination of the melodic line in rock music to a pulsating, relentless rhythm has an hypnotic effect that causes people to lose touch with reality. Bob Larson states: "The steady pounding can cause the mind to go into a state of daydreaming in which it loses touch with reality. This in turn causes the dancer or the listener to lose touch with the value system related to reality. Any monotonous, lengthy, rhythmic sound induces various stages of trances. It is quite obvious to any qualified, objective observer that teenagers dancing to rock often enter hypnotic trances. When control of the mind is weakened or lost, evil influences can often take possession. Loss of self-control is dangerous and sinful. In a state of hypnosis the mind of the listener can respond to almost any suggestion given it. Such compulsive behavior is indicated by the rising tide of promiscuity and by the increasing rebelliousness of modern youth."[54]

Janis Joplin, a popular rock singer who committed suicide, described the tremendous power of rock music she experienced following her first appearance at the Avalon, a San Francisco ballroom. "I couldn't believe it, all that rhythm and power. I got stoned just feeling it like it was the best dope in the world. It was so sensual, so vibrant, loud, crazy. I couldn't stay still; I have never danced when I sang, but there I was moving and jumping. I couldn't hear myself, so I sang louder and louder. By the end I was wild."[55]

There is no way to insulate the bodily responses from the pulsating and pounding power of rock music, because it impacts directly on the body, bypassing the mind. Marye Mannes is quoted by the *Washington Post* as saying that rock music is "the new illiteracy, and the young love it. They love it because they would rather feel than think. It is easier. It is easier for those who cater for them. For, to blast the senses—to blow the mind—you don't need training. You don't need knowledge. You don't even need talent. All you need is a boundless ego, a manic temperament, and the loudest amplifying equipment you can get. Then you can do your own thing." She concludes: "If the essence of creative expression is to bring meaning and beauty into life, then the sound and the fury of the new illiteracy is bent on destroying both."[56]

The physical damage to the eardrums caused by the excessive volume rock is discussed at some length in Chapter 8 by Tore Sognefest. Studies on hearing loss indicate that listening to rock, whether through a Walkman, discotheques, or concerts, has become a widespread hazard. The problem has assumed such alarming proportions that consumer activists and audiologists have proposed that local governments should enforce a 100-decibel level on rock played in clubs.[57]

PART 2
A CHRISTIAN RESPONSE TO ROCK MUSIC

The capacity of rock music to alter the mind and to cause several physical reactions, including sexual arousal, should be of great concern to Christians. After all, Christianity entails a holistic response to God through the consecration of our mind, body, and soul to Him (1 Cor 6:19; 1 Thess 5:23; Rom 12:2). It is through the mind that we offer to God "a rational service" (Rom 12:1; in Greek *logike*) and make moral, responsible decisions. Scripture summons us to abstain from anything that impairs our mind (1 Pet 1:13; 4:7; Eph 5:18), because through the daily "renewal of the mind," we "put on the new nature, created after the likeness of God in true righteousness and holiness" (Eph 4:24; cf. Col 3:10; Rom 12:2).

Rock Music Largely Unchallenged. What has been the church's response to the challenge posed by the physical and psychological problems caused by rock music? Negligible. Why? Calvin Johansson explains the reason with unusual insight. "The reason the [rock] music has largely gone unchallenged is the subjective notion that the notes, harmony, and rhythm of such songs contain no worldview, moral ethos, or life outlook. It is felt that music does not reflect a moral, philosophical, or theological position. Hence, the church has naively and simplistically split asunder the medium (music) and the message (text). Some Christians have embraced the music of rock (or a derived version of it) while disavowing the text!"[58]

Is such a split feasible? The answer is NO, for three major reasons. First, as we have seen, rock music makes its impact *musically rather than lyrically.* This means that in whatever version rock music is heard, it alters the mind and stimulates the body through its hypnotic beat. Poison kills no matter how it is administered. By the same token, the rock beat impacts on the mind and body whether the lyrics are sacred or secular.

Second, as Johansson puts it, "Christian rock of whatever category is still rock since its message remains the same, now having moved from bars, dance halls, and clubs to the chancel. We have not only given nihilistic rockers a forum to peddle their wares, but we do it for them."[59] If a Christian rock band looks and sounds like the secular counterpart, its music can hardly be an alternative because *the sound is the same.* In reality, the Christian band is promoting secular rock by exposing people to a modified version of it.

Third, the music and lyrics of rock are the product of the same worldview, value system, and pantheistic religious experience. The ethos of rock communicated through the music is supported by the text, and vice versa. "There are no rules, There are no laws," Jim Morrison declares.[60] "I am an anti-Christ, I am an anarchist," Johnny Rotten affirms.[61] The famous art historian H. R. Rookmaaker notes that rock music has emerged "with a thumping rhythm and shouting voices, each line and each beat full of angry insult to all Western values."[62] This means that the adoption of rock music in any form represents an endorsement of the social and religious values associated with such music.

An Unholy Alliance. There is today an unholy alliance between Christian and secular rock bands. Not only are Christian performers crossing over to the secular market, but so-called Christian magazines are listing and promoting the names of the Christian groups that look and sound like their secular counterpart.

Group, which calls itself *The Youth Ministry Magazine,* often carries a feature known as "CCM: A Sound Alternative." The list gives the names of the popular, secular rock groups together with the names of the Christian bands that sound alike. The caption reads: "If you like to listen to___ then you'll probably enjoy___."

In one issue, *Group* placed at the top of the list a secular rock group classified as *Punk/Thrash Music.* The name itself indicates the kind of music played by that group. Several Christian bands are listed as the "CCM Sound Alikes" to this aberrant group. Note what *Newsweek* had to say about the "Christian" sound-alike band: "They play the kind of music that parents love to hate. It is loud, disgusting, without redeeming social merit. There are *no melodies, no harmonies*, no singing—just a relentless flood of raunchy, rapped-out lyrics, punched home by a steady barrage of blaring guitars and synthesized beats."[63]

Can this band that sounds and behaves like its secular counterpart, be legitimately considered a "Christian alternative"? The Christian alternative is to confront the world with the purity and power of the Gospel, not to conform to its values and practices.

When the Babylonian captors asked the Israelites to entertain them, saying: "Sing us one of the songs of Zion!" (Ps 137:3), the people responded: "How shall we sing the Lord's song in a foreign land?" (Ps 137:4). Note that the Israelites did not say, "Let us sing them one of our sacred songs in the Babylonian music style so that we might convert them to the Lord!" No, their response was that they could not sing the Lord's song to entertain the ungodly. "The Israelites knew it was wrong to take that which belonged to the Lord and profane it by entertaining the unbelievers. Today, not only is the Lord's song used to entertain the heathen, but the heathen's music is being employed as the Lord's song [to entertain the Christians]."[64]

Knowing Our Enemy. To successfully meet the challenge of secular influences like rock music, it is imperative for the church to know what it is up against. Wise playing in sports always entails knowing the strengths and weaknesses of the competitors.

The Old Testament prophets knew their opposition. They understood how the cultural influence of the surrounding pagan nations had led

God's people into apostasy and they boldly called upon the people to repent, because God would not tolerate their disobedience. Similarly, the New Testament abounds with admonitions not to be "conformed to this world" (Rom 12:2; Eph 6:12; 2 Pet 1 and 2). John admonishes us to "love not the world, neither the things that are in the world" (1 John 2:15, KJV).

To effectively withstand the cultural pressure of our times and retain our Christian identity, we, like the godly people of Bible times, must understand the perverted values and practices of our culture. In the context of this study, we must understand the true nature of rock music—a music that, as we have seen, embodies a spirit of rebellion against God and the moral principles He has revealed for our lives today.

Reasons for Avoiding Rock Music. The fundamental reason for the church to avoid rock music in any version is its power to alter the mind. We have found that rock music itself, apart from its lyrics, can alter the mind through its relentless beat. A disciplined Christian lifestyle calls for the avoidance of mind-altering music or drugs which impairs the mental judgment, thus favoring irresponsible behavior.

In his book *A Return to Christian Culture*, Richard S. Taylor offers a sensible perspective on the Christian choice of music: "There are music forms, whether secular or sacred, which create moods of pensiveness, of idealism, of awareness of beauty, of aspiration, and of holy joyousness. There are other forms of music which create moods of recklessness and sensual excitement. Surely it does not take much judgment to know which forms are most appropriate for religious functions."[65]

It is unfortunate that good judgment is often lacking on the part of those who promote the adoption of rocky types of music, even for Christian worship. Most likely these people are not aware of the mental and physical impact of rock music. They ignore that Christian lyrics do not neutralize the sensual effect of the rock beat.

When Christian singers use for their songs the methods employed by rock musicians to make the sound sensual, they "do not realize or deliberately ignore the fact that this is no longer ministry, but pure, sensual, flesh-gratifying entertainment."[66] "When hymns are so rhythmically irresistible that hand-clapping, dancing, or patty-caking is the routing response, we may be having fun, but such songs are ultimately self-defeating. Any music that has an overbearing rhythmic drive which induces excess and unrestrained bodily response pleasures self. It gives 'me' a rollicking good time. But it lacks the discipline necessary for maturation. When attention is riveted to fleshly response, then church music has succumbed to an infantile self-centeredness."[67]

The Problem with "Crossover" Artists. The lack of spiritual maturity promoted by rock music in its various versions, may be partly responsible for those Christian artists who cross over into secular rock. This is an easy step to take by those performers who have already been playing the same rock music, though with different words.

The Christian commitment to Christ leaves no room for Christian artists to cross over into the secular rock scene. It is simply a matter of choosing whom they want to serve. Some mistakenly believe that they can worship the god of rock at the concert and the Rock of Ages at the church. Ralph Novak, a music commentator, offers us a fitting example of this trend. He writes for *People* the following perceptive description of a popular crossover Christian performer: "She has made a smooth transition from a rock-tinged gospel to a gospel-tinged rock. She sounds confident and vibrant. For those who like to dance and pray at the same time, her stuff can't be beat."[68]

Can a Christian engage in erotic dancing and praying at the same time? Such a mixture of good-evil is becoming increasingly common today. We must not forget that this was the strategy used by Satan to cause the Fall of man. Speaking of Adam's Fall, Ellen White writes: "By the mingling of evil with good, his mind had become confused, his mental and spiritual powers benumbed. No longer could he appreciate the good that God had so freely bestowed."[69]

The pressure to accept the good-evil mixture is especially felt today in the field of religious music. Lloyd Leno, who prior to his untimely death served as music professor at Walla Walla University, wrote: "The mass media has so thoroughly conditioned the masses with a diet of dance rhythm-oriented music, that anything but this seems bland and dull. This has resulted in something akin to an obsession among many Seventh-day Adventist gospel music composers and performers to cloth all gospel music with some kind of dance beat. Although some groups are more cautious or 'conservative,' the standard fare of many groups includes thinly disguised hybrid forms of dance styles such as waltz, swing (fox trot), country Western, soft rock, and folk rock. . . . It is quite obvious that these groups are using models whose goals are not compatible with Christian principles."[70]

If Leno was alive today to observe the music scene in some Adventist churches, he would add "Hard rock" to the list. In my itinerant ministry around the world, I have been confronted on several occasions with Adventist rock bands playing the kind of music one would expect to hear in night clubs or discos, but not in a church. Such a music would have been strongly condemned in all Adventist churches thirty years ago, but today some members do not see anything wrong with it. Why? Simply because their moral sensitivity has been dulled by the rock music that is blaring everywhere in our society. It is like frogs placed in water that is gradually heated. Eventually they boil to their death without sensing the danger.

Some Churches Recognize the Problem. While some Christians are compromising by adopting modified versions of rock music, others recognize the problem and break away from it. It is encouraging to read about the increasing number of Christian churches and recording artists who recognize that some Contemporary Christian Music (CCM) misrepresent Christ in its sound and lyrics. In his book, *At the Cross Road,* Charlie Peacock, an award-winning recording artist, producer, and songwriter of CCM, provides a stirring account of some of the churches and artists who have recently severed their connection with the CCM because they can no longer compromise their principles.

In November 1997, the People's Church of Salem, Oregon, announced its plans to terminate the Christian music festival, known as "Jesus Northwest" which has drawn capacity crowds for the past 21 years. The announcement came as a surprise in the form of a letter of repentance written by Rev. Randy Campbell, pastor of the People's Church and the festival director. He wrote: "We humbly repent before the Lord and ask for forgiveness of the body of Christ for inadequately representing Christ in our ministry, message, and methods."[71]   The letter acknowledges that much of what is done within the contemporary Christian music industry "(for example, ministry direction, decision-making methods, even the message itself) is often driven by marketing—not the mind of the Lord."[72]

On October 31, 1997, veteran CCM recording artist Steve Camp declared to be "burdened and broken over the current state of CCM" and released an essay in poster form accompanied by 107 theses entitled "A Call for Reformation in the Contemporary Christian Music Industry." He concludes his essay urging readers to "come away from an industry that has all but abandoned Christ and forge, by God's grace, what it was always meant to be . . . a ministry. Pray on this."[73]

In the Seventh-day Adventist church we have had several success-ful rock performers who have abandoned altogether the rock scene after joining the church. Two of them, Louis Torres from the USA and Brian Neumann from South Africa, prior to their conversion, played in popular rock bands that performed nationally and internationally. You can read the gripping conversion story of David Neumann in Chapter 14 of this symposium. You will be greatly inspired to read how the Holy Spirit convicted his heart and led him from the addiction to rock music to the worship of the Rock of Ages.

Another performer is Rick Shorter, who was former director of the Broadway show "Hair." When he became a Seventh-day Adventist, he faced the temptation to compromise. As a professional vocalist and guitarist, he felt that he could use his talents by converting old rock songs into new gospel songs. But he decided against it. Horter stated: "At first I thought I could rehash some old rock and soul songs and make them into gospel music. But now I realize there can be no compromise with the world—its music, its entertainment, or its philosophies."[74]

As he reflected on his former life which included acquaintances with such popular rock stars as Janis Joplin, Jimmy Hendrix, and Jim Morrison, he gave this warning to young people: "There is absolutely nothing to that kind of life. I just wish that I could get the message across to the kids whose heads are into Rock. They see the surface glitter, not the emptiness inside."[75]

A Christian Response to Rock Music. In formulating a Christian response to rock music, it is important to remember what we stated at the outset, namely, that the defining characteristics of good music is the balance between three basic elements: melody, harmony, and rhythm. We have found that rock music reverses this order, by making rhythm its dominant element that overshadows the harmony and melody.

Christians should respond to rock music by choosing instead the good music that respects the proper balance among melody, harmony, and rhythm. The proper balance among these three may well correspond to the proper balance in our life among the spirit, mind, and body.

In their book *Music in the Balance*, Frank Garlock and Kurt Woetzel present a concept that was new to me, but which I find worth considering. They explain graphically that

MELODY responds to the SPIRIT
HARMONY responds to the MIND
RHYTHM responds to the BODY.[76]

The part of music to which the Spirit responds is the melody. This is suggested by Ephesians 5:18-19 where Paul admonishes believers to "be filled with the Spirit, addressing one another in psalms and hymns and spiritual songs, singing and making melody." The parallelism suggests that "making a melody" is equivalent to singing psalms, hymns, and spiritual songs. Singing the melody (the tune) of a religious song, not only in church, but also while driving, working, walking, or even taking a shower, expresses our joy and praise to the Lord who fills us with His Spirit.

The part of music to which our mind responds is the harmony. This is because harmony is the intellectual part of music. Virtually anyone can produce a simple melody, but it takes extensive musical training to write and understand the various chords (parts). A good sounding harmony can be arranged only by a trained musician. The harmony, as suggested by the meaning of the word, harmonizes the melody and rhythm.

The part of music to which the body responds is the rhythm. The word "rhythm" derives from the Greek word *reo,* which means "to flow" or "to pulse" (John 7:38). The rhythm is the pulse of the music which finds an analogical correspondence to the pulse of the heartbeat.

The Pulse of the Heart and the Rhythm of Music. Garlock and Woetzel perceptively suggests that "the analogy between the pulse [of the body] and the rhythm [of the music] will help any desirous Christian to gain discernment in his choice of music."[77] To illustrate this concept they provide this helpful chart:

"Too much (or erratic) pulse	Body is sick
Too much (or erratic) rhythm ...	Music is sick
No pulse	Body is dead
No rhythm	Music is dead
Pulse under control	Body is well
Rhythm under control	Music is 'well'"[78]

The analogy between the pulse of our body and the rhythm of music is recognized by medical doctors. John Diamond, a medical doctor quoted earlier, wrote: "Our bodies have a pulse, and so does music. In a healthy state, we are in touch with our 'inner pulse,' which Dr. Manfred Clynes so well describes as 'the key to the empathy we experience with a composer.' . . . The phenomenon of the inner pulse . . . is in effect an internally conducted beat."[79]

Rhythm, as noted earlier, is the physical part of music. As in the human body the pulsation of the heartbeat must be within a normal range for the body to be well, so in music the rhythm must be balanced for the music to be good. The problem with rock music is that the rhythm or beat dominates in order to appeal primarily to the physical and sensual aspect of human nature.

This physical, sensual impact of the rock rhythm is widely recognized by scholars. In his book *Sound Effects, Youth, Leisure, and the Politics of Rock 'n' Roll,* English sociologist Simon Frith emphatically states: "The sexuality of music is usually referred to in terms of its rhythm—it is the beat that commands a direct physical response."[80] The same view is clearly expressed in David Tame's book, *The Secret Power of Music*: "When pulsation and syncopation are the rhythmic foundation of the music at a dance hall, the movements of the dancers can invariably be seen to become very sensual."[81]

Order in the Christian Life. By stimulating the physical, sensual aspect of the body, rock music throws the order of the Christian life out of balance. Tame often refers to what he calls "one timeless axiom . . . as in music, so in life."[82] As Christians we can reverse the axiom and say: "As in life, so in music." In other words, the order of priorities of the Christian life with the spiritual first, the mental second, and the physical third, should be reflected in the music itself.

"The Christian who is preoccupied with and spends most of his efforts on the physical (the body) is sensual rather than spiritual. The child of God who exerts most of his energies on improving the mind, to the neglect of his spiritual and physical needs, places undue emphasis on intellectual pursuits. The Christian with a Scriptural order and balance in his life emphasizes the spiritual first (Matt 6:33), the intellectual or emotional second (2 Cor 10:5), and the physical last (Rom 13:14)."[83]

The proper order among the spiritual, mental, and physical aspects of our Christian life should be reflected in Christian music. Garlock and Woetzel develop this correlation very cogently: "Just as the spiritual considerations of life receive priority by the balanced Christian, so the melody (that part of music to which the spirit responds) must dominate music in the Christian's life. Similarly, the harmony (that part of music to which the mind and emotions respond) needs to have a supportive role in music, just as the mind and emotions play a secondary role in the Christian experience. Last, and most obvious, the rhythm (that part of music to which the body responds) must be under strict control in music, just as the body and its desires need to be disciplined in the Christian's life."[84]

The challenge we all face in our Christian life is to keep our body in the proper relationship to the mind and spirit. Paul refers to this struggle when he said: "But I discipline my body and bring it into subjection, lest, when I have preached to others, I myself should be disqualified" (1 Cor 9:27; NKJV). Like Paul, we need to discipline our body by avoiding those things that feed only our carnal nature. We need to cultivate a taste for the right kind of music that respects the proper balance among the melody, harmony, and rhythm. Such music reinforces the proper order of the Christian life among the spiritual, mental, and physical.

Making Hymns Meaningful. There are plenty of traditional and contemporary hymns that respect the proper balance and reinforces our Christian values. But, some people complain that hymns are dull and boring. Could it be that the problem lies, not with the hymns, but with the new appetite that some have developed for pop music? Could it be that such an appetite has so dulled the musical sensitivity of some people that they are no longer able to appreciate sacred music? A spiritual appetite must be developed before one can enjoy spiritual music, but this does not happen overnight.

The problem, however, is not always a perverted appetite. Some-times traditional hymns seem dull because the congregational singing is lifeless. The solution to this problem is to be found not in adopting the sound of secular music, but in finding a dynamic and spiritual song leader who can inspire the congregation to sing wholeheartedly. The same hymn that sounds dull when sung in a monotonous way becomes vibrant and inspiring when sung with enthusiasm.

Hymns become meaningful to the congregation when all participants—the song director, the minister, the accompanist, and, of course, the congregation—awaken to the enormous blessing which awaits them as they sing from the heart with great dedication and concentration.[85]

To help in this process, attention can be called to the author of the words of the hymn, or to the composer of its music. Some significant aspects of the hymn's message can be brought out; then one can invite the congregation to sing the hymn with fresh meaning and understanding.

Imaginative changes in the manner of singing can make even familiar songs more interesting. Sometimes the song leader can invite the congregation to sing acapella. One verse can be sung by women and another by men. In other instances the congregation can accompany the choir, singing group, or soloist. There are endless ways of singing old hymns with new fervor and excitement.

A Ground-swelling of Contemporary Hymns. Those who complain that the church hymnal is old, and want to sing new songs, will be pleased to learn that during the past few decades there has been a ground-swell of hymn writing in the United States, Britain, and other countries around the world.[86] The hymn writers and hymn-tune composers of our times are men and women of talent, commitment, and dedication. They represent different Christian denominations, and their songs fill new hymnals that can enrich the worship experience of all Christians.

Mention should be made of The Hymn Society of the United States and Canada[87] which was founded in 1922. Since then, the Society has been actively involved in promoting the composition of new hymns which are published in their periodical called *The Hymn*. Their annual conference is held each summer in different parts of the North America and attracts hymn writers and hymn-tune composers from many countries and of different Christian denominations.

The Hope Publishing Company[88] deserves special commendation for encouraging hymn writers to submit their new songs for publication. These new collections are published each year and made available to the general public.

To introduce new hymns and to learn to appreciate more fully the older ones, a Hymn Festival can be organized. This can be a time of great inspiration and joyous celebration when the importance of hymns for the life of the church and national events like Thanksgiving can be rediscovered. In 1999 a special Hymn Festival was organized at Andrews University to celebrate the last Thanksgiving of the century. It was truly a service of great beauty and gratitude for God's unspeakable gifts of mercy, love, and joy to His sons and daughters.

CONCLUSION

In his book *The Secret Power of Music*, David Tame concludes his analysis of rock music with words that fittingly express the conclusion of this present study. He wrote: "Rock has unquestionably affected the philosophy and lifestyle of millions. It is a global phenomenon; a pounding, pounding destructive beat which is heard from America and Western Europe to Africa and Asia. Its effects upon the soul is to make nigh-impossible the true inner silence and peace necessary for the contemplation of eternal verities. Its 'fans' are addicted, though they know it not, to the 'feel good,' egocentricity-enhancing, para-hypnotic effects of its insistent beat."[89]

Tame is not a religious educator, but a musicologist who traces in a scholarly fashion the influence of music on man and society from the time of the ancient civilization to the present. Yet he strongly believes that rock music poses a serious threat to the very survival of our civilization. "I adamantly believe that rock in *all* of its forms is a critical problem which our civilization *must* get to grips with in some genuinely effective way, and without delay, if it wishes long to survive."[90]

In many ways Tame's assessment of rock music perfectly agrees with the conclusions that have emerged during the course of our investigation conducted in the last four chapters into the philosophical, historical, religious, and musical aspects of rock music.

Philosophically, we found in Chapter 2 that rock music rejects the biblical transcendental view of God, promoting instead a pantheistic conception of the supernatural as an impersonal power which the individual can experience through the hypnotic rhythm of rock music, drugs, and sex.

Historically, we noted in Chapter 3 that rock music has gone through an easily discernible hardening process, blatantly promoting, among other things, a pantheistic/hedonistic worldview, an open rejection of the

Christian faith and values, sexual perversion, civil disobedience, violence, satanism, occultism, homosexuality, and masochism.

Religiously, we saw in Chapter 4 that rock music has led to the rejection of the Christian faith and to the acceptance of a new kind of religious experience. The latter involves the use of rock music, sex, drugs, and dance to transcend the limitation of time and space and to connect with the supernatural.

Musically, we have shown in this chapter that rock music differs from all other forms of music because of its driving, loud, relentless beat. Scientific studies have shown that the rock beat can alter the mind and cause several physical reactions, including sexual arousal.

The factual information we have gathered about the nature of rock music during the course of this investigation makes it abundantly clear that such music cannot be legitimately transformed into Christian music by changing its lyrics. In whatever version, rock music is and remains a music that embodies a spirit of rebellion against God and the moral principles he has revealed for our lives.

By stimulating the physical, sensual aspect of the human nature, rock music throws the order of the Christian life out of balance. It makes the gratification of the carnal nature more important than the cultivation of the spiritual aspect of our life.

By consciously striving for a physical impact, "Christian" rock reduces spiritual truths to a physical experience. Listeners are deceived into believing that they had a spiritual encounter with the Lord, when in reality that experience was only physical excitement.

Christians should respond to rock music by choosing instead good music that respects the proper balance among melody, harmony, and rhythm. The proper balance among these three reflects and fosters the order and balance in our Christian life among the spiritual, mental, and physical components of our beings. Good and balanced music can and will contribute to keep our "spirit and soul and body . . . sound and blameless at the coming of our Lord Jesus Christ" (1 Thess 5:23).

At the threshold of a new century and a new millennium, Christians have an unprecedented opportunity to build upon their rich religious music heritage. At a time when the trend is to replace sacred hymns with secular songs that stimulate people physically rather than elevating them spiritually, it is well to remember that God summons us to worship Him in "the beauty of holiness" (1 Chron 16:20; cf. Psalm 29:2; 96:9).

Holiness in worship avoids repetitious trivia in sound and words. Holiness in worship avoids the degenerate beat and crooning style of pop artists. Holiness in worship demands commitment to the highest reasonable standards of performance. Holiness in worship is truly worshipping the Lord with our utmost in reverence and respect.

Our worship music should reflect the music we expect to sing in the fellowship of the Father and Son in the world to come. Are the Father, Son, and Holy Spirit honored by our music? Does our music reflect the peace, purity, and majesty of our God? Can we imagine singing our church music one day when we stand before the indescribable majesty of the triune God? Paul reminds us that "Our citizenship is in heaven" (Phil 3:20, NIV). This means that every aspect of our lives, including our music, should be seen as a preparation for that glorious experience in the New Earth, where "one pulse of harmony and gladness beats throughout the vast creation."[92]

ENDNOTES

1. Allan Bloom, *The Closing of the American Mind* (New York, 1987), p. 69.

2. Quentin J. Schultze, *Dancing in the Dark* (Grand Rapids, MI, 1991), p. 151.

3. Aaron Copland, *What to Listen for Music* (New York, 1957), p. 40.

4. Ibid., p. 46.

5. Jay Cannon, *Striving for Excellence* (Oakbrook, IL, 1989), p. 5.

6. Tim Fisher, *The Battle for Christian Music* (Greenville, SC, 1992), p. 68.

7. Jay Cannon (note 5), p. 10.

8. See Lawrence Walters, "How Music Produces Its Effects on the Brain and Mind," *Music Therapy* (New York, 1954), p. 38.

9. Tim Fisher (note 6), p. 79.

10. Bob Larson, *The Day Music Died* (Carol Stream, IL, 1972), p. 15.

11. Tim Fisher (note 6), p. 69.

12. Bob Larson (note 10), p. 16.

13. Quentin J. Schultze (note 2), p. 151.

14. Charles T. Brown, *The Art of Rock and Roll* (Englewood Cliffs, NJ, 1983), p. 42.

15. Gene Grier, *A Conceptual Approach to Rock Music* (Valley Forge, PA, 1976), p 30.

16. Ibid., p. 61.

17. Bob Larson, (note 10), pp. 9, 12. Emphasis supplied.

18. Simon Frith, *Sound Effects, Youth, Leisure, and the Politics of Rock 'n' Roll* (New York, 1981), p. 14.

19. Daniel and Bernardette Skubik, *The Neurophysiology of Rock,* published separately as an appendix in John Blanchard, *Pop Goes the Gospel: Rock in the Church* (Durham, England, 1991), p. 191. Emphasis supplied.

20. Verle L. Bell, "How the Rock Beat Creates an Addiction," in *How to Conquer the Addiction to Rock Music* (Oakbrook, IL, 1993), p. 82.

21. Daniel and Bernardette Skubik (note 19), p. 187.

22. John Diamond, *Your Body Doesn't Lie* (New York, 1979), p. 101.

23. Ibid., pp. 159-160.

24. Stephen Halpern, *Tuning the Human Instrument* (Belmont, CA, 1978), p. 45. Emphasis supplied.

25. Don Campbell, *The Mozart Effect. Tapping the Power of Music to Heal the Body, Strengthen the Mind, and Unlock the Creative Spirit* (New York, 1997), p. 67.

26. Ibid.

27. Interview, *Entertainment Tonight,* ABC, December 10, 1987. Quoted in Leonard Seidel, *Face the Music* (Springfield, VA, 1988), p. 26.

28. Interview in *Newsweek* (January 4, 1971), p. 25.

29. *Fort Lauderdale News* (March 6, 1969), p. 14.

30. *Rolling Stones* (January 7, 1971), p. 12.

31. *USA Today* (January 13, 1984), p. 35.

32. Daniel and Bernardette Skubik (note 19), pp. 187-188.

33. Anne H. Rosenfeld, "Music, the Beautiful Disturber," *Psychology Today* (December 1985), p. 54.

34. Bob Larson (note 10), p. 123.

35. Calvin M. Johansson, *Discipling Music Ministry: Twenty-First Century Directions* (Peabody, MA, 1992), pp. 50-51.

36. Ibid.

37. Ibid., p. 52.

38. See Lawrence Walters, "How Music Produces Its Effects on the Brain and Mind," in *Music Therapy* (New York, 1954), p. 38; Arthur Winter, M. D., and Ruth Winter, *Build Your Brain Power* (New York, 1986), pp. 79-80.

39. Ira A. Altshuler, *A Psychiatrist's Experiences With Music as a Therapeutic Agent: Music and Medicine* (New York, 1948), pp. 270-271.

40. G. Harrer and H. Harrer, "Musik, Emotion und Vegetativum," *Wiener Medizinische Wochenschrift* 45/46 (1968).

41. Bob Larson (note 10), p. 110.

42. Quoted in Leonard Seidel, *Face the Music* (Springfield, VA, 1988), p. 64.

43. John Diamond (note 22), p. 164. Emphasis supplied.

44. Ibid. Emphasis supplied.

45. Jeffery Arnett, "Heavy Metal and Reckless Behavior Among Adolescents," *Journal of Youth and Adolescents* (1991), p. 6.

46. William J. Schafer, *Rock Music* (Minneapolis, MN, 1972), p.76. See also C. H. Hansen and R. D. Hansen, "Rock Music Videos and Antisocial Behavior," *Basic and Applied Social Psychology,* 2:4 (1990), pp. 357-370; Phyllis Lee Levine, "The Sound of Music," *New York Times Magazine* (March 14, 1965), p. 72.

47. *Newsweek* (February 16, 1976), p. 24. Emphasis supplied.

48. Stephen Halpern (note 24), p. 103.

49. Timothy Leary, *Politics of Ecstasy* (New York, 1965), p. 165.

50. *Hit Parader* (January 1968), p. 12.

51. *Melody Maker* (October 7, 1967), p. 9.

52. *Hit Parader Yearbook,* No. 6 (1967). Emphasis supplied.

53. Bob Larson (note 10), p. 111.

54. Ibid.

55. Quoted by Joel Dreyfuss, "Janis Joplin Followed the Script," *Wichita Eagle* (October 6, 1970), p. 7A.

56. Quoted by Lawrence Laurent, "ABC New Format Proves Successful," *The Washington Post* (July 19, 1968), p. C7.

57. Ralph Rupp, an audiologist at the University of Michigan Speech Clinic, proposed that local governments should enforce a 100-decibel level on rock played in clubs. (Cited by Jeff Ward, "Cum On Kill the Noize!" *Melody Maker* 48 [December 8, 1973], p. 3.) See also "Nader Sees Deaf Generation from Excessive Rock 'n' Roll," *New York Times* (June 2, 1969), p. 53.

58. Calvin M. Johansson (note 35), p. 25.

59. Ibid.

60. David A. Noebel, *Rock 'n' Roll: A Prerevolutionary Form of Cultural Subversion* (Tulsa, OK, n.d.), p. 3.

61. Ibid., p. 10.

62. R. H. Rookmaaker, *Modern Art and the Death of a Culture* (Downers Grove, IL, 1970), p. 188.

63. Jim Miller, "Hymning the Joys of Girls, Gunplay and Getting High," *Newsweek* (February 2, 1987), p. 70. Emphasis supplied.

64. Frank Garlock and Kurt Woetzel, *Music in the Balance* (Greenville, SC, 1992), p. 108.

65. Richard S. Taylor, *A Return to Christian Culture* (Minneapolis, MN, 1973), p. 87.

66. Frank Garlock and Kurt Woetzel (note 64), p. 93.

67. Calvin M. Johansson (note 35), p. 73.

68. Ralph Novak, "People's Picks & Pans," *People* (24 June, 1985), p. 20.

69. Ellen G. White, *Education* (Mountain View, CA, 1952), p. 25.

70. H. Lloyd Leno, "Music and Morality," *Adventist Review* (February 26, 1976), pp. 7-8.

71. Charlie Peacock, *At the Crossroad: An Insider's Look at the Past, Present, and Future of Contemporary Christian Music* (Nashville, TN, 1999), p. 15.

72. Ibid.

73. Ibid., p. 16.

74. Jiggs Gallager, *Insight,* special editon.

75. Ibid.

76. Frank Garlock and Kurt Woetzel (note 64), p. 57.

77. Ibid., p. 59.

78. Ibid.

79. John Diamond (note 22), p. 156.

80. Simon Frith (note 18), p. 240.

81. David Tame, *The Secret Power of Music* (New York, 1984), p. 199.

82. Ibid., p. 15.

83. Frank Garlock and Kurt Woetzel (note 64), p. 62.

84. Ibid., p. 63.

85. The material of this section, "Making Hymns Meaningful," is adapted from an essay "The Music of Worship" prepared by Elsie Buck, who is currently serving as the President of the International Adventist Musicians Association.

86. Ibid.

87. The address for *The Hymn Society of the United States and Canada* is Boston School of Theology, 745 Commonwealth Avenue, MA 02215-1401.

88. Hope Publishing Company, 380 South Main Place, Carol Stream, IL 60188.

89. David Tame, *The Secret Power of Music* (Rochester, VT, 1984), p. 204.

90. Ibid.

91. Ibid.

92. Ellen G. White, *The Great Controversy Between Christ and Satan* (Mountain View, CA, 1950), p. 678.

Chapter 6
AN ADVENTIST THEOLOGY OF CHURCH MUSIC
by
Samuele Bacchiocchi

The controversy over the use of pop music in the worship service is fundamentally theological, because music is like a glass prism through which God's eternal verities shine. Music breaks this light into a spectrum of many beautiful truths. The hymns sung and the instruments played during the church service express what a church believes about God, His nature, and His revelation for our present life and future destiny.

Music defines the nature of the worship experience by revealing the manner and object of worship. When music is oriented toward pleasing self, then worship reflects our culture's elevation of people over God. The hedonistic bent of our culture can be seen in the increasing popularity of various forms of rock music used for church worship, because they provide easy self-gratification.

Many Christians complain that the traditional hymns of the church are dead, because they do not appeal to them anymore. By contrast, contemporary religious rock music gives them a "kick"—a pleasurable sensation. Those who clamor for church music that offers personal gratification ignore the fact that they are seeking for a self-centered physical stimulation rather than a God-centered spiritual celebration of His creative and redemptive activities.

In Chapter 2 we noted a close connection between music and theology. During Christian history the production of music has been largely influenced by the evolution of the understanding of God. The historical shift from the transcendental understanding of "God beyond us" during the medieval period, to the immanental conception of "God for us" during the sixteenth century reformation, and to "God within us" perception from the seventeenth-century to our times is reflected in the gradual evolution of church music from the medieval chant to the Lutheran chorale to today's "Christian" rock.

The modern manifestation of a strong immanental "God within us" conception has caused people to seek an immediate emotional experience of God through the stimulus of rhythmic and loud pop music. Such music, often used during the church service, reflects to a large extent the theological outlook of the congregation and, most likely, of the denomination which it represents.

Insufficient Theology. The increasing number of Christian churches, in general, and SDA churches, in particular, that are adopting new worship styles where various forms of rock music are performed, suffer from a condition that may be diagnosed as "theological impoverishment." The defining characteristic of this condition is the choice of music on the basis of personal taste and cultural trends rather than on clear theological convictions.

The problem has been recognized even by some contemporary Christian musicians. In his thought-provoking book *At the Cross Roads* (1999), Charlie Peacock, an award-winning recording artist, producer, and songwriter of such popular songs as "Every Heartbeat" (recorded by Amy Grant), frankly acknowledges that Contemporary Christian Music (CCM) has been operating "under insufficient theology."[1] He writes: "What is missing from CCM is a comprehensive theology of music, in general, and a theology of CCM artistry, industry, and audience, in particular. In order to begin to rethink contemporary Christian music, we will first have to recognize the necessity of developing a comprehensive theology."[2]

Peacock finds that the theologies of contemporary music "often miss the mark" because they are based on personal tastes or popular demand rather than biblical teachings. "Without God's thoughts and God's ways, we are left with our own dim and insufficient ideas. If we willfully choose to neglect the work of building truthful theologies for our callings, we will find ourselves waving good-bye to the brightness which illuminates life. We will find ourselves stumbling blindly down the way which seems right to a man but leads to nothing but darkness."[3]

The challenge of rethinking the theological underpinning of contemporary music affects not only the CCM movement, but Christian churches, in general, including the Seventh-day Adventist church. All too often the popular songs sung during the church service are based on an inadequate or even heretical theology oriented toward self-satisfaction. This is true not only of pop songs but also of some traditional hymns.

An example is the song, "We Get Lifted Up,"[4] which begins: "I've learned a little secret that you may already know." The secret turns out to be that praising the Lord "does as much for us as it does for Him 'Cause we get lifted up.'" The refrain repeats the same message: "We get lifted up, we get lifted up, we get lifted up when we praise the Lord; Oh, we get lifted up, we get lifted up, we get lifted up when we praise the Lord." The second stanza begins, "I used to think my praise was only meant to serve the King," but now we have discovered that praising the Lord "does as much for us as it does for Him."

Indeed, worship does lift us up. But if the reason for worship is just to get an emotional lift, then worship becomes a self-centered gratification rather than God-centered adoration. Ultimately we sing about ourselves rather than about God's glory, beauty, and holiness manifested in creation and redemption.

Feeling-oriented Music. Inadequate and misleading theology is often present also in children songs. For example, in the popular children series *Psalty,* produced by Maranatha Music, the smallest child asks: "Psalty, I'm so little. How can I praise the Lord?" Psalty replies: "Can you jump up and down? Can you get down on the ground? Can you shout with all your might, 'Praise the Lord?' If you do that with all your heart, then you can praise the Lord." The next song with a decidedly contemporary sound begins with all the children singing: "I'm gonna jump down / turn around / touch the ground / and praise the Lord."

The false message of this song is typical of the feeling-oriented music and worship. We do not praise God simply by jumping up and down or shouting His name. Praising God is not simply a matter of external exercises, but an internal, heartfelt response.

It is amazing that many adults are content to sing simple choruses fit for children. In fact, many churches have come to ignore the hymnal, opting instead for easily memorizable choruses which can be sung and danced as if one were at a party. "I'm-happy-happy-happy-all-the-day," is repeated a dozen of times. Another example, "I've got a feeling everything's gonna be all right. I've got a feeling everything's gonna be all right. I've got a feeling everything's gonna be all right, all right, all right, all right."

Such choruses are not only trite, but also heretical by making one's feeling, rather than God's promises, the basis of certainty. "In worship . . . faith, not feeling, should be the frame of reference. A faith practiced on the basis of feeling is no faith at all. Such songs may be fun to sing and make us feel good, but their effect on worship and life is devastating."[5]

Obscure Spirituality. The emphasis of many contemporary religious songs on "me," "my," and "I" reflects the self-centered theology which is so prevalent today. In his article "Gospel Music Finds Its Amazing Grace," Philip Gold points out that the message of contemporary religious songs "rarely varies: I'm OK, you're OK, God's OK, and it's gonna be OK."[6]

The self-centered theology of contemporary songs is reflected in those lyrics which contain only vague and obscure references to spiritual things. Take, for example, the popular contemporary Christian song "You Light Up My Life." The song speaks of a nebulous *you,* which could easily be a reference to a boyfriend, lover, husband, or wife, or possibly the Lord.

> And you light up my life.
> You give me hope, to carry on.
> You light up my days and fill my nights with song.
> It can't be wrong when it feels so right,
> 'Cause you—you light up my life.

Because of its nebulous theology, this song is sung in virtually any setting, from Las Vegas casino halls to evangelistic crusades "as a background song during an invitation to accept Jesus Christ as Savior."[7]

The implications of this so-called Christian song is that if it feels right, it cannot be wrong. If it feels good, do it! Incidentally, this was the nature of Eve's temptation. She found that the forbidden fruit tasted "good," so she took it and "gave some to her husband" (Gen 3:5-6). The Bible warns us through examples and precepts that our feelings are not a safe moral guide for Christian conduct, because our carnal minds are at enmity with God (Rom 8:7).

Another example of obscure spirituality is Amy Grant's popular song, "Who to Listen To":

> Don't take a ride from a stranger
> No way to know where they go
> You may be left on a long dark road
> Lost and alone
> Don't you recall what your Mama told you
> You've got to learn hot from cold.

This song hardly teaches substantive spiritual values. It gives no biblical direction or purpose to people. Note the comments of a Boston newspaper reporter who reviewed one of Amy's concerts where she sang "Who to Listen To": "'You want to sing, sing out! You want to dance, dance your brain out! Tonight we celebrate!' With those words, she [Amy Grant] kicked off her own brand of revival meeting at the Worchester Centrum Monday night. . . . For nearly two hours, she kept the spirit moving—laying down strong but gentle vocals over a blend of electronic pop that seemed better suited for a dance party than a church. 'Who to Listen To,' one bouncy number, has even figured in a 'Miami Vice' episode."[8]

Music fit for "Miami Vice" is not suitable for worship in God's sanctuary. This is especially true for the Seventh-day Adventist church, where the music used in the worship service should express its theological identity as a prophetic movement called to prepare a people for the soon-coming Savior. In fact, many songs in the Adventist hymnal embody such distinctive beliefs as creation, the Sabbath, the atonement, Christ's heavenly priesthood, the judgment, the Second Advent, and the world to come.

Objectives of This Chapter. This chapter attempts to rethink the theological basis that should guide the choice of music used in Adventist worship services. Specifically, we consider how the three distinctive Seventh-day Adventist beliefs of the Sabbath, Christ's ministry in the heavenly sanctuary, and the Second Advent should impact the choice and the performance of music during the divine service.

The chapter is divided into three parts. The first part examines church music in the context of the Sabbath. An important point made in this section is that the Sabbath, as holiness in time, effectively challenges believers to respect the distinction between the *sacred* and the *secular,* not only in time, but also in such areas as church music and worship.

The second part looks at church music in the context of Christ's intercessory ministry in the heavenly sanctuary. This study proposes that the triumphant and majestic music of the heavenly choirs described in the book of Revelation, should shine through the music, prayers, and preaching of the church on earth.

The third part focuses on church music in the context of the certainty and imminence of Christ's Second Advent. A significant point of this section is that the vision of the soon appearing of the Rock of Ages, with the greatest band of angels this world has ever seen, should fire up the imagination of members to sing with joyful anticipation and of musicians to compose new songs that can rekindle the Blessed Hope in believers' hearts.

What is presented in this chapter is a first feeble attempt to address a most important subject which has been largely ignored. The author is not aware of any significant study produced by Adventist scholars who examine church music in the context of the distinctive SDA beliefs. This means that the theological reflections presented in this chapter represent an initial attempt to lay a foundation upon which competent Adventist scholars hopefully will build upon in the future.

Part I
CHURCH MUSIC
IN THE CONTEXT OF THE SABBATH

The Seventh-day Adventist church draws inspiration for her music and worship from three major doctrines: (1) the Sabbath, (2) Christ's atoning sacrifice and His ministry in the heavenly sanctuary, and (3) the certainty and imminence of Christ's return. Each of these beliefs helps to define the nature of Adventist worship and music.

Unfortunately, the ongoing debate over the use of pop music in Adventist worship largely ignores the theological presuppositions that should undergird the worship experience of Adventist believers. Some Adventist worship leaders are pushing for the adoption of pop music in Adventist worship services strictly on the basis of personal taste and cultural considerations. But the music and worship style of the Adventist church cannot be based solely on subjective tastes or popular trends. The prophetic mission and message of the church should be reflected in her music and worship style.

The music and worship style of most Adventist churches is largely based on uncritical acceptance of the worship style of other denominations. In his book *And Worship Him,* Norval Pease, my former professor of worship at the Andrews University Seventh-day Adventist Theological Seminary, states: "We are Adventists, and we must approach worship as Adventists. A worship service that meets the needs of Methodists, Episcopalians, or Presbyterians may be unsatisfactory for us."[9]

The answer to the Adventist worship renewal is not found in the adoption of religious rock music, but in a re-examination of how our distinctive Adventist beliefs should impact the various parts of the church service, including music. Such an ambitious undertaking is beyond the limited scope of this chapter which focuses primarily on the music aspect of the worship service.

The Sabbath Offers Reasons for Worship. Of the three major biblical doctrines that identify the Seventh-day Adventist church, the Sabbath occupies a unique place because it provides the basis for the true worship of God. Such a basis is to be found in the three fundamental truths that the Sabbath contains and proclaims: namely, that the Lord has *created us perfectly,* He has *redeemed us completely*, and He will *restore us ultimately.* These three fundamental meanings of the Sabbath are examined at great length in my two books *Divine Rest for Human Restlessness* and *The Sabbath Under Crossfire*. The reader is referred to these studies for an exposition of the theology of the Sabbath.

To worship means to acknowledge and praise the worthiness of God. Would God be worthy of praise if He had not originally created this world and all its creatures perfectly and made provision for their ultimate restoration? No one praises a manufacturer that produced a car with mechanical problems without taking responsibility for repairing them. Similarly, it would be hard to find reasons to praise God with songs, prayers, and sermons if He had not created us perfectly and redeemed us completely.

The Sabbath worship service is an occasion for believers to celebrate and rejoice over the magnitude of God's achievements: His wonderful creation, His successful redemption of His people; and His manifold manifestations of constant love and care. These are fundamental themes that should inspire the composition and the singing of hymns of praise to God.

Some of these themes appear in Psalm 92, which is "A Song for the Sabbath." Here the believers are invited to celebrate the Sabbath by giving thanks, singing praises, and playing the lute, the harp, and the lyre (Ps 92:3). The purpose of this joyful celebration is to declare God's steadfast love and faithfulness (Ps 92:2), to praise the great works of His creation (Ps 92:4-5), and to acknowledge God's care and power (Ps 92:12-15).

The Celebration of God's goodness and mercy constitutes the basis for all the music and worship offered to God on any day of the week. On the Sabbath, however, the music and the worship experience reach the fullest expression, because the day provides both the time and the reasons for joyfully and gratefully celebrating God's creative and redemptive love.

The Conflict Between True and False Worship. To appreciate the importance of Sabbath worship, of which music is a major component, we need to note that in a sense the Bible is the story of the conflict between true and false worship. God's summon to "put away the foreign gods" (Gen. 35:2), which occurs in the first book of the Bible, is reiterated in different forms in all subsequent books. In Revelation, the last book of the Bible, the summon is renewed through the imagery of three flying angels.

These angels call upon "every nation and tribe and tongue and people" (Rev 14:6), on one hand, to renounce the perverted system of worship promoted by "Babylon," "the beast and its image" (Rev 14:8-11), and on the other hand to "fear God and give him glory, for the hour of his judgment has come," and to "worship him who made heaven and earth, the sea and the fountains of water" (Rev 14:7).

This solemn call to abandon the false worship of Babylon and to restore the true worship of God is presented in Revelation 14 as part of the preparation for "the harvest of the earth" (Rev 14:15), when the Lord shall come to gather the believers and punish the unbelievers. This preparation entails the abandonment of the false worship promoted by Babylon and the restoration of the true worship by God's people.

We noted in chapter 4 that the apocalyptic imagery of the false worship promoted by Babylon is derived from the historical chapter of Daniel 3, which describes an event of prophetic endtime significance. On the Plain of Dura, all the inhabitants of the Babylonian empire were called to worship the golden image of King Nebuchadnezzar. A fiery furnace was prepared for those who refused to do homage to the golden image. Twice Daniel mentions that "every kind of music" (Dan 3:7,10) was used to cause all classes of people from all the provinces of the empire to corporately worship the golden image (Dan 3:10).

The eclectic music produced by "the sound of the horn, pipe, lyre, trigon, harp, bagpipe," and other instruments, served to induce the people "to fall down and worship the image" (Dan 3:15). Could it be that, as with ancient Babylon, Satan is using today "every kind of music" to lead the world into the endtime false worship of the "beast and its image" (Rev 14:9)? Could it be that a Satanic stroke of genius will write gospel songs that will have the marking of every taste of music: folk music, jazz, rock, disco, country-western, rap, calypso, etc.? Could it be that many Christians will come to love this kind of gospel song because it sounds very much like the music of Babylon?

The summon of the Three Angels' Message to come out of spiritual Babylon, by rejecting its false worship, could also well include the rejection of the music of Babylon. Soon the whole world will be gathered for the final showdown in the antitypical, apocalyptic Plain of Dura and "every kind of music" will be played to lead the inhabitants of the earth to "worship the beast and its image" (Rev 14:9).

The Music of Babylon. The use of music to promote the end-time false worship is suggested by the description of the final overthrow of Babylon: "So shall Babylon the great city be thrown down with violence, and shall be no more; and the sound of harpers and minstrels, of flute players and trumpeters shall be heard in thee no more" (Rev 18:21-22).

The final silencing of the musicians of Babylon suggests that their music plays an active role in promoting false worship. It is instructive to note the contrast between the music of Babylon, which is primarily instrumental, with minstrels (professional entertainers), and the music of the heavenly choirs, which is primarily vocal. The only instrument used to accompany the heavenly choirs is the harp ensemble. No flutes or trumpets accompany them. Why? As we shall see, the timbre of the harp blends harmoniously with the collective human voices. The use of other instruments would overshadow the singing.

The apocalyptic description of the music of Babylon reminds us of the instruments used by rock bands. Their music is so loud that the lyrics can hardly be heard. The reason, as we have seen in earlier chapters, is to stimulate people physically through the loud, incessant beat. This is the music that the Lord ultimately will silence at the overthrow of apocalyptic Babylon. By contrast, the triumphant music of eternity is driven, not by the hypnotic beat of percussion instruments, but by the marvelous revelation of God's redemptive accomplishments, which inspires the redeemed to sing their hearts out. To this point we shall return shortly.

An Antidote Against False Worship. The mission of the church at this time, as portrayed effectively by the three apocalyptic angels, is to promote the *true worship* of "him who made heaven and earth, the sea and the fountains of water" (Rev 14:7). The Sabbath is a most effective means to promote the restoration of true worship, because it calls upon people to worship Him who in six days "made heaven and the earth, the sea, and all that is in them" (Ex 20:11).

By focusing on God's creative and redemptive accomplishments, the Sabbath functions as an antidote against false worship. It challenges men and women to worship not their human achievements and pleasures, but their Creator and Redeemer.

The temptation to worship human realities such as money (Matt 6:24), power (Rev 13:8; Col 3:5), and pleasure (Rom 6:19; Titus 3:3), has been present in every age. Today the problem is particularly acute, because the triumph of modern science and the hedonistic bent of our culture have led many people to worship personal profit and pleasure rather than God's power and presence.

The pleasure syndrome of our time can be seen in the church's worship practice. People have become so attuned to amusement that they also expect church music to be entertaining, self-satisfying, and stimulating. The Sabbath can serve as an antidote against the search for pleasure in worship by reminding believers that God invites them on His Holy day to come into His sanctuary, not to seek for their "own pleasures" (Is 58:13), but to delight in the goodness of His creative and redemptive love.

Holiness in Time as Holiness in Church Music. As holiness in time, the Sabbath effectively challenges believers to respect the distinction between the *sacred* and the *secular,* not only in time, but also in such areas as church music and worship. After all, music and worship constitute an important aspect of the observance of the Sabbath.

The fundamental meaning of the holiness [Hebrew *qadosh*] of the Sabbath, which is frequently affirmed in the Scriptures (Gen 2:3; Ex 20:11; Ex 16:22; 31:14; Is 58:13), is the "setting aside" of the twenty-four hours of the seventh day to culvitate the awareness of God's presence in our lives. It is the manifestation of God's presence that makes time or space holy.

The holiness of the Sabbath is to be found, not in the structure of the day which is the same as the rest of the weekdays, but in God's commitment to manifest in a special way His holy presence through the Sabbath day in the life of His people. Isaiah, for example, pictures God as refusing to be present at the Sabbath assembly of His people, because of their "iniquity" (Is 1:13-14). God's absence makes their worship experience not an adoration but an "abomination" or a "trampling of my courts" (Is 1:12-13).

As the symbol of God's free choice of His special time to manifest His holy presence, the Sabbath can constantly and effectively remind believers of their special divine election and mission in this world. *Holy Day* calls for a *holy people*. As the Sabbath stands as the *Holy Day* among the weekly days, so the believer who keeps it is constantly invited to stand as God's chosen *holy person* among a secularly minded and perverse generation. In other words, as the Bible puts it, Sabbathkeeping serves as "a sign between me and you throughout your generations, that you may know that I, the Lord, sanctify you" (Ex 31:13; cf. Ezek 20:12).

The Mixing of the Sacred with the Secular. The distinction between the *sacred* and the *secular,* which is embedded in the Sabbath commandment, is foreign to those Christians who view their Lord's Day as a *holiday* rather than a *Holy Day.* In Western Europe, less than ten percent of Catholics and Protestants go to church on Sunday. The vast majority of Christians choose to spend their Lord's Day seeking personal pleasure and profit. Even in America, where church attendance runs close to fifty percent, the same Christians who on Sunday morning go to church, in the afternoon will most likely go to the shopping mall, ball games, restaurants, or other places of entertainment.

The mixing of sacred with secular activities, on what many Christians view as their Lord's Day, facilitates the mixing of sacred with secular music in church worship itself. The common contributory factor is the loss of the sense of the sacred—a loss which affects many aspects of the Christian life today.

For many people, nothing is sacred anymore. Marriage is viewed a *civil contract* that can be easily terminated through the legal process rather than a *sacred covenant* witnessed and guaranteed by God Himself. The church is treated as a *social center* for entertainment, rather than a *sacred place* for worship. The preaching draws its inspiration from *social issues* rather than the *Sacred Word.* By the same token, church music is often influenced by the *secular rock beat,* rather than by the *sacred Scriptures.*

Cultural Relativism. The adoption of modified versions of rock music for church worship is symptomatic of a larger problem, namely, the loss of the sense of the sacred in our society. The process of secularization, which has reached new heights in our time, has gradually blurred the distinction between sacred and secular, right and wrong, good and bad. "All values and value systems, regardless of their conflicting perspectives, are equally valid. Right and wrong are reduced to mere opinion, one is as good as the other. Truth is not fixed but changeable, relative to the whims which define it."[10]

The cultural relativism of our time has influenced the church especially in the field of aesthetics, such as music, which has become but a matter of personal preference. "I like rock, you like classical—so what?" One is supposed to be as good as the other. For many, there is no longer a distinction between sacred and secular music. It is simply a matter of taste and culture.

The subjectivism in the field of aestetic stands in stark contrast to the objective, non-negotiable doctrinal beliefs which are passionately defended by evangelical Christians. Dale Jorgensen correctly observes that "The same preacher who believes that he is obligated to preach objective righteousness in morality, often implies that 'anything goes' in the music of the church. This is one area where naturalistic humanists find, perhaps with good reason, a wide crack in the Christian door."[11]

The Sabbath challenges believers to close the door to the humanistic pressure of cultural relativism by reminding them that the distinction between the sacred and the secular extends to all the facets of Christian life, including church music and worship. *Using secular music for the church service on the Sabbath is to treat the Sabbath as a secular day and the church as a secular place.* Ultimately, no real worship is offered to

God, because true worship entails recognizing the boundaries between what is sacred for God's use and what is secular for our personal use.

Part 2
CHURCH MUSIC IN THE CONTEXT
OF THE HEAVENLY SANCTUARY

For many Christian churches, worship service centers on what Christ has already accomplished in the *past* through His perfect life, atoning death, and glorious resurrection. By contrast, Seventh-day Adventist worship centers *not only on these past* redemptive accomplishments of our Savior, *but also on His present ministry* in the heavenly sanctuary and *on His future coming* to bring to consummation His redemption. Thus, all three dimensions of Christ's ministry—past, present, and future—are involved in Adventist worship.

Meeting with the Lord. It is noteworthy that the three distinctive Adventist doctrines—the Sabbath, the Sanctuary, and the Second Advent—share a common denominator, namely, *meeting with the Lord.* On the Sabbath we meet the invisible Lord in *time.* In the Heavenly Sanctuary we encounter by faith the ministering Savior in *place.* At the Second Advent we shall be reunited with the visible Lord in *space.*

Meeting with the Lord in *time* on His Sabbath day, in *place* in His holy Sanctuary, and in *space* on the glorious day of His coming should constitute the focal points of Adventist worship. When Adventists assemble for worship, their desire should be to meet the Lord. By faith they should wish to meet the Lord, not only at Calvary on the Cross, where He paid the penalty of their sins, but also at the throne of God in heaven itself, where He ministers on their behalf.

In his book *Sing a New Song! Worship Renewal for Adventists Today,* Raymond Holmes wrote: "In our [Adventist] worship we enter the heavenly sanctuary by faith and are able to see the world, the purpose of the church, the ministry of our Lord, and our own lives from God's all-encompassing perspective and not just from our own limited, self-centered, and narrow point of view."[12]

The focus of Adventist worship should be on the heavenly sanctuary where Jesus continually ministers in the heavenly liturgy on behalf of His people. "We have such a high priest, one who is seated at the right hand of the throne of the Majesty in heaven, a minister in the sanctuary and the true tent which is set up not by man but by the Lord" (Heb 8:1-2). It is because we have such a High Priest ministering in heaven that Hebrews says: "Let us then with confidence draw near to the throne of grace, that we may receive mercy and find grace to help in time of need" (Heb 4:16).

Church Worship to Reflect Heavenly Worship. The invitation to "draw near to the throne of grace" is obviously an invitation to worship by offering to our Lord our prayers, praises, and songs. The church on earth joins heavenly beings in praising Christ: "Let us continually offer up a sacrifice of praise to God, that is, the fruit of lips that acknowledge his name" (Heb 13:15).

The music and worship of the church on earth should draw its inspiration from the music and worship of the heavenly sanctuary, because the two are united by the worship of the same Creator and Redeemer. Hebrews invites believers to "come to Mount Zion and to the city of the living God, the heavenly Jerusalem, and to the innumerable angels in festal gatherings, and to the assembly of the first born who are enrolled in heaven" (Heb 12:22-23).

What a challenge for the church of the last days to let the glory and majesty of the heavenly worship shine through its music, prayers, and preaching. As Richard Paquier suggests, "something of the royal majesty and glory of the risen One who ascended to heaven has to come through in the worship of the church."[13]

When glimpses of the majesty and glory of the risen Savior and heavenly High Priest come through the music and worship of the church, there will be no need to experiment with religious rock, drama, or dance to revitilize church worship. The vision of the Lord's glory and majesty provides all the dramatic ingredients believers could ever wish for an exciting worship experience.

The Worship of the Heavenly Sanctuary. To catch a glimpse of the majestic worship conducted in the heavenly sanctuary, we turn to the book of Revelation where we find the largest number of choral ensembles to be found anywhere in the Bible. Scholars who have studied the music of Revelation have come up with different numbers of hymn texts in the book. Oscar Cullman has identified six hymns (Rev 5:9; 5:12; 5:13; 12:10-

12; 19:1-2; and 19:6),[14] while Michael Harris enumerates seven (Rev 4:8-11; 5:9; 7:10; 11:17-18; 12:10-11; 15:3; and 15:4b).[15] Forrester Church and Terrance Mulry identify eleven hymns in Revelation (Rev 1:5-8; 4:11; 5:9-11; 5:12-13; 11:17-18; 12:10-12; 15:3-4; 18:22-23; 19:1-9; 22:16-17; and 22:20).[16]

The exact number of hymns and choruses performed in Revelation is less important than their witness to the important role that music plays in the eschatological worship of God in the heavenly sanctuary. The three major choirs that participate in the heavenly worship are (1) the 24 elders (Rev 4:10-11; 5:8-9; 11:16-18; 19:4); (2) the countless multitude of angels and redeemed (Rev 5:11-12; 7:9-12; 14:2-3; 19:1-3, 6-8); and (3) the all-inclusive ensemble of every creature in heaven and earth (Rev 5:13).

The text of the hymns is very instructive. The chorus of the 24 elders sings first before God's throne a hymn about His *creative power*: "Worthy art thou, our Lord and God, to receive glory and honor and power, for thou didst create all things, and by thy will they existed and were created" (Rev 4:10-11). Then they sing before the Lamb a hymn accompanied by harps about His *redemptive accomplishments*: "Worthy art thou to take the scroll and to open its seals, for thou wast slain and by thy blood didst ransom men for God from every tribe and tongue and people and nation, and thou made them a kingdom and priests to our God, and they shall reign on earth" (Rev 5:9-10).

Finally, the twenty-four elders sing before God about the *vindication of the redeemed* and the inauguration of the eternal kingdom: "We give thanks to thee, Lord God Almighty, who art and who wast, that thou has taken thy great power and begun to reign. The nations raged, but thy wrath came, and the time for the dead to be judged, for rewarding thy servants, the prophets and saints, and those who fear thy name, both small and great, and for destroying the destroyers of the earth" (Rev 11:17-18; cf. 19:4). One notices a thematic progression in the hymns of the 24 elders, from the praising of God's creation to that of Christ's redemption and the final vindication of His people.

Similar ascriptions of praises are found in the hymns sung by the countless multitude of angels (Rev 5:11-12) and by the redeemed (Rev 7:9-12; 14:2-3; 19:1-3; 19:6-8). "After this I looked, and behold, a great multitude which no man could number, from every nation, from all tribes and peoples and tongues, standing before the throne and before the Lamb, clothed in white robes, with palm branches in their hands, and crying out with a loud voice, 'Salvation belongs to our God who sits upon the throne, and to the Lamb!'" (Rev 7:9-10).

In his dissertation, published under the title *A Theology of Music for Worship Derived from the Book of Revelation,* Thomas Allen Seel finds a crescendo in the participation of the heavenly choirs. "The chorus of the 24 elders appears to lead the larger choirs as the action in the text builds in a mighty crescendo of participation and sound; it initiates with the chorus of the 24 elders singing, followed by an antiphonal response of the creatures of heaven, and culminates when these antiphonal forces participate in a joined response with the remainder of creation, including the Redeemed. Together they corporately direct their praise to the Godhead."[17]

The dynamics of the antiphonal and responsorial responses of the various groups reveal an amazing unity. "They respond in an orderly and balanced manner which witnesses the totally complete, uncompromising unity of all of the Godhead's creation. Worship in the Apocalypse is 'genuinely congregational' and inclusively unites variegated levels of creation into a sea of doxological praise to the Godhead."[18]

Triumphant Music Without Beat. A careful study of the various hymns of Revelation reveals that in spite of all the references to the suffering of God's people, the book still may prove to be one of the happiest compositions ever written. As *The Interpreter's Bible* comments: "The music of eternity [in Revelation] sends its triumphant joy back into the life of time. The justification of glorious Christian music in the world is always justification by faith . . . . The writings of Paul also have this characteristic of bursting into song. You can judge an interpretation of the Christian religion by its capacity to set men singing. There is something wrong about a theology which does not create a triumphant music."[19]

The triumphant music of Revelation is inspired, not by the hypnotic beat of percussion instruments, but by the marvelous revelation of God's redemptive accomplishments for His people. As the worshippers of the heavenly sanctuary are privileged to review the providential way in which Christ, the Lamb that was slain, has ransomed people of every nation, they sing with dramatic excitement in their doxological praise of the Godhead.

Worship leaders, who are urging the use of an array of drums, bass guitars, and rhythmic guitars to give a rocky beat to their church music, should notice that both in the Jerusalem Temple and in the heavenly sanctuary, no percussion instruments were allowed. The only instrument used by the heavenly choirs is a harp ensemble (Rev 5:8; 14:2). The reason, as Thomas Seel explains, is that "the distinctive timbre of the harp in worship blends harmoniously with the worshippers' collective voices. It should be noted that the instrumental support does not supplant the importance of the words of the text, nor does it contain a mixture of diverse instruments. The instrumental ensemble contains a singular type of instrument [the harp] which blends with the voice."[20]

No Secular Music Allowed in the Temple. The distinction between sacred and secular music which is present in the heavenly sanctuary was also evident in the Jerusalem Temple. In the next chapter on "Biblical Principles of Music," we shall see that only a selected group of Levites made up the Temple choir. They played *only four instruments* at specific times during the service: the trumpets, cymbals, lyres, and harps (1 Chron 15:16; 16:5-6). Of the four, only the last two, the lyre and harps (both string instruments that blended with human voices), were used to accompany the singing.

The trumpets were used only to give various signals, such as when the congregation was to prostrate or the choir was to sing during the presentation of burnt offerings (2 Chron 29:27-29). The cymbals were used to announce the beginning of a song or of a new stanza. "Contrary to common opinion, the cymbals were not used by the precantor to conduct the singing by beating out the rhythm of the song."[21] The reason is that the music in ancient Israel, as Anthony Sendrey has shown, lacked a regular beat and a metrical structure.[22] It is evident that there was no possibility for any Jew who could play an instrument to be invited to join the Temple rock band and turn the service into a music festival.

In his doctoral dissertation presented at Cambridge University and published under the title *The Lord's Song: The Basis, Function and Significance of Choral Music in Chronicles*, John Kleinig notes: "David determined the particular combination of instruments to be used in worship. To the trumpets which the Lord had ordained through Moses, he added the cymbals, lyres, and harps (1 Chron 15:16; 16:5-6). The importance of this combination is emphasized by the insistence in 2 Chronicles 29:25 that the instruments for sacred song, like the place of the musicians in the temple, had been instituted at the Lord's command. It was this divine command which gave them their significance and power."[23]

In 2 Chronicles 29:25, it explicitly states that king Hezekiah "stationed the Levites in the house of the Lord with cymbals, harps and lyres, according to the commandment of David and Gad the king's seer and of Nathan the prophet; for the commandment was from the Lord through his prophets." By appealing to the prophetic directives of Gad and Nathan, the author of Chronicles emphasizes the fact that David's addition of the cymbals, harps, and lyres to the use of the trumpet (Num 10:2) was not based on the king's personal taste, but on a commandment "from the Lord."

Sacred Music for a Sacred Place. Those who believe that the Bible gives them the license to play any instrument and music in church, ignore the fact that the music at the Temple was not based on personal taste or cultural preferences. This is indicated by the fact that other instruments like timbrels, flutes, pipes, and dulcimers could not be used in the Temple, because of their association with secular entertainment. This principle was respected also in the synagogue and early church, as shown in the next chapter on "Biblical Principles of Music."

It is evident that nothing is morally wrong with the use of instruments like the timbrel or flutes. The reason they were excluded from the Temple's orchestra is simply because they were commonly used for entertainment. Women's dancing in the Bible was usually accompanied by the playing of timbrels, which seem to have been hand drums, like the modern tambourines, made up of a wooden frame on which a single skin was stretched.

Had the instruments and the music associated with dancing been used in the Temple, the Israelites would have been tempted to turn the Temple into a place of entertainment. To prevent this thing from happening, instruments and music associated with entertainment were excluded from the Temple. This exclusion extended to the participation of women in the music ministry of the Temple, because, as we shall see in the next chapter, their music consisted mostly of dancing with timbrels—a music that was unfit for sacred worship.

In his book *Music of the Bible in Christian Perspective,* Garen Wolf points out that "the use of tabret, timbrel, toph, and dancing by women or men had no connection with worship in the Temple, but rather for the purpose of show, ecstacy and secular entertainment or for religious music making outside the Temple."[24]

Music was rigidly controlled in the Temple worship to ensure that it would be in harmony with the sacredness of the place. Just as the Sabbath is a holy day, so the Temple was a holy place, where God manifested his presence "among the people of Israel" (Ex 29:45; cf. 25:8). Respect for God's holy day and holy place of worship, demanded that no music or instruments associated with secular life be used in the Temple.

The connection between the Sabbath and the sanctuary is clearly affirmed in Leviticus 19:30: "You shall keep my Sabbaths and reverence my sanctuary: I am the Lord." Keeping the Sabbath is equated with reverence in God's sanctuary, because both are sacred institutions established for the worship of God. This means that secular music that is inappropriate for the Sabbath is also inappropriate for the church, and vice versa. Why? Simply because God has set aside both of them for the manifestation of His holy presence.

Lessons from the Temple's Music. Four major lessons can be drawn from the music performed at the Jerusalem Temple as well as in the heavenly sanctuary. First, church music should respect and reflect the sacredness of the place of worship. This means that percussion instruments and entertainment music which stimulate people physically are out of place in the church service. Out of respect for the presence of God, such music was not allowed in the Temple services, nor is it used in the liturgy of the heavenly sanctuary. In the next chapter, we shall see that the same was true in the worship service of the synagogue and the early church. This consistent witness of scripture and history should serve as a warning to the church today, when the adoption of pop music for worship is becoming the "in" thing to do.

Second, the music of both the earthly and heavenly Temples teaches us that instrumental accompaniments are to be used to aid the vocal response to God and not to drown the singing. In Revelation, it is the harps' instrumental ensemble that accompanies the singing of the choirs, because the harp's sound blends well with the human voice, without supplanting it. This means that any loud, rhythmic music that drowns the sound of the lyrics is inappropriate for church worship.

Third, church music should express the delight and the joy of being in the presence of the Lord. The singing of the various choirs in Revelation is heartfelt and expressive. They sing with a "loud voice" (Rev 5:12; 7:10) and express their emotions, saying "Amen. Hallelujah" (Rev 19:4).

A balance must exist between the emotional and intellectual sides of life in religion and worship. "Musical expression in worship must have an emotional and intellectual aspect because that is the nature of man, the nature of music, and the nature of religion. At its best, music should demonstrate this life-religion-music unity in worship by a well-proportioned, reasoned, feeling approach to composition."[25]

Reverence in God's Sanctuary. Last, church music should be reverential, in tune with the sacred nature of worship. It is significant that of the eight words used in the New Testament to express a worship response to God, only one of them is used in Revelation.[26] It is the Greek word *prokuneo,* which is commonly translated "to worship" or "to prostrate." The term appears 58 times in the New Testament, 23 of which occur in Revelation.[27]

The term *prokuneo* is compound of two roots: *pros* meaning "toward" and *kuneo* meaning "to kiss." When combined, they imply the honor and respect demonstrated toward a superior. Time and again we are told in Revelation that heavenly beings "fell down and worshipped Him" (Rev 4:10; 5:14; 7:11; 11:17; 15:4; 19:4).

It is significant that John the Revelator uses only *prokuneo* to describe the reverential worship of end times. The reason could be the need to warn the end-time generation not to be misled by the false worship of Babylon, characterized by feverish excitement. God is holy and we worship Him with deep respect, awe, and affection. Both in the Jerusalem Temple and in the heavenly sanctuary, God is worshipped with great reverence and respect. The same attitude should be manifested in our worship today, because God does not change.

Today we live in a world of feverish activity, constant entertainment, and close familiarity. This is reflected also in some of the contemporary pop music that treats God with frivolity and irreverence. The worship in the earthly and heavenly Temples teaches us that we need to bow in humility before our great God. Sacred music can help to quiet our hearts and souls so that we can more clearly recognize who our God really is and respond to Him in reverence.

Part 3
CHURCH MUSIC IN THE
CONTEXT OF THE SECOND ADVENT

The belief in the certainty and imminence of Christ's return is the driving force of the Adventist church worship and lifestyle. To be an Adventist Christian means, first and foremost, to live looking forward to the glorious day of Christ's coming. Peter urges this forward look: "Set your hope fully upon the grace that is coming to you at the revelation of Jesus Christ" (1 Pet 1:13). Paul eloquently expresses this forward look: "One thing I do, forgetting what lies behind and straining forward to what lies ahead, I press on toward the goal for the prize of the upward call of God in Christ Jesus" (Phil 3:13-14).

Pilgrim's Outlook. To live with this forward look means to view our present life as a pilgrimage, a journey to a better land. The writer of Hebrews notes that Abraham and all past true believers were pilgrims, with no permanent home on this earth. "They admitted that they were aliens and strangers on earth. People who say such things show that they are looking for a country of their own. If they had been thinking of the country they had left, they would have had opportunity to return. Instead, they were longing for a better country—a heavenly one. Therefore God is not ashamed to be called their God, for he has prepared a city for them" (Heb 11:13-16, NIV).

Someone has said that twentieth-century Christians are "the best-disguised set of pilgrims this world has ever seen." Many Christians have come to view this world as the "living room" in which to live as though Christ may never come, rather than the "waiting room" to the world to come.

The forward look to the future Kingdom of God challenges us not to invest present religious or political institutions with permanent value and functions because they are not the method by which the Kingdom of God is to be established. It challenges us to recognize that when Jesus comes, all of our human institutions, including our churches, will come to an end.

We must build for the future while recognizing that the future does not belong by right to what we build. The ultimate effect of living with a forward look is to view all our institutions and personal decisions in the light of the Advent of our Lord.

Worship in Anticipation. The expectancy of Christ's soon coming gives a special texture to Adventist worship and music. Through worship we break through the barriers of time and space and experience a foretaste of the blessedness of the future heavenly worship that awaits us at the glorious coming of the Lord. The writer of Hebrews speaks of this vital function of worship: "You have come to Mount Zion and to the city of the living God, the heavenly Jerusalem, and to innumerable angels in festal gathering, and to the assembly of the first-born who are enrolled in heaven" (Heb 12:22-23).

Communal worship with believers enables us to temporarily forget and transcend the unpleasant realities of this present life and to catch a glimpse of the blessedness of the world to come. The music, the prayers, the proclamation, and the witness of and fellowship with other members can give us a foretaste of the future heavenly Jerusalem and the festal gathering of God's children. Such an experience nourishes and strengthens the Advent Hope in our hearts by giving us a vision and a foretaste of the glories of the Second Advent.

The expectancy of Christ's coming gives a sense of urgency to the Adventist church worship. Hebrews admonishes believers "to stir up one another to love and good works, *not neglecting to meet together,* as is the habit of some, but encouraging one another, and *all the more as you see the Day drawing near*" (Heb 10:24-25).[28]

The need to assemble together for worship and mutual encouragement is presented in this passage as all the more pressing as the Day of Christ's Coming draws near. The nearer we draw to the return of Christ, the more intense will be Satan's efforts to undermine the work of God in our lives and in this world. "Woe to you, O earth and sea, for the devil has come down to you in great wrath, because he knows that his time is short!" (Rev 12:12). The inspiration and encouragement we receive from worshiping together with fellow believers can help us to hold fast to our faith and hope in the soon-coming Savior.

Advent Music. Church music plays a vital role in strengthening the faith and nourishing the hope of Christ's coming. Through hymn singing, believers rehearse the day when they will see Jesus and speak with Him face to face. "Face to face shall I behold Him, Far beyond the starry sky; Face to face in all His glory I shall see Him by and by."

It is not surprising that the new *Seventh-day Adventist Church Hymnal* has 34 hymns about the Second Advent.[29] They far outnumber the hymns about any other subject, including the 18 hymns about the Sabbath.[30] The music and text of the Advent hymns express a variety of moods. For example, "O, we see the gleams of the golden morning Piercing through the night of gloom" envisions the excitement at the appearing of the Lord in the golden sky. "O Lord Jesus, how long, how long Ere we shout the glad song? Christ returneth, Hallelujah!" expresses the longing and impatience to see the Lord. "O it must be the breaking of the day!" gives the reassurance that the end-time signs are fast-fulfilling.

"Lift up the trumpet and loud let it ring" challenges believers to boldly proclaim that "Jesus is coming again." "We have this hope that burns within our hearts" captures in a marvelous way the belief that the "time is here, When the nations far and near Shall awake, and shout, and sing, Hallelujah! Christ is King." "When the roll is called up yonder, I'll be there" enthusiastically reaffirms the commitment to be ready for the day "When the trumpet of the Lord shall sound, and time shall be no more."

Advent Inspiration. The glorious vision of Christ's return has inspired the composition of many faith-instilling hymns that have enriched church life and worship through the centuries. Today, as we stand at the threshold of the Lord's return and "see the Day drawing near" (Heb 10:25), the Blessed Hope should inspire the composition of new songs that can rekindle the flame and encourage believers "to live sober, upright, and godly lives in this world, [while] awaiting our blessed hope, the appearing of the glory of our great God and Savior Jesus Christ" (Titus 2:13).

New upbeat Advent songs are needed today to appeal especially to the younger generation that has been captivated by the fast moving, rhythmic, loud, electronically amplified sounds and uninhibited lyrics of rock music. To reach the younger generation is a formidable task, because in many cases their senses have become so dulled by their overexposure to the loud, rhythmic sounds of rock music that they can no longer hear "the still small voice." In his *Decline of the West*, Oswald Spengler gave an ominous warning years ago: "In the last stages of a civilization all art becomes nothing but titillation of the senses (nerve excitement)."[31]

Indeed, today we live in the very last stage of the end-time civilization when "the titillation of the senses" through the rock idiom has invaded even the evangelical community, including an increasing number of Adventist churches. Rock music provides for many a deceptive substitute for the inner feelings of "love, joy, and peace" that comes when the Holy Spirit works in our lives (Gal 5:22).

Our challenge today is to help our rock-and-roll generation capture the vision of that glorious day that is coming when they will be able to experience the most exciting audiovisual extravaganza they have ever imagined—the glorious coming of the Rock of Ages. The band of angels that will accompany Him will produce the most thundering sounds this planet has ever heard. The splendor of His presence and the vibrations from the sound of His voice will be so powerful as to annihilate the unbelievers and to bring new life to believers.

Such a glorious event can fire up the imagination of musicians today to compose new songs that will appeal to many who are looking for meaning and hope in their lives. A song that comes to mind is "Welcome Home Children," by Adrian King. The song helps to capture the delight and emotional excitement of the glorious day that is coming when "heaven's gates will open wide and all who love the Lord will enter in." The Lord Himself will greet His children, saying, "Welcome home children, this is a place I prepared for you. Welcome home children, now that your work on earth is through. Welcome home children, you who have followed so faithfully."

New Advent songs, like "Welcome Home Children" which are theologically correct and musically inspiring, can enrich the worship experience of believers and appeal to those who are receptive to the working of the Holy Spirit in their lives.

My son, Gianluca, informs me that "Welcome Home Children" is a CCM song. We used this song in a video recording entitled "Sabbath in Songs," in which two outstanding lyric tenors join me in presenting the Sabbath through words and songs. The fact that I used the song without being aware that it was a CCM production shows that contemporary songs can have music and lyrics suitable for worship.

CONCLUSION

We noted at the outset that music is like a glass prism through which God's eternal truths shine. Through church music, a whole spectrum of biblical truths can be taught and proclaimed. Throughout church history people have learned through music the great truths of the Christian faith and the claims of Christ upon their lives.

In an attempt to bring about worship renewal, many evangelical churches today are adopting religious rock songs on the basis of personal taste and cultural trends rather than on clear theological convictions. The result is that some popular songs sung during church services have an inadequate or even heretical theology oriented toward self-satisfaction.

The choice of appropriate church music is crucial especially for the Seventh-day Adventist church, because through her music she teaches and proclaims the end-time truths entrusted to her. Regretfully, the music and worship style of most Adventist churches is largely based on the uncritical acceptance of the worship style of other churches.

To provide a theological basis for the choice and performance of music during the worship service of Adventist churches, we have considered in this chapter the implications of the Sabbath, Christ's ministry in the heavenly sanctuary, and the Second Advent. We have found that each of these three distinctive Adventist beliefs contributes in its own unique way to the definition of what church music should be like.

The Sabbath teaches us to respect the distinction between the *sacred* and the *secular,* not only in time, but also in such areas as church music and worship. At a time when cultural relativism has influenced many churches to blur the distinction between sacred and secular music, the Sabbath teaches us to respect such a distinction in all the facets of Christian life, including church music and worship. To use secular music for the church service on the Sabbath is to treat the Sabbath as a secular day and the church as a secular place.

The study of the music and liturgy of the Jerusalem Temple, as well as the heavenly sanctuary, has been very instructive. We have found that out of respect for the presence of God, percussion instruments and entertainment music which stimulate people physically were not allowed in the Temple services, nor are they used in the liturgy of the heavenly sanctuary. For the same reason, percussion instruments and music that stimulates people physically rather than elevating them spiritually are out of place in the church today.

Worship in the earthly and heavenly temples teaches us also that God is to be worshipped with great reverence and respect. Church music must not treat God with frivolity and irreverence. It should help to calm our souls and respond to Him in reverence.

Belief in the certainty and imminence of Christ's coming should be the driving force of the Adventist lifestyle and church music. The soon-appearing of the Rock of Ages, with the greatest band of angels this world has ever seen, can fire up the imagination of musicians today to compose new songs to appeal to those who are looking for meaning and hope in their lives.

At the threshold of a new millennium, the Seventh-day Adventist church faces an unprecedented challenge and opportunity to re-examine the theological basis for the choice and performance of its music. We hope and pray that the church will respond to this challenge, not by accepting uncritically contemporary pop music which is foreign to the mission and message of the church, but by promoting the composition and singing of songs that fittingly express the hope that burns within our hearts (1 Pet 3:15).

ENDNOTES

1. Charlie Peacock, *At the Cross Roads: An Insider's Look at the Past, Present, and Future of Contemporary Christian Music* (Nashville, TN, 1999), p. 72.

2. Ibid., p. 70.

3. Ibid., pp. 72-73.

4. Hal Spencer and Lynn Keesecker, "We Get Lifted Up," *Works of Heart* (Alexandria, IN, 1984), p. 44.

5. Calvin M. Johansson, *Discipling Music Ministry: Twenty-First Century Directions* (Peabody, MA, 1992), p. 52.

6. Philip Gold, "Gospel Music Industry Finds Its Amazing Grace," *Insight* (December 17, 1990), p. 46.

7. Frank Garlock and Kurt Woetzel, *Music in the Balance* (Greenville, NC, 1992), p.124.

8. "Spirit of Pop Moves Amy Grant," *Boston Herald* (April 9, 1986), p. 27.

9. Norval Peace, *And Worship Him* (Nashville, TN, 1967), p. 8.

10. Calvin M. Johansson (note 5), p. 42.

11. Dale A. Jorgenson, *Christianity and Humanism* (Joplin, MO, 1983), p. 49.

12. C. Raymond Holmes, *Sing a New Song! Worship Renewal for Adventists Today* (Berrien Springs, MI, 1984), p. 41.

13. Richard Paquier, *Dynamics of Worship* (Philadelphia, PA, 1967), p. 22.

14. Oscar Cullman, *Early Christian Worship* (Philadelphia, PA, 1953), p. 8.

15. Michael Anthony Harris, *"The Literary Function of the Hymns in the Apocalypse of John,"* Ph.D. Dissertation, Baptist Theological Seminary (Louisville, KY, 1988), p. 305.

16. F. Forrester Church and Terrance J. Mulry, *Earliest Christian Hymns* (New York, 1988), p. x.

17. Thomas Allen Seel, *A Theology of Music for Worship Derived from the Book of Revelation* (Metuchen, NJ, 1995), p. 84.

18. Ibid., p. 126.

19. George A. Buttrick, ed., *The Interpreter's Bible* (Nashville, TN, 1982), vol. 12, p. 420.

20. Thomas Allen Seel (note 18), p. 124.

21. John W. Kleinig, *The Lord's Song: The Basis, Function and Significance of Choral Music in Chronicles* (Sheffield, England, 1993), p. 82.

22. Anthony Sendrey, *Music in Ancient Israel* (London, England, 1963), pp. 376-377.

23. John W. Kleinig (note 21), p. 78.

24. Garen L. Wolf, *Music of the Bible in Christian Perspective* (Salem, OH, 1996), p. 145.

25. Calvin M. Johansson, *Music and Ministry: A Biblical Counterpoint* (Peabody, MA, 1986), p. 67-68.

26. See, Ralph P. Martin, *The Worship of God* (Grand Rapids, MI, 1982), p. 11.

27. See, James Strong, *The Exhaustive Concordance of the Bible* (New York, 1890), p. 1190.

28. Emphasis supplied.

29. *The Seventh-day Adventist Hymnal* (Washington, D C, 1985), p. 783.

30. Ibid., p. 787.

31. As quoted by Jack Wheaton, "Are Jazz Festivals Killing Jazz?" *Pro/Ed Review* 1 (April/May 1972), p. 19.

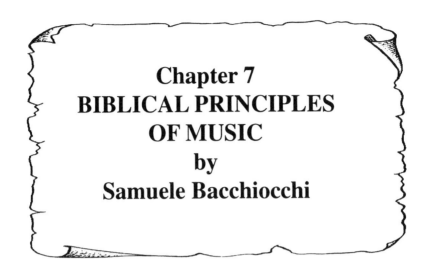

Chapter 7
BIBLICAL PRINCIPLES
OF MUSIC
by
Samuele Bacchiocchi

The story is told of a man who, during an election campaign, had a bumper sticker which read, "My mind is already made up. Please do not confuse me with the facts." This story reminds us of the ongoing debate over the use of "Christian" rock music for worship or evangelism. Many Christians have strong opinions in favor of or against the use of such music.

As Christians we cannot afford to close our minds to the search for biblical truths, because we are called to grow in "grace and knowledge" (2 Pet 3:18). Sometimes we think we know all that the Bible teaches on a certain doctrine, but when we begin investigating it, we soon discover how little we know.

This has been my experience. The many months I have spent examining the biblical references to music, singing, and musical instruments, have made me aware of the fact that the Bible has far more to say about music, especially church music, than I had ever imagined. It is a privilege to share this learning experience with all those who are eager to understand more fully the biblical principles of music.

Objectives of This Chapter. The overall objective of this chapter is to distill from the Bible some basic principles regarding appropriate music for the church service and private use. The task is not easy because the Bible is not set up as a doctrinal manual with a section devoted exclusively to music. Instead, the Bible is a source book with over 500 references scattered throughout about music, musicians, singing, and musical instruments. The challenge is not where to find these references, but how to draw from them principles applicable to us today.

No attempt is made to trace the history of music in the Bible, as several scholarly studies already address this subject. Our goal is to look at music in the Bible theologically rather than historically. What we seek to understand is the nature and function of music in the social and religious lives of God's people. More specifically, we want to ascertain what distinction, if any, the Bible makes between sacred and secular music. Was rhythmic music associated with dancing and entertainment ever used in the Temple, the synagogue, or the early church?

This chapter is divided into three parts. The first part examines the importance of music in the Bible, especially singing. Three major questions are addressed: (1) When, where, how, and why should we sing? (2) What does it mean to "make a joyful noise unto the Lord"? (3) What is the "New Song" that believers are to sing?

The second part of this chapter focuses on the ministry of music in the Bible. The investigation begins with the music ministry in the Temple and then continues with that of the synagogue and finally the New Testament church. The results of this investigation are significant because they show that, contrary to prevailing assumptions, the Bible makes a clear distinction between sacred and secular music. Percussion instruments, rhythmic music with a beat, and dancing were never part of the music ministry of the Temple, the synagogue, or the early church.

The third part of this chapter examines what the Bible teaches about dancing. The question we address is whether or not the Bible sanctions dance as a positive component of church worship. This is an important question because supporters of pop music appeal to some biblical references to dance to justify their use of rhythmic dance music in the church. By way of conclusion, a brief summary will be given of the biblical principles that have emerged in the course of this study.

Part 1
THE IMPORTANCE OF SINGING IN THE BIBLE

The importance of music in the Bible is indicated by the fact that God's creative and redemptive activities are accompanied and celebrated by music. At creation we are told that "the morning stars sang together, and all the sons of God shouted for joy" (Job 38:7). At the incarnation, the heavenly choir sang: "Glory to God in the highest, and on earth peace among men with whom he is pleased!" (Luke 2:14). At the final consummation of redemption, the great multitude of the redeemed will sing: "Hallelujah! For the Lord our God the Almighty reigns. Let us rejoice and exult and give him glory, for the marriage of the Lamb has come, and his Bride has made herself ready; it was granted her to be clothed with fine linen, bright and pure" (Rev 19:6-8).

The Singing of Creation. The response of the natural world to the majestic glory of God's created works is often expressed in terms of singing. This clearly shows that singing is something which God welcomes and in which He delights. Numerous examples show God's creation being invited to sing praises to God.

"Let the heavens rejoice, let the earth be glad; let the sea resound, and all that is in it; let the fields be jubilant, and everything in them. Then all the trees of the forest will sing for joy; they will sing before the Lord" (Ps 96:11-12; NIV). "Let the rivers clap their hands, let the mountains sing together for joy; let them sing before the Lord" (Ps 98:8-9; NIV). "Praise the Lord, all his works everywhere in his dominion" (Ps 103:22; NIV).

We read about the birds singing because God provides them with water (Ps 104:12). The heavens, the lower parts of the earth, the mountains, the forest, and every tree breaks forth into singing unto the Lord (Is 44:23). The wilderness, the cities, and the inhabitants of the rock sing and give glory to God (Is 42:1-12). Even the desert shall blossom and "rejoice with joy and singing" (Is 35:2).

All these metaphorical allusions to the animated and inanimate creation singing and shouting praises to God indicate that music is something that God ordains and desires. If these were the only references in the Bible, they would be sufficient for us to know that music, especially singing, has an important place and purpose in God's universe.

Human Singing. More wonderful than all of nature singing is the invitation extended to human beings to sing. "O Come, let us sing to the Lord; let us make a joyful noise to the rock of our salvation!" (Ps 95:1). "Sing praises to the Lord, O you his saints, and give thanks to his holy name" (Ps 30:4). "Oh that men would praise the Lord for his goodness, and for his wonderful works to the children of men" (Ps

107:8; KJV). Jesus once said that if people would not praise Him, "the very stones would cry out (Luke 19:40).

The Bible specifically mentions that singing should be directed to God. Its purpose is not personal gratification, but God's glorification. Moses said to the people: "I will sing to the Lord, for he has triumphed gloriously" (Ex 15:1). David declared: "I will extol thee, O Lord, among the nations, and sing praises to thy name" (2 Sam 22:50). Similarly, Paul exhorts the believers to sing and make melody "to the Lord with all your heart" (Eph 5:19). God and the praising of His people are so wrapped up together that God Himself is identified as "my song": "The Lord is my strength and *my song*" (Ex 15:2).

Music in the Bible is not only *for* God, it is also *from* God. It is God's gift to the human family. In praising God for His deliverance, David says: "He put a new song in my mouth, a hymn of praise to our God" (Ps 40:3. NIV). Thus, music can be inspired by God, just as His Holy Word. A telling proof is the fact that the longest book of the Bible is Psalms—the hymn book of God's people in Bible times. This means that sacred music is not only a human artistic expression. We may differ on the style or types of music, but no Christian can legitimately be opposed to music per se, because music is part of God's gracious provision for the human family.

Music Essential to the Total Human Well-Being. The first statement that we find in the Bible on any given subject has a foundational value. This seems to be true also in the case of music. Only a few generations from Adam and Eve, the Bible tells us that three sons were born to Lamech and his two wives, Adah and Zillah. Each son is introduced as "the founding father" of a basic profession. "Adah bore Jabal; he was the father of those who dwell in tents and have cattle. His brother's name was Jubal; he was the father of all those who play the lyre and pipe. Zillah bore Tubal-cain; he was the forger of all instruments of bronze and iron" (Gen 4:20-22).

It is evident that these three brothers were the founding fathers of three different professions. The first was a farmer and the third a tool-maker. Both agriculture and industry are essential to human existence. Sandwiched between the two is the musical profession of the middle brother. The implication seems to be that human beings are called, not only to produce and consume food and goods, but also to enjoy aesthetic beauty, such as music.

The American classical pianist Sam Totman sees in this verse an indication of God's provision for aesthetic human needs, besides the physical and material ones. He writes: "Here, within the compass of but a few verses, God reveals that the provision of man's material needs is not enough; in addition, man must have an outlet for his aesthetic sensitivities. Even from the beginning music was more than a mere pastime which could be viewed as something pleasant but essentially unnecessary. Simply stated, God has created in man a certain aesthetic need which can be best satisfied in music, and in his love and wisdom he has provided for this need."[1]

From a biblical perspective, music is not merely something potentially enjoyable. It is a gift provided by God to fully meet human needs. The very existence of music should give us reason to praise God for lovingly providing us with a gift through which we can express our gratitude to Him, while experiencing delight within ourselves.

The Reason for Singing. In the Bible religious music is God-centered, not self-centered. The notion of praising the Lord for entertainment or amusement is foreign to the Bible. No "Jewish" or "Christian" music concerts were performed by bands or singing artists at the Temple, synagogue, or Christian churches. Religious music was not an end to itself, but as a means to praise God by chanting His Word. An amazing recent discovery, discussed later, is that the entire Old Testament was originally intended to be chanted (sung).

Singing in the Bible is not for personal pleasure nor for reaching out to the Gentiles with tunes familiar to them. It is to praise God by chanting His Word—a method known as "cantillation." Pleasure in singing comes not from a rhythmic beat that stimulates people physically, but from the very experience of praising the Lord. "Praise the Lord, for the Lord is good; sing praise to his name, for that is pleasant" (Ps 135:3; NIV). "How good it is to sing praises to our God, how pleasant and fitting to praise him" (Ps 147:1. NIV).

Singing unto the Lord is "good" and "pleasant," because it enables believers to express to Him their joy and gratitude for the blessings of creation, deliverance, protection, and salvation. Singing is seen in the Bible as an offering of thanksgiving to the Lord for His goodness and blessings. This concept is expressed especially in Psalm 69:30-31: "I will praise God's name in song and glorify him with thanksgiving. This will please the Lord more than an ox, more than a bull with its horns and hoofs" (NIV).

The notion that *singing praises to the God is better than sacrifice* reminds us of a similar concept, namely, that obedience is better than sacrifice (1 Sam 15:22). Singing praises to God by chanting His Word is not only a pleasant experience; it is also a means of grace to the believer. Through singing, believers offer to God a worship of praise, enabling them to receive His enabling grace.

The Manner of Singing. To fulfill its intended function, singing must express joy, gladness, and thanksgiving. "Sing to the Lord with thanksgiving" (Ps 147:7). "I will praise thee with the harp for thy faithfulness, O my God; I will sing praises to thee with the lyre, O Holy One of Israel. My lips will shout for joy, when I sing praises to thee" (Ps 71:22-23). Note that singing is accompanied by the harp and lyre (often called psaltery—Ps 144:9; 33:2; 33:3), and not with percussion instruments. The reason, as noted in Chapter 6, is that string instruments blend with the human voice without supplanting it.

In numerous places the Bible indicates that our singing should be emotional with joy and gladness. We are told that the Levites "sang praises with gladness, and they bowed down and worshipped" (2 Chron 29:30). Singing should be done not only with gladness but also with the whole heart. "I will give thanks to the Lord with my whole heart" (Ps 9:1). If we follow this biblical principle, then our singing of hymns or praise songs in church should be joyful and enthusiastic.

To sing enthusiastically, it is necessary for the grace of God to be applied to the believer's heart (Col 3:16). Without divine love and grace in the heart, singing becomes as a sounding brass and a tinkling cymbal (1 Cor 13:1). The person who has experienced the transforming power of God's grace (Eph 4:24) can testify that the Lord has "put a new song in my mouth, a song of praise to our God" (Ps 40:3).

The music of an unconverted, rebellious heart is to God an irritating noise. Because of their disobedience, God said to the children of Israel, "Take away from me the noise of your songs" (Am 5:23). This statement is relevant in a day of loud amplification of pop music. What pleases God is not the volume of the music, but the condition of the heart.

"Make a Joyful Noise unto the Lord." The reference to the volume of the music reminds us of the admonition to "make a joyful noise unto the Lord"—a phrase that occurs with slight variations seven times in the KJV version of the Old Testament (Ps 66:1; 81:1; 95:1-2; 98:4, 6; 100:1). These verses are often used to defend the use of loud rock music in the church.

I have preached in churches where the music of the band was amplified at such high decibels that my eardrums were in pain for several days afterwards. This is the price I sometimes have to pay for preaching the Word of God in those churches that have introduced music bands with high-power amplification systems. Sometimes their huge speakers are placed right on the platform close to the ears of the preacher.

The defense for the use of deafening sound in the church service is that God does not really care about how we sound, as long as we make a joyful noise unto Him. Since rock bands with their electronic equipment produce a powerful, thundering loud noise, it is alleged that God is made very happy by such "joyful noise."

Before examining those Bible texts where the phrases "joyful noise" or "loud noise" appear in some mistaken translations, it is important to remember that in Bible times there was no electronic amplification. What was loud in Bible times, would be very normal today. The volume of music produced by the human voice or musical instruments *without amplification* does not increase in proportion of the number of participants.

Ten trumpets do not make ten times the noise or volume of one trumpet. In his book on the *Psychology of Music*, Carl Seashore devotes an entire chapter to the subject of volume. He writes: "The addition of one or more tones of the same intensity tends to increase the total intensity in the volume, but only to a slight degree. For example, if we have a piano tone of 50 decibels and we add to that another tone of the same intensity, the combined effect will be about 53 decibels. If we add a third tone, the total intensity is likely to be 55 decibels. Thus the addition to the total intensity decreases with the number of units combined; and in every case the increase is small in comparison with the original intensity of one element."[2]

What this means is that the singers that David appointed to "offer praises to the Lord with the instruments" (1 Chron 23:5) could produce at most a sound volume of about 70 or 80 decibels, because they had no amplification possibilities. The usual choir was rather small, consisting of a minimum of 12 adult male singers, accompanied by few string instruments. The level of volume depended on the distance between the singers and the congregation. By contrast, today a four-man rock group with the right amplification system can output a sound power in the 130-140 decibel level, which can upstage a jumbo jet at takeoff.

The "loud noise" in Bible times was not loud enough to harm people physically. Today the possibility of being hurt by excessive volume is a constant possibility. "Most ear doctors say that we should not listen to anything above the 90 decibels on the sound scale. Many rock music groups, both secular and Christian, play at 120-125 decibel level! (Keep in mind that the SST Concord Supersonic jet hits just over 130 decibels when leaving Washington's Dulles Airport.) 'Your bodies are the temple of the Holy Spirit' (1 Cor 6:19). Certainly that text is applicable to this point. We are to be good stewards of our eardrums, too."[3]

Does Loud Noise Praise God? Do those Bible texts that speak about making "a joyful noise" or "a loud noise" unto the Lord teach us that God is pleased with the excessive amplification of the human voice or musical instruments during the worship service? Hardly so. This conclusion is largely drawn from a mistranslation of the original Hebrew terms commonly translated as "noise." In his book, *The Rise of Music in the Ancient World,* Curt Sachs answers this question: "How did ancient Jews sing? Did they actually cry at the top of their voices? Some students have tried to make us believe that such was the case, and they particularly refer to several psalms that allegedly bear witness of singing in fortissimo. But I suspect them of drawing from translations rather than from the original."[4]

The phrase "make a joyful noise" is a mistranslation of the Hebrew *ruwa*. The term does not mean to make an indiscriminate loud noise, but to shout for joy. The God of biblical revelation does not delight in loud noise per se, but in joyful melodies. A good example is found in Job 38:7 where the same word *ruwa* is used to describe the sons of God who "shouted for joy" at creation. The singing of the heavenly beings at creation can hardly be characterized as "loud noise," because "noise" presupposes unintelligible sound.

The mistranslation of *ruwa* as "noise" has been caught by the translators of the New International Version (NIV), where the term is consistently translated as "shout for joy" rather than "make a joyful noise." For example, in the KJV Psalm 98:4 reads: "Make a joyful noise unto the Lord, all the earth: make a loud noise, and rejoice, and sing praise." Note the more rational translation found in the NIV: "Shout for joy to the Lord, all the earth, burst into jubilant song with music" (Ps 98:4). There is a world of difference between "making a loud noise unto the Lord," and "shouting for joy" or "bursting into jubilant song." Singing jubilantly with the full volume of the human voice is not noise making, but an enthusiastic expression of praise.

Another self-evident example of mistranslation is found in Psalm 33:3 which in the KJV reads: "Sing unto him a new song; play skilfully with a loud noise." The latter phrase is contradictory, because music skillfully played can hardly be described as "loud noise." One wonders why the translators of the KJV did not see the contradiction. The NIV correctly renders the verse: "Sing to him a new song; play skillfully, and shout for joy" (Ps 33:3).

Two Old Testament references indicate that sometimes music can degenerate into noise making. The first reference is found in Amos 5:23 where God rebukes the unfaithful Israelites: "Take away from me the noise of your songs; to the melody of your harps I will not listen." A similar warning is found in Ezekiel's prophecy against Tyre: "And I will cause the noise of thy songs to cease; and the sound of thy harps shall be no more heard" (Ezek 26:13).

In both texts the word "noise" correctly translates the Hebrew *hamown,* which occurs eighty times in the Old Testament and is commonly translated as "noise" or "tumult." The NIV correctly uses the word "noisy": "I will put an end to your noisy songs, and the music of your harps will be heard no more." God views such music as "noise" because it is produced by a rebellious people.

In one instance in the New Testament, the word "noise" is used in conjunction with music produced by professional mourners. We read in Matthew 9:23-24: "And when Jesus came into the ruler's house, and saw the minstrels and the people making a noise, He said unto them, 'Give place; for the maid is not dead, but sleepeth.' And they laughed him to scorn." In this case the music and the wailing are correctly characterized as "noise," because they consisted of incoherent sounds.

On this occasion the Greek verb *thorubeo* refers to the musical wailing and noise making by minstrels and the crowd. The fact that Christ characterizes such music as "noise" suggests that the Lord does not approve of loud musical noise in a worship service. "It was a semitic custom to hire professional mourners to wail, and sing and beat percussion instruments and play mournfully over the dead. . . . Although this verse definitively connects noise making with music in the New Testament, it does not implicate that in the New Testament dispensation we should make noise unto God with our religious music."[5]

The review of relevant texts indicates that the Bible does not sanction making a joyful noise unto the Lord, or any kind of noise making for that matter. God's people are invited to break forth in singing with power and joy. God does care about how we sing and play during the worship service. God has always demanded our best, when making an offering to him. As He required the burnt offerings to be "without blemish" (Lev 1:3), so it is reasonable to assume that He expects us to present Him with the very best musical offering. There is no biblical basis for believing that the loud, noise-making music or questionable lyrics are acceptable to God.

The Place and Time of Singing. The Bible instructs us to sing, not only in God's House, but also among unbelievers, in foreign countries, in time of persecution, and among the saints. The writer of Hebrews says: "In the midst of the congregation I will praise thee" (Heb 2:12). The Psalmist admonishes to "Sing to the Lord a new song, his praise in the assembly of the faithful" (Ps 149:1). Paul affirms "I will praise thee among the Gentiles, and sing to thy name" (Rom 15:9). Isaiah exhorts to praise God in the islands (Is 42:11-12). While in jail, Paul and Silas were "praying and singing hymns to God" (Acts 16:25).

The frequent references to praising God among the heathens or Gentiles (2 Sam 22:50; Rom 15:9; Ps 108:3) suggest that singing was seen as an effective way to witness for the Lord to unbelievers. However, there are no indications in the Bible that the Jews or the early Christians borrowed secular tunes and songs to evangelize the Gentiles. On the contrary, we shall see below that the entertainment music and percussion instruments common in the pagan temples and society were conspicuously absent in the worship music of the Temple, synagogue, and early Christian gatherings. Both Jews and early Christians believed that secular music had no place in the house of worship. This point becomes clearer as we proceed with this study.

Singing, in the Bible, is not limited to the worship experience, but extends to the totality of one's existence. Believers who live in peace with God have a constant song in their hearts, though the singing may not always be vocalized. This is why the Psalmist says: "I will praise the Lord all my life; I will sing praise to my God as long as I live" (Ps 146:2; 104:33. NIV). In Revelation those who come out of the great tribulation are seen standing before God's throne, singing with a loud voice a new song which says: "Salvation belongs to our God who sits on the throne, and to the Lamb" (Rev 7:10). Singing praises to God is an experience that begins in this life and continues in the world to come.

The "New Song" of the Bible. Nine times the Bible speaks of singing "a new song." Seven times the phrase occurs in the Old Testament (Ps 33:3; 40:3; 96:1; 98:1; 144:9; 149:1; Is 42:10) and twice in the New Testament (Rev 5:9; 14:3). During the preparation of this manuscript, several subscribers to my "Endtime Issues" newsletter have emailed messages, arguing that for them the contemporary pop religious music is the prophetic fulfillment of the biblical "new song," because pop songs have "new" lyrics and tunes. Others believe that Christians are required to sing new songs and, consequently, musicians constantly must compose new hymns for the church.

There certainly is a continuing need for new hymns to enrich the worship experience of the church today. However, a study of the "new song" in the Bible reveals that the phrase "new song" refers not to a new composition, but to a new experience that makes it possible to praise God with new meaning. Let us look first at a couple of passages from the Old Testament which help us define the meaning of the "new song." The Psalmist says: "He lifted me out of the slimy pit, out of the mud and mire; he set my feet on a rock and gave me a firm place to stand. He put a new song in my mouth, a hymn of praise to our God" (Ps 40:2-3, NIV). In this text, the "new song" is defined by the appositional phrase as "a hymn of praise to our God." It is the experience of deliverance from the slimy pit and of restoration upon solid ground that gives David reason to sing old hymns of praise to God with new meaning.

The "new song" in the Bible is not associated with simpler lyrics or more rhythmic music, but with a unique experience of divine deliverance. For example, David says: "I will sing a new song to you, O God; on the ten-stringed lyre I will make music to you, to the One who gives victory to kings, who delivers his servant David from the deadly sword" (Ps 144:9-10. NIV). It is the experience of deliverance and victory that inspires David to sing with a new sense of gratitude the hymns of praises.

The same concept is expressed in the two references to the "new song" found in the New Testament (Rev 5:9; 14:2). The twenty-four elders and the four living creatures sing a "new song" before the Throne of God. The song praises the Lamb "for thou wast slain and by thy blood didst ransom men for God" (Rev 5:9).

On a similar note in Revelation 14, the redeemed join the elders and the living creatures in singing "a new song before the throne" (Rev 14:3). We are told that "no one could learn that song" except those "who had been redeemed from the earth" (Rev 14:3). What makes this song new, is not the new words or melody, but the unique experience of the redeemed. They are the only ones who can sing it, not because the words or melody are difficult to learn, but because of their unique experience. They came out of the great tribulation; thus they can express their praise and gratitude to God in a way no one else can do.

The Greek word translated "new" is *kainos,* which means new in quality and not in time. The latter meaning is expressed by the Greek word *neos.* The *Theological Dictionary of the New Testament* clearly explains the difference between the two Greek words *neos* and *kainos.* "*Neos* is what is new in time or origin, . . . *kainos* is what is new in nature, different from the usual, impressive, better than the old.* "[6]

Only the person who has experienced the transforming power of God's grace can sing the new song. It is noteworthy that Paul's famous exhortation in Colossians 3:16 to "sing psalms and hymns and spiritual songs" is preceded by his appeal to "put off the old nature with its practices and have put on the new nature, which is being renewed in knowledge after the image of its creator" (Col 3:9-10). The "new song" celebrates the victory over the old life and old songs; at the same time, it expresses gratitude for the new life in Christ experienced by believers.

Part 2
THE MINISTRY OF MUSIC IN THE BIBLE

In discussing the importance of music in the Bible, we have focused so far on the role of singing in the personal spiritual experience. Very little has been said of the ministry of music conducted first in the Temple, and then in the synagogue, and finally in the early church. A brief examination of the public ministry of music during Bible times offers significant lessons for church music today.

(1) The Music Ministry in the Temple

Many of those involved in contemporary music ministry appeal to the different styles of music of the Old Testament for "doing their own thing." They believe that music produced by percussion instruments and accompanied by dancing was common in religious services. Consequently, they maintain that some styles of rock music and dancing are appropriate for church services today.

A careful study of the function of music in the Old Testament reveals otherwise. For example, in the Temple musicians belonged to the professional clergy, played only on limited and special occasions, and used only few specific musical instruments. There was no possibility to turn the Temple service into a music festival where any Jewish "rock band" could play the entertainment music of the time. Music was rigidly controlled in the Temple. What is true of the Temple was later true also of the synagogue and the early church. This survey will help us to understand that in music, as in all areas of life, God does not give us the license to "do our own thing."

The Institution of the Music Ministry. The transition from the unsettled, nomadic life in the desert to a permanent lifestyle in Palestine under the monarchy afforded the opportunity for developing a music ministry that would meet the needs of the worshipping congregation at the Temple. Prior to this time the references to music are primarily in conjunction with women singing and dancing to celebrate special events. Miriam led a group of women in singing and dancing to celebrate the overthrow of the Egyptians (Ex 15:1-21). Women played and danced for the conquering David (1 Sam 18:6-7). Jephthah's daughter met her father with timbrels and dance upon his return from battle (Judg 11:34).

With the establishment by David of a professional music ministry of Levites, music making was restricted to men. Why women were excluded from serving as musicians in the Temple is an important question that has baffled scholars. We shall comment upon it shortly. Women did continue making music in the social life of the people.

The book of Chronicles describes with considerable detail how David organized the music ministry of the Levites. An insightful analysis of how David accomplished this organization is provided by the doctoral dissertation of John Kleinig, *The Lord's Song: The Basis, Function and Significance of Choral Music in Chronicles.*[7] For the purpose of our study, we limit ourselves to a brief summary of those features that are relevant for the ministry of music today.

According to the first book of Chronicles, David organized the music ministry in three stages. First, he ordered the heads of the Levitical families to appoint an orchestra and a choir to accompany the transportation of the ark to its tent at Jerusalem (1 Chron 15:16-24).

The second stage occurred after the ark had been safely placed in its tent in his palace (2 Chron 8:11). David arranged for the regular performance of choral music at the time of the daily burnt offerings with choirs in two different places (1 Chron 16:4-6, 37-42). One choir performed under the leadership of Asaph before the ark in Jerusalem (1 Chron 16:37), and the other under the leadership of Herman and Jeduthun before the altar in Gibeon (1 Chron 16:39-42).

The third stage in David's organization of the ministry of music occurred at the end of David's reign when the king planned for the more elaborate music service that would be conducted at the temple that Solomon was to build (1 Chron 23:2 to 26:32). David established a pool of 4,000 Levites as potential performers (1 Chron 15:16; 23:5). From this group he formed a professional Levitical choir of 288 members. The Levite musicians accounted for more than ten percent of the 38,000 Levites. "Some kind of examination was probably necessary for the process of selection, since musical ability is not always inherited."[8]

David himself was involved together with his officials in the appointment of twenty-four leaders of the watches, each of whom had twelve musicians for a total of 288 musicians (1 Chron 25:1-7). These in turn were responsible for the rest of the selection of the musicians.

The Ministry of the Musicians. To ensure that there would be no confusion or conflict between the sacrificial ministry of the priests and the music ministry of the Levites, David carefully delineated the position, rank, and scope of the ministry of the musicians (1 Chron 23:25-31). The performance of the ministry of music was subordinate to the priests (1 Chron 23:28).

The nature of the ministry of the musicians is graphically described: "They shall stand every morning, thanking and praising the Lord, and likewise at evening, and whenever burnt offerings are offered to the Lord on sabbaths, new moons and feast days, according to the number required of them, continually before the Lord" (1 Chron 23:30-31).

The context suggests that the musicians stood somewhere in front of the altar, since their music performance coincided with the presentation of the burnt offering. The purpose of their ministry was to thank and praise the Lord. They announced the Lord's presence to His assembled people (1 Chron 16:4), reassuring them of His favorable disposition toward them.

In 1 Chronicles 16:8-34 we find a remarkable hymn of praise that was sung by the Temple choir. "This song consists of portions of Psalms 105, 96, and 106, which were reworked and recombined to produce this remarkable liturgical text. The song itself begins and ends with a call to thanksgiving. A concluding petition and doxology are appended in 1 Chronicles 16:35-36. We thus have in 1 Chronicles 16:8-34 a carefully crafted composition which has been placed there to demonstrate the basic pattern of thanksgiving which David instituted for performance by the singers in Jerusalem."[9]

Successful Music Ministry. The music ministry at the Temple was successful for several reasons which are relevant for our church music today. First, the Levite musicians were mature and musically trained. We read in 1 Chronicles 15:22 that "Kenaniah the head Levite was in charge of the singing; that was his responsibility because he was skillful at it" (NIV). He became director of music because he was an accomplished musician able to instruct others. The concept of musical skill is mentioned several times in the Bible (1 Sam 16:18; 1 Chron 25:7; 2 Chron 34:12; Ps 137:5). Paul also alludes to it when he says: "I will sing with my spirit, but I will also sing with my mind" (1 Cor 14:15, NIV).

The choir consisted of a minimum of twelve adult male singers between the ages of thirty and fifty (1 Chron 23:3-5).[10] Rabbinical sources report that the musical training of a Levitical singer took at least five years of intensive preparation.[11] The biblical principle is that music leaders must be mature with an understanding of music, especially today as we live in a highly educated society.

Second, the music ministry at the Temple was successful because its musicians were prepared spiritually. They were set aside and ordained for their ministry like the rest of the priests. Speaking to the leaders of the Levite musicians, David said: "Sanctify yourselves, you and your brethren . . . So the priests and the Levites sanctified themselves" (1 Chron 15:12, 14). The Levite musicians were given a sacred trust to continually minister before the Lord (1 Chron 16:37).

Third, the Levite musicians were full-time workers. 1 Chronicles 9:33 states: "Now these are the singers, the heads of father's houses of the Levites, dwelling in the chambers of the temple free from other service, for they were on duty day and night." Apparently the Levites' ministry of music entailed considerable preparation, because we read that "David left Asaph and his brethren there before the ark of the covenant of the Lord to minister continually before the ark as each day required" (1 Chron 16:37). The biblical lesson is that ministers of music must be willing to work diligently in preparing the music needed for the worship service.

Lastly, the Levite musicians were not singing artists invited to entertain the people at the Temple. They were *ministers of music*. "These are the men whom David put in charge of the service of song in the house of the Lord, after the ark rested there. They ministered with song before the tabernacle of the tent of meeting" (1 Chron 6:31-32). Through their musical service the Levites *"ministered"* to the people. In five other instances in the Old Testament, the Levites are said *to minister* to the people through their music (1 Chron 16:4, 37; 2 Chron 8:14; 23:6; 31:2).

The ministry of the Levite musicians is well defined in 1 Chronicles 16:4: "Moreover he appointed certain of the Levites as ministers before the ark of the Lord, to invoke, to thank, and to praise the Lord, the God of Israel." The three verbs used in this text—"invoke," "thank," and "praise"—suggest that the music ministry was a vital part of the worship experience of God's people.

An indication of the importance of the music ministry can be seen in the fact that the Levite musicians were paid out of the same tithes given for the support of the priesthood (Num 18:24-26; Neh 12:44-47; 13:5, 10-12). The biblical principle is that the work of a minister of music should not be "a labor of love," but a ministry supported by the tithe income of the church. It stands to reason that if a lay person volunteers to help in the music program of the church, such service does not need to be remunerated.

Summing up, the music ministry at the Temple was conducted by experienced and mature Levites who were trained musically, prepared spiritually, supported financially, and served pastorally. As Kenneth Osbeck observes: "To minister musically in the Old Testament was a great privilege and a most responsible service. This is still true of a church music-ministry today. In a very real sense we are New Testament Levites. Therefore these principles established by God for the Levitical priesthood should be noted as valid guidelines for music leaders in a New Testament church."[12]

The Levitical Choir and the Sacrificial Ritual. The book of Chronicles presents the musical ministry of the Levites as part of the presentation of the daily offering at the Temple. The ritual consisted of two parts. First came the blood ritual which was designed to atone for the sins of the people through the transference of the blood of the sacrifice to the Holy Place (2 Chron 29:21-24). This service created the ritual purity necessary for God's acceptance of His people and the manifestation of His blessing upon the congregation. During this ritual no songs were sung.

Once the rite of atonement was completed, the burnt offering was presented upon the altar. This ritual signalled God's acceptance of His people and the manifestation of His presence. John Kleinig explains that "As the sacrifices were being burnt upon the altar, the trumpets, which announced the Lord's presence, called for the prostration of the congregation in His presence, and the song of the Lord was sung by the musicians [2 Chron 29:25-30]. Thus, the choral service came after the rite of atonement had been completed. It did not attempt to secure a favorable response from the Lord but presupposed such a response as something already given. The musicians proclaimed the Lord's name during the presentation of the sacrifices, so that he would come to His people and bless them, as He had promised in Exodus 20:24 and demonstrated in 2 Chronicles 7:1-3."[13]

The function of the music during the sacrificial ritual was not to overshadow or replace the sacrifice itself, but to enlist the involvement of the congregation at certain designated moments during the service. In other words, the Israelites did not go to the Temple to hear the Levite bands performing in sacred concert. Instead, they went to the Temple to witness and experience God's atonement for their sins. The music that accompanied the atoning sacrifice invited them to accept and celebrate God's gracious provision of salvation.

At a time when many Christians choose their churches in accordance with the musical style of worship, we need to remember that in the Bible, the music was never an end to itself. In the Temple the music served enhanced the sacrificial service by enlisting the participation of the congregation at certain specific moments. In the synagogue and the early church, music reinforced the teaching and proclamation of the Word of God. To be true to the biblical witness, our church music must support the teaching and preaching of God's Word, and not overshadow it.

The Musical Instruments of the Temple. David instituted not only the times, place, and words for the performance of the Levitical choir, but he also "made" the musical instruments to be used for their ministry (1 Chron 23:5; 2 Chron 7:6). This is why they are called "the instruments of David" (2 Chron 29:26-27).

To the trumpets which the Lord had ordained through Moses, David added the cymbals, lyres, and harp (1 Chron 15:16; 16:5-6). The importance of this combination as divinely ordained is indicated by the fact that this combination of instruments was respected for many centuries until the destruction of the Temple. For example, in 715 B. C., King Hezekiah "stationed the Levites in the house of the Lord with cymbals, harps, and lyres, according to commandment of David and of Gad the king's seer and of Nathan the prophet; for the commandment was from the Lord through his prophets" (2 Chron 29:25).

The trumpets were played by the priests and their number ranged from two in the daily worship (1 Chron 16:6; Num 10:2) to seven or more on special occasions (1 Chron 15:24; Neh 12:33-35; 2 Chron 5:12). "In worship at the Temple the trumpets gave the signal for the prostration of the congregation during the presentation of the burnt offering and the performance of the choral service (2 Chron 29:27-28). . . . While the Levitical musicians faced the altar, the trumpeters stood facing them in front of the altar (2 Chron 5:12; 7:6)."[14] This arrangement highlighted the responsibility of the trumpeters to give the signal for the congregation to prostrate and for the choir to sing.

The cymbals consisted of two metal plates with reflexed rims about 10-15 inches wide. When struck together vertically, they produced a ringing, tinkling sound. Some appeal to the use of cymbals to argue that Temple music had a rhythmic beat like rock music today, and, consequently, the Bible does not forbid percussion instruments and rock music in the church today. Such an argument ignores the fact that, as Kleinig explains, "the cymbals were not used by the precantor to conduct the singing by beating out the rhythm of the song, but rather to announce the beginning of the song or a stanza in the song. Since they were used to introduce the song, they were wielded by the head of choir on ordinary occasions (1 Chron 16:5) or by the three heads of the guilds on extraordinary occasions (1 Chron 15:19). . . . Since the trumpets and the cymbals were played together to announce the beginning of the song, the players of both are called the 'sounders' in 1 Chronicles 16:42."[15]

In his book *Jewish Music in Its Historical Development*, A. Z. Idelsohn notes that in the worship of the Temple only one pair of cymbals were used and that by the leader himself. "The percussive instruments were reduced to one cymbal, which was not employed in the music proper, but merely to mark pauses and intermissions."[16] In a similar vein, Curt Sachs explains,"The music in the Temple included cymbals, and the modern reader might conclude that the presence of percussion instruments indicate rigid beats. But there is little doubt that the cymbals, as elsewhere, marked the end of a line and not the beats inside a verse. . . . A word for rhythm does not seem to exists in the Hebrew language."[17] The term "Selah," which occurs in some psalms to mark the end of a stanza, may indicate the place where the cymbals were struck.

The third group of musical instruments was comprised of two string instruments, the lyres and the harps, which were called "the instruments of song" (2 Chron 5:13) or "the instruments of God's song" (1 Chron 16:42). As indicated by their descriptive name, their function was to accompany the songs of praise and thanksgiving to the Lord (1 Chron 23:5; 2 Chron 5:13). The musicians who played the harps and the lyres would themselves sing the song to their own accompaniment (1 Chron 9:33; 15:16, 19, 27; 2 Chron 5:12-13; 20:21).

In his book *The Music of the Bible in Christian Perspective*, Garen Wolf explains that "String instruments were used extensively to accompany singing since they would not cover up the voice or the 'Word of Jehovah' which was being sung."[18] Great care was taken to ensure that the vocal praise of the Levitical choir would not be overshadowed by the sound of the instruments.

Restriction on Musical Instruments. Some scholars argue that instruments like drums, timbrel (which was a tambourine), flutes, and dulcimers were kept out of the Temple because they were associated with pagan worship and culture, or because they were customarily played by women for entertainment. This could well be the case, but it only goes to show that there was a distinction between the sacred music played inside the Temple and the secular music played outside.

A restriction was placed on the musical instruments and art expression to be used in the House of God. God prohibited a number of instruments which were allowed *outside* the Temple for national festivities and social pleasure. The reason is not that certain percussion instruments were evil per se. The sounds produced by any musical instrument are neutral, like a letter of the alphabet. Rather, the reason is that these instruments were commonly used to produce entertainment music which was inappropriate for worship in God's House. By prohibiting instruments and music styles, like dancing, associated with secular entertainment, the Lord taught His people to distinguish between the sacred music played in the Temple, and the secular, entertainment music used in social life.

The restriction on the use of instruments was meant to be a binding rule for future generations. When King Hezekiah revived Temple worship in 715 B.C., he meticulously followed the instructions given by David. We read that the king "stationed the Levites in the house of the Lord with cymbals, harps, and lyres, according to the commandment of David . . . for the commandment was from the Lord through his prophets" (2 Chron 29:25).

Two and a half centuries later when the Temple was rebuilt under Ezra and Nehemiah, the same restriction was applied again. No percussion instruments were allowed to accompany the Levitical choir or to play as an orchestra at the Temple (Ezra 3:10; Neh 12:27, 36). This confirms that the rule was clear and binding over many centuries. The singing and the instrumental music of the Temple were to differ from that used in the social life of the people.

Lessons from the Temple Music. What lessons can we learn from the music of the Temple? The absence of percussion musical instruments and of dancing bands in the music of the Temple indicates, as noted earlier, that a distinction must be made between the secular music used for social entertainment and the sacred music employed for worship service in God's House.

No "Jewish Rock Bands" were at the Temple to entertain the people with loud rhythmic music, because the Temple was a place of worship and not a social club for entertainment. Percussion instruments like drums, tambourines, timbrels or tabrets, which were commonly used for making entertainment music, were absent in the Temple music. Only the cymbals were used, but in a limited way. They marked the end of a stanza and the cessation of the singing.

The lesson for us today is evident. Church music should differ from secular music, because the church, like the ancient Temple, is God's

House in which we gather to worship the Lord and not to be entertained. Percussion instruments which stimulate people physically through a loud and relentless beat are as inappropriate for church music today as they were for the Temple music of ancient Israel.

A second lesson is that the musical instruments used to accompany the choir or the singing of the congregation should not cover up the voice. Like the string instruments used in the Temple, musical instruments used in the church today should support the singing. Musical instruments should serve as a hand-maiden to the Word of God which is sung and proclaimed. This means, for example, that organ music should not be so loud as to drown the voice of the congregation.

On numerous occasions I have been in churches equipped with powerful electronic organs that are played so loud that the voice of the congregation cannot be heard. Biblical principle indicates that the function of the organ is to support the singing of the congregation; not to cover it up. This principle applies not only to organ music, but to any other instrument or an orchestra that accompanies a choir or a singing congregation.

Some argue that if we are to follow the example of the Temple, we need to eliminate in the church such instruments as the piano and the organ, because they are not string instruments. Such an argument ignores the distinction between a biblical principle and its cultural application.

The biblical principle is that instrumental music accompanying the singing should aid the vocal response to God and not drown it. In Bible times this was best accomplished by the use of string instruments. Note that trumpets and cymbals were used in the Temple, but not to accompany the Levitical choir. Nothing was wrong with these instruments. They simply were not seen as suitable to accompany the singing, presumably because they do not blend well with the human voice, besides supplanting it.

Another point is that instruments like the organ or the piano were unknown in Bible times. Were we to exclude from our life today all that the Bible does not explicitly mention, we should not eat pizza, apple pie, or ice cream.

The important biblical principle is that music in God's House, both instrumental and vocal, must respect and reflect the sacredness of the place of worship. When instruments are used to accompany the singing, they should support the human voice without supplanting it.

(2) The Music Ministry in the Synagogue

The function of music in the synagogue differed from that of the Temple, primarily because the two institutions had different purposes. The Temple was primarily where sacrifices were offered on behalf of the whole nation and of individual believers. The synagogue, on the other hand, emerged most likely during the Babylonian exile as the place where prayers were offered and scripture was read and taught. While there was only one Temple for the whole nation, according to the Talmud, there were 394 synagogues located in Jerusalem alone in Jesus' time.

The difference in function between the Temple and the synagogue is reflected in the different roles that music played in these two institutions. While the music of the Temple was *predominantly vocal,* with string instruments aiding the singing, the music of the synagogue was *exclusively vocal,* without any instruments. The only exception was the *shofar*—the ram-horn that served as a signal instrument.

In the Temple the ministry of music was in the hands of professional musicians. Their choral music was an accessory to the sacrificial ritual. We might say that the music was *"sacrifice-centered."* The participation of the congregation was limited to affirmative responses as "Amen," or "Hallelujah." By contrast, in the synagogue the service, including the music, was in the hands of lay persons and their music was, as Curt Sachs call it, "logenic,"[19] that is, *"Word-centered."*

Little evidence suggests that musical instruments were ever used in the synagogue service. We know that after the A.D. 70 destruction of the Temple, the only instrument used in the synagogue service was the *shofar.* The reason, as Eric Werner explains, was "partly because of the hostility of the Pharisees to instrumental music, and partly because of the deep mourning for the Temple and the land, and the disappearance of the Levitical functions, including the provision of music for the sanctuary. . . . The exclusion of instruments from Jewish worship remained in force generally for many centuries; only at the loss of political power by the rabbis in the nineteenth century Emancipation, did instrumental music once again appear in the (liberal) synagogue, and the exclusion still remains in force where, as in modern Israel, orthodox rabbis retain some power."[20]

Blurring of Music and Speech. The distinction between music and public speech was blurred in the synagogue, because the word-centered worship migrated back and forth between speech and song. The musical ambiguity of the synagogue service was caused by the fact that much of the service consisted of prayers and the public reading of the Scriptures, which often took the form of chanting, known as "cantillation."

"The concept that the entire Old Testament was originally intended to be chanted (sung) is a new concept to church musicians and pastors, but it is a long established fact among scholars of Bible music. The reason that it is such a well-kept secret is that we tend to ignore what we do not understand."[21]

"The intonations or cantillations, mentioned as far back as the first century, were cast into a system of modes or formulae, one for each of the books of the Bible intended to be publicly read. . . . Little is known about when the transition from declamatory to musical reading was first evidenced, except that the Psalms were sung in temple worship. Idelsohon and Werner both believe that the chanting of Scripture, in one form or another, went back perhaps as far back as Ezra (fifth century B.C.), and that its eventual complexity and organization was the result of hundreds of years of crystallization."[22]

"The Talmud scorns those who read the Scriptures without melody and study the words without singing. Service, based on reading the Holy Books, was musical throughout, alternating between the cantor's chant and the tunes of the congregation. In both forms it was what we call *cantillation,* though not in the stagnant monotone of a Christian lesson, but rather in the noble fluency of Gregorian melodies."[23]

One of the surprising discoveries of recent years is that the accents of the Masoretic Hebrew Text are musical notations. This made it possible for Suzanne Haik-Vantoura to decipher the ancient music of the Bible, which was found to consist of a seven-note diatonic scale, strikingly similar to our modern diatonic scale.[24]

Relevance of Synagogue Music for Today. What lessons can we learn from the ministry of music at the synagogue? Are we required to chant scripture today as the Jews have historically done in the synagogue? No. Nothing in the Bible commands us to sing the Scriptures. This does not exclude the possibility of learning scripture by means of the "Scripture song" and "Psalm-singing." In fact, considerable efforts have been done in recent times to set to music numerous Psalms and Bible passages.

We have seen that the ministry of music at the synagogue was largely a ministry of the Word. The Jews came together to the synagogue in a rather informal setting to pray, read, and sing the Scriptures. For them, music was not an end to itself, but a means of praising the Lord by chanting His Word and thus learning His revealed will.

At a time when much of CCM is deficient in scriptural content and Christian artists often draw the attention of the people to their singing abilities rather than to the teachings of God's Word, it is good to remember that the music of the synagogue, which Jesus Himself sang, was *"Word-centered"*—it was designed to teach and proclaim the great Scriptural truths.

Does our church music help us to hear the Word of God clearly? Remember that "faith comes from hearing the message, and the message is heard through the word of Christ" (Rom 10:17, NIV). Church music should help us hear the Word of God through its sound, the character of the composition, and its lyrics.

Another important lesson is that the music of the Temple and synagogue was distinct from that of the pagan society. While much of the music played in the pagan society was improvised, "the rigid training of the Levites as described by Josephus and rabbinical sources left little room for spontaneous improvisation. . . . In this respect the Temple [and the synagogue] music must have been untypical of Middle Eastern music, in which improvisation is normally indispensable."[25]

(3) The Music Ministry in the New Testament

To speak about a music ministry in the New Testament may seem completely out of place. The New Testament is silent about any "musical" office in the church. Outside the book of Revelation, in which music is part of a rich eschatological drama, only a dozen passages refer to music.

None of these passages, however, gives us a clear picture of the role that music played in church services during New Testament times. This is not surprising, because New Testament believers did not see their worship gatherings as being much different from those of the synagogue. Both were conducted in an informal setting, with lay people leading out in the prayer, reading, singing, and exhortation. The New Testament references to worship gatherings reflect to a large extent the worship service of the synagogue, as scholarly studies have established.[26] The fundamental difference between the two was the messianic proclamation, which was present only in the Christian worship.

Of the twelve references to music in the New Testament, five refer to it metaphorically (Matt 6:2; 11:17; Luke 7:32; 1 Cor 13:1; 14:7-8) and, consequently, are not relevant to our study. The remaining seven shed important light, especially when they are seen within the broader context of the synagogue worship, which was known and practiced by the Christians.

Four references to music are found in the Gospels. Two mention instrumental music and dancing in conjunction with the mourning for the death of a girl (Matt 9:23) and the celebration upon the return of the Prodigal Son (Luke 15:25). Two passages are parallel and mention Christ singing a hymn with His disciples at the conclusion of the Last Supper (Matt 26:30; Mark 14:26). Most likely this was the second portion of the Jewish Hallel sung at the completion of the Passover meal. It consisted of Psalms 113 to 118.

One text refers to Paul and Silas singing while in jail (Acts 16:25). We have no way of knowing whether they sang psalms or newly composed Christian hymns. The above examples tell us that music accompanied various activities in the social and religious life of the people, but they do not inform us about the role of music in the church.

Instructions Regarding Music. Few instructions regarding church music are found in the Epistles. James states that if a person is cheerful "Let him sing praise" (James 5:13). The implication is that singing should spring from a cheerful heart. Presumably the singing of praises occurred not only privately at home, but also publicly in the church. Other texts suggest that the singing of hymns of praise was a feature of the church service.

More specific information comes to us from Paul, who provides us with insights into the role of music in the New Testament worship services. In the context of his admonitions regarding ecstatic manifestations at the Corinthian church, Paul calls for a balance in music making by urging that singing be done with the mind as well as the spirit: "I will sing with the spirit and I will sing with the mind also" (1 Cor 14:15). Apparently some sang ecstatically without engaging the mind. Senseless singing is like senseless speech. Both dishonor God. As Paul says: "God is not a God of confusion but of peace" (1 Cor 14:33).

Paul's admonition to sing with the mind, or with understanding, is relevant for us today, when the singing done in some charismatic churches consists of emotional outbursts of ecstatic shouting which no one can understand. Our singing must be with understanding because God expects from His intelligent creatures "a rational worship" (Rom 12:2—*logike,* that is, "logical" in the Greek).

Singing should be for spiritual edification and not for physical stimulation. Paul says: "When you come together, each one has a hymn, a lesson, a revelation, a tongue, or an interpretation. Let all things be done for edification" (1 Cor 14:26). This text suggests that the church service was rather informal, like that of the synagogue. Each one contributed something to the worship experience.

Some members contributed a hymn to the service. Most likely a hymn was a newly composed song of praise directed to Christ. Bible scholars have identified several Christ-centered hymns in the New Testament. The important point is that the singing, like all parts of the church service, was to edify the congregation. The biblical principle, then, is that church music should contribute to the spiritual edification of the believers.

Psalms, Hymns, and Spiritual Songs. The two remaining Pauline texts (Eph 5:19; Col 3:16) are the most informative about music in the New Testament. Paul encourages the Ephesians to "be filled with the Spirit, addressing one another in psalms and hymns and spiritual songs, singing and making melody to the Lord with all your heart" (Eph 5:18-19). In a similar vein, the apostle admonishes the Colossians: "Let the word of Christ dwell in you richly, teach and admonish one another in all wisdom, and sing psalms and hymns and spiritual songs with thankfulness in your hearts to God" (Col 3:16).

Both passages provide the earliest indication of how the apostolic church differentiated between the psalms, hymns, and spiritual songs. It is hard to draw hard-and-fast distinctions between these terms. Most scholars agree that the three terms loosely refer to the various forms of musical compositions used in the worship service.

The psalms most likely are those of the Old Testament, though there may have been some Christian additions. The hymns would be newly composed songs of praise directed to Christ. Some evidence for these Christ-centered hymns appears in the New Testament (Eph 5:14; 1 Tim 3:16; Phil 2:6-11; Col 1:15-20; Heb 1:3). The spiritual songs probably refer to spontaneous praise songs which the inspiring Spirit placed on the lips of the enraptured worshipper (1 Cor 14:15).

The phrase "addressing one another in psalms and hymns and spiritual songs" suggests that the singing was interactive. Presumably some of the singing was responsorial, with the congregation responding to the song leader. The singing was to be done with "thankfulness" and "with all your heart." Through their singing, Christians expressed their whole-hearted gratitude "to the Lord" for His marvellous provision of salvation.

Christ-Centered Hymns. While in the synagogue the singing was "word-centered," that is, designed to praise God by chanting His Word; in the New Testament church the singing was "Christ-centered," that is, designed to extol Christ's redemptive accomplishments.

A good example of a "Christ-centered" hymn is found in 1 Timothy 3:16, which consists of an introductory sentence ("Great indeed, we confess, is the mystery of our religion"), which is followed by six lines:

He was manifested in the flesh,
vindicated in the Spirit,
seen by angels,
preached among the nations,
believed in the world,
taken up in glory.

This hymn embodies in a cryptic way the fundamental truths of the Gospel message. As Ralph Martin explains, "By a series of antithetical couplets in which a second line complements the thought of the first line, the Gospel message . . . is set forth. It treats of the two world orders, the divine and human; and shows how Christ has brought together the two spheres by His coming from the glory of the Father's presence into this world ('revealed in the flesh': cf. John 1:14; Rom 8:3) and by His lifting up of humanity back again into the divine realm. Thus heaven and earth are joined, and God and man reconciled."[27]

The celebration of Christ's redemption is the basic theme of other New Testament hymns (Phil 2:6-8; Col 1:15-20; Heb 1:3), and especially in the book of Revelation. We noted in the previous chapter that the angelic choir around God's Throne sings a new song saying: "Worthy art thou to take the scroll and to open its seals, for thou wast slain and by thy blood didst ransom men for God, from every tribe and tongue and people and nation, and hast made them a kingdom and priests to our God" (Rev 5:9-10). The

"Christ-centered" singing done by the church on earth reflects the "Lamb-centered" singing done by the living creatures in heaven.

A Pagan Witness. A most telling evidence of "Christ-centered" singing by the early church is found in the private correspondence between the Roman Governor Pliny and the Emperor Trajan. In a letter written in A.D. 112, Pliny reported to the emperor that he tortured some young Christian deaconesses in order to find out what possible crimes were committed by Christians in their religious gatherings.

To his surprise, Pliny found that "The sum total of their guilt or error amounted to no more than this. They had met regularly before dawn on a fixed day to chant verses alternately among themselves in honor of Christ as if to a god, and also to bind themselves by oath, not for criminal purpose, but to abstain from theft, robbery and adultery, to commit no breach of trust and not to deny a deposit when called upon to restore it."[28]

What an inspiring pagan testimony about early Christian worship! Christians became known for singing to "Christ as if to a god," and for binding themselves to follow His example in their lifestyle of purity and honesty. It is evident that the main theme of their songs was Christ. They witnessed for the Lord by singing about Him and living godly lives in His honor.

The witness of the New Testament singing is relevant for us today. Is our singing "Christ-centered" like that of the apostolic church? Does our church music praise the Savior for His past, present, and future redemptive accomplishments? Does it give us a greater appreciation for Christ's creative and redemptive love?

If you are tempted to listen to rock music, ask yourself: Do the beat, rhythm, and lyric of this music help me to appreciate the purity, majesty, and holiness of Christ? Does it magnify His character? Does it have appropriate words, a pure tone, and a lovely melody? Music about Christ should be like Christ, reflecting the purity and loveliness of His character.

No Instrumental Music in the Early Church. None of the New Testament references to music examined above makes any allusion to musical instruments used by New Testament Christians to accompany the singing. Apparently Christians followed the tradition of the synagogue in prohibiting the use of musical instruments in their church services because of their pagan association.

Undoubtedly Paul understood that music could be an effective resource to help the church fulfill the overwhelming tasks of evangelizing the Gentiles. He knew what would work in attracting people. He says: "For Jews demand signs and Greeks seek wisdom" (1 Cor 1:22). But he chose not to use Gentile or Jewish idioms to proclaim the Gospel. Why? Because he wanted to reach people, not by giving them what they wanted, but by proclaiming to them what they needed. "But we preach Christ crucified, a stumbling block to the Jews and folly to Gentiles, but to those who are called, both Jews and Gentiles, Christ is the power of God" (1 Cor 1:23-24).

The outright condemnation of musical instruments, sometimes even of the harp and the lyre, is present in the writings of numerous early Christian authors. In his dissertation on *Musical Aspects of the New Testament,* William Smith concludes his survey of the critical attitude of church leaders toward the use of musical instruments by listing several reasons, of which the first three are as follows:

"(a) Most important of all, at least ostensibly, seems to be the association of instruments with the worship of heathen cults.

(b) The employment of instruments at secular excesses as the theater and the circus.

(c) The sensuality of instrumental music and its aesthetic effects."[29]

Contrary to the current philosophy that rock music can be adopted and adapted to reach the secular society, the early Christians distanced themselves not only from secular songs but also from the musical instruments used for secular entertainment and pagan worship. In his book *The Sacred Bridge,* Eric Werner concludes his study of music in the early church: "Up to the third century, the Christian sources reflect almost the same attitude toward Hellenistic music as contemporary Judaism. The very same distrust of instrumental accompaniment in religious ceremonies, the same horror of flute, *tympanon* [drum], and cymbal, the accessories of the orgiastic mysteries are here in evidence."[30] The same point is emphasized by the *The New Grove's Dictionary of Music and Musicians* in its description of the early church: "The ban on dance in the worship service shows that rhythm did not have much of a place in the liturgy."[31]

We cannot approve the early Christians' radical rejection of all musical instruments for church services simply because they were used by the pagans in social and religious life. Yet we must commend them for recognizing the danger of bringing into the church the music and instruments which were associated with a pagan lifestyle.

The early church understood the fundamental truth that adopting pagan music, and the instruments used to produce it, could eventually corrupt the Christian message, identity, and witness, besides tempting people to fall back into their pagan lifestyles. Eventually this is what happened. Beginning from the fourth century when Christianity became the religion of the empire, the church tried to reach the pagans by adopting some of their practices, including their music. The result has been the gradual secularization of Christianity, a process that is still continuing today. The lesson of history is clear. To evangelize people with their secular idioms, ultimately results in the secularization of the church itself.

Part 3
DANCE IN THE BIBLE

There are conflicting opinions concerning dance and its use in the worship service of ancient Israel. Historically the Seventh-day Adventist church has maintained that the Bible does not sanction dancing, especially in the context of the worship service. In recent years, however, the question has been reexamined, especially by Adventist youth leaders who claim to have found biblical support for dancing.

Shall We Dance? A good example of this new trend is the symposium *Shall We Dance? Rediscovering Christ-Centered Standards.* This research was produced by twenty contributors and is based on the findings of the "Valuegenesis Study." This study is the most ambitious project ever undertaken by the Adventist church to determine how well the church transmits its values to the new generation.

The back cover of *Shall We Dance?* indicates that the book is "jointly sponsored by the Department of Education of the North American Division of Seventh-day Adventists, the John Hancock Center for Youth Ministry, La Sierra University, and La Sierra University Press." The combined sponsorship by four major SDA institutions suggests that the content of the book reflects the thinking of major Adventist institutions.

For the sake of accuracy, it must be stated that the opening statement of the introduction says: "The book is *not* an official statement of the Seventh-day Adventist Church regarding standards and values. Rather it is an invitation to open discussion regarding lifestyle issues. Hopefully even better biblical principles will become the bedrock for our distinctive lifestyle as we move from the peripheral, but ever-present issues to the weightier matters of living the Christian life."

The clarification that the "book is *not* an official statement of the Seventh-day Adventist Church" is reassuring, because, in my view, some of the conclusions hardly encourage the development of "even better biblical principles." A case in point are the four chapters devoted to dance and written by four different authors. These chapters present a very superficial analysis of the Biblical references to dance. For example, the chapter entitled "Dancing with a User-Friendly Concordance," consists primarily of a listing of twenty-seven Bible references to dancing, without any discussion whatsover. The author assumes that the texts are self-explanatory and supportive of religious dancing. This is indicated by the fact that he closes the chapter, asking: "How could we dance before the LORD today? What type of dance would it be? Why do people dance nowdays?"[32] Surprisingly the author ignores that no dancing ever took place in the religious services of the Temple, synagogue, or early church.

The conclusions derived from an examination of the biblical view of dancing are concisely stated in five principles, the first of which says: "Principle 1: Dance is a component of divine worship. When we study Scripture we find that what it says about dance and dancing is not only *not* condemnatory, but in some cases positively prescriptive: 'Praise him with trumpet sound; praise him with lute and harp! Praise him with timbrel and dance; praise him with strings and pipe'(Ps 150:3-4)."[33]

The author continues: "A half hour with a good concordance leaves the lingering impression that there is more to a truly Biblical perspective on dance than has previously met our Adventist eyes. Of some 27 references to dance (dance, danced, dances, dancing) in the Scriptures, only four occur in a clearly negative context, and even these references nowhere describe dancing as the object of God's displeasure."[34]

This chapter presents this surprising challenge to the Adventist church: "As challenging as it is to our notion of respectability and decorum, it seems evident that Adventists should give new thought and study to the inclusion of dance as part of the worship of God, at least in selected communities and on special occasions."[35]

Three Major Flaws. After spending not "a half hour" but several days examining the biblical data relevant to dance, I find this conclusion unsubstantiated and its challenge unnecessary. For the sake of clarity, I wish to respond to the position that "dance is a component of divine worship" in the Bible by submitting what in my view are three major flaws of his methodology:

(1) The failure to prove that dancing was indeed a component of divine worship in the Temple, synagogue, and early church;

(2) The failure to recognize that of the twenty-eight references to dance or dancing in the Old Testament, only four refer without dispute to religious dancing, and none of these relate to worship in God's House;

(3) The failure to examine why women, who did most of the dancing, were excluded from the music ministry of the Temple, synagogue, and early church.

No Dance in the Worship Service. If it were true that "dance is a component of divine worship" in the Bible, then why is there no trace of dancing by men or women in the worship services of the Temple, the synagogue, or the early church? Did God's people in Bible times neglect an important "component of divine worship"?

Negligence does not seem to be the reason for the exclusion of dance from the divine service, because we noted that clear instructions were given regarding the ministry of music in the temple. The Levitical choir was to be accompanied only by string instruments (the harp and the lyre). Percussion instruments like drums and tambourines, which were commonly used for making dance music, were clearly prohibited. What was true for the Temple was also true for the synagogue and later for the early church. No dancing or entertainment music was ever allowed in God's House.

Garen Wolf reaches this conclusion after his extensive analysis of "Dance in the Bible": "First, dancing as part of the Temple worship is nowhere traceable in either the first or the second Temple. Second, of the 107 times these words are used in the Bible [Hebrew words translated as "dance"], only four times could they be considered to refer to religious dance. Third, none of these references to religious dance were in conjunction with the regular established public worship of the Hebrews."[36]

It is important to note that David, who is regarded by many as the primary example of religious dancing in the Bible, never instructed the

Levites regarding when and how to dance in the Temple. Had David believed that dancing should be a component of divine worship, no doubt he would have given instructions regarding it to the Levite musicians he chose to perform at the Temple.

After all, David is the founder of the music ministry at the Temple. We have seen that he gave clear instruction to the 4,000 Levite musicians regarding when to sing and what instruments to use to accompany their choir. His omission of dancing in the divine worship can hardly be an oversight. It rather tells us that David distinguished between the sacred music performed in God's House and the secular music played outside the Temple for entertainment.

An important distinction must be made between religious music played for entertainment in a social setting and the sacred music performed for worship in the Temple. We must not forget that the whole life of the Israelites was religiously oriented. Entertainment was provided, not by concerts or plays at a theater or circus, but by the celebration of religious events or festivals, often through folk dancing by women or men in separate groups.

No romantic or sensually oriented dancing by couples ever occurred in ancient Israel. The greatest annual dance took place, as we shall see, in conjunction with the Feast of Tabernacles, when the priests entertained the people by doing incredible acrobatic dances the whole night. What this means is that those who appeal to the biblical references to dance to justify modern romantic dancing inside or outside the church ignore the vast difference between the two.

Most people who appeal to the Bible to justify modern romantic dancing would not be interested in the least in the folk dancing mentioned in the Bible, where there was no physical contact between men and women. Each group of men, women, and children did its own "show," which in most cases was a kind of march with rhythmic cadence. I have seen "The Dance Around the Ark" by the Coptic priests in Ethiopia, where many Jewish traditions have survived, including Sabbathkeeping. I could not understand why they called it "dance," since it was merely a procession by the priests who marched with a certain rhythmic cadence. To apply the biblical notion of dance to modern dance, is misleading to say the least because there is a world of difference between the two. This point becomes clearer as we survey the references to dance.

The References to Dance. Contrary to prevailing assumptions, only four of the twenty-eight references to dance refer without dispute to religious dancing, but none of these have to do with public worship conducted in the House of God. To avoid burdening the reader with a technical analysis of the extensive use of the six Hebrew words translated "dance," I will submit only a brief allusion to each of them.

The Hebrew word *chagag* is translated once as "dance" in 1 Samuel 30:16 in conjunction with the "drinking and dancing" of the Amalekites. It is evident that this is not a religious dance.

The Hebrew word *chuwl* is translated twice as "dance" in Judges 21:21, 23, with reference to the daughters of Shiloh who went out to dance in the vineyards and were taken as wives by surprise by the men of Benjamin. Again there is no doubt that in this context this word refers to a secular dance done by unsuspecting women.

The Hebrew word *karar* is translated twice as "dance" in 2 Samuel 6:14 and 16 where it states, "And David danced before the Lord with all his might . . . Michal the daughter of Saul looked out of the window, and saw King David leaping and dancing before the Lord." More is said about the significance of David's dance below. In this context it suffices to note that "these verses refer to a religious type of dance outside the context of the Temple worship. The word *karar* is only used in Scripture in these two verses, and is never used in conjunction with Temple worship."[37]

The Hebrew word *machowal* is translated six times as dance. Psalm 30:11 uses the term poetically: "Thou hast turned for me my mourning into dancing." Jeremiah 31:4 speaks of the "virgins of Israel" who "shall go forth in the dance of the merrymakers." The same thought is expressed in verse 13. In both instances the references are to social folk dancing done by women.

"Praise Him with Dance." In two important instances, *machowal* is translated as "dance" (Psalms 149:3 and 150:4). They are most important because in the view of many people they provide the strongest biblical support for dancing as part of church worship. A close look at these texts shows that this popular assumption is based on a superficial reading and inaccurate interpretation of the texts.

Linguistically, the term "dance" in these two verses is disputed. Some scholars believe that *machowl* is derived from *chuwl*, which means "to make an opening"[38]—a possible allusion to a "pipe" instrument. In fact this is the marginal reading given by the KJV. Psalm 149:3 states: "Let them praise his name in the dance" [or "with a pipe," KJV margin]. Psalm 150:4 reads: "Praise him with the timbrel and dance" [or "pipe," KJV margin].

Contextually, *machowl* appears to be a reference to a musical instrument; in both Psalm 149:3 and 150:4, the term occurs in the context of a list of instruments to be used for praising the Lord. In Psalm 150 the list includes eight instruments: trumpet, psaltery, harp, timbrel, string instruments, organs, cymbals, clashing cymbals (KJV). Since the Psalmist is listing all the possible instruments to be used to praise the Lord, it is reasonable to assume that *machowal* also is a musical instrument, whatever its nature might be.

Another important consideration is the figurative language of these two psalms, which hardly allows for a literally interpretation of dancing in God's House. Psalm 149:5 encourages people to praise the Lord on the "couches." In verse 6, the praising is to be done with "two-edged swords in the hands." In verses 7 and 8, the Lord is to be praised for punishing the heathen with the sword, binding kings in chain, and putting nobles in fetters. It is evident that the language is figurative because it is hard to believe that God would expect people to praise Him by standing or jumping on couches or while swinging a two-edged sword.

The same is true of Psalm 150 which speaks of praising God, in a highly figurative way. The psalmist calls upon God's people to praise the Lord "for his mighty deeds" (v. 2) in every possible place and with every available musical instrument. In other words, the psalm mentions the *place* to praise the Lord, namely, "his sanctuary" and "his mighty firmament"; the *reason* to praise the Lord, namely, "for his mighty deeds . . . according to his exceeding greatness" (v. 2); and the *instruments* to be used to praise the Lord, namely, the eight listed above.

This psalm makes sense only if we take the language to be highly figurative. For example, there is no way in which God's people can praise the Lord "in his mighty firmament," because they live on earth and not in heaven. The purpose of the psalm is not to specify the *location* and the *instruments* to be used to praise for church music. Nor it is intended to give a license to dance for the Lord in church. Rather, its purpose is to invite *everything* that breathes or makes sound to praise the Lord *everywhere*. To interpret the psalm as a license to dance, or to play drums in the church, is to misinterpret the intent of the

Psalm and to contradict the very regulation which David himself gave regarding the use of instruments in God's House.

Celebration Dance. The Hebrew word *mechowlah* is translated seven times as "dance." In five of the seven instances the dance is by women who celebrate a military victory (1 Sam 18:6; 21:11; 29:5; Jud 11:34; Ex 15:20). Miriam and the women danced to celebrate the victory over the Egyptian army (Ex 15:20). Jephthah's daughter danced to celebrate her father's victory over the Ammonites (Jud 11:34). Women danced to celebrate David's slaughter of the Philistines (1 Sam 18:6; 21:11; 29:5).

In the remaining two instances, *mechowlah* is used to describe the naked dance of Israelites around the golden calf (Ex 32:19) and the dance of the daughters of Shiloh in the vineyards (Jud 21:21). In none of these instances is dance a part of a worship service. Miriam's dance may be viewed as religious, but so were the dances performed in conjunction with the annual festivals. But these dances were not seen as a component of a divine service. They were social celebrations of religious events. The same thing occurs today in Catholic countries where people celebrate annual holy days by organizing carnivals.

The Hebrew word *raquad* is translated four times as "dance" (1 Chron 15:29; Job 21:11; Is 13:21; Ecc 3:4). Once it refers to how "children dance" (Job 21:11). Another is to "satyr dancing" (Is 13:21), which may refer to a goat or a figure of speech. A third instance is a poetic reference "to a time to dance" (Ecc 3:4), mentioned in contrast "to a time to mourn." A fourth reference is to the classic example of "King David dancing and making merry" (1 Chron 15:29). In view of the religious significance attached to David's dance, special consideration is given to it shortly.

Dance in the New Testament. Two Greek words are translated as "dance" in the New Testament. The first is *orcheomai,* which is translated four times as "to dance" with reference to the dancing of Herodias' daughter (Matt 14:6; Mark 6:22) and a children's dance (Matt 11:17; Luke 7:32). The word *orcheomai* means to dance in a rank-like or regular motion and is never used to refer to religious dance in the Bible.

The second Greek word translated as "dance" is *choros.* It is used only once in Luke 15:25 with reference to the return of the prodigal son. We are told that when the elder son came close to the house "he heard music and dancing." The translation "dancing" is disputed because the Greek *chorus* occurs only once in this passage and is used in extra-biblical literature with the meaning of "choir" or "group of singers."[39] At any rate, this was a family reunion of a secular nature and does not refer to religious dancing.

The conclusion that emerges from the above survey of the twenty-eight references to dance is that dance in the Bible was essentially a social celebration of special events, such as a military victory, a religious festival, or a family reunion. Dance was done mostly by women and children. The dances mentioned in the Bible were either processional, encircling, or ecstatic.

No biblical references indicate that men and women ever danced together romantically as couples. As H. Wolf observes, "While the mode of dancing is not known in detail, it is clear that men and women did not generally dance together, and there is no real evidence that they ever did."[40] Furthermore, contrary to popular assumptions, dance in the Bible was never done as part of the divine worship in the Temple, synagogue, or early church.

Dancing in Pagan Worship. Most indications of religious dancing in the Bible have to do with the apostasy of God's people. There is the dancing of the Israelites at the foot of Mount Sinai around the golden calf (Ex 32:19). There is an allusion to the dancing of the Israelites at Shittim when "the people began to play harlot with the daughter of Moab" (Num 25:1). The strategy used by the Moabites women was to invite Israelite men "to the sacrifice of their gods" (Num 25:2), which normally entailed dancing.

Apparently the strategy was suggested by the apostate prophet, Balaam, to Balak, king of Moab. Ellen White offers this comment: "At Balaam's suggestion, a grand festival in honor of their gods was appointed by the king of Moab, and it was secretly arranged that Balaam should induce the Israelites to attend. . . . *Beguiled with music and dancing*, and allured by the beauty of heathen vestals, they cast off their fealty to Jehovah. As they united in mirth and feasting, indulgence in wine beclouded their senses and broke down the barriers of self-control."[41]

There was shouting and dancing on Mount Carmel by the prophets of Baal (1 King 18:26). The worship of Baal and other idols commonly took place on the hill with dancing. Thus, the Lord appeals to Israel through the prophet Jeremiah: "Return, faithless people; I will cure you of back-sliding. . . . Surely the idolatrous commotion on the hills and mountains is a deception" (Jer 3:22-23, NIV).

David Dancing Before the Lord. The story of David dancing "before the Lord with all his might" (2 Sam 6:14) while leading the procession that brought the ark back to Jerusalem is viewed by many as the most compelling biblical sanction of religious dancing in context of a divine service. In the chapter "Dancing to the Lord," found in the book *Shall We Dance?,* Timothy Gillespie, Seventh-day Adventist youth leader, writes: " We can dance to the Lord like David, reflecting an outburst of excitement for the glory of God; or we can introspectively turn that excitement inward, reflecting on ourselves and our selfish desires."[42] The implication of this statement seems to be that if we do not dance unto the Lord like David, we repress our excitement and reveal our self-centeredness. Is this what the story of David's dance teaches us? Let us take a close look at it.

To say the least, David's dance before the ark poses serious problems. In the first place, David "was girded with a lined ephod" (2 Sam 6:14) like a priest and "offered burnt offerings and peace offerings before the Lord" (2 Sam 6:17). Note that the ephod was a sleeveless linen waistcoat garment to be worn only by the priests as an emblem of their sacred office (1 Sam 2:28). Why did David choose to exchange his royal robes for those of a priest?

Ellen White suggests that David revealed a spirit of humility by laying aside his royal robes and attiring "himself in a plain linen ephod."[43] This is a plausible explanation. The problem is that nowhere does the Bible suggest that the ephod could be legitimately worn by someone who was not a priest. The same holds true when it comes to sacrifices. Only the Levite priests had been set aside to offer sacrifices (Num 1:50). King Saul was severely rebuked by Samuel for offering sacrices: "You have done foolishly; you have not kept the commandment of the Lord your God" (1 Sam13:13). By offering sacrifices dressed like a priest, David was assuming a priestly role in addition to his kingly status. Such an action cannot be easily defended biblically.

David's Behavior. More problematic is David's manner of dancing. Ellen White says that David danced "in reverent joy before

God."[44] Undoubtedly this must have been true part of the time. But it would appear that during the dance, David may have become so excited that he lost his loin cloth, because Michal, his wife, rebuked him, saying: "How the king of Israel honored himself today, uncovering himself today before the eyes of his servants' maids, as one of the vulgar fellows shamelessly uncovers himself!" (2 Sam 6:20). David did not dispute such an accusation nor did he apologize for what he did. Instead, he argued that he did it "before the Lord" (1 Sam 6:21), and that he was prepared to make himself even "more contemptible" (1 Sam 6:22). Such a response hardly reveals a positive aspect of David's character.

Perhaps the reason David was not troubled by his uncovering during the dance is that this kind of exhibitionism was not uncommon. We are told that Saul also in an ecstatic dance "stripped off his clothes, and he too prophesied before Samuel, and lay naked all that day and all that night" (1 Sam 19:24; cf. 10:5-7, 10-11).

It is a known fact that at the time of the annual festivals, special dances were organized where priests and nobles would perform acrobatic feats to entertain the people. There is no mention, however, of the priests uncovering themselves. The most famous dance was performed on the last day of the Feast of Tabernacles, and it was known as the "Dances of the Water-Drawing Festival."

The Talmud offers a colorful description of this Water-Drawing dance which was performed in what is known as the women's court of the Temple: "Pious men and men of affair danced with torches in their hands, singing songs of joy and of praise, and the Levites made music with lyre and harp and cymbals and trumpets and countless other instruments. During this celebration, Rabbi Simeon ben Gamaliel is said to have juggled eight torches, and then to have turned a somersault."[45]

Dances done by men or by women in Bible times, within the context of a religious event, were a form of social entertainment rather than part of a worship service. They could be compared to the annual carnival celebrations that take place today in many Catholic countries. For example, during the three days before Lent, in countries like Brazil, people organize extravagant carnival celebrations with endless types of colorful and sometimes wild dancing, similar to the Mardi Gras in New Orleans. No Catholic would consider such dances as part of the worship services.

The same is true for the various types of dances mentioned in the Bible. They were social events with religious overtones. Men and women danced, not romantically as couples but separately in processional or encircling dances. In view of the religious orientation of the Jewish society, such folk-type dances are often characterized as religious dances. But there is no indication in the Bible that any form of dance was ever associated with the worship service in God's House. In fact, as noted below, women were excluded from the music ministry of the Temple, apparently because their music was associated with dancing and entertainment.

Women and Music in the Bible. Why were women excluded from the music ministry of the Temple, first, and of the synagogue and early church later? Numerous biblical passages refer to women singing and playing instruments in the social life of ancient Israel (Ex 15:20-21; 1 Sam 18:6-7; Jud 11:34; Ezra 2:64-65; Neh 7:66-67), but no references in the Bible mention women participating in the worship music of God's House.

Curt Sachs notes that "Almost all musical episodes up to the time of the Temple describe choral singing with group dancing and drum beating. . . . And this kind of singing was to a great extent women's music."[46] Why then were women excluded from the music ministry of the Temple, when they were the main music makers in the Jewish society?

Scholars who have examined this question suggest two major reasons. One reason is musical in nature and the other sociological. From a musical perspective, the style of music produced by women had a rhythmic beat which was better suited for entertainment than for worship in God's House.

Robert Lachmann, an authority on Jewish cantillation, is quoted as saying: "The production of the women's songs is dependent on a small store of typical melodic turns; the various songs reproduce these turns—or some of them—time and again. . . .The women's songs belong to a species, the forms of which are essentially dependent not on the connection with the text, but on processes of movements. Thus we find here, in place of the rhythm of cantillation and its very intricate line of melody, a periodical up and down movement."[47]

Women's music was largely based on a rhythmic beat produced by tapping with the hand the tabret, toph, or timbrel. These are the only musical instruments mentioned in the Bible as being played by women and they are believed to be the same or very similar. The tabret or timbrel seems to have been a hand drum made up of a wooden frame around which a single skin was stretched. They were somewhat similar to the modern tambourine.

"It is interesting to note," writes Garen Wolf, "that I have not been able to find a single direct reference to women playing the *nebel* [the harp] or the *kinnor* [the lyre]—the instruments played by men in the music worship of the temple. There can be little doubt that their music was mostly of a different species than that of the male Levite musicians who performed in the Temple."[48]

The tabret or timbrel was played largely by women in conjunction with their dancing (Ex 15:20; Jud 11:34; 1 Sam 18:6; 2 Sam 6:5, 14; 1 Chron 13:8; Ps 68:25; Jer 31:4). The timbrel is also mentioned in connection with strong drink (Is 5:11-12; 24:8-9).

Secular Nature of Women's Music. From a sociological perspective, women were not used in the ministry of music of the Temple because of the social stigma attached to their use of timbrel and the entertainment-oriented music. "Women in the Bible were often reported as singing a non-sophisticated kind of music. Usually at its best it was for dancing or funeral mourning, and at its worst to aid in the sensuous appeal of harlots on the street. In his satire about Tyre, Isaiah asks: 'Shall Tyre sing as an harlot?' (Is 23:15. KJV; or as rendered in the margin, 'It shall be unto Tyre as the song of an harlot')."[49]

It is noteworthy that female musicians were extensively used in pagan religious services.[50] Thus, the reason for their exclusion from the music ministry of the Temple, synagogue, and early Christian churches was not cultural, but theological. It was the theological conviction that the music commonly produced by women was not suitable for the worship service, because of its association with secular and, sometimes, sensual entertainment.

This theological reason is recognized by numerous scholars. In his dissertation on *Musical Aspects of the New Testament,* William Smith wrote: "A reaction to the extensive employment of female musicians in the religious and secular life of pagan nations, was doubtless a very large factor in determining Jewish [and early Christian] opposition to the employment of women in the musical service of the sanctuary."[51]

The lesson from Scripture and history is *not* that women should be excluded from the music service of the church today. Praising the Lord with music is not a male prerogative, but the privilege of every child of God. It is unfortunate that the music produced by women in Bible times was mostly for entertainment and, consequently, not suitable for the divine worship.

The lesson that the church needs to learn from Scripture and history is that secular music associated with entertainment is out of place in God's House. Those who are actively involved in pushing for the adoption of pop music in the church need to understand the biblical distinction between secular music used for entertainment and sacred music suitable for the worship of God. This distinction was understood and respected in Bible times, and it must be respected today if the church is to remain a sacred sanctuary for the worship of God rather than becoming a secular place for social entertainment.

CONCLUSION

Several important biblical principles relevant to church music today have emerged during the course of this study. An attempt will be made to summarize them by way of conclusion.

Music has a special place and purpose in God's universe. It is a divine gift to the human family through which human beings can express their gratitude to God while experiencing delight within themselves. Pleasure in singing comes not from a rhythmic beat that stimulates people physically, but from the very experience of praising the Lord. "How good it is to sing praises to our God, how pleasant and fitting to praise him" (Ps 147:1. NIV).

Singing is seen in the Bible as an offering of thanksgiving to the Lord for the blessings of creation, deliverance, protection, and salvation. We found this concept expressed especially in Psalm 69:30-31: "I will praise God's name in song and glorify him with thanksgiving. This will please the Lord more than an ox, more than a bull with its horns and hoofs."

God does care about how we sing and play during the worship service. He is not pleased with unintelligible "loud noise," but with orderly, melodious, and intelligible singing. Those Bible texts that speak about making "a joyful noise" or "a loud noise" unto the Lord do not teach us to praise God with excessive amplification of the human voice or musical instruments during the worship service. Such a notion is derived from a mistranslation of *ruwa* as "loud noise." The correct translation as found in the NIV is "shouting for joy."

Music ministry is to be conducted by people who are trained, dedicated, and spiritually minded. This lesson is taught by the Temple's music ministry, which was performed by experienced and mature Levites who were trained musically, prepared spiritually, supported financially, and served pastorally. This principle established by God for Temple musicians is applicable to ministers of music today.

Music is to be God-centered, not self-centered. The notion of praising the Lord for entertainment or amusement is foreign to the Bible. Percussion instruments which stimulate people physically through a loud and relentless beat are as inappropriate for church music today as they were for the Temple music in ancient Israel.

We found that the music in the Temple was "sacrifice-centered," that is, designed to praise God for the provision of forgiveness and salvation through the sacrificial offerings. In the synagogue, the music was "Word-centered," that is, intended to praise God by chanting His Word. In the early church the music was "Christ-centered," that is, designed to extol Christ's redemptive accomplishments.

The Bible does not support the kind of romantic or sensual dancing which is popular today. Nothing in the Bible indicates that men and women ever danced together romantically as couples. We have found that dance in the Bible was essentially a social celebration of special events, such as a military victory, a religious festival, or a family reunion. Most of the dancing was done by women who were excluded from the music ministry of the Temple, synagogue, and early church because their entertainment music was deemed unsuitable for the worship service.

The biblical principles of music outlined above are especially relevant today, when the church and the home are being invaded by various forms of rock music which blatantly rejects the moral values and religious beliefs espoused by Christianity. At a time when the distinction between sacred and secular music is blurred, and many are promoting modified versions of secular rock music for church use, we need to remember that the Bible calls us to "worship the Lord in the beauty of holiness" (1 Chron 16:29; cf. Ps 29:2; 96:9).

No entertainment type of music was allowed in the Temple, synagogue, and early church. The same should be true in the church today.

Those who disagree and want to adopt pop music for their church services are free to have their own music. But let those who hold to the authority of Scripture keep to music that praises God in a way which is neither sensational nor sensual—a music which reflects the beauty and purity of God's character and celebrates His marvelous creative and redemptive accomplishment for the human family. May the Lord give us the discernment and desire to fill our homes and churches with music that meets His approval, rather than the applause of the world.

ENDNOTES

1. Quoted in the *Banner of Truth* (January 1977), p. 13.

2. Carl E. Seashore, *Psychology of Music* (New York, 1968), p. 135.

3. Tom Allen, *Rock 'n' Roll, the Bible and the Mind* (Beaverlodge, Alberta, Canada, 1982), p. 156.

4. Curt Sachs, *The Rise of Music in the Ancient World* (New York, 1943), p. 80.

5. Garen L. Wolf, *Music of the Bible in Christian Perspective* (Salem, OH, 1996), p. 349.

6. Johannes Behm, *"Kainos," Theological Dictionary of the New Testament*, Gerhard Kittel, ed. (Grand Rapids, MI, 1974), vol. 3, p. 447.

7. John W. Kleinig, *The Lord's Song: The Basis, Function and Significance of Choral Music in Chronicles* (Sheffield, England, 1993).

8. Ibid., p. 57.

9. Ibid., p. 67.

10. See, Joachim Jeremias, *Jerusalem in the Time of Jesus* (Philadelphia, PA, 1969), pp. 173 and 208.

11. See, *Babylonian Talmud, Hullin 24*. The text is discussed by A. Z. Idelsohn, *Jewish Music in Its Historical Development* (New York, 1967), p. 17.

12. Kenneth W. Osbeck, *Devotional Warm-Ups for the Church Choir* (Grand Rapids, MI, 1985), pp. 24-25.

13. John W. Kleinig (note 7), p. 113.

14. Ibid., p. 80.

15. Ibid., p. 82-83.

16. A. Z. Idelsohn (note 11), p. 17.

17. Curt Sachs, *Rhythm and Tempo* (New York, 1953), p. 79.

18. Garen L. Wolf (note 5), p. 287.

19. Curt Sachs (note 4), p. 52.

20. Eric Werner, "Jewish Music," *New Grove Dictionary of Music and Musicians*, ed. Stanley Sadie (New York, 1980), vol. 9, p. 623.

21. Garen L. Wolf (note 5), p. 351.

22. Harold Best and David K. Huttar, "Music in Israelite Worship," *The Complete Library of Christian Worship,* ed. Robert E. Webber (Peabody, MA, 1993), vol. 1, p. 229.

23. Curt Sachs (note 4), p. 90.

24. Suzanne Haik-Vantoura, *The Music of the Bible Revealed,* trans. Dennis Webber (Berkeley, CA, 1991), p. 32.

25. Eric Werner (note 20), vol. 9, p. 622.

26. See, for example, C. W. Dugmore, *The Influence of the Synagogue upon the Divine Office* (London, England, 1944).

27. Ralph P. Martin, *Worship in the Early Church* (Grand Rapids, MI, 1964), pp. 48-49.

28. As cited by F. Forrester Church and Terrance J. Mulry, *Earliest Christian Hymns* (New York, 1988), p. ix.

29. William Sheppard Smith, *Musical Aspects of the New Testament* (Amsterdam, Holland, 1962), p. 53.

30. Eric Werner, *The Sacred Bridge* (Hoboken, NJ, 1984), p. 317.

31. *The New Grove's Dictionary* (note 20), vol. 9, p. 364.

32. Steve Case, "Dancing with a User-Friendly Concordance," in *Shall We Dance? Rediscovering Christ-Centered Standards*, ed. Steve Case (Riverside, CA, 1992), p. 101.

33. Bill Knott, "Shall We Dance?" in *Shall We Dance? Rediscovering Christ-Centered Standards*, ed. Steve Case (Riverside, CA, 1992), p. 69.

34. Ibid.

35. Ibid., p. 75.

36. Garen L. Wolf (note 5), p. 153.

37. Ibid., p. 148.

38. See, for example, Adam Clarke, *Clarke's Commentary* (Nashville, n. d.). vol. 3, p. 688.

39. *"Choros,"* *A Greek-English Lexicon of the New Testament,* ed. William F. Arndt and Wilbur Gingrich (Chicago, IL, 1979), p. 883.

40. H. M. Wolf, "Dancing," *The Zondervan Pictorial Encyclopedia of the Bible,* ed. Merrill C. Tenney (Grand Rapids, MI, 1976), vol. 2, p. 12.

41. Ellen G. White, *The Story of Patriarchs and Prophets* (Mountain View, CA, 1958). p. 454. Emphasis added.

42. Timothy Gillespie, "Dancing to the Lord," in *Shall We Dance? Rediscovering Christ-Centered Standards*, Steve Case, ed. (Riverside, CA, 1992), p. 94.

43. Ellen G. White (note 40), p. 707.

44. Ibid.

45. Cited in "Dance," *The Universal Jewish Encyclopedia* (New York, 1942), vol. 3., p. 456.

46. Curt Sachs (note 4), p. 90.

47. Cited by Curt Sachs (note 4), p. 91.

48. Garen L. Wolf (note 5), p. 144.

49. Ibid.

50. For discussion and illustrations from pagan antiquity regarding the employment of female musicians in the social and religious life, see Johannes Quasten, "The Liturgical Singing of Women in Christian Antiquity," *Catholic Historical Review* (1941), pp. 149-151.

51. William Sheppard Smith, *Musical Aspects of the New Testament* (Amsterdam, 1962), p. 17. See also Eric Werner (note 30), pp. 323-324; A. Z. Idelsohn (note 11), p. 18; Philo, *De Vita Contemplativa* 7; Babylonian Talmud *Berakot* 24a.

Chapter 8
THE EFFECTS
OF
ROCK MUSIC
by
Tore Sognefest

Tore Sognefest is a professional musician and pianist. During the 1980s he had his own rock band which was well-known in Norway. He earned a Master's degree in music from the Academy of Music in Bergen, Norway, where he taught music for several years.

Sognefest has authored a popular book *The Power of Music*. He is a popular lecturer invited by different denominations to conduct music seminars. Currently he is serving as the Principal of a Seventh-day Adventist secondary school in Norway.

The current controversy over the effects of rock music is largely based on aesthetic, social, religious, and/or political concerns rather than on scientific studies of its mental and physical effects on humans. Subjective evaluations of music can give rise to endless controversies, because they are based on personal taste and/or cultural considerations.

We are reminded of the attempts that Hitler made to eliminate the "primitive" and Negroid traits of black music by establishing norms to determine what constituted suitable music for the German people. Among other things, the Third Reich decreed: "The so-called jazz compositions may contain no more than 10% syncopation. The rest must consist of a natural legato flow completely void of the hysterical rhythmic turns so typical of the music of the barbarian races which appeal to the dark instincts so foreign to the Germanic race (the so-called 'riffs')."[1]

It is evident that the Third Reich did not succeed in eliminating "the hysterical rhythmic" music of "the barbarian races," because it was only a few years after the fall of Hitler's empire that rock music came into existence with a stronger rhythmic driving beat than jazz. Today, the effects of rock music are criticized not only by some politicians, preachers, and social analysts, but also by accomplished musicians.

For example, the well-known Norwegian concert pianist Kjell Bekkelund, stated: "The pop-culture represents a basic human lie. It portrays human beings without problems and restrictions, dreaming about new sexual conquests, social careers, and acceptance by 'the upper crust.' It is guilty of unlimited degradation of the woman, considering her only as a sex object. The goal of the pop industry, in my opinion, seems to create individuals that 'do not have to think.'"[2]

Some may wish to question the personal opinions of music critics like Bakkelund because they are based on subjective evaluation of pop music. It is therefore imperative to look at scientific studies on the effects of rock music on the human body.

Objectives of This Chapter. Based on several recent and significant, scientific studies, this chapter examines the physical and mental effects of rock music on human beings. Due to length limitations, only a sampling of the studies is cited.

The chapter is divided into two parts. The first deals in a more general way with the influence of music on the human body. It considers, especially, how music affects the functioning of the brain, the hormone production, and the rhythms of the body.

The second part examines some of the specific effects of the irregular, relentless, loud rock beat on the human body. Specific reference is made to how the rock beat places the human body under stress by increasing the pulse rate, the blood pressure, and the production of adrenaline. Consideration is also given to the impact of the deafening noise of rock music on the hearing.

Part 1
THE INFLUENCE OF MUSIC

Natural laws govern the chemistry of body and mind as well as the physical and mental effects of music. These laws have been studied with scientific experiments and careful observations. When measuring the effects of music stimuli, researchers look for such physiological responses as the increased pulse rate and the electrical resistance of the skin. Of course, a spontaneous music experience involves much more than a measurable physical response. Nevertheless, it is the physical presence of sound that influences our reactions.

Most people do not pay much attention to the laws of music and ignore the impact that music makes on their physical, social, and mental health. Today the choice of music is largely determined by personal taste. This trend reflects the consumeristic orientation of our society where many people stuff themselves uncritically with inferior "junk food" which causes numerous psychological as well as physical disorders, such as the lack of concentration and learning disabilities among school children and young students. The same uncritical attitude is found in the consumption of inferior and harmful music.

Sound Waves and the Brain. To appreciate the effects of music, we need to be aware of the basic processes that take place in the human ear at the sound of music. The sound waves (vibrations) hitting the ear drum are transformed into chemical and nerve impulses which register in our mind the different qualities of sounds we are hearing. What many do not know is that "the roots of the auditory nerves—the nerves of the ear—are more widely distributed and have more extensive connections than those of any other nerves in the body.... [Due to this extensive networking] there is scarcely a function of the body which may not be affected by the pulsations and harmonic combinations of musical tones."[3]

The investigation into the influence of music on the human body has largely been conducted by a branch of medicine known as "music therapy." In 1944, The Music Research Foundation was established in Washington, DC., in order to explore and develop new methods for controlling human behavior and emotions. The American government funded this research because of the acute need for psychiatric treatment of the war veterans who suffered injuries connected with shell shock during World War II.

A most important discovery was soon made. Researchers found that music is registered in the part of the brain which normally is stimulated by emotions, bypassing the brain centers dealing with intelligence and reason. Ira Altschuler, one of the researchers, explains that "Music, which does not depend upon the master brain (centers of reason) to gain entrance into the organism, can still arouse by way of the thalamus—the relay station of all emotions—sensations and feelings. Once a stimulus has been able to reach the thalamus, the master brain is automatically invaded."[4]

What this means is that "music attacks the nervous system directly,"[5] bypassing the master brain. Some researchers are of the opinion that the sense of hearing, more than the other senses, makes the greatest impact on the autonomous nervous system through its auditory pathways.[6] Though conclusions of various studies differ, the common denominator is that auditory stimuli directly affect the nervous system.

Studies have shown that the impact of music on the nervous system and the emotional changes brought about by the thalamus directly or indirectly affect such processes as the heart rate, respiration, blood pressure, digestion, hormonal balance, and moods and attitudes.[7] This helps us understand why the relentless driving beat of rock, directly impacting the body, can have such a wide range of physical and emotional effects.

Music and Hormone Production. Even Ruud, sound researcher and music professor at The Institute of Music, University of Oslo, Norway, maintains that an understanding of the automatic connection between music and emotional reactions poses some problems, because one can hardly generalize the concept of music or use such elementary models to explain psychological problems.[8] While recognizing the conceptual limitations of music, other researchers have reached some specific conclusions.

It is a well-known fact that the endocrine system regulates not only the functions of the internal organs, like the heart and the respiratory organs, but also the endocrine glands. These glands are controlled by the thalamus which is closely connected with our emotions. Mary Griffiths, a physiologist, explains that "the hypothalamus controls the excretions of the thyroid gland, the adrenal cortex and the sexual glands. Thus it influences the speed of metabolism . . . as well as the production of sex hormones. . . . Hypothalamus has a marked effect on the release of the autonomous responses brought about by fear, anger, and other emotions."[9]

Ruud points to recent research which proves that music might influence the monthly cycle of women. One study has also found an increase of the luthenizing hormone (LH) while listening to music.[10] Other studies indicate that music releases adrenaline and possibly other hormones. It also influences the electric skin resistance of the body which, in turn, affects and governs the moods of a person.[11]

While it is true that the response to music varies with each individual, thus making it difficult to generalize its effects, the fact remains that the music industry and the world of business know how to use music to create or change moods and to sell merchandise.

The Effects of Rhythm. A Russian scientist, Ivan P. Pavlov, conducted experiments on the effects of music on dogs. He published the results of his experiments around the beginning of the century. His research contributed significantly to the development of the field of behavioral psychology in America. Pavlov conducted tests on the reflex reactions of his dogs to rhythm. He found that when he played rapid rhythms his dogs reacted with excitement; slower rhythms had a calming effect. When exposed to syncopated rhythms, the nervous systems of the dogs seemed manipulated, and they appeared to be confused and did not know how to react. The asynchronic rhythms made them very bewildered.

Long before the emergence of rock music, European concert audiences were given a foretaste of the effects of rhythm when Igor Stravinsky's symphonic work "Rite of Spring" was performed in Paris in 1913. This composition caused a violent reaction. Shortly after its opening movement, the audience seemed to be in a state of shock. The music consisted of a series of discords coupled with disconnected and incoherent and violent rhythms. It took only a few minutes before the concert hall was boiling with rebellion. After ten minutes, fighting broke out between those who disliked the music and those who liked it.

One might wonder whether it was the hard rhythms of the music or the protest against this new kind of music that caused the uproar. Similar reactions occurred a few years later when Arnold Schönberg's atonal twelve-note music (music without fixed tonality, neither major nor minor keys) hit the European concert public like a lightning bolt. This break from the old music traditions seems to have heralded a new age characterized by experimentation with hard rhythms.

Today, hard rhythms, like those of rock music, no longer cause popular uproars. On the contrary, many have become addicted to them. The driving beat of rock music is dominating the everyday life of young people in many parts of the world. Social analysts are greatly concerned because it seems that only through a heavily pulsating rock beat is it possible to get through to the young people. Ruud also expresses this concern: "My concern is that pretty much all music for children and youth must be rhythmically appealing in order to break through the sound barriers. This in turn shuts them out from other types of listening experience."[12]

Consonance or Dissonance? Critics of rock music generally appeal to the harmful physical effects of its rhythm which overshadows the melody and lyrics. They explain that good music should consist of a combination and balance among five basic elements:

Melody: Tones arranged to make a tune.

Tone color: The quality of the sound produced by instruments or the voice.

Harmony: The stacking of tones so as to create chords.

Rhythm: A specific allotment of time given to a note or syllable in a verse and the time meter of a composition of music.

Tempo: The speed of the rhythm in which the piece is to be played or sung.

Every one of these five elements consists of rhythmic vibrations and/or rhythmic cycles. Each note vibrates at specific frequencies. A middle "A" vibrates 440 times per second. The tone color is dependent upon the combination of the vibrations of the natural overtones inherent in each note.

Harmony has to do with the combination of notes in a vertical relationship. Intervals like thirds, fifths, or sixths appear to the listener as harmonic or consonant compared with seconds and sevenths which sound discordant because of the frequency relationship between the notes. A perfect fifth and a perfect octave sound very harmonious due to the mathematical simplicity present in their relationship. If we mix other notes of varying frequencies, other combinations and qualities of sound appear either in the direction of consonance or dissonance.

Exposure to music with "harmonic" rhythms reinforces the rhythmic cycles of the human body, synchronizing nerve messages, enhancing coordination, and harmonizing moods and emotions.

By contrast, exposure to music with "disharmonic" rhythms—"whether it be the 'tension' caused by dissonance or 'noise' or the unnatural swings of misplaced rhythmical accents, syncopation, and polyrhythms, or inappropriate tempo—can result in a variety of changes including: an altered heart rate with its corresponding change in blood pressure; an overstimulation of hormones (especially the opiates or endorphins) causing an altered state of consciousness from mere exhilaration on one end of the spectrum to unconsciousness on the other; and improper digestion."[13]

Our body's association with certain elements of music is so profound that "short of numbing the entire brain, neurologists have been unable to suppress rhythmic ability. Doping either side of the brain, or many regions at once, still leaves the patient able to count and clap in time."[14]

The studies on the effects of "disharmonic" rhythms on the human body help us to understand better why the emphatic rhythm of rock music exercises such an hypnotic influence on the lives of so many people today.

Various Uses of Music. Music has been used for different purposes during the course of human history. One function has been to ease the monotony of labor by synchronizing the movements of workers. In fact, many folk songs originated in this way. This is especially true of the Negro Spirituals which trace their origins to the work songs of the African Americans in slavery. Tests conducted in places of work have shown that unless the music is adjusted to the particular environment and type of work, precision and accuracy suffer.[15]

In the Soviet Union, an institute for medical and biological studies reported test results showing that music rhythm and tempo had an immense impact on the human organism. "Specially selected music increases the working capacity of the muscles. At the same time, the tempo of the movements of the worker changes with the change of the musical tempo. It is as if the music determines a good rapid rhythm of movement."[16]

Rhythm has also been used to excite people during religious rituals. This has been true for the festive celebrations of the ancient wild orgies of the Dionysius cult, the war and religious dances among the American Indians, and the voodoo rites of West Africa. These repetitive, rhythmic, and monotonous dances usually result in trance-like reactions.

The shamans use drum patterns to achieve contact between human-ity and the occult dimensions. Ruud observes: "It looks like the tension-regulating elements of rhythm are consciously being used. During the gradual progress of the ritual the rhythmic tension is regulated so that it corresponds to the spirit of that particular disease. The tension-building music is contrasted by a freer and more syncopated form designed to serve as a kind of release towards the end of the ritual.[17]

In many cultures, music is used also for healing. The "medicine man" plays a rhythmical pattern which has a hypnotic effect on the mind of the patient. Western psychologists may find this phenomenon difficult to explain. Ruud notes that "when such a healing ritual actually works we might find it difficult to assess the role of the music, especially for those of us who are rooted in the present educational-psychological orientation. This kind of music psychology might not accept the claims that music possesses universal qualities that effect the listener regardless of culture and education.[18]

Music Rhythm and Body Rhythm. Music with a strong rhythm causes a senso-motoric reaction in the human body. When soldiers get tired, a rousing march creates increased energy. In his book *Music in Hospitals*, Van de Wall, explains: "Sound vibrations acting upon and through the nervous system give shocks in rhythmical sequence to the muscles, which cause them to contract and set our arms and hands, legs and feet in motion. On account of this automatic muscular reaction, many people make some movement when hearing music; for them to remain motionless would require conscious muscular restraint."[19]

Rhythmic elements are definitely present in the human body and in other organisms. Psychologist Carole Douglis states: "We are essentially rhythmic creatures. Everything, from the cycle of our brain waves to the pumping of our heart, our digestive cycle, sleep cycle— all work in rhythms. We are a mass of cycles piled one on top of another, so we are clearly organized both to generate and to respond to rhythmic phenomena."[20]

Every human being functions according to a rhythmic tempo. This is partly related to the rhythm of the heart, which runs between 60 and 120 beats per minute. A normal pulse runs between 70 and 80 beats per minute. Some studies indicate that people seem to function best when they associate with persons who have a similar rhythmic "tempo." We tend to react unfavorably to people who are either too keyed up or too slow.[21]

These rhythmic or cyclic phenomena may be observed on all levels of biological organization. Within an organism, processes appear that are not only accidental and self-controlled, but also self-amplifying and essential to life, like the brain activities, the heartbeats, and the respiratory cycle. All these life-important rhythms are synchronized with other cellular activities and cooperate harmonically with all the other bodily functions.[22]

Problems occur when we tamper with cycles and body rhythms. This is a well-known fact in medicine. When the body is exposed to many and continuous disharmonic stimuli, several of the stress mechanisms of our body are put in a state of alert. If these defense mechanisms are overly strained, the natural harmony of the biological rhythms is disturbed. This causes disharmony and may lead to collapse. Unless the balance is restored, the stress situation may result in a fundamental pathological disorder.

Researchers have observed a connection between disturbance of the body rhythms and such diseases as diabetes, cancer, and respiratory ailments. Since most regulatory mechanisms are neutral in origin, it is not surprising that many pathological alterations could also occur in neutral structures. In the case of brain cells, this "disordering" can manifest itself not only in the physical state of neurons but also in the harmony of their functioning. Consequently, the behavior of the organism may become seriously affected.[23]

We find examples of this kind if we deprive persons of sleep or let drops of water constantly hit their forehead, a method used in torture of prisoners. Researcher David A. Noebel says that the rhythm in rock music creates an abnormally high secretion of sex and adrenaline hormones and may cause changes in the blood-sugar levels and the amount of calcium in the body.[24]

Since the brain receives its nourishment from the blood sugar, its function decreases when the blood sugar is directed to other parts of the body to stabilize the hormonal balance. At the point when insufficient blood sugar reaches the brain, moral judgment is greatly reduced or even completely destroyed. This is what happens when the rhythm of rock music changes the blood-sugar levels in the body.

Part 2
THE EFFECTS OF ROCK MUSIC

To better understand the effects of rock music on the human body, it is important to know first of all how the music rhythm works. The rhythmic element of music consists of measurements of time divided into bar cycles. The most common time units are groups of bars containing two beats (double time), three beats (triple time), or four beats (quadruple time). In quadruple time (like 4/4 time), the main natural accents fall on beats one (the primary accent or stress) and three (the secondary accent or stress). The primary accent on one is, of course, the stronger of the two. This could be illustrated as follows: **ONE, two, THREE, four**.

In rock music and similar forms, the accent pattern is reversed, so that beats two and four are accented instead of one and three, as pictured in the measure that follows: **one, TWO, three, FOUR**. By reversing the order, rock makes the rhythm the most important part of the sound and creates a conflict with the body's natural rhythmic cycles. This effect, known as "back beat" or "break beat," causes nervous tension (a "high") because it goes against the rhythm of the heart beat and other rhythms of the body.

Addictive Power of Rock. The "high" caused by the irregular rock rhythm increases the heart rate, weakens a subject's strength, and has addictive power. Psychiatrist Verle Bell offers a graphic explanation of how the rock beat causes addiction: "One of the most powerful releases of the fight-or-flight adrenaline high is music which is discordant in its beats or chords. Good music follows exact mathematical rules, which cause the mind to feel comforted, encouraged, and 'safe.' Musicians have found that when they go against these rules, the listener experiences an addictive high."[25]

Bell continues noting that "like unscrupulous 'diet' doctors who addicted their clients to amphetamines to ensure their continued dependence, musicians know that discordant music sells and sells. As in all addiction, victims become tolerant. The same music that once created a pleasant tingle of excitement no longer satisfies. The music must become more jarring, louder, and more discordant. One starts with soft rock, then rock 'n' roll, then on up to heavy metal music."[26]

John Diamond, a New York physician, has conducted numerous experiments on the effects of rock music. In 1977, he served as president-elect of the International Academy of Preventive Medicine. He found that rock music is the most serious form of noise pollution in the United States. Particularly harmful is the rock music which employs an "anapestic" beat, where the last beat is the loudest, such as "da da DA." According to Diamond, this kind of music can "heighten stress and anger, reduce output, increase hyperactivity, weaken muscle strength and could play a role in juvenile delinquency."[27]

Body's Rhythm under Stress. These behavioral disorders occur, according to Diamond, because rock music causes a breakdown in the synchronization of the two sides of the brain so that the symmetry between the two cerebral hemispheres is lost. He conducted an experiment in a New York factory where rock music was played all day. When the music was switched to non-rock, Diamond found that plant productivity increased by 15% while the number of errors made decreased by the same number.[28]

Diamond published his findings in the book *Your Body Doesn't Lie*. He explains that the anapestic beat, characteristic especially of rock music, is disruptive because it is the opposite of the heartbeat and thus places the normal body's rhythm under stress. This results in perceptual difficulties and manifestations of stress. In young people these manifestations may include decreased performance in school, hyperactivity and restlessness, decreased work output, more errors, and general inefficiency. In adults the symptoms include reduced decision-making capacity on the job, a nagging feeling that things just are not right, and the loss of energy for no apparent reason.[29]

In his own laboratory, Diamond tested the effects of rock music by measuring the strength in the deltoid muscle of the arm. He found that a normal man could withstand about 45 pounds of pressure on the arm, but this was reduced by about a third when the anapestic beat was played in the background.[30] The purpose of Diamond's research was not to seek a ban on rock music, but to warn people against its dangers. He surmised: "Rock music is not going to kill anybody, but I really doubt if Mick Jagger is going to live as long as Pablo Casals or Segovia."[31]

Russian researchers came to similar conclusions. They found that rock music has "a tremendously harmful psychic effect."[32] Addressing a rally of Russian youth, the medical team who conducted the experiments announced that rock music was "like a series of alarm signals, causing surges of concentrated energy which must be released somewhere."[33] The energy is channeled into brawls and fights which, the Russian doctors pointed out, is a common feature of Western rock concerts.[34]

Even Ruud explains how loud and rhythmic rock music creates a need for muscular reactions and bodily movements: "If the stimulus of sound via the brain stem and the limbic system is unable to express itself in terms of physical motion, it may result in unfortunate stress symptoms, that is, an increased alertness and alarm preparation in the system that find no release. Seeing that this condition is dependent on the intensity of the stimulus, we may understand why people exposed to noise would be prone to experience stress symptoms. Loud and syncopated music will likewise create extensive limbic activity plus vegetative and hormonal reactions, or stress reactions. These forces might be neutralized by means of dance."[35]

The Pulse Rate. An important measurable effect of the rock beat is its influence on the rhythm of the heart, irrespective of whether the body is in motion or not. Ann Ekeberg, a secondary college teacher and music researcher, involved some of her colleagues—music teachers—in experiments with their students. Before the test, each student's pulse was recorded. Then a hard rock record was played for 5 minutes. During the test, students remained quiet in their seats. At the end of the test, the pulse rates were checked again and an average was recorded. The result showed an increase in the pulse rate of 7-12 beats per minute while rock music was played.

The six columns below represent the school classes which participated in Ekeberg's experiment. The dark gray column represents the pulse rate before the rock music was played and the light grey column the pulse rate after the students had listened to 5 minutes of hard rock.

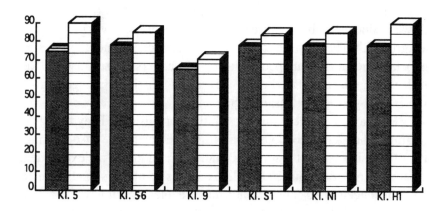

To test the validity of Ekeberg's results, I conducted my own tests on my students at the Bergen SDA secondary school in Norway. We recorded an average increase in pulse rate of 10 beats per minute when the students listened to "Hell's Bells" by the group AC/DC. When we played an "Air" by Bach, the pulse rates went as low as 5 beats per minute below their normal pulse. The difference of 15 heartbeats per minute is quite remarkable. It is fair to say that I chose two very different pieces of music.

It is noteworthy that students who were fans of AC/DC had stronger responses than those who disliked the music. The test proves that various types of music affect us physically in different ways. The excess energy generated by the rock beat causes the heart to beat faster, even when the subject is sitting still on a chair. This may explain why rock fans find it difficult to sit still while listening to pulse-accelerating music. Their accumulated energy craves for some kind of release.

The Norwegian music professor Even Ruud conducted similar tests on the effects of rock music at the Karajan Music Institute in Salzburg. He found: "Syncopated rhythms are especially able to cause extra systolic beats, beats that come too soon. It is also possible to increase the pulse rate by dynamic changes, like the crescendo and decrescendo of a drum roll. . . . Physiological reactions are dependent on the type of music being played. Forms like dance music or marches tend to trigger motoric responses, while other forms seem to cause changes in respiration and pulse rates."[36]

Increased Production of Adrenaline. Roger Liebi, a Swiss musician and expert in biblical languages, maintains that an increase in pulse rate also increases the blood pressure. In turn, this leads to an increase in the production of adrenalin. This process is a defense mechanism against stress, which helps to keep the body on the alert by increasing the blood flow in the muscles and easing the intake of oxygen.[37]

If the pulse stress continues, as with a lengthy rock concert with loud and monotonous music, an excessive amount of adrenalin is produced, which the enzymes of the body are unable to dispose of. The result is that some of the adrenalin changes into another chemical called adrenochrome ($C_9H_9O_3N$). This is actually a psychedelic drug similar to LSD, mescaline, STP, and psylocybin. Adrenochrome is a somewhat weaker composition than the others, but tests show that it creates a dependency similar to other drugs. "One cannot therefore be astonished when the public at rock concerts or in discotheques get 'high,' go into a trance and lose self-control."[38]

The increased secretion of hormones caused by rock music is confirmed by other studies. David Noebel, a medical researcher, explains: "Under rock music, the secretion of hormones is more pronounced . . . which causes an abnormal imbalance in the body's system, lowers the blood sugar and calcium levels and impairs judgement."[39] He cites medical research indicating that "The low frequency vibrations of the bass guitar, along with the driving beat of the drum, affect the cerebrospinal fluid, which in turn affects the pituitary gland, which in turn directs the secretions of hormones in the body."[40]

Human reaction to rock music is so overwhelming that neurologists have been unable to suppress the physical response to its rhythms. Experiments have been made to dope each half of the brain or several areas of the brain simultaneously, but the patient still responds to beat of the rhythm.[41]

Pulsating Light Effects. The rhythmic stimuli of rock music can be intensified with pulsating lights. For example, laser and strobe lights used in discotheques and in rock concerts intensify and amplify rhythmic manipulation. Jean-Paul Regimbal, a Canadian researcher, explains how the phenomenon works: "Lights that constantly change their color and intensity disturb the ability for orientation and the natural reflexes. When the change between light and dark takes place six to eight times per second the sense of depth is seriously impaired. If this happens 26 times per second the alpha waves of the brain do change, and the ability to concentrate is weakened. Should the frequency of change between light and dark exceed this and last for a considerable length of time, one's control over the senses might cease completely. For this reason it is no exaggeration to claim that rock combined with light effects results in a downright 'rape of one's consciousness.'"[42]

Bäumer, a German researcher, comments on the effects of such manipulation on the bodily functions (especially at extreme levels): "The person enters an ecstatic state with epileptic-like cramps, in which he or she screams, bites, roars with laughter, urinates, and tears his or her clothes in an intense feeling of joy and happiness."[43] For this reason, people prone to epileptic seizures are warned to stay away from discotheques where strobe lights are being used, seeing that these pulsating lights tend to cause seizures.

A combination of lights and sounds intensify the effects of the rhythm, because the body is unable to decide whether the in-coming rhythms are compatible with its own. The secret behind rhythmic manipulation is found in the sound and light waves that affect the nervous system by acting like sequential shocks to the muscles, causing the arms and legs to move. This explains why people at a rock concert find it hard to resist the urge to move. To remain immobile would require considerable restraining effort.

The above phenomena are easily observed in the popular rock culture and rave parties where light and sound are used in rapid alternation, with monotonous and repetitive patterns, in order to make the maximum effect on the audience.

Peter Bastian, a well-known Danish musician and teacher at The Royal Music Academy of Copenhagen, describes how relatively simple and peripheral elements can manipulate individuals so that their behavior changes unconsciously. "I once observed a somewhat scary scene involving a boy and a slot machine. The music from the machine contained a subliminal message in the form of heartbeats that gradually increased their frequency. The boy got more and more excited and finally threw himself at the machine.—He couldn't 'hear' the heartbeats, but the 'message' had its effect.[44]

Ann Ekeberg refers to a similar example. During a rock concert in Sweden, panic gripped the audience and three persons were trampled to death while many others were hurt. While the police and paramedics tried to revive the sufferers, the youthful crowd hurled all sorts of swear words and insulting remarks at them. In an interview, Jan Agrell, a Swedish professor and a specialist in mass psychosis, commented on this behavior: "A crowd possessed by mass psychosis behaves like a stampeding herd of buffaloes, and you will not be able to get through to them. . . . Pop music has magic power and causes people to act in unison."[45]

A Deafening Noise. Volume is a most important element in rock music. Stacks of equipment are needed to produce the required amount of amplification in order to make the desired physical impact. Volume for volume's sake is a defining trademark of hard rock. Lemmy Kilminster, of the popular rock band "Motorhead," told *Hit Parader* that his group wanted to see "blood coming out of everyone's ears, if possible. Nothing dangerous, just enough to let us know they are having a good time."[46] If rock music must be played so loud to cause blood to come out of people's ears to ensure that "they are having a good time," then it can hardly be said that there is "nothing dangerous" about it. On the contrary, numerous scientific studies have shown that the high noise level of rock music can harm the body in several ways.

In controlled experiments, Andrew Neher discovered that rhythmic drumming has neuro-physiological effects, resulting in auditory driving responses (changes in the electric potential in the brain) which can be measured on the electro-encephalograph.[47] Neher added that subjective responses included "fear, astonishment, amusement, back pulsing, muscle tightening, stiffness in the chest, tone in background, humming, rattling, visual and auditory imagery."[48] Such responses are hardly compatible with the spirit of Christianity.

For many years, the medical profession has warned that loud rock music can cause problems, especially hearing loss. In 1967, Charles Lebo, a medical researcher, presented a paper on the subject to the California Medical Association. The highlights of his speech were reported in the magazine *High Fidelity*: "The very sound of this amplified art form may present as great a trauma to the inner ear as the general quality of the music often does to the inner man."[49]

Lebo made sound measurements of rock music in two San Francisco establishments where he recorded noise levels between 100 to 119 decibels at the rock joints. He found that the noise levels "were capable of producing both temporary and permanent inner ear damage in the musicians and audience."[50] He concluded: "Since the inner ear damage of the type produced by noise exposure is cumulative and permanent, the desirability of lower levels of amplification for this type of live music is apparent."[51]

Even Ralph Nader, a well-known American consumer activist, became involved in this issue and proposed that Congress should classify rock music above certain prescribed decibels as a "public nuisance."[52] He concluded: "Acoustic trauma from rock 'n' roll music is emerging as a very threat to the hearing quality of young people who expose themselves to substantial durations of this music by live rock groups with high amplification."[53]

Impaired Hearing. Ralph Rupp, an audiologist at the University of Michigan Speech Clinic, agrees with Nader that local government should enforce a 100-decibel level on rock played in clubs.[54] He warned against headphones: "Unfettered by parental monitoring, they may pulse to the rock ritual with such an abandon that permanent damage to the inner ear is almost assured."[55]

Many young people spend their days completely wrapped in a sound blanket through the use of a Walkman outfit, portable "sound blasters," and other forms of stereo systems at home as well as in discotheques and other places of entertainment. The long-term effects of constant listening to loud rock music cannot be determined.

In 1992, the Norwegian Broadcasting Company, NRK, ran some tests aimed at the problem of loud sounds and impaired hearing. The three tests showed that 40% or 50% or 70% of musicians experienced loss of hearing due to the extreme volumes at rehearsals and performances. Many found it difficult to hear general conversation, and some were plagued with a constantly piercing tone generated in the ear (tinnitus).

Some rock concerts may reach volume levels of 110-135 decibels, while the threshold for damage to the hearing stands at 85 decibels. This is not a problem limited to the performers only; it affects the listeners as well. The walkman is regarded as one of the worst culprits.

Hearing tests on persons enlisting in the military services in Norway revealed a marked degree of hearing loss among the youth. These impairments proved to become increasingly noticeable with age. Researchers are of the opinion that this problem is a social catastrophe of alarming dimensions. All kinds of loud music, even powerful passages from a symphony orchestra, might pose problems, but the electrically amplified music is definitely the greatest problem.

Manufacturers of sound systems know fully well what effects sound amplification has on people. Geoffrey Marks, director of Cerwin Vega, a loudspeaker production plant in Los Angeles, acknowledges that tests show that one becomes sexually aroused when dancing to music at a volume of 100-120 decibels.[56] When asked if disco music might have a similar effect, he said, "Absolutely! If the sound system performs properly we can manipulate it so that people get sexually aroused. But the volume must be right. It is also important that the bass has the right effect. The bass is what actually governs and directs our feelings. It penetrates our body and affects our nerves. We have tested this particular volume on people and have seen how they respond with rapid sexual arousal. They seem to find it hard to resist. The low bass frequencies have a powerful influence on body and emotions."[57]

The music industry is obviously capitalizing on the effects of the strong vibrations of the bass especially present in rock music in order to induce the physical stimulation many are seeking for. These vibrations hit below the belt, causing the listener to lose the benefits of his or her controlling mechanisms. For this reason, the manufacturers continuously strive to improve the effects of the kilowatts so that the physical effects may reach ever increasing heights.

Evidence for the negative effects of rock music comes from different sources and countries. In closing, I cite a report filed from Moscow by correspondent Martin Walker for the English newspaper *Times on Sunday*. Walker reports that a Russian research project *Sovyetskaya Rossiya* made "a stunning discovery" regarding rock music. "The wilder the music, the lower is the young people's working ability."[58]

Professor G. Aminev, head of the psychology department at Bashkiria University, found that "Heavy metal listeners are affected by the psycho-physiological mechanisms of addiction. If they are isolated from such music for a week their general level of health declines, they become more irritable, their hands start to tremble and their pulse becomes irregular. Some of them refused to continue with our experiments after the third day. This means that we are witnessing a certain kind of illness. It seems that rock music does not only have a psychological influence but a biochemical one too, for it seems connected with the appearance of the morphine type substances which induce 'pleasure.'"[59]

Professor Aminev continues explaining that studies of Russian school children exposed to heavy-metal discos showed "a worsening of memory, loss of attention, a fall in reading speeds, and an increase in aggressiveness and stubbornness."[60]

CONCLUSION

Scientific investigations have shown that music affects the heart rate, respiration, blood pressure, digestion, hormonal balance, neural networks of the brain, rhythms of the human body, moods, and attitudes. The enormous influence of music on the physical, mental, and emotional aspects of our body should be of great concern to Christians who accept the summons to consecrate their whole being as "a living sacrifice, holy and acceptable to God" (Rom 12:1).

The irregular, relentless, and loud beat of rock music places the human body under stress by increasing the pulse rate, blood pressure, and production of adrenalin, and by impairing the hearing quality of people. More importantly, we have found that rock music does not just tickle the ear—it jams the brain like a freight train.

The constant repetition, the incessant beat, and the avalanche of decibels makes rock music capable of blasting the emotions and the mind. By impairing the functioning of the mind, rock music makes it impossible to reflect on truth, honesty, integrity, and, above all, to offer a "rational [*logike* in Greek] worship" (Rom 12:1).

ENDNOTES

1. Josef Skvoreck, *Comments on "Bass-saksofonen"* (Cappelen, 1980), pp.11-12.

2. Kjell Bekkelund, "Pop og antipop," *Berlingske Tidende* (June 6, 1964).

3. Edward Podolsky, *Music for Your Health* (New York, 1945), pp. 26-27.

4. Ira A. Altshuler, "A Psychiatrist's Experiences with Music as a Therapeutic Agent," *Music and Medicine* (New York, 1948), pp. 270-271.

5. Erwin H. Schneider, ed., *Music Therapy* (Lawrence,1959), p. 3.

6. G. and H. Harrer, "Musik, Emotion und Vegetativum," *Wiener Medizinische Wochenschrift*, no. 45/46 (1968).

7. See Willem Van de Wall, *Music in Hospitals* (New York, 1946), pp. 15-20; G. and H. Harrer (note 6), pp. 45-46; Edward Podolsky (note 3), p. 131; Arthur Guyton, *Functions of the Human Body* (Philadelphia, 1969), pp. 332-340.

8. Even Ruud, *Musikk som kommunikasjon og samhandling* (Oslo, Norway, 1990), p. 263.

9. Mary Griffiths, *Introduction to Human Physiology* (New York, 1974), pp. 474-475.

10. Even Ruud (note 8), p. 44.

11. See Ira A. Altshuler (note 4), p. 270; Doris Soibelman, *Therapeutic and Industrial Use of Music* (New York, 1948), p. 4.

12. Even Ruud, *Musikken—vårt nye rusmiddel?* (Oslo, Norway,1983), p. 17.

13. Carol and Louis Torres, *Notes on Music* (New York, 1990), p. 19.

14. Michael Segell, "Thythmatism," *American Health* (December 1988), p. 60.

15. Doris Soibelman (note 11), p. 47.

16. Leonid Malnikov, "USSR: Music and Medicine," *Music Journal*, 82 (November 1970), p.15.

17. Even Ruud (note 8), p. 45.

18. Ibid., p. 43.

19. Willem Van de Wall (note 7), p. 15.

20. Carole Douglis: "The Beat Goes On," *Psychology Today* (November 1987), p .42.

21. Ibid., pp. 37-42.

22. See Gervasia M. Schreckenberg and Harvey H. Bird, "Neural Plasticity of MUS musculus in Response to Disharmonic Sound," *Bulletin, New Jersey Academy of Science* 32, no. 2 (Fall 1987), p. 8.

23. Ibid., p. 9.

24. Cited by Ann Ekeberg, *För Sverige—på tiden* (Stockholm, 1991), p. 53.

25. Verle L. Bell, "How the Rock Beat Creates an Addiction," in *How to Conquer the Addiction to Rock Music* (Oakbrook, IL, 1993), p. 82.

26. Ibid.

27. "Medico Finds Root of Many Evils in a Pesty Rock Beat," *Variety* 288 (September 28, 1977), p. 77.

28. Ibid.

29. John Diamond, *Your Body Doesn't Lie* (New York, 1979), p. 49. See also Roman Kozak, "Can Certain Music Harm One's Health?" *Billboard* 92 (February 23, 1980), p. 53.

30. John Diamond (note 29), p. 160.

31. Ibid., p. 49.

32. "Soviet Doctors Blast Rock's 'Harmful Effect,'" *Variety* 314 (March 28, 1984), p. 32.

33. Ibid.

34. Ibid.

35. Even Ruud (note 12), p. 254.

36. Ibid., p. 260.

37. Roger Liebi, *Rock Music! The Expression of Youth in a Dying Era* (Zürich, 1989), p. 4.

38. Ibid.

39. David Noebel is quoted in *Contemporary Christian Music* (August-September 1981), p. 26.

40. Ibid.

41. Michael Segell (note 14), p. 60.

42. Jean-Paul Regimbal and others, *Le Rock'n Roll viol de la conscience par des messages subliminaux* (Genéve, 1983), pp. 17-18.

43. U. Bäumer, *Wir wollen nur deine Seele, Rockszene und Okkultismus: Daten—Fakten—Hintergründe,* vol. 2 (Bielefeld, Germany, 1986), p. 102.

44. Peter Bastian, *Inn i Musikken* (Stockholm, 1987), p. 46.

45. Ann Ekeberg (note 24), p. 58.

46. *Hit Parader* (February 1982), p. 12.

47. Andrew Neher, "Auditory Driving Observed with Scalp Electrodes in Normal Subjects," *EEG and Clinical Neurophysiology* 13 (1961), pp. 449-451.

48. Ibid., p. 451.

49. "Acoustic Trauma from Rock and Roll," *High Fidelity* 17 (November 1967), p. 38.

50. Ibid.

51. Ibid.

52. "Nader Sees Deaf Generation from Excessive Rock 'n' Roll," *New York Times* (June 2, 1969), p. 53.

53. Ibid.

54. Cited by Jeff Ward, "Cum On Kill the Noize!" *Melody Maker* 48 (December 8, 1973), p. 3.

55. Ibid.

56. Interview in *Vecko Revyn,* no. 41 (1979), p.12.

57. Ibid.

58. *Times on Sunday* (June 7, 1987), p. 17.

59. Ibid.

60. Ibid.

Chapter 9
HOW POP MUSIC
ENTERED THE CHURCH
by
Calvin M. Johansson

Calvin M. Johansson is Professor of Music at Evangel University in Springfield, Missouri. He earned his Master of Sacred Music at Union Theological Seminary and his doctorate in Musical Arts at Southwestern Baptist Theological Seminary.

A well-known lecturer, he has authored numerous articles and two books: *Music and Ministry: A Biblical Counterpoint,* and *Discipling Music Ministry: Twenty-First Century Directions.* Both of these books are widely used for university and seminary courses on church music and worship. His parish ministry as music director and organist spans a period of over forty-five years.

It is remarkable that a book such as this should still be thought important enough to be published at this juncture in history. Fifty years after the advent of rock 'n' roll, questioning the validity of rock is considered as decidedly uncool, even naive. Rock, highly instrumental in revolutionizing the most revered values of American society, is now an established and accepted fact—a major part of the national musical scene. Take away rock and its spin-offs and one has little musical activity left. Not only is it the most popular music in the United States; it is the most popular music in the world. One hears the unmistakable sounds of its strident tangle of ingredients everywhere.

Objectives of This Chapter. This chapter is divided into two parts. The first examines some of the factors which contributed to the gradual acceptance of pop music into the Christian church. Attention is given to the inadequate evangelical criticism of rock music and to the influence of the secular culture upon the church.

The second part of the chapter considers some of the characteristics of the societal worldview which have favored the flourishing of rock music. Consideration is given to materialism, amoralism, hedonism, and relativism. These popular ideologies, which stem from the naturalistic movement of the seventeenth century, have fostered a climate conducive to the acceptance of rock music. Rock, in turn, has promoted the disintegration of Judeo-Christian values.

Part 1
HOW POP MUSIC ENTERED THE CHURCH

In the 1950s and 1960s when rock was just emerging, it was commonplace for preachers and societal critics alike to lambaste the form. Respected musicians of the "classical" type stayed away from it, and music education programs ignored it. Dire warnings pronounced the consequences of rock. "Rock music will rot the minds of our youth," we were told. Lamentably, these prophets turned out to be right in more complex and interwoven ways than they imagined.

Early Rock Criticism. In those early years, it was fashionable for pastors and evangelists to spend time and energy on the evils of rock 'n' roll. As a college student, I remember how David Wilkerson, noted *Teen Challenge* founder, left in the middle of one of his crusade meetings to go after a rock drummer, the son of one of the local church members, who was playing a gig in a local bar during service time. The congregation shared Wilkerson's concern and stayed in an attitude of prayer and meditation while Wilkerson dealt with the youth. When Wilkerson returned, however, he came without the young man. He reported: "I have never seen a young man so under conviction." Wilkerson (and many like him) considered rock to be a serious threat to spiritual health.

As a matter of fact, the evangelical religious establishment took rock so seriously in those early years that special ministries arose to counter its spreading popularity and influence. One of the first anti-rock pamphlets published was David Wilkerson's own *The Devil's Heartbeat: Rock and Roll!*[1] Here he listed 16 sins that he attributed to rock music.

Other evangelists like Bob Larson, a converted rock musician, the Peters Brothers, and Craig and Mary Harrington were energetically teaching and preaching caution regarding this new musical form. Seminars, special meetings, and crusades abounded as preachers everywhere railed against the new form.

Criticism Flawed. Unfortunately, the reformers' message had a fatal flaw that would prove to be its undoing. The emphasis tended toward examining texts and dissecting record covers (graphics). They criticized the life style of rock musicians; the drugs; the illicit and pornographic sex natural to the rock scene; the emphasis on Satanism, witchcraft, and cults; the subliminal messages; backward masking; couple dancing; and lewd and suggestive performance practice. In other words, they criticized everything except the music itself! Besides mentioning the "beat" and slight concern for instrumentation, the music was essentially ignored.

Christians refrained from criticizing the music of rock for several reasons: their unfamiliarity with aesthetic principles; lack of knowledge of musical grammar; indifference toward or downright dislike of "classical" music; an upbringing, hence a familiarity, with the pop music genre of the first part of the 20th century; a failure to come to grips with the appeal of rock for Christian young people; an unwillingness to pay the price for a thoroughgoing biblically based musical aesthetic; and/or the inability to apply scriptural principles to music.

In addition, religious-rock critics somehow intuitively knew that if they denigrated the music itself, most of their own music would have to go. I remember vividly how struck I was with the dichotomy between the anti-rock sentiment and the pro-rock singing in a service held by a well-known evangelist. How could this be? The answer lies in understanding of the nature of music.

Because music was believed to be of little consequence and quite unable to bring forth the content of intent, one merely had to analyze text, musicians' life-styles, or performance practice, for example, to ascertain its suitability. The music itself then could be in any style as long as words were appropriate. Many well-meaning critics fell into this trap. Often they would end their commiserations with examples of "good" rock with Christian words. Otherwise it was similar to or at least heavily influenced by the very rock music they were opposing.

A whole new pop genre arose from an obvious need to reject anti-faith textual content while retaining the musical form—a kind of have your-cake-and-eat-it-too approach to the dilemma. Soon the wholesale flood of rock, "Christian" and non-Christian alike, began its inexorable takeover of Christian worship as the power of the young people of the 60s, 70s, and 80s began to flourish.

Inconsistent Criticism. In addition, confused Christian leaders waffled on their anti-rock stances. From initially reviling rock, Wilkerson eventually recanted after realizing that he was actually using "soft rock" in his own meetings. Among his new guidelines was a fourth one which stated, "It is unscriptural to criticize another's taste in music."[2] All that he had previously taught and preached, he now countermanded. Rock was acceptable because music was beyond criticism. Musically autonomous in their own right, individuals were free to do as they pleased.

Amazingly, three years later Wilkerson reversed himself again: "I cringe when I hear parents and ministers say, 'Don't judge.' I say they had better obey God's Word and judge righteous judgment, before they lose their children to the seductions of this age. Parents are now so easy and nonchalant about the music their kids listen to. They say, 'Well, each generation has its own style of music. We don't like it, but it seems the kids like it. And they do sing about Jesus, so it must be all right.' What incredible spiritual blindness! If the music of devils gets kids up front to make a decision, it is acceptable. How very dangerous. One of the reasons God's Spirit was lifted from the Jesus Movement of the last decade was their refusal to forsake their old music. They gave up pot, heroin, alcohol, promiscuous sex, and they even gave up perverted lifestyles. But they refused to give up their beloved rock."[3]

Wilkerson's inconsistency plays right into the hands of rock enthusiasts. Differences among people are one thing. But when a respected evangelist can't make up his own mind, perhaps all of it is only a matter of opinion. If a religious leader's teaching moves back and forth and back again, credibility and trust are lost. Disrepute is brought upon the whole field of biblical/musical judgments. Not surprisingly, the relativists claim victory.

Waning Resolve. Even more common are Christians who initially resisted the incursions of rock into the church but gradually relinquished their misgivings. As the years pass, the weariness of doing battle takes its toll. The attitude of the wider culture toward the acceptance and the promulgation of rock as the musical norm of our time has convinced all but the most ardent critic that rock's musical styles are here to stay. "If you can't lick 'em, join 'em" became a common position.

Of course, this trend toward easing into the mainstream is not limited to music. For example, Jerry Falwell's no-holds-barred posture concerning homosexuality has been toned down. The pressure to legitimatize homosexuality as just an alternate lifestyle appears to have changed Falwell's approach.

In an atmosphere of blaring Christian rock, Falwell at the Liberty University chapel hour recently explained his new view with language which *Time* reported as sounding "a bit strange. 'We can have friendship with homosexuals,' he says. 'You need to learn that. . . . If we are to have a real Christian witness to millions of gay and lesbian people we have to use our language carefully.'" And so he does, using the politically correct term "gay" rather than the harsher language used previously. He apologized for his former attitude to "200 gay people of faith" in a meeting with Soulforce, an ecumenical homosexual group directed by the Rev. Mel White, a homosexual activist.[4]

Undoubtedly, Falwell has not changed his basic belief. But his new rhetoric is an indication of the tremendous power that culture wields. The best example of the weakening resolve of religious leaders toward rock and rock-influenced music is also the least noticeable because broadly accepted change comes slowly. Spread over decades, movement takes place in an evolutionary fashion. Church music changes are no different.

The vast majority of youthful churchgoers know little of the tumultuous transformation caused by the rock revolution. To question such a normal part of daily aesthetic life is astounding. Because young people have grown up with rock, it is normal. Older people, bombarded as they are by blatant sounds from every quarter, eventually get used to the din. Their aesthetic sensitivity becomes hardened, and the whole issue simply fades away. "What was all the fuss about years ago," they wonder.

Evangelical Tendency Toward Musical Accommodation. There is another compelling reason for the eventual acceptance of rock by evangelicals. The 20th-century evangelical church has always used popular musical forms. Evangelicals' easy familiarity with popular forms made rock's eventual acceptance almost a foregone conclusion. The wonder is that it took so long.

While many churches currently are engaged in incorporating the most recent popular religious music into their services of worship, such a phenomenon is relatively recent for denominations like Presbyterian, Methodist, Lutheran, and Episcopalian. But the more aggressive evangelistic denominations, such as Baptist, Pentecostal, and Christian and Missionary Alliance, adopted a pragmatic approach from the outset. They used anything from culture which brought about the desired result.

Consequently, evangelistic denominations pattern their music after the fashionable, secular, musical forms popular with the culture of the times. The gospel song is a prime example. Taking its cue from Stephen Foster songs, campfire melodies, YMCA songs, and the like, it eventually incorporated many popular musical idioms and traits from Tin Pan Alley and Hollywood. This music was commensurate with the developing popular music industry.

Thousands upon thousands of these religious songs were written, strictly speaking, as the religious counterpart of the secular popular forms of the day. With their toe-tapping, catchy air, people enjoyed singing them. Texts were direct, experiential (emphasizing the first person), and generally limited to salvation themes. This form neatly bridged the gap between light musical fare and heavy textual themes.

If the gospel song had been recognized early on for what it is and had been dealt with accordingly, the evangelical church might now be a bit wiser concerning the present pop foray. Donald Hustad has noted, "I have tended to feel that my friend Calvin Johansson's sharp indictment of the gospel song was overdrawn. . . . But, in this instance, Calvin's indictment was prophetic. The *deja vu* genie let out of the bottle—the genie of commercial pop religious music propagated by modern entertainment performance and media—has become a dragon which would challenge St. George. Is it possible that the church must now finally break its tie to secular pop music, and especially with the religious copycat businesses (radio, TV, concerts, recordings, videos, publishing) for all the reasons Johansson has given—especially these three: (1) because of the exceedingly primitive nature of much modern popular music, which has become so strong a cultural icon that it cannot serve another master (God); (2) because copying the ever-changing styles of contemporary pop (from country to rock to rap to karioke to reggae) both suggests and insures that the church's only identity is that of novelty-seeker; and (3) because such copying can only continue to encourage the fracturing of the church along generational lines."[5]

Rock Influences Church Pop. Denominations which adopted the popular pragmatic philosophy of the gospel-song movement were poised to accept the church music spin-offs of the rock-music revolution almost by osmosis. Tuned in to pop cultural developments, it took virtually no time at all for someone to ask the inevitable question: "Why not talk to young people about Jesus in their own language, and with the sound of their own music?"[6]

The question that had driven religious, popular, Christian music for 50 years was again being invoked. In hundreds of churches across the land, the music which had caught the fancy of the younger set was poised to make the jump from rock concert, bar, and club to the chancel.

In spite of all the time, money, and effort spent to counter it, rock music swept away all the objections. Regardless of what was said or done, no preaching or zealot-led, album-fed bonfires could effectively keep this perceived evil at bay. Inconsistent evangelical criticism, a long-term continuing erosion of resolve, and an evangelical pragmatic philosophy all contributed to the acceptance of rock as a basis for a new pop church music.

Interestingly, though liberal denominations had no particular problem with accepting pop in everyday secular life, they made every effort to maintain historic musical standards in worship. For the most part, pop forms, particularly rock, were not even an issue. But when membership roles dwindled significantly and younger worshipers who had grown up with rock became more influential, the pragmatism of survival and of placating taste suggested taking another look.

With a cue from the larger church-growth movement, liberal churches eventually began to adopt the musical forms used by evangelicals. For Roman Catholics, the watershed event which allowed for the admittance of popular music into the liturgy was the second Vatican Council (1962-1965). More than 1500 years of musical tradition were set aside as guitars magically appeared to accompany the Catholic pop version of evangelical Jesus music.

The church was ill prepared to deal with this incursion of popular music for two reasons. First, many churches do not have a clear understanding of what it means to be "in the world but not of it," musically speaking. Moreover, the pilgrim mentality necessary to maintaining such a posture is out of fashion.

Thinking of the church as the Body of Christ which ministers in and to the world without being corrupted or unduly influenced by it is a concept alien to those who have "accommodation" as their *modus oper-andi*—a tempting position in a world which is changing at almost an exponential pace and in a world which has come to treat change as not only a fact of life but a way of life. Tradition becomes an enemy (except when nostalgia is a factor).

The second reason that the church was unprepared to deal with the rock revolution was its misunderstanding of the power of culture.

The Power of Culture. Anthropologists define culture as the sum total of everything there is to know about a people: their beliefs, practices, understanding, and symbols; their food, bathing suits, education, families, religion, music, hairpieces, burial customs, work, war, tatoos, morality, forks, and language. Life is not only lived in a culture. Life is culture. Culture is the environment into which a child is born and reared, the aggregate state in which life is lived. No one escapes culture for everyone is a part of it.

The overwhelming power that culture exercises upon an individual or social structure is not generally understood, at least to its full extent. Instead of people possessing culture, it is culture which possesses them. There is no way to escape it. We imagine ourselves to be free and independent, yet we are bound by laws, customs, and mores.

Even the Amish, who have purposively isolated themselves from the wider culture, cannot escape it entirely. Income taxes, tools forged in modern factories, buggies running on the latest rubber formulations over a road made by modern earth-moving equipment, public schools, and stores all attest to the difficulty of escaping their environment. It is not a distortion to say that we are prisoners of culture. No matter how much we fantasize about being free, that dream is mostly illusory.

Certain areas of life exist in which decisions can be made which go contrary to the prevailing cultural grain. Some of these decisions are obvious. Christians believe that they continue to have an obligation to uphold the Ten Commandments, for example, though the wider culture has largely rejected them. Even here, however, the influence of culture is so strong that Christians are not immune to culture's ability to subtly redefine the moral center of the average believer.

Culture's overwhelming power is hard to discern because it is formidably difficult to analyze culture from within. Yet that is exactly what Christians are called to do. It requires Herculean effort, special insight, and sensitivity. Such a task will be successful only to the extent that one relies on divine revelation.

Who Controls Culture? The operative question is "Who controls culture?" Is it a purely neutral, human endeavor? Is it Satan's playground? Or does God control human activity? Regardless of how the answers are nuanced, scripture provides ample evidence that though God is in ultimate control, He allowed humans to choose good or evil in the Garden.

Having chosen evil, our now fallen race is clearly prejudiced toward that evil and remains under Satan's influence. Healing the breech caused by the fall occurs as men and women accept God's offer of salvation. Yet, even then, the regenerate retain vestiges of the Adamic. Sin, selfishness, and sloth still operate. St. Paul's dilemma of doing what he knows he should not and not doing what he knows he should is every Christian's cross. Perfection is still far off.

Scripture is replete with admonitions to beware of the world system. "Never give your hearts to this world or to any of the things in it. A man cannot love the Father and love the world at the same time. For the whole world system, based as it is on men's primitive desires, their greedy ambitions and the glamor of all they think splendid, is not derived from the Father at all, but from the world itself."[7] "Who gave himself for our sins, that he might deliver us from this present evil world, according to the will of God and our Father."[8]

"Ye adulterers and adulteresses, know ye not that the friendship of the world is enmity with God? whosoever therefore will be a friend of the world is the enemy of God."[9] We could go on and on. The Word does say that "God so loved the world," but that was the motivation behind His giving His Son to redeem the fallen world. Culture needs to be viewed with great wariness.

A Normless Culture? Culture is driven more by the unregenerate than the regenerate, as seen by an analysis of the norms of our society. Our nation has drifted so far from Judeo/Christian ideals that our Post-Modern culture has been referred to as "Post-Christian." It is an apt label. At every juncture, Christian values have been softened and/or obliterated.

It is one thing to have an individual president behave immorally and unethically. It is quite another to note the acceptance of such behavior by the population. Will Herberg's 1968 statement, "Today's culture comes very close to becoming a non-moral, normless culture,"[10] should be amended to read, "Today's culture is, in most quarters, a non-moral, normless culture."

The intervening years have brought us to the point where traditional values can no longer be assumed. The glue that holds our culture together has broken down. Normlessness has become our new "norm." And rock music is one of the prime instigators.

Driving the re-valuing revolution is the operative underlying worldview of society. The Church is, of course, part of culture. But it is also supposed to be supra-cultural—above culture—speaking to the world from a supernatural vantage point. If it is both of culture and above culture, it is absolutely imperative that it continually monitors the wider culture's movements in order to crosscheck them with its own divine standards and assumptions.

What Values Drive Our Culture? The church does speak out on issues which are clearly, even blatantly, unchristian; murder and gross immorality are still believed to be wrong. However, the places that need the most careful watching are the more subtle attitudes and innuendos of culture which signal drifts from a Judeo/Christian center.

The question is: "What is the real, down-to-earth, working worldview of our culture?" "What are the assumptions which make us the people we are?" "How do they work themselves out in the daily life of our nation?" And finally, "How do these assumptions compare with those of a biblically based worldview?"

The conglomerate philosophic center of a nation defines its culture more than anything else. Some cultures eat with spoons, and others eat with forks and use knives as pushers, but these are only peripherally significant. The important issues change the basics of life. Value systems which reflect the collective thought of a people must be noted and responded to by the Church.

Even though the worldview of a nation is not a unified, clearly articulated, or agreed upon set of assumptions, the average acted-upon understandings of most people are enough to ascertain the worldview assumptions which drive a particular culture. These characteristics must be apprehended.

Part 2
SOCIETAL WORLDVIEW CHARACTERISTICS

All things considered, the operative worldview molding our national life is naturalism. In biblically based theism, God-ordained objective principles govern life. These originate with God and are given to us in law and grace, principle and example.

Naturalism. In the 17th century, the first chinks appeared. Thinkers reduced God's status to that of absentee landlord, an entity removed from the world. Although theoretically He still existed, He became of little importance in daily life. Known as deism, the absent clockmaker worldview, God (the clockmaker) created the world, wound it up, and then left it alone to run on its own.

The concept of an absent, uninvolved God led people to conclude that the human race is coldly alone. Nietzsche's proposal that God was dead did not seem farfetched. Further, it was not a stretch to postulate that God was not only absent, but perhaps never existed. Thus, naturalism. There is no God. The only eternal entity is matter. Humans must make the best of their chance existence because there is no overall purpose or design to life. Humans are mere products of Mother Nature and have the right to live as their individual subjective tastes desire.

Naturalism is now the dominant worldview philosophy which drives Western culture (as well as societies under the West's strong influence). Arising in the 18th century, it has finally come of age. Spawning many permutations, including some major world-changing ones (such as secular humanism, Marxism, nihilism, existentialism, and new age thought), naturalism seems to be here to stay. "It dominates the universities, colleges and high schools. It provides the framework for most scientific study. It poses the backdrop against which the humanities continue to struggle for human value, as writers, poets, painters and artists in general shudder under its implications. . . . no rival worldview has yet been able to topple it."[11]

The philosophic assumptions of naturalism affect society significantly. The general characteristics which describe our national life are the result of naturalism. The basic core beliefs of people stem from certain central assumptions. Societal characteristics are part of a larger overall scheme. Some may appear to be harmless; but as a part of naturalism, they are deadly.

Materialism. Naturalism's contention that only matter is eternal puts a priority on things. Such an emphasis is not found in theism. Our preoccupation with buying and selling, with obtaining and storing, is a glorification of a central naturalistic assumption that "what you see is what you get."

The cosmos is reality; life after death, non-existent. Life's significance is bound together with that which is sensual. Celebrating the eternal stuff of existence in material things plays into this theme of the priority of possessions. Goods are a way of life.

Amoralism. It is not surprising that naturalism embraces an ambiguous view of morality. Naturalism is not merely against the concept of theistic morality—it holds that there is no absolute moral standard in the first place. Morals are essentially a private matter. If one wishes to adopt a certain standard, that is fine for that individual. On the other hand, someone else may believe in no moral standards at all. Since morality is a human invention, one is free to invent morals. Neither position, it is believed, is superior to the other. Naturalism is morally neutral.

Naturalism has had a devastating effect on people's understanding of the power of music to influence character. The ancient Greek doctrine of *ethos* and the early church's circumspect attitude toward music has become unacceptable to modern society. Stripped of any foundational absolutist assumptions, naturalism's tenets of no moral right and wrong affect all disciplines. Who would argue that music affects character when there is no such thing as character in the first place? Amorality has had the effect of dismissing centuries of ethical/musical concerns.

Never mind that most of the children and young people who have committed heinous crimes in the last two decades have invariably been attracted to rock music. Such anecdotal evidence is unscientific, but that does not make it unreliable or unimportant. Music must not be regarded as an entity without a moral component, yet that is exactly what naturalism infers.[12]

Selfism and Hedonism. Naturalism has no frame of reference except the natural evolutionary world driven by chance processes of evolution. Humans are prisoners of a mistress we do not know except for some vague notion of a connection to eternal, impersonal cosmic molecules. Life has no outside-imposed purpose or meaning from some higher order of being. The individual positions his center of existence in the only thing that makes any sense.

Given the mechanistic orientation and emptiness of the naturalistic order, the self is all he has. Making life more bearable by escaping the determined world of impersonal natural selection is one way to fill the emptiness of existence. Of the many forms that escape takes, a prime way is to seek out pleasure.

Entertainment has become a national pastime with millions of dollars and millions of hours spent on sports, Hollywood productions, and the popular music "industry." The desire to please ourselves while we have the chance is entirely consistent with the naturalistic assumption that there is no larger life, no heavenly city to aspire to at death. Living for the moment in an escape mode seems to be a logical way to forget the capriciousness of the past and the grimness of the future.

Hedonism holds that pleasure is the highest good. Enjoyment and fun are laudable pursuits. And why not? No absolute levels of pursuit exist in naturalism. It is a worldview turned in on itself. The individual, though he is in some way determined, authenticates his existence by ordering his own world around self and doing it in the least taxing, most pleasing manner.

Relativism. Naturalism takes a dim view of absolutes. This worldview, more than any other, has promoted one of the most visible characteristics of the age in which we live—relativism, a philosophy which avoids authority and opts for taste. Since the 1950s, relativism has been a major player in the daily lives of millions of people. Naturalism, in the past 50 years, has trumpeted the superiority of a sweeping relativistic subjectivity. Its love affair with the subjective is a matter of necessity rather than choice. Having no place to go for absolute standards and values, subjective invention became its only option.

In a way, naturalism's foundation is its biggest dilemma. Its insistence that there is no God (and all that implies) is central to its proclamations. Carried to its logical conclusion, naturalism ends in nihilism, a negation of everything. But life as we know it could not be lived nihilistically. Negating things like traffic lights or poison mushrooms does not prevent one from paying the price should they be ignored. So it is with naturalism. Although ultimate authority is dismissed, areas exist in which we need to trust experts. We should do better to let a trained pilot fly a 747 rather than a non-pilot. A surgeon is better qualified to operate on a toe than a plumber is. In naturalism, a certain chameleon-like transformation allows for objective changes in application. Yet in the area of aesthetics, naturalism's penchant for the subjective is clearly inviable. Taste, pure and simple, is the operative way musical selection is made.

Rock's Influence on Culture. Undoubtedly, naturalistic presuppositions fostered a climate in which rock music flourished. Materialism, amoralism, selfism, hedonism, and relativism supported the musical sounds of rock and its textual philosophy. However, it is too facile to conclude that rock was simply a result of naturalism and subsequent more extreme worldviews. The relationship between rock and worldview assumptions is complex. Rock was as much a cause as an effect. It had an agenda, and that agenda, inculcated in its texts and more importantly in its music, served to mold culture in its own worldview image. Rock was used to further the secular humanism of a godless and naturalistic worldview.

Rock musicians had immense power. The music served as a catalyst to launch the most sweeping popular revolution of value systems the Western world had ever seen since the time of Christ. Traditional notions of morality, ethics, aesthetics, and societal values based on Judeo/Christian theism were turned upside down.

Robert Bork notes this flip-flopping of societal values: "We are now two nations. These are not, as Disraeli had it, the rich and the poor, or, as presidential commissions regularly proclaim, whites and blacks. Instead, we are two cultural nations. One embodies the counterculture of the 1960s, which today is the dominant culture. . . . The other nation, of those who adhere to traditional norms and morality, is now a dissident culture."[13] Singers and musicians became the heroes and idols of the target audience, the young. Absorbing countercultural values through the music they listened to, the young brought their value system along with them when they matured into adulthoood.

Most evangelical church youth of the 60s were amenable to the suspicion of parents, pastors, and teachers concerning rock. That did not keep them from assimilating it, however. Because it was heard everywhere young people went, they could hardly avoid it. As time went on and rock became more and more extreme in its text and music, everyone, including adults, was swept along by the tide. Eventually, it was taken for granted—a fact of life.

The real danger of rock is not that it will take over the music of worship completely—religious hip-hop, punk, and heavy metal congregational fare. The real danger is more subtle. The great danger is the insidious influence of rock music on the music of Christian worship and on the daily listening habits of those who patronize the Christian music field.

The church is not in any imminent danger of its vocal music taking on acid rock characteristics, although some churches have done so. Of course, dozens of CCM soloists, bands, and ensembles are thoroughgoing rockers. But for the most part, the influence of rock on congregational music should be the greatest concern.

Rock and Religious Pop. Presently, the Church's biggest dilemma is in the wider field of worship music, which has been influenced by rock music. Popular religious music is flooding the church as never before. Most of this music cannot be categorized as out-and-out rock. Yet the musical formulations are quite out of character for music that is supposed to be a reflection of the gospel.

A closer look at this large body of music indicates that although it is not strictly rock, it does have many of the characteristics of popular music. While very few churches would tolerate the incursion of hip-hop into worship, for example, most are coming to welcome music with a decidedly pop air. It is, therefore, more useful to consider the broader category of popular music (which includes rock) in Chapter 10, rather than the more narrow genre of rock. Looking at pop forms as a whole cuts across demarcation lines of sub-categories and looks at the broad spectrum of the religious pop music field.

We need to consider pop music as a genre, as a class, and as a style. Such criticism is distinctly out of fashion, that question supposedly having been settled in pop's favor thirty years ago. But history has shown that wholesale accommodation to culture changes the gospel. Who would dispute the claim that lighter, more "fun" music on the part of evangelicals has accompanied a simultaneous reduction of piety and discipline?

Granted, such a state ought not be laid at the feet of music alone. Other factors have contributedto it: a feel-good approach to faith, a culture of trivialization, an easing of moral constraints, the breakdown of the family unit, distrust of authority, an erosion of belief in the sovereignty of God, and so on. But on balance, music has had a disproportionate influence on the life of the church.

We Live in a Pop Culture. When the music histories of the 20th century are written, the most prominent musical feature to emerge will be a large scale shift from art music to popular music. The dramatic change can be chronicled by noting the waning interest in classical music as the century wore on. This is not to say that classical music is dead, but its future is at best uncertain. It may eventually be found only as a museum artifact should our present value system continue.

Community-concert associations, arts councils, and the like were forced into programming more and more pop concerts in order to attract the audience necessary to stay afloat. Even the most prestigious symphony orchestras resorted to adding pop attractions or a separate pop concert series in order to keep the orchestra financially viable. Choral societies as well as church choirs which sang a high standard of repertoire dwindled in number.

Popular singers of the first half of the century kept some modicum of vocal beauty in their singing (Bing Crosby and Dennis Day, for example), while the last half of the century experienced vocal sounds that became increasingly ugly. Machines made mass marketing of recordings a multi-million-dollar enterprise. Pop soloists and groups after World War II served to revolutionize western life in every way. Doing so gave them, with the help of commercial marketing strategists, a stranglehold on the molding of musical taste. College and university curricula reflected lagging interest, as did the disappearance of the neighborhood piano teacher. All in all, the century showed that music cannot be divorced from the developing traits of a society. The values of a people show up in what they sing and play.

ENDNOTES

1. David Wilkerson, *The Devil's Heartbeat: Rock and Roll!* (Philipsburg, PA, n.d.).

2. David Wilkerson, *Confessions of a Rock 'n' Roll Hater!* (Lindale, TX, 1982), p. 3.

3. David Wilkerson, *Set The Trumpet to Thy Mouth* (Lindale, TX, 1985), pp. 91-92.

4. John Cloud, "An End to the Hatred," *Time* (November 1, 1999), p. 62.

5. Donald Hustad, *The Merry Go Round Goes Round* (unpublished paper, Hardins-Simmons University Symposium, 1994), pp. 4-5.

6. Pat Boone in Paul Baker, *Why Should the Devil Have All the Good Music* (Waco, TX, 1979), p. *vii.*

7. John 2:15-16, Phillips.

8. Galatians 1:4, KJV.

9. James 4:4, KJV.

10. Will Herberg, "What Is the Moral Crisis of Our Time?" *The Intercollegiate Review* 2 (Fall 1986), p. 9.

11. James Sire, *The Universe Next Door: A Basic Worldview Catalogue,* 3rd ed. (Downers Grove, IL, 1997), pp.71-72.

12. See William Kilpatrick, *Why Johnny Can't Tell Right from Wrong* (New York, 1993), pp. 172-189.

13. Robert H. Bork, "True Conservatism," *The Intercollegiate Review* (Spring 1999), p. 6.

Chapter 10
POP MUSIC
AND THE GOSPEL
by
Calvin M. Johansson

Calvin M. Johansson is Professor of Music at Evangel University in Springfield, Missouri. He earned his Master of Sacred Music at Union Theological Seminary and his doctorate in Musical Arts at Southwestern Baptist Theological Seminary.

A well-known lecturer, he has authored numerous articles and two books: *Music and Ministry: A Biblical Counterpoint,* and *Discipling Music Ministry: Twenty-First Century Directions.* Both of these books are widely used for university and seminary courses on church music and worship. His parish ministry as music director and organist spans a period of over forty-five years.

One cannot get around it. What the church does represents what the church is. A congregation that lies to the city council is showing off its Christianity (or lack of it). A church board that deceives the pastor is giving a witness of its faith. A Christian-education program which is all but nonexistent is dysfunctional in working out the Great Commission!

So all-encompassing is biblical theism that everything the church embraces becomes an analogue of its faith. That is why the actions of the church are so important. It speaks not only for itself, but for its Lord. When it acts in ways that are contrary to its very covenant, such actions are still perceived as representing God. When its actions are consistent with its faith, such actions likewise represent the Almighty. Whatever we do in word or deed, good or bad, becomes a working symbol of life in Christ.

Since we cannot avoid witnessing, the only question that remains concerns the content of the witness. If the symbol is virtuous, consistent with the faith in every way, the witness will be positive. The gospel will be promoted and glory will be given to God. However, when the witness or symbol is inconsistent with God's Word, when it shows (via its own language medium) characteristics which are opposite to the traits of the gospel, then the symbol brings disrepute on the full gospel. Such representations do much harm to the cause of Christ. They need to be rejected. Whether it's heretical preaching, sentimentalized calendar art, or inappropriate music, the quality of witness is determined by its integrity to gospel principles in its own medium.

An analysis of the characteristics of popular music, [1] a genre which includes many styles, must of necessity be quite general. The traits mentioned here are endemic to all of them. It should also be noted that within each category of popular music, from rap to Broadway to CCM, there are levels of worth. Music is not all of the same quality.

Obviously, the broad category of popular music in no case has the standard of excellence found in art music, a music of great integrity and depth. If it did, it would by definition no longer be popular music. "Pop," as I am using the term, refers to that which is made for the express purpose of becoming popular at the expense of those compositional traits which yield a music of artistic greatness.

Objectives of This Chapter. This chapter attempts to help the reader understand the fundamental differences between the values and goals of pop music and those of the Gospel. Eight specific areas are compared and contrasted. The analysis of these areas show that pop music is inimical to the gospel and can ultimately pervert its meaning and relevance for today.

Church Music as a Symbol. Music is often thought of as a text lubricator, a means to worship, a kind of background halo hanging over the congregation, or even an emotional stimulant which punctuates preaching. Church music, however, is something quite different. The very least that church music should do is to further the gospel. Although this influence of the music may be totally subconscious, we should not take it for granted. To do so may be perilous. Too many believe that the gospel furthered by music is found in the text itself apart from the music. They consider the music merely as accoutrement to the text. This is a misunderstanding of the comprehensive nature of the reach of church music.

Church music has a powerful propensity for communicating via its own language medium—notes, rhythm, harmony, texture—something much larger than itself. Trying to split the message of church music from its medium simply is not possible, even though that mistake is often made.

Acknowledged or unacknowledged, church music is a symbol. It is a symbol of Christianity, Christian theism, or, in short, the gospel. It is a symbol, not because of style or quality, but because of its use. That is, the word "church," used adjectivally, describes the use to which church music is put. Since "church" is a description of the whole Christian enterprise, "church" (or "Christian") music is music which likewise describes Christianity.

(1) Entertainment Versus Edification

The first and most obvious trait of all pop music is that it is entertaining, a fact generally missed by those who use religious pop music in worship. Nevertheless, entertainment is at its very heart. Myopic and narcissistic, pop is oriented around musical pleasure based on individualistic whim and caprice rather than on objective musical value and worth. No matter how vehemently people deny it, pop entertains. That is why it exists.

Pop musicians know this and readily design their renditions to be frivolous, if not witless. This fun music with its constant bombardment of musical silliness tends to reform the listener in its own image, a result which eventually may turn out to be anything but "fun." Again, easygoing, breezy, informal, mad, wild, secular, or Christian, pop music has at least one thing in common—it entertains.

Pop's musical composition insures that this is so. Entertainment occurs when music is crafted devoid of musical reason. Harmony, melody, rhythm, and timbre are shaped to be fun and viscerally stimulating. Without theoretical depth, pop utilizes a construction which is empty of serious musical thought. It is one-sided, costing the listener little in the way of intellectual investment. Sweet, sour, saccharine, or belligerent, pop washes over the listener with gay abandon. Its purpose, its *raison d'être,* is to amuse.

The Gospel Is Not Entertainment. Gut-wrenching, life-changing redemption has little in common with amusement. Jesus' sacrifice was not an idle pastime. Nor is the life He calls us to either frolicsome or filled with tomfoolery. Christians are called to a life that is painful at times and yet is sometimes full of unspeakable joy. The Christlife was never intended to be frivolous or supercilious. Further, the worship of the Saviour, the One who suffered, died, and rose again to give us new life, ought not reflect popular culture's contemporary predilection for trivialization.

Worship which focuses on providing the worshiper a rollicking good time is sacrilege. In accommodating the gospel to society's love of entertainment, worship is turned around 180 degrees. Even though we believe such worship is directed toward God, in reality it is directed toward people. What we utilize in worship is that which pleases us, the created. We want things we like—things which feed our selfish drive for having a good time. Naturalism's hedonistic tendencies end up in the house of the Lord. In fact, worship which is based on its entertainment quotient is idolatrous. The worshiper is worshiping self.

It should be obvious that to use popular music of any type in worship simply turns worship into entertainment, no matter what category, stripe, style, or subspecies of music it is. Whether rock, CCM, swing, or ragtime is used, the end result will be the same: convoluted worship, trivialization of the faith, and immaturing of the believer.

On the other hand, great music edifies the listener. The composer invests in the work musical traits which call the listener to reflect seriously on levels of musical content that go beyond the temporal. With emotional and intellectual balance as a result of competent craft, musical depth in great music sympathetically resonates within the heart and mind of the listener in the manner of a gestalt.

Those who give their whole beings to a piece of fine music are translated to realms beyond description. They are enlightened and moved. These experiences leave them with a sense of wonderment. In the manner of general revelation, the listener is built up and edified. Far beyond entertainment, fine music brings one face to face with a world which reflects God's glory.

(2) Novelty Versus Creativity

Popular Music Is Novel. It relies on facile decoration (often obnoxiously obvious!) to provide the illusion of true creativity. It requires constant changing because it doesn't wear well. The Top 40 are a case in point. Continual dropping and adding of titles indicate how the genre needs the momentum of change to stay alive.

Disposability supports a kind of fad approach to composition which pop music must have in order to survive. Integrity defaults to expendability. Pop music cannot tolerate the degree of creativity that art music demands because then it would cease to be pop. Novelty depends upon hype and gimmicks, plentiful in the annals of pop history.

Some of the more extreme innovations are not only novel; they are bizarre. Biting the head off a dove or amplifying the throbbing thump of an ear-splitting trap set may be novel, but certainly they have little to do with creativity. The latter may be defined as making with imagination and integrity. Imagination comes from the innate talent and vision that an artist possesses.

The competence of compositional craft determines the work's integrity. Both imagination and craft are necessary. It is a fallacy to think of creativity (in the sense we are using the term) as simply "newness." In fact, creativity only exists as it mirrors, haltingly to be sure, the creativity of Almighty God. When God looked back upon the world that He made in the initial creation, the Bible says that "God saw every thing that he had made, and, behold, it was very good" (Gen 1:31, KJV). This is a statement of quality. The creation was not only created, it was created good. More than that, it was created with a high degree of excellence; it was created *very* good.

Creative Excellence. God, the "Maker of heaven and earth," saw fit to tell us of His creatorship at the outset of His revelation to us. Further, He tells us that we are made in His image. Among the various ways that His image is shown in us, certainly the one which stands out among all the others is the fact that we have been made in the image of a creator. When reading the Bible from the beginning, the narrative begins with the fact of God's existence. Then there is a recounting of the initial creation. When we come to verse 26 of Genesis 1, the only things we have been told about Him is that He exists and that He is a creator. "Let us make man in our image, after our likeness" leads to the logical conclusion that we have been made *creators* in the likeness of a *Creator.*

Creativity is no small thing. It is the first thing we know about God and the first thing we know about humans, which gives it a certain priority. The councils which framed the creeds (such as the Nicene and Apostles' creeds) recognized the importance of God's creatorship by affirming it at the outset of each formulation: "We believe in one God, the father, the almighty, *maker* of heaven and earth." And again "I believe in God, the Father almighty, *maker* of heaven and earth."

When using God's creativity as a model, it is imperative to note that whatever He made, it was made excellently. Even more to the point, the products of God's creativity were not banal, trite, mad, or wild. They were not casual, hackneyed, or stereotyped. They were not easygoing, trifling, silly, or wacky. Nor were they disposable or expendable. To be sure, when Adam and Eve disobeyed in the garden, all of creation was brought under the curse of sin. But even so, we see a level of creation which defines for us creative excellence.

Pop Music Lacks Creative Excellence. Popular music does not aspire to the highest degree of creative excellence. It is too facile, too obvious. It lacks the musical craft and imagination of great music. While some pop songs may be better than others, none rise to the level of excellence found in serious music. It may be novel, but it does not have Godly creativity.

Since pop has no musical depth (as in art music), the inevitable conclusion is that pop creativity and Godly creativity run counter to one another. This makes pop an inadequate medium for theistic witness. Since one of God's main attributes is His excellent creativity, we testify about Him best when our church music witness is deeply creative. Novel church music may be fun to listen to, but musically it suggests that the Christian faith is similarly slick. It implies that the author of such a superficial faith is likewise a creative lightweight— hardly a fitting representation of God Almighty.

We know that Jesus, as agent of creation, literally holds the universe(s) together by the power of His word. *Creatio continua,* God's continuing creation, speaks eloquently of His power to sustain what He originally created, and that that sustainability is just as creative as the original creation. Moreover, God chooses to work through humans in the continuation of creation. He has given us a creation mandate to fulfill the potential He placed in the world at the beginning. Hence, humans are arms of God's *creatio continua.*

If humans are to be God's creative agents, the Church should realize that it too is part of God's creative call. The Body of Christ on the earth, in its representation of what it means to witness to God's grace, should include works of the highest creativity of which humans are capable. The corporate worship of the Church is its collective witness. Can one omit the musical means of Godly creativity and expect good witness through forms which are absolutely poverty stricken?

Popular culture has so captured the minds *and* hearts of the Church that, without a second thought, worship has become stripped of much musical creativity. This lowers the standards of the Church in order to meet the approval of the wider culture. Ought the Church be a warmed-over version of the society it is trying to save? That does not make sense. What is needed is firm resolve. A beginning would be to avoid pop church music which is reminiscent of our culture's infatuation with the novel. We should rely instead on that which has inculcated in it the Godly attribute of high creativity.

(3) Immediate Gratification Versus Delayed Gratification

The general aesthetic principle upon which pop is based is immediate gratification. This principle, more than any other, defines the genre. Every aspect of the musical structure, whether melody, harmony, rhythm, texture, or form, is built upon the notion of supplying musical gratification in the quickest, most direct manner. Little aesthetic subtlety exists in pop. Just as our culture is one of credit card immediacy NOW, so pop mirrors culture by being a music of expeditious indulgence NOW.

Immediate Gratification. The music of pop is conspicuously easy to assimilate. This fact alone accounts for the rapidity with which it wears out. The musical components of pop rarely outlive the listener's interest in them. They are composed for easy assimilation which provides no significant challenge to the listener. That which is fully comprehended is as interesting as yesterday's newspaper. Nostalgia excepted, new songs supplant the old in an endless parade because the aesthetic principle of immediate gratification demands constant turnover if the genre is to be perpetuated.

Leonard Meyer has shown that when musical goals are "reached in the most immediate and direct way,"[2] aesthetic value is slight. In addressing pop and art music, Meyer suggests that the difference between "art music and primitive music lies in speed of tendency gratification. The primitive seeks almost immediate gratification for his tendencies whether these be biological or musical. Nor can he tolerate uncertainty. And it is because distant departures from the certainty and repose of the tonic note and lengthy delays in gratification are insufferable to him that the tonal repertory of the primitive is limited, not because he can't think of other tones. It is not his mentality that is limited, it is his maturity. Note, by the way, that popular music can be distinguished from real jazz on the same basis. For while 'pop' music whether of the tin-pan-alley or the Ethelbert Nevin variety makes use of a fairly large repertory of tones, it operates with such conventional cliches that gratification is almost immediate and uncertainty is minimized."[3]

The speed of tendency gratification is an indicator of musical value. Pop's goal-inhibiting tendencies are negligible; art music's are significant. To the degree that the final tonic, for example, is creatively worked toward, the ultimate arrival of the concluding cadence, postponed until the subtly crafted digressions have been worked through, is the degree of value a piece has attained.

If there ever was an aesthetic principle which perfectly matched a culture, it is this principle of immediate gratification. From "How to Play the Piano in Ten Easy Lessons" to instant mashed potatoes to contractual theology to sex outside of marriage, the prevailing attitude of our culture is to consummate desire with an immediacy which finds delay repugnant.

Such practice cuts across the broad cultural front and is strongly ingrained in the collective psyche. It is clearly seen in the casual attitude toward fornication and adultery. If immediate gratification has bent morality to its own norms, how much more should we expect that it has done the same to society's aesthetic appreciation. This is why pop is a musical analogy of our culture's values.

Delayed Gratification. The opposite corollary of immediate gratification is delayed gratification. It is one of the key aesthetic principles employed in the creating of music of integrity and worth. My experience over a lifetime of rehearsing college and church choirs has been that music of delayed gratification wears well over weeks and months of rehearsal. But popular music of whatever ilk does not fare as well. Choristers tire of rehearsing its predictable tunes and harmonies.

In spite of any technical difficulty, when musical components exude obvious musical patterns that are trite, the very thing that makes the music popular in the first place is the thing which kills it in rehearsal. The same can be said for careful listening. Pieces which can be assimilated without travail, so to speak, do not have the power to engage the listener for long.

The mystery is gone, the challenge dissipated, the music plastic. But music built on delayed gratification has built into it distance, adventure, and challenge. The joy of anticipation is a propellant toward eventual gratification. The process of listening is one of looking forward, of new discovery, of finding in the music a similitude with the human condition.

A Gospel Principle. Delayed gratification is a major gospel principle. Consistent with God's dealing with humanity, the New Testament continues the Old Testament pattern of progressive revelation. From the earliest encounter with Abraham to the ascension of our Lord, "that which is to come" always entices us. Hebrews 11 chronicles heroes of the faith who died in the hope of receiving that which was promised.

The New Testament reveals that Christians will someday sit down at the Messianic banquet. Some day, there will be no pain, no sorrow; some day, we will receive an incorruptible body; some day, the lion and the lamb will lie down together. Christ has died. That is part of the historical record. It is true that Christ is risen, but there is also the hope that Christ will come again. Christians live in hope. We do not now receive everything coming to us. We wait until the fullness of time. That is delayed gratification.

Some day we will be completely vindicated. But not now. Included in God's dealing with us is a time line. Life is a process; our Christian experience is a journey. Though we are fully sons and daughters of our Lord at conversion, more is to come. If the Christian life is anything at all, it is a process of maturing—a process of becoming conformed to the image of the Son. That takes time. Full gratification is delayed. The travail of making us into what God wants us to be a mark of our Christian human condition.

The concept of delayed gratification is also a basic life principle. It is the way God made the natural world. Life comes from seed, then growth toward maturity. The end of life is encapsulated in time. It doesn't happen all at once. Additionally, progress toward the eventual goal is impeded by difficulties and detours. These incursions make life a difficult road to travel. Nonetheless, rightly understood, the rigors of life have a purpose because they give meaning and shape to existence.

Pop Music Is Not the Musical Gospel. These considerations should cause us to reject the present headlong acceptance of immediate gratification as basic life strategy. It is not how God designed life. Nor is it the model for the Christian walk. Aesthetic works based on immediate gratification are unable to aspire to greatness because they are out of step with Godly design. As a life principle, a gospel principle, and an aesthetic principle, immediate gratification fails.

Put in this light, why is the Christian church so enamored with pop music? Based as it must be on immediate gratification, pop is incapable of being the musical gospel. Its medium of notes, rhythm, and harmony is unable to display general revelatory gospel witness. Pop music simply has little in common with the gospel.

Worship is an activity which ought to be consonant with scripture and with the Christian walk. The fact that much worship is being filled with forms of music built on the aesthetic principle of immediate rather than delayed gratification is grievous. Such has all the ear marks of pop worship and has more in common with the world than with heaven. Worship inconsistent with the gospel is, once more, no worship at all.

(4) Low Standards Versus High Standards

Popular music's standard is determined by the lowest common denominator of public taste. Music for the populace means music which rises no higher than the inclination of the least astute listener. It is predisposed toward the lowering of musical appreciation because it does not call for the hearer to rise to a higher level of musical competence.

Low Standards. What is provided is on the basis that it will not be too cultured, too erudite. Twentieth-century pop music decreases the level of musical sophistication. It reflects the adamic nature of sloth and laziness and fosters a declining ability to compose, play, and sing well. People need high aspirations to excel. The problem with pop is that, as a genre, it is fixated on mediocrity.

Conversely, music of artistry assumes the normalcy of high expectations. Composers don't write "down" to an audience, even at the subconscious level. Unlike pop composition, which exists within an assumed framework of the necessity of mass acceptability, art music expects the listener to rise to the standard set by art work. The hearer does not determine the aesthetic level of the composer's craft. Rather, the composition is made to reflect the very highest aesthetic excellence.

Whether performers or audiences "understand" or "like" the piece is not relevant to the compositional process. If the work is at too high a level, the audience is invited to rise to that level. There is no dumping down, no writing down. Great music calls us to be our best musical selves. Its assumption is that people have the ability to make friends with the highest and best forms of art. Quality comes first.

High Standards. Scripture, too, calls for high standards. These are easily seen, for example, in the Ten Commandments and in the Lord's requiring Israel to remain separate from surrounding cultures. Not so readily perceived, perhaps, are the New Testament standards under grace. Not being accountable to the ceremonial law might seem to indicate a free-for-all. Because humans look at the outward appearance but God looks at the heart, is behavior a concern any longer?

Jesus Himself gives us direction in Matthew 5. Under the law, adultery and murder were forbidden but under His reign lust and anger are also prohibited. It seems clear that a higher standard is set under grace. Now a person's heart is an additional battleground on which right must prevail. Further, all that Jesus had to say about personal purity, practicing the God-controlled life, giving good for evil, discipline, and the call to leave everything for the cause of Christ shows unequivocally that grace calls us to a higher standard than the law ever did. In other words, grace fulfills the law.

This being the case, little support is shown for popular culture's propensity for the lowest common denominator. By accepting the basest cultural standards, the norm simply degrades society. If the gospel call is to high standards, then Christians have a duty to promote them wherever they have the opportunity.

High Standards in Church Music. In worship especially we should expect the high standards of scripture to be borne out in the works of our hands. Music in church must be of a caliber that rises above the low musical standards of the world. Simply because a song is liked is no reason to use it. People may be comfortable with it, but acceptance by a cultural milieu of populists and adamic principles placed by God in the natural world, principles which are cross-cultural and timeless, may be circumvented.

Composers and performers are able to do whatever they desire without concern for the musical worth of what they are doing. While this may appear to be freedom, it really is license. It has a cost: poor music. The statement over the court house in Worcester, Massachusetts, is noteworthy: "Obedience to law is liberty." Extreme subjectivity is an invitation to anarchy. That is the situation in pop music from a compositional basis. Doing that which is right *in one's own eyes* may seem like artistic freedom. It isn't. It is artistic chaos.

Biblical theism, on the other hand, is essentially an objective worldview. God is the boss. His Word rules. While He gives us choice, it is choice with consequences. We will pay the penalty for choosing wrongly. Despite the fact that God is mystery and that His Word may be interpreted incorrectly, Erik Routley has asserted that on all matters of importance, God speaks in scripture, if not by direct reference, then by inference. No scripture is of private interpretation. Such subjectivity is extremely dangerous. The objective nature of God's dealing with humankind ought not be lost.

Theistic objectivity is important because it is a means by which aesthetic worth can be established. Pop practice, based as it is on subjective taste, is a musical genre consistent with naturalistic assumptions and is contrary to theism. This is one reason why pop music, secular or Christian, is unable to be a musical analogue of the gospel. Its nature is so far removed from the locus of biblical revelation that it is actually an anti-gospel form. Great music is based on objective theistic norms. Pop is based on subjective naturalistic ones. Acknowledged or not, pop's presuppositions do incalculable harm to musical art. They do even more harm to the cause of Christ.

Objective Divine Revelation. God's revelation to humankind is not a figment of subjective imagination but a matter of objective reality. Reordering of the world via supernatural directive is entirely consistent with the fact of God's sovereignty. Such interference in the affairs of humans is both authoritarian and commensurate with biblical theism. As creatures, we are obliged to discover the parameters of the Creator's dealing with us—a discovery which is more informed by God's determinations than ours.

Our relationship to God is fundamentally objective. A theist's relationship to the world is similar. This is not to suggest that there is no human tint to what is observed and known; rather, godly precepts and principles exist apart from human observation. Living in a subjectively driven world is difficult. Relativism so infects the atmosphere in which we live that objective judgments are next to impossible to execute, let alone consider.

But consider them we must. If we countenance a crack in one area, it is bound to spread to others. Using objective musical judgments on the music of worship is important. Allowing music ministry to run on the subjective musical taste of worshipers will broaden to other faith/life territory. Because popular music is taste driven, it has a tremendous propensity toward individual subjectivity.

People in control of the musical contents of worship who are unable to see through popular culture and who do not know or do not recognize basic objective aesthetic rudiments choose music on the basis of preference. The objective nature of theism is then musically thwarted. Worship promotes a music which is fundamentally out of sync with the biblical record. In choosing subjectivity over objectivity, worship is based more on subjective taste than on objective value—a human-centered focus. Worship centered on humans becomes worship of humans.

(5) Commercialism Versus Non-Commercialism

Pop music is firmly ensconced in commercial enterprise. Since acceptability determines sales, the music work is influenced by consumers' demand. The imaginative and technical characteristics of popular music as a whole are shaped by what a songwriter knows about the general expectations of the audience. Even musicians who attempt something that is far afield, even bizarre, do not do so without considering its impact on the audience.

Market Driven. Naturally sub-categories of listeners in the pop field are numerous; some are attuned to acid rock, others to country or perhaps CCM, hip-hop, or gangsta rap. Whatever the sub-style, composers are well aware of what it takes to "turn on" their audience.

Successful writers of popular music are recognized not on the basis of the inherent, objective aesthetic worth of their songs but on how many recordings have been sold or tickets purchased. Crowd-pleasing is a must in the popular field. Fads in vogue today will, of necessity, mutate or be supplanted tomorrow. Yet the style has an innate cyclical nature which makes it a natural for commercial, consumer-driven enterprise, so it is easy to see why the fickle changeability of the public is so pronounced.

Business has exploited the transient nature of pop. Recently the music arm of Time Warner and EMI announced a 20 BILLION dollar merger.[4] Considering the millions that are spent each year on popular music of all stripes, these giants sense further money-making potential in the field. Publicly traded, these businesses know that the bottom line is shareholder earnings. If there ever was a question about the profit motive in popular music, it can now be laid to rest. Even the so-called Christian Contemporary Music field is dominated by a few conglomerates.[5] Art is out. Money is in.

The language used to describe popular music shows its business orientation. Pop music is a product. It belongs to an industry. Song writers are providers and their songs commodities. The music they write and the bands who perform it are mass merchandized for maximum penetration and saturation in a market. Musical production must be vendible. If it doesn't sell, a song is finished. Hence, taste makers try to insure that a particular piece will be profitable.

Air time, performer exposure, advertisements, and widespread media coverage whip up enthusiasm for a new song or album. The costs are enormous, but with standard entrepreneurial practice, the potential for even greater returns is recognized. Pop music is no different from any other manufactured device. It is beholden to business for its very life.

Obviously, composers have to earn a living just like everyone else. The difference between pop and art music that the composer writes, however, is that the former is an entity which has been shaped by the necessity of being acceptable. To insure this, imaginative and technical characteristics of the music are influenced by what the composer knows the public want—who, it might be added, are neither sensitive nor able musicians themselves.

On the other hand, the classical composer, taking on a commission for a new work, does not tie his compositional technique to the foibles of the commissioner. Although parameters are often given to the composer (such as length or performance forces), no composer worth his salt would allow his musical integrity to be compromised by strictures to his compositional technique. The making of a genuine work of art is not tied to acceptability.

The composer of art music maintains control over the compositional process. Moreover, its success is not dependent on making money for huge corporations. Its success is determined by its adherence to an objective aesthetic criteria—imagination and technique achieved with creative excellence. While pop is thoroughgoing commercial music, great art has a life of its own, independent of saleability. Its essence lies in aesthetic goodness.

The Gospel Is Not a Business. Profit is not its motive. Storing up this world's goods or thinking of the kingdom of God as a temporal entity is antithetical to gospel teaching. Material possessions are seen in scripture as a hindrance to achieving God's best. Yet contemporary business practices are often used as models for church organization and development.

The whole church-growth movement borrows heavily from commerce. Terminology ("sinners" are out, "unchurched" is in), methodology (congregations are consumers), and staff organization (the pastor is the CEO) all come from the business model. A church based on this paradigm is bound to earthly, pragmatic, industrial thinking. Biblical methods are subsumed under an avalanche of "modern" ones. The Body of Christ turns into a firm.

The business model works well for the pop-music industry. Treating music as a product allows it to control the art work from beginning to end. Even in the Christian music world, profit motive and shareholder return motivate the industry. All major labels are now owned by profit-driven conglomerates: Zomba, Gaylord Entertainment, and Time Warner.

Worship has taken on a commercial flavor. Not only does business serve as a model for the church, but commercialism has strongly affected the quality of congregational musical composition in worship. Songs with a commercial aesthetic are being sung, and some churches sing nothing but this type of music. Tightly controlled licensing of these songs protect the rights of the copyright owners.

Thus, churches have to pay a royalty to use most CCM songs, either directly or through licensing companies such as Christian Copyright Licensing International (CCLI). Now the drive to make money makes church services "markets." Although the gospel is inherently noncommercial, commercialism shapes the church's worship when religious pop music is used.

(6) Indulgent Versus Disciplined

Popular music of all kinds is musically undisciplined. Its compositional traits tend toward the facile, the manipulative, the effect. It opts for indulgence and eschews restraint. Without compunction, pop goes for the jugular; aesthetic contemplation, tempered and ordered by reason, is replaced by hedonistic titillation. Popular music provides emotionalistic satisfaction in the manner of a cheap thrill. What is missing is the arduous journey toward the arrival. The travail of birthing something valuable is anathema to pop.

To change the sentimental syrupy melodies of Tin Pan Alley, the brash vulgarity of rock's tunes, the coarseness of country, or the bedlam of rap, a more disciplined compositional approach would change the locus of the genre so that it would be unrecognizable. Pop cannot tolerate musical discipline. Its form has become more and more unruly. Heavy metal and acid will be supplanted by even more audacious effrontery because pop breeds disorder.

Music of Excellence Must Be Disciplined. For example, certain notes of the diatonic scale have voice-leading tendencies which limit the composer's choices. These tendencies come from the natural pull of steps and half steps within the context of the piece's texture. They exist whether we agree with them or not, but good writing demands that they be taken into account. We can ignore them. To do so results in a degradation of quality.

The same can be said for the aggregate processes of composition. One writes in the tension between law and freedom. That tension is compositional discipline. Without it, music becomes either bound or indulgent; hence, great music always resides in the discipline between freedom of expression and the restraint of principle.

Called to be disciples, Christians have a duty to embrace discipline. It is the mark of a disciple. Christian discipline is intended to affect not only religious things like prayer or Bible reading; it also ought to impact family life, driving habits, diets, and leisure time.

Included in such a comprehensive list is music and worship. For composition to be good, to be a symbol of the gospel, and to be useful in worship, it must shun indulgence. The antidote to compositional indulgence is compositional discipline.

Worship Needs Disciplined Music. Our permissive society is so prone to having its desires satisfied that it is a shock when they are denied. Yet, the gospel is about the fulfillment of one's self-denial. "If any man will come after me, let him deny himself, and take up his cross, and follow me" (Matt 16:24, KJV).

Dietrich Bonhoeffer realized this in his book of *The Cost of Discipleship.* Cheap grace might be fun and entertaining, but costly grace is the grace of the gospel. The counter measure to worship which tends to musical indulgence is the inclusion of disciplined forms in the service of worship. Songs which are more ascetic and classic than romantic and popular promote the kind of discipline necessary to foster maturity. When a parishioner inquired of the late Dr. Erik Routley why he couldn't have particular music in church, he answered, "You can't have it because it is not good for you."

(7) Prettiness/Grotesqueness Versus Beauty/Truth

Pop music endeavors to be pretty (as in the case of pre-WWII popular forms), flamboyant, downright grotesque, or even perverted (as in the case of the post-WWII pop). Needing immediate punch without listener exertion calls pop to be direct and without listener discomfiture. Ease of consumption means just that—assimilation without aesthetic travail. In order to meet this requirement, pop's appeal must be instantly apparent; it has little time to make its case. The first impression of a song either makes or breaks it. Therefore, the music needs some kind of hook to arrest listener interest. That necessity is met by designing the piece around an element which most directly appeals to a specific audience. Early pop music settled on making the tune "pretty," meaning openly affected, gushing, sentimental, or "nice."

Later, other forms of pop grabbed listeners by exploiting outlandish rhythms, or by featuring unmusical vocal or other sounds so loudly that they tended to mesmerize the listener. Whatever the case, popular music had little depth because it had to expose itself in a manner which held nothing in reserve. The important general impression of the first few bars of a song allowed no highbrow aesthetic impediments to come between the song and its potential audience. It had to opt for a single, apparent, superficial characteristic which made its case without question. From prettiness to sordidness, pop makes its unambiguous stand.

Great Music Takes Another Tack. The concept of great music is to engage the listener in a consideration of the beautiful. Such an engagement requires the composer to invest levels of imagination and craft which, when contemplated, reveal themselves in an endless array of wonderment and awe.

Artistic beauty has little to do with pleasantness. It goes beyond surface decoration and deals with reality. Artists reveal beauty, not by making something pretty (or as is the case with anti-art, by making it singularly kooky), but by making something wholesome. Musical beauty is very much akin to the Hebrew concept of beauty. "How beautiful are the feet of them that preach the gospel of peace, and bring glad tidings of good things!" (Rom 10:15, KJV). Feet are not universal symbols of physical beauty. Quite the contrary. The theistic view holds that good action makes something beautiful.

Integrity and exemplary action result in beauty. Musical beauty is the result of composition which is put together well and has a requisite component of artistic goodness. As universal aesthetic principles are held to and worked out with imagination and integrity, the art work exudes beauty. Thus, art can deal with unpleasant subjects and yet show classic beauty. For example, Benjamin Britten's *War Requiem* is beautiful in its investigation of the horrors of war. Art music's beauty is not the result of making the piece sound attractive but in making it artistically excellent.

The Bible, too, finds beauty and truth in good action. Integrity and wholesomeness yield beauty—beauty that is not merely the outward appearance of a face, for example, but the inner workings of character. The result of doing the right thing may not appear "pleasant," but it will always be "beautiful."

Church Music Mirrors the Gospel. The church needs music programs which disavow prettiness and embrace beauty. Saccharine sweet church music, along with increasingly strident popular forms, need to be eliminated. Worship, if it is to be "worth" something, needs music that mirrors the gospel. Although the crucifixion is not a pretty picture, it is a beautiful one. The reality of Jesus' pain and sorrow is not avoided or glossed over in the gospel accounts.

Jesus, the Lamb of God, central to God's redemptive purpose (a purpose planned from the foundation of the world), did what needed to be done and did it well. Gospel-inspired music needs to give the same attention to its substance and style. Rather than focusing on the outward appearance, as is done in pop music, composers need the kind of compositional conscientiousness that yields profundity of craft. The inner workings of church composition should at least display an affinity for compositional character which is inspired by the integrity of gospel truth. The music of a church indicates more than musical preference—it is the people's collective testimony.

(8) Aesthetic Imbalance Versus Gospel Balance

A key aesthetic concept is the principle of a balanced unity and variety. Such a theorem is fundamental to art of all kinds. Every piece of music ever composed comes under its broad reach: rock, pop, sacred, thrash, or classical. The extent to which a piece fulfills an artistic balance between its unifying devices and its varying ones, we can ascribe worth (as far as this principle goes) to the composition.

This aesthetic principle was placed by God in the natural world. When we look at the leaves of a white oak tree, we can ascertain that every leaf is clearly a white oak leaf. There are no red oak or maple leaves on a white oak. Unity prevails throughout the tree.

Aesthetic Imbalance. Unity is a mark of God's creation; it gives cohesion to every created thing. On the other hand, too much cohesion stifles inventiveness and invites boredom. If we carefully look again at our white oak tree, we notice that while all the leaves are white oak leaves, no two of them are exactly the same. So here we have not only unity but also variety. If only variety were at work, absolute chaos would result. The fact that God made the world well connected yet varied within that connectedness is a clue as to how artistic works ought proceed. Both parts of the proposition are necessary. Unity and variety need to exist in beneficent balance.

Since pop is a music of immediate gratification, it must have some way to accomplish that immediacy. A primary one is to make the music overly repetitious. Pop music is overunified. Certain elements are repeated again and again for the sake of easy assimilation. It might be the reiteration of a cliched harmonic formula repeated *ad nauseam* or a melodic fragment (similarly uninventive) repeated over and over again. Both are without the benefit of meaningful technical variety.

Hardly any pop music exists without the steady hammering of percussion or percussive devices in an incessant cacophony of noise. It is essential for pop to have something about its musical elements which overunifies the form. Much pop of the last several decades gives nihilistic and anarchistic impressions to the listener. Almost always this is accomplished through wild and orgiastic-like singing, playing, and electronic decibel overkill. Even if one can get through this level of chaos, one is bound to find few levels of technical excellence. The impression of complete pandemonium is accomplished through repetition violently, even savagely, executed.

Aesthetic Balance. The best music has aesthetic balance between unity and variety. The numerous ways this can be accomplished marks the profundity of great composition. Musicians committed to honest creativity have at their fingertips a wealth of possibilities which cannot be plumbed even in a lifetime.

God has made the world an inspiration for every composer. At every turn, one finds evidence of the tremendous variety within creation's overall unity. Composers shouldn't try to circumvent God's way of doing things. Listeners also have an obligation to encourage the highest and best arts—those with a balanced unity and variety.

If God so made the world that there is a balance between sameness and difference in nature, we should expect a certain consistency in His dealings with us.

One can readily see unity and variety at work in human relationships with the Almighty. God made us all one family (unity), yet each person in that family is unique (variety). His dealings with each of us are tailored to what He knows of our contextual condition. His relationship with each one is personal and individual.

On the other hand, God has certain limits beyond which He will not go. God will not tolerate the breaking of His laws. All who are redeemed must come through Jesus because He is the only mediator between God and humanity. The variety in His individual dealings with humankind must come within the unity of laws He has laid down. There a is just balance between treating all humans the same and treating each one differently.

God Does Have a Balance. On a deeper level, we find balance in what are essentially mysteries. Humans are so finite and God so infinite that He ultimately resorts to paradox in relating to His creatures. God is at once up and down, inside and out. He is immanent yet transcendent, loving yet our judge. Scripture tells us that the first will be last and the last first; that in losing our lives, we find them. In weakness we are strong, and in giving we receive.

Life (resurrection) comes via death (crucifixion). God directs the affairs of human beings, yet He allows us to choose. He is absolute sovereign, yet He gives us free will. One hymn says, "I sought the Lord, and afterward I knew He moved my soul to seek him, seeking me."[6] Calvinists and Arminians have been arguing the relative merits of opposite positions for centuries. Each armed with biblical chapter and verse eventually arrive at an impasse. These are inexplicable mysteries.

God has a balance between sovereignty and free will, but it is a balance incomprehensible to the finite mind. Both sides of each paradox are fully and completely true. The sides are not watered down to meet in the "middle." The balance is something only the infinite can comprehend. The best we can do is acknowledge the mystery.

What is germane to our consideration here is that music is the best language we have for dealing with mystery. It was Van Cliburn who echoed what musicians have known for centuries: "The other arts, though highly inspirational, are not as mysterious as music, for music is something you cannot see, you can only hear it and feel its impact. I believe it was Plato who said, 'Music is to the mind what air is to the body.'"[7]

Church Music Must Have a Balance. Unfortunately, not all music is able to deal with mystery equally. Pop music is made purposefully light and direct so that there is little ambiguity. That is its exact ethos. Not intent on searching out great mysteries, it aims instead to entertain. Music of creative excellence and aesthetic balance is able to search out the hidden meanings behind the musical symbols. Exactly what happens is a mystery.

Somehow great art touches a nerve deep in the recesses of the heart and mind. We are transported to realms beyond the temporal. In being lifted up, we touch something of the transcendent. The musical and gospel balance between unity and variety ultimately gives way to a balance that is "explained" only by faith.

Church music desperately needs musical art that reinforces the depths of aesthetic wonderment in faith. Entertaining and titillating the congregation with pop music is a sure way to promote infantilism. Church music of excellence, delayed gratification, and a balanced unity/variety is the gospel in musical action. It belongs in worship. The transcendent nature of great music has so much to give—it is unacceptable to substitute pop music for it.

Summary. The foregoing comparison between the traits of pop music and the characteristics of the gospel can be summarized as follows:

Pop Characteristics	Gospel Characteristics
Entertainment	Edification
Novelty	Creativity
Immediate Gratification	Delayed Gratification
Low Standards	High Standards
Subjective Worldview	Objective Worldview
Commercial	Non-Commercial
Indulgent	Disciplined
Pretty/Grotesque	Beauty/Truth
Aesthetic Imbalance	Gospel Balance

The two lists are strikingly opposite one another. Pop characteristics are antipathetic to gospel characteristics. It seems obvious that a music (pop) which is so unlike the thing it is supposed to represent (the gospel) is unable to embody the gospel in its medium of witness (music). Hence, pop is useless in spiritual endeavor. If it is used, it does the cause of Christ much harm by painting an untrue picture of what the Christian life is.

Because the power of music is so strong, worship music which is consistently entertaining, novel, immediately gratifying, standardless, subjective, commercially-driven, undisciplined, pretty or grotesque, and unbalanced, plants the idea in the Christian that faith is like these things. One cannot go to church week after week and be fed religious pop without being negatively affected.

If the enemy were to devise a strategy to keep Christians from realizing their spiritual potential, he could do no better than to include in his plan the use of pop in worship. Yet the incursion of worship and praise music after the model of pop is an accomplished fact in many churches.

Revival of Worship Music Needed. A revival of wholesome worship music is needed. To degrade worship into a religious mimicry of pop culture is not only heartbreaking but an outrage. Every religious leader and congregant should do all in his or her power to protect the integrity of worship. How we worship affects the Body of Christ.

Products of firms like Integrity Music, Inc., Maranatha! Music, or EMI provide not only the general traits of pop, but the more extreme traits of various types of rock music. Driving beats, consistent syncopation, funk-like harmonies, back beats, and clipped, unlyrical "melodic" lines combine in strident cacophony.

The overall musical impression is one of bodily looseness, visceral rhythmic manifestations, and sexual gyration. The vocal timbre called for by this music tells the whole story. Just listen to a professional recording. Hard, harsh, unfocused vocal sounds are the norm. Lyrical beauty gives way to stridency—even brutal screaming. Tension-produced gutteral utterances do horrendous damage to the vocal mechanism. They also damage the aesthetic sensitivity of the listener. No one can listen to this music for long before the decibel overload and the nihilistic sounds corrode one's ability to respond to great music. Adherents of rock dismiss such pronouncements. They tend to call such music simply high-energy music.

For the Christian two things are worth noting: first, rock musicians generally allow that rock is for dance (we're not talking folk dance); second, the definition of musical rhythm implies flow. Ironically, the incessant hammering of rock's beat inhibits flow. This type of repetitive pounding immobilizes true rhythm. The rock beat paralyzes and incapacitates the listener into trancelike states of reflexivity. Very little energy resides in immobility.

The Need to Evaluate Worship Music. Worship leaders should analyze the Praise and Worship music they are giving their congregations. It is understandable for busy people to get caught up in an assembly's preferences (shaped as they are by their daily listening habits) and in the stupendous marketing schemes of Praise and Worship providers.

But music directors, pastors, and others need to evaluate what is happening. Believing that anything a worship company publishes is fine because it publishes "Christian" material is foolish. So-called Christian publishers actually ought to be screened more carefully than others because their materials are used in worship.

Conversely, the gospel list of edification, creativity, delayed gratification, high standards, non-commercialism, discipline, beauty/truth, and gospel balance are traits which can be found in great music. If music directors and pastors wish to find a music which exhibits these traits, they need go no farther than music which is compositionally excellent. Such music need not be complex. It just needs to be good.

Societal Aesthetic Decline. In addition to concern for the quality of worship music, a larger, more inclusive concern exists. The cause of the difficulty with musical standards in the church is, at bottom, the aesthetic decline of the population at large. If the average level of musical appreciation were commensurate with the norms of great music, music directors and pastors would not foist pop music on their congregations. Because people either prefer or tolerate popular music, it has been provided. Because the church has bought into the consumer societal model, people eventually get what they want.

One solution to the dilemma is for the church to encourage the making of, performing of, and listening to great music in the everyday life of the average citizen. The church would surely wage an intensive educational campaign if people were losing their ability to read the Bible. Similarly, the church should mount a drive to reinvigorate music-education programs, amateur music making, local symphonies and choruses, and piano lessons. It should discourage the purchase of pop in favor of "classical" music. It is shortsighted to believe that the Body of Christ has no business with the very things that are causing it so much trouble. We are called to be salt in the world.

Throughout these pages, it has been stressed that popular music is made for entertainment. It is amusement music. The title of one giant company tells it all—Gaylord Entertainment. Word Records and Thomas Nelson were purchased by Gaylord Entertainment for $120 million in January of 1997.[8] The leadership of Gaylord Entertainment obviously felt that the new acquisitions would enhance their product line. It is naive to believe that such musical styles can shed their entertainment stripes and all of a sudden no longer entertain simply because they are used in worship. Calling entertainment music "ministry" doesn't change its entertaining ethos. It is dishonest to imply that religious pop is anything other than entertainment.

CONCLUSION

The foregoing comparative analysis between the values of the gospel and those of pop music has shown that the overall tone of the gospel shuns popularity. A perusal of Jesus' teachings shows a stringency unacceptable to the crowds He taught. Think about His views on worldly possessions or revenge or turning the other cheek. Recall that although the multitudes loved His miracles, they eventually crucified Him.

Wanting an earthly king to put things right, they were not prepared to deal with Jesus' ideas on the Kingdom. Our Lord knew this. He could not have made plainer the gospel position: "Enter ye in at the strait gate: for wide is the gate, and broad is the way, that leadeth to destruction, and many there be which go in thereat: Because strait is the gate, and narrow is the way, which leadeth unto life, and few there be that find it" (Matt 7:13-14, KJV).

Jesus acknowledged that few will choose that Kingdom, the narrow way that leads to life. It has no popular appeal. On the other hand, many will choose the wide gate that leads to destruction. It is the popular way with no Kingdom requirements. The gospel of Christ is a gospel of the hard way, the long way, the disciplined way. Although salvation is free, there is a personal cost in serving God with standards to uphold and right choices to make. The gospel was not watered down for easy acceptability; nor has it been changed to appeal to the adamic nature. The conclusion is inescapable. The gospel was not intended to be "popular."

If the gospel was not made for popularity, it is senseless to put it to musical forms which are made for popularity. In doing so, we promote a different gospel. That is the point of this discussion. Music is not the issue. The gospel is the issue. The problem with pop is not merely that it is poor music; the danger of pop is its diabolical ability to denude the gospel and delude the believer. If there ever was a reason to abandon pop in the sanctuary, this is it. Pop transforms into a caricature of itself whatever it touches—even the gospel.

ENDNOTES

1. Some months after Ken Meyer's book *All God's Children and Blue Suede Shoes* was published (1989), I received a phone call from him. During the conversation he assured me that he had had no knowledge of my *Music and Ministry: A Biblical Counterpoint* (Peabody, MA, 1986) when writing his book, in spite of the fact that both of us, independently, had come to similar conclusions concerning pop music characteristics.

2. Leonard Meyer, "Some Remarks on Value and Greatness in Music," in *Aesthetic Inquiry: Essays on Art Criticism and the Philosophy of Art,* ed. Monroe C. Beardsley and Herbert M. Schueller (Belmont, CA, 1967), p. 263.

3. Ibid., p.178.

4. Christopher Cooper, "Venerable or Not, EMI Was Bound to Be Absorbed," *The Wall Street Journal* (January 25, 2000), section A, p. 13.

5. Ted Olsen, "Will Christian Music Boom for New Owners?" *Christianity Today* (April 28, 1997), p. 80.

6. "I Sought the Lord," *The Hymnal 1982* (New York, 1985), number 689.

7. Van Cliburn, "Great Music a Gift from God," *Arts in Religion* 19 (Winter 1969), p. 3.

8. Ted Olsen, "Will Christian Music Boom for New Owners?," *Christianity Today* (April 28, 1997), p. 80.

Chapter 11
ROCK MUSIC
AND
EVANGELISM
by
Güenter Preuss

Güenter Preuss is currently serving as a full-time Director of Music for the Baden-Wuerttemberg Conference of Seventh-day Adventists in Germany. From 1985 to 1995 he was Chairman of the Music Department at the Adventist College and Theological Seminary at Collonges-sous-Salève, in France. He will shortly defend his doctoral dissertation on reformed hymnody between 1700 and 1870 at the Sorbonne University in Paris.

Preuss has written several studies on music in the synagogue, in the early church, and in youth evangelism. He is actively involved in helping young people overcome their addiction to rock music and make good musical choices.

Shakespeare's dictum, "To be or not to be," can be paraphrased today to read "To rock or not to rock." The battle over whether or not rock music should be used for church worship and evangelism is being fought across denominational lines. This is true not only in America but also in many Western countries, including my own country of Germany.

The use of rock music, especially at Adventist youth rallies in Germany, is creating enormous polemics. For example, on June 19, 1999, a youth rally was organized in Nurnberg which was attended by 1,900 people. A rap song was played for the special music before the sermon.

While some of the youth were delighted by that music, others sent letters of protest to the conference and union officers, who apologized for what had happened. Unfortunately, this was not an isolated incident as Adventist rock bands have become a regular feature at youth rallies.

Some Adventist CCM artists—rock, pop and gospel singers—passionately defend the use of their music for church worship and evangelistic outreach.[1] Others strongly protest against what they perceive to be the music of Babylon. Contenders on both sides of the music debate are pondering their strategies in order to win converts to their cause.

The ongoing debate affects me deeply because music has always been the passion of my life. For the past 15 years I have served, first, as Chairman of the Music Department of the Adventist College and Theological Seminary at Collonges-sous-Salève in France (1985-1995), and, then, as Music Director of the SDA Baden-Wuerttemberg Conference in Germany (1995-2000). I am one of the founders of the European "Adventist Music Society" (1999). The recent invasion of loud pop music into our Adventist churches, especially at youth rallies, has caused me to spend countless hours examining rock music from social, moral, physiological, psychological, and biblical perspectives. This essay represents a brief summary of some aspects of my research.

Objective of This Chapter. This chapter addresses this fundamental question: Can rock music, in whatever form, be used to keep youth within the church and to reach out to secular-minded people outside the church?

It would be presumptuous to assume that this chapter provides the definitive answer to such a hotly debated issue. The best I can hope for is to stimulate a constructive dialogue among church musicians, youth leaders, and administrators. In addressing this divisive issue, it is imperative to learn to disagree without becoming disagreeable to one another.

The chapter is divided in two parts. The first part parts defines the terms and the issues of the current debate over the use of rock music. The second part focuses specifically on the use of rock music to evangelize the secular-minded people, especially the young. Special attention is given to some of the popular arguments used to defend the use of rock music in evangelism.

Part 1
DEFINING THE TERMS

A meaningful analysis of the current debate over the use of rock music for church worship and evangelism presupposes an understanding of the issues involved and of the meaning of the terms used. Thus we attempt first to define the major terms and concepts around which the debate revolves.

Sacred Music. A good place to start is with the definition of "sacred music." There are those who contend that music per se is neither sacred or secular—it is a neutral thing.[2] For them, what makes music "sacred" is not its style, but its lyrics. This popular view is flawed both historically, theologically, and scientifically. Historically, it ignores the fact that the music performed at the Temple, synagogue, and early church was different from the music played at social events for entertainment. As shown in Chapter 7, "Biblical Principles of Music," the music and the instruments associated with dancing and entertainment were excluded from the Jewish and Christian places of worship.

Theologically, the notion that music is a neutral thing is negated by the Christian call to sanctification (1 Thess 5:23)—a call that encompasses all the realms of life, including music. Sanctification presupposes a separation from the world in order to be set aside and consecrated to the service of God. Whatever is used for the service of God is sacred, that is, set aside for holy use. This is true not only of music but of speech as well. The profane language used in the street is inappropriate in church. In the same way, rock music used in bars or nightclubs to stimulate people physically cannot be used in the church to elevate people spiritually.

From a biblical perspective, mixing the sacred with the profane is an abomination to the Lord (Prov 15:8; 15:26; Is 1:13; Mal 2:11). To use the rock idiom in the church or in evangelism means "to offer strange fire before the Lord" (Lev 10:1. KJV), or, as the New English version renders it, "unauthorized fire." Paul emphasizes this principle: "Take no part in the unfruitful works of darkness, but instead expose them" (Eph 5:11).

Scientifically, the notion that music is neutral is discredited by research on the physiological, psychological, and social effects of music. The "neutralists" could be likened to the members of "The Flat Earth Society." They should try their theory on music therapists, psychologists, behavioral scientists, or even on surgeons and dentists who use music as an anasthestic. The power of music to alter the mind and affect the body is a well-established scientific fact.

Sacred music reflects the majesty, harmony, purity, and holiness of God in its melody, harmony, rhythm, text, and performance practices. Its goal is not to entertain or draw attention to the performer's ability, but to glorify God and to inspire believers to conform to the image of God. This is true also of evangelistic music which focuses on God's saving grace and its transforming power in the life of penitent sinners.

Rock Music. Defining rock music is a most difficult task because, during its half-century of existence, it has generated a whole tribe of children and grandchildren. The old "Stones" are still "Rolling," and they have become the literal grandfathers of the newest techno and rap freaks. The old man, called "Rock 'n' Roll," married all kinds of famous women who have given birth to milk-and-coffee babies, such as jazz-rock, classic-rock, latin-rock, polit-rock, and others.

No drug has been left untouched leading to psychedelic, acid rock, and ecstasy-punched rave parties. Techno freaks claim that "their" music is a world of its own, not just another "rock" style. In reality, however, Techno shares the common characteristics of rock music and sets new records in noise, tempo, and ecstatic effects.

The basic musical elements of rock, including "Christian" rock, are volume, repetition, and beat. It is a music designed not to be heard, but to be felt, to be drowned in. "Turn on, dive in and drop out" is the motto and the effect searched for. Its main instruments are amplified electrical guitars, electrical bass, drum set with a dominating one-beat, often accentuated on the second and the fourth beat. Keyboard instruments like piano and synthesizers are often added.

Rock music conveys a physically driven feeling called "groove." This feeling is caused by a slight difference in timing between the main "one-beat" in the drums and the "offbeat" effect of the other instruments or the singers. This "groove feeling" compels people to dance. Some "bang" it out with the whole body.

Rock singing does not use the techniques of classical music based on a relaxed larynx and rich harmonic overtones. Instead, it employs high-pitched strained voicing, using "shout and scat" techniques in order to obtain a top level of emotional touch. The lyrics are secondary to the music.

Scientists speak about "signal listening,"[3] which means that the mention of a word or a short phrase suffices to evoke the topic and to stir up the listener's emotions. Each one of the hundreds of different youth culture groups have their own "signal" vocabulary.

Most rock music does not seek a balance in composition among the melody, harmony, and rhythm. The music is dominated by a relentless rhythmic beat and general loudness which are designed to penetrate the bodies of the listeners with emotional stimulation, while disconnecting, at least in part, their master brain.[4] Gotthard Fermor, a German Protestant theologian who is a strong defender of "Christian" rock, acknowledges that all the elements of rock music are designed to generate an agitated trance.[5]

The capacity of rock music to alter the mind and stimulate the body raises an important question: Can the rock idiom, in whatever version, be legitimately used to worship God in the church and to evangelize the unsaved outside the church? The conclusion of this investigation is NO, for the simple reason that the *medium affects the message*. The medium we use to worship God and proclaim the Gospel determines the quality of our evangelistic efforts and the nature of the message to which people are won.

Contemporary Christian Music. To define Contemporary Christian Music (CCM) is not an easy task, because it comes in a variety of species like the famous 57 brands of Heinz soup. Not all CCM is rock music, although the two are often confounded. It is estimated that about ninety percent of CCM comes in a wide variety of rock styles. The multicolored spectrum of this industry reaches out from the "pastel" of folk, youth-choir music, country, chanson, ballad, gospel, to the "brighter tones" of folk rock, country rock, gospel rock, and, finally, the incredible "blinding colors" of Christian hard core, heavy metal and techno.

Between these extremes is the "glitter" of rap, hip-hop, latin, reggae—all "sanctified" through "Christian" lyrics and an ever-increasing audience of believers and unbelievers. Major Christian bookstores have a large section on music that usually is divided into the following categories: *Contemporary*, which includes every type of popular music; *Praise Worship*, which covers a wide range of rock styles; *Rap, Country, Hard, Alternative, Techno-Drive*, the last three of which include harsh rock styles such as punk, metal, ska, retro, industrial, etc.; *Southern Gospel and Black Gospel*, which incorporate a wide variety of heavy beat music.

Musically speaking, most "Christian" rock is no different from secular rock, except for the lyrics. All the various styles of rock from soft rock to hard rock, acid rock, punk rock, metal rock, rap, etc., are available in a "Christian" version. The deception is self evident. Christians addicted to the secular rock beat can satisfy their craving for rock just by listening to a "Christian" version.

Related to CCM, and dependent upon it, is Contemporary Worship Music (CWM). Many of the same artists involved in CCM are also active in CWM, often recording in the same secular corporations. The significant difference is in the lyrics, which are more biblically based. An example is the song "How Majestic Is Your Name" by Michael W. Smith. Mainly it represents a type of soft rock. Two major problems with CWM is that it generally incorporates rock rhythms with a heavy bass line and is very repetitious. Jesus warned against using vain repetitions in worship (Matt 6:7). This type of music is adopted by more and more Adventist young people who are organizing bands and, in some cases, achieving professional status.[6]

Liberals Versus Conservatives. The debate over the use of modified rock music in church worship and evangelism involves two groups. On the one side are the so-called "Liberals," who say: "We must keep our youth in the church"; "We must update"; "We must use new methods to reach the secular mind." The Liberals tend to overemphasize God's love and forgiveness in order to justify the use of questionable methods of evangelism.

On the other side of the debate are the so-called "Conservatives," who say: "Do the youth dictate what we are to do?" "Where is the message of the Bible when we lower our standards?"; "Can we convert the world by bringing worldly music into the church?"

"Liberals" accuse "Conservatives" of being "Puritan body haters." "You cannot bear enjoyment," they say. In some cases, the criticism is valid. Some "conservatives" view the Christian life as gloom and doom. They label as sinful any legitimate expression of joyful excitement. This is not right because Christians who have experienced Christ's redeeming grace have reason to shout for joy.

The real issue behind the whole debate is the method of interpreting the Bible. While the "Conservatives" are sometimes accused of interpreting Paul's warnings against worldliness too narrowly, the "Liberals" can be accused of taking David's dance out of context in order to justify rock evangelism. Each side tends to find rational and biblical reasons for their positions.

Part 2
ROCK MUSIC AND EVANGELISM

To define the role of music in evangelism is problematic for two major reasons, one biblical and the other contemporary. From a biblical perspective, music is never used as a medium for evangelizing the Gentiles. The only Bible text which could be twisted to support a form of music evangelism is Acts 16:25, where we are told that Paul and Silas, while languishing in a jail at Philippi, were "singing hymns to God, and the prisoners were listening to them."

We are not told whether the singing was intended as a witness to the prisoners or as an expression of confidence in God's protection. Most likely both motives were present. Whatever the motives were, this text offers little insight into the apostolic use of music for evangelism.

In the rest of the Bible, music is always presented in the context of the worship of God and not of evangelistic outreach to the Gentiles. As shown in Chapter 7, the music in the Temple was "sacrifice-centered," praising God for the provision of salvation through the sacrificial offering. In the synagogue, the music was "Word-centered," praising the Lord by chanting the very words of Scripture.

In the early church, music was "Christ-centered," extolling Christ's redemptive accomplishment. Any evangelistic impact of the worship music was indirect. Gentiles who heard God's people singing in some instances may have been attracted and converted to the worship of the true God. No explicit indications, however, suggest that music was ever used as a means to attract Gentiles to the Christian faith.

Ecumenical Music. From a contemporary perspective, the role of music in evangelism is a problem because ecumenism discourages proselytizing among Christian churches. Today evangelism is defined more in terms of interconfessional communion than of proclamation of the Gospel as understood by different denominations. Christian rock artists, stemming from different churches, espouse virtually the same expression of a minimal Gospel. Doctrinal differences do not really matter and should not be expressed in song. What matters is joining together in praising the Lord. Even the whole "pop life style" is often regarded by theologians as something "authentic" that should be accepted rather than condemned.[7]

Evangelistic music, instead of bringing people from the world to Christ, often brings the world's agenda into the church, thus undermining the identity and mission of the church. Music, in general, and evangelistic rock music, in particular, stand in danger of becoming a sign of the times by participating in the destruction of the very Christian values it wants to communicate.

Evangelistic Music Versus Church Music. Many believe that evangelistic music should be different from church music because its goal is to reach people where they are. This creates a gap between evangelistic and worship music, which, if not properly controlled, can ultimately result in the establishment of new churches characterized by their new worship styles. The process can be graphically described.

First, there is the conviction that secularized people must be reached by means familiar to them ("pick them up where they are"). By doing this, a gap is created between the music service at the evangelistic crusade and that of the weekly worship service at the church. This leads to the second step which involves changing the old-fashioned worship style at the church into a new "modern" style in order to accommodate the secular-minded people who are brought into the church.

The result is step three, when societal trends set the agenda for the church which becomes caught in a never-ending race trying to keep up with the latest fad. Today the church chooses "Christian" rock music, tomorrow it will adopt "Christian" drama, and the following day "Christian" lottery or gambling. Incidentally, all of these activities are already taking place within some churches. The end result is that the evangelistic rock music that was intended to reach and change the people of the world ultimately transforms the church itself into the likeness of the world.

But the spiral of change does not stop here. The fourth step occurs when pluralism develops within each denomination. Groups sharing the same tastes organize themselves in separate congregations. Then comes the last step when different churches with the same worship styles approach each other to form a new denomination.

New Worship-Style Denominations. Today a number of new denominations have come into existence, not because of the discovery of new biblical truths, but because of new worship styles that better satisfy the expectations of the baby-boomer generation. The market-driven "seeker-churches" and the "body-oriented" charismatic movements constitute new brands of evangelism that claim to be role models for the Christian world to follow.

The issue is no longer dogmatic unity but worship unity.[8] Music becomes more important than biblical teachings, because the goal is to give people what they want to experience now rather than what they need to know to become citizens of God's eternal Kingdom.

This process helps us understand why the adoption of pop music is becoming a hot issue within the Seventh-day Adventist Church. Many of its members fear that the adoption of a new style of worship, driven by pop music, ultimately will undermine the church's prophetic claim. They are concerned that if the current trend continues, Adventists, who are known as "the people of the Book," eventually will become known as "the people of rock," like many contemporary evangelical churches.

The solution to the dilemma is to be found not in eliminating any distinction between evangelistic and church music, but in keeping the two in close proximity. There is a need for a "decrescendo" of musical styles in each evangelistic meeting, from a more lively type of music to more meditative music, which predisposes people to reflect on the truths of God's Word presented at the meetings.

Two Strategies. The debate over whether "to rock or not to rock" in evangelism largely stems from two opposite strategies. One strategy is "Message-oriented"—the church must preach the message of salvation without looking for results that could be generated by the use of pop music. The second strategy is "Seeker-friendly," believing that it must adopt the idiom of the people to be reached.

The "Seeker-friendly" Christians defend the use of rock music in evangelism because they believe that rock is part of today's culture and thus is needed to penetrate the rock generation. They justify their strategy by referring to Jesus who has sent us into the world (John 17:18), and to Paul, who said: "To those outside the law I became as one outside the law" (1 Cor. 9:21). Unfortunately, they ignore the second half of the verse: "not being without law toward God but under the law of Christ" (1 Cor. 9:21).

"The law of Christ" did not allow Paul to use the popular Greek choral songs or Roman plays to reach the masses.

Had Paul been a "Seeker-friendly" strategist who was determined to reach the masses using their philosophical or musical idioms, then he would have become a popular evangelist, drawing capacity crowds wherever he went. But this was hardly the case. In his letters he tells us that almost everywhere he met opposition, persecution, even stoning sometimes. To survive, he often fled from place to place. The reason is that Paul chose to preach the Gospel, not by couching it in the popular idioms of the Roman culture, but by proclaiming it in clear and compelling words.

With prophetic insight Paul warned that in the last days some will adopt a compromising strategy. "For the time is coming when people will not endure sound teaching, but having itching ears they will accumulate for themselves teachers to suit their own likings" (2 Tim 4:3). The mention of "itching ears" reminds one of the use of pop music today to satisfy the "itching ears" of the rock generation.

On the opposite side, we have today the "Message-oriented" Christians who carefully analyze any innovative method before using it, because for them what counts is the proclamation of the message. "We are to preach, not to look for success," they say. Jesus was also almost alone at the end, yet His apparent defeat became His greatest victory.

A negative attitude toward innovative methods that can enrich church worship and improve the effectiveness of the evangelistic outreach is deplorable. Christ Himself was a keen observer of the culture of His people and borrowed from it valuable object lessons for his teaching. Like Christ, we need to be sensitive to the contemporary culture, including music, and borrow whatever can be legitimately used to reach men and women with the message of salvation.

Music and Culture. The music used in church and in evangelism must be sensitive to culture. This is true not only in Western countries but also in developing countries, where, sometimes, missionaries ignore the native music and expect the people to learn and adopt Anglo hymns. That raises a question: Is the music of our worship services and evangelistic campaigns serving only the prevailing culture or enhancing also the content of the message? Our goal should be to meet both objectives. We need to carefully analyze the culture and borrow those elements that can enhance the preaching of the full message. God's message needs to be heard in a way that is relevant to people, but it must not be distorted by idioms like rock music, that contradict its values.

Evangelistic music needs to be both "Seeker-friendly" *and* "Message-oriented." It needs to be understood by the listener, but it must not distort the message. Evangelistic music can borrow valuable material from everywhere (from the past and from other countries), but it must avoid the music that fails to portray the beauty of Christ's character and the seriousness of the whole plan of salvation. Most rock music fails to give a "sacred shiver."

Evangelistic music must reflect Christ's courage in confronting the culture of His time with the principles of God's Kingdom. Christ did not meet the expectations of His contemporaries, not even those of His disciples. Similarly, Paul summons believers to confront the world with the principles of the Gospel, rather than conforming to its values (Rom 12:1).

The use of rock music in evangelism should be avoided because it reminds young people of their rebellious past. It can serve as a regression tool towards their own childhood, as psychologists explain it.[9]

By using rock in evangelism, Christians contribute to the general increase of physical stimulations and aggressiveness.[10] Happiness is mixed with erotic undertones and joy with aggressiveness.[11] We should be messengers of God's real joy and peace.

The use of rock in evangelism is inappropriate, not only because its values are inimical to the Christian faith, but also because it represents a pantheistic and syncretistic form of religion which invites its followers to plug into the supernatural by means of dance, sex, and drugs. Using such a medium in evangelism is like introducing "strange fire" in God's House.

Rock Music Draws the Crowds. A major argument used to defend the use of rock music in evangelism is the fact that it draws huge crowds at pop Gospel concerts. No one disputes this fact. But this is hardly surprising since rock has become an indispensable part of today's youth culture. Many teenagers are so immersed in rock music that a Gospel concert where this music is played provides them with an outlet to enjoy their music without the condemnation of their parents or church.

Pop Gospel concerts do not call enough for spiritual or moral commitment. They mainly offer young people what they want—entertainment. Pop gospel musician John Allen acknowledges the danger of such concerts: "It seems undeniable that most of the audience is there simply to enjoy the music, not to think hard about anything: and there is a real danger of the emergence of a 'Greenbelt Christians,' consisting of semi-converted, shallowly committed teenagers whose Christianity means little more than that the enjoyment of festival-going."[12]

We live today in a pleasure-oriented society, where people have a much greater appetite for what is amusing and pleasing than for what is edifying. Empiric research has shown that adolescents tend to listen less and less carefully even to their own music.[13] It is becoming increasingly difficult to motivate people to attend meetings where the only attraction is God and the study of His Word. But this must never become an excuse for giving people what they want.

Our biblical mandate is to present to people what they need to hear: God's plan and expectations for their lives. The claim that rock music draws the crowds is irrelevant from a biblical perspective. Our real concern is to be true to principle, not to be popular.

If apostolic Christianity was to be judged by the number of people converted, then it was hardly a successful movement. Why? Because by the end of the first century, all the evangelistic efforts conducted over a period of almost seventy years, had converted only about 0.6 percent of the population of the Roman empire. This amounted to one million Christians in a population of about 181 million.[14] By contrast, in the fourth century when Christianity became a popular movement and pagans entered the church by the thousands, the result was spiritual decline and apostasy of the church. This shows that numbers can be deceptive. Massive conversions sometimes bespeak of spiritual decline and apostasy.

Only Rock Music Reaches Teenagers. We hear people constantly saying: "Teenagers today will not come to church. We can only reach them with rock music." Is this true? Surprisingly, there are many evangelical churches where no rock music is played, and yet they are filled with young people. Could it be that those who are clamoring for rock music are not the *unsaved* after all?

John Blanchard raises these pointed questions: "Is it true that it is the *unsaved* who insist on the music? Or it is nearer the truth to say that it is young *Christians* who enjoy it so much that they insist on it? Is it true that the unconverted friends of Christians adamantly refuse to attend any evangelistic presentation except a musical one? Or is it truer to say that they are almost never asked? Isn't it true that young Christians invite friends to Gospel concerts as a first resort rather than as a last resort?"[15]

If the reports are correct that thousands of young people are saved every year through "Christian" rock music, then one wonders where they are? If the claim about mass conversion made by so many rock groups is correct, then we should see a noticeable decrease in violence, drug use, civil disobedience, and premarital sex. Unfortunately, this is not the case. The reality is that this music of entertainment confirms patterns of aggressiveness and violence.

Rock Music Produces Excellent Results. Promoters of "Christian" rock music claim that God is blessing their efforts and thousands of young people are saved. Mylon LeFevre, known as "The Solid Rocker," claims that tens of thousands have signed their decision card at his concerts: "There are 52,000 people who have signed a little cards that says, 'Tonight, for the first time, I understand who Jesus is and how He does things, and I want Him to be my Lord.'"[16]

The popular Christian press reports similar accounts of mass "decisions" registered at pop Gospel concerts. We are thankful for every soul who is saved regardless of the method of evangelism. There is no reason to doubt that some of the rock bands are genuinely concerned for the salvation of young people through their music and concerts. But the fact that God uses such means to save people is not of itself an indication that every means that works is biblically valid. I believe that people are saved, not because of Christian rock, but *in spite of* it.

Franky Schaeffer perceptively points out: "The excuse that 'sometimes people are saved' is no excuse at all. People have been saved in concentration camps because God can bring good from evil, but this does not justify the evil."[17] Moses obtained excellent results when he struck the rock at Kadesh-barnea and produced enough water for all the Israelites and their livestock (Num 20:1-20). Yet God punished him for what he did.

Evangelistic methods must be tested, not by their results, but by their faithfulness to biblical principles. When evangelism is not controlled by biblical teaching, then it becomes a performance in manipulative skills, rather than a manifestation of the power of truth. True salvation comes through the proclamation of true doctrine. A corrupted or watered down presentation of the Gospel through a rock concert makes the decisions suspect.

Paul Blanchard reports on a survey of 1,829 young people conducted by his organization in England, Wales, Scotland, and Northern Ireland. The young people came from seven major denominations. "The poll indicated that of the 1,829 young people concerned, only thirty-nine, or 2.1%, were converted at a Gospel concert. (Even this tiny figure almost certainly gives an exaggerated picture; the poll did not ask whether the musical presentation was the specific means of conversion)."[18]

The reports of mass "decisions" for Christ made at pop Gospel concerts are suspect, not only because of the message but also because of the atmosphere created by the music itself. Powerful music can produce emotional decisions, but a biblical conversion is not the result of an emotional, unthinking response. It involves a genuine repentance wrought by the Holy Spirit through the preaching of the biblical Gospel.

At most pop Gospel concerts, the music is so loud and raucous that the words are hardly heard. How can the Gospel be presented in its convicting power when the words can hardly be heard? This exposes the contradiction of the defenders of "Christian" rock. On the one hand, they claim that the lyrics make the music Christian, yet, on the other hand, the lyrics can hardly be heard. If they were serious about their claim, they would reduce the volume of the instrumental music so that the message of the songs could be heard clearly and distinctly.

The big question is whether rock music really communicates the Gospel without distortion. After all, it is vitally important for the Gospel to be biblically received. The acceptance of the Gospel presupposes the use of the *mind*. "You shall love the Lord your God with all your heart, and with all your soul, and with all your *mind*" (Mark 12:30). In view of the fact that in biblical psychology, heart, soul, and mind are used interchangeably to refer to the intellect, the mental response to God is paramount. Rock music, however, is designed to be felt, not to be heard. Its appeal is to the body and not to the mind. How then can a person understand the Gospel through rock when its music bypasses the mind? The rock fan may understand the rock signals (whatever they mean), but he can hardly understand the Gospel.

Practical Suggestions for Youth Rallies. In planning for youth rallies like concerts or music festivals, several considerations should be kept in mind. First of all, the motivation of the event should not be to imitate the popular rock scene. We need to seek healthy alternatives to the music played in discotheques and night clubs. Of course, friends can and should be invited, but they should be informed about the special nature of the event.

In planning for the music program, two considerations should be kept in mind. What thought associations will the music produce and what what will be the possible physical impact? Organizers should ensure that the music is played with moderate loudness.[19] A pleasant but sober atmosphere should characterize the meeting. Emphasis should be on a strong spiritual message, and on congregational singing rather than on performing bands. Creative playfulness should be a self-evident fact and reality. Young people need to experiment. We must inspire and challenge the youth, while being open to some unusual results. But youth leaders should never abandon their responsibility of providing loving guidance.

The volume of the instruments accompanying the singing should be very moderate. They should support the singing and not supplant it. Often I have seen that young people do not become enthusiastically involved in singing is because the music is too loud and they cannot hear their voices. The song leader directing the congregational singing should ensure that the musicians follow his directives in keeping the volume under control.

Clapping, tapping, and swinging are out of place in the church, but they could be allowed in a moderate way at outdoor rallies. Great care should be taken, however, to prevent the unruly behavior charac-teristic of rock concerts, with stamping, whistling, yelling, etc. The instrumentalists, the song leader, and the speakers should work to-gether to ensure that the singing and the preaching reflect the distinc-tive characteristic of Adventist meetings. Times of joy should alternate with times of meditation, and even quietness.

The program should start with fresh and lively music to arouse interest and establish a good contact with the people. The function of the music is to serve as a servant of the Word. Simple heart-to-heart preaching and short biblical messages should be the main emphasis in any youth evangelistic program. At the end, the music should be calmer and medita-tive, inviting the youth to renew their commitment to the Lord.

Youth cultures split into more and more different global cells such as bikers, surfers, fun sporters, etc. Each one has its own musical language. This offers an opportunity to create specific Christian or Evangelical or Adventist musical subculture. Convincing presentations will at least reach the earnest seekers among today's youth.

Musicians, pastors, and teachers should gather young people around them and plan together how to create an authentic Adventist music program suitable for church service and evangelism. They should take the time to choose together appropriate music for the occasion. Classical music presented with enthusiasm and quality can still impress young people. The same goes for carefully performed folk styles.[20]

CONCLUSION

The search for an effective way to reach secular-minded people with the Gospel has led many church leaders and musicians to adopt various versions of rock music for communicating the Christian message.[21] We commend the motives of these people, but we question the legitimacy of their method for several reasons.

Rock music is not a neutral vehicle for Christian lyrics. The music itself is a powerful language. Rock music in evangelism works on imagination and on thought associations, as any music. But rock music misrepresents the claims of the Gospel by encouraging worldly values. It makes people believe that they are all right, when in reality they desperately need a radical change in their lives—a conversion experience. As a medium which promotes instant gratification, violence, drugs, sex, and pantheistic self-redemption, rock music perverts the message of the Gospel simply because the medium affects the message.

Rock music in evangelism undermines the effort to construct a strong moral foundation in the youth. Instead of promoting self-control, temperance, respect for authority, and purity, it teaches self-indulgence, intemperance, disobedience, pleasure seeking, and immature behavior.

Rock music impairs the discriminatory sense of right and wrong built within our conscience. The constant puffing up of emotions destroys guilt barriers. It wraps people up in a guiltless and shameless self-satisfaction that ultimately makes the recognition of evil impossible. Christ calls for the recognition of our lostness in order that we might receive His gracious provision of salvation. Listeners should capture a glimpse of divine awe in order to sense God's calling to a complete commitment, to a change in life-style, including music habits.

Rock evangelism confirms the "rock religion" which fosters a mixture of half-conscious religious feelings and behaviours that tend towards ecstasy and the occult. It is imperative for Christians to keep a safe distance from such idolatrous practices.

Rock music also has a strong physical impact mainly through its volume and pounding beat. The music needs to be loud in order to be "felt" by the listeners. The pounding beat of rock leads to dancing, stamping, or head banging. The result of this heavy load of sound energy is that the mind switches off and leaves the field to the emotions to take over. Christians should not allow their minds to be impaired by sounds or drugs, because it is through their minds that they honor God by living sanely and soberly.

God's proven method of evangelism is the "foolishness of preaching" (1 Cor 1:21. KJV). He has committed to us the message of reconciliation (2 Cor 5:18). Our responsibility is not to contaminate this message with worldly idioms, like rock music. There is no need for the manipulation and stimulation of rock music to save people. Evangelism has been and is greatly aided by Christlike music presented by Christlike performers; but ultimately, it is the proclamation of the Word of God, accompanied by the convicting power of the Holy Spirit, that brings people into a saving relationship with Jesus Christ. May our evangelistic efforts be centered on the Rock of Ages, rather than on the rock music of our age.

ENDNOTES

1. The individual testimonies are impressive. Jeff Trubey, "Making Waves," *Adventist Review* (July 17, 1997), pp. 8-13.

2. John Blanchard, *Pop Goes the Gospel: Rock in the Church* (Durham, England, 1991), p. 24.

3. See, Dörte Hartwich-Wiechell, *Pop-Music* (Koln, Germany, 1974), p. 30. She speaks of the small units that people need in order to be stimulated by pop music.

4. Wolf Muller-Limmroth, "Neurophysiologische und psychomentale Wirkungen der Musik" ("Neurophysiological and Psychomental Effects of Music"), in *Musik und Medizin* 2 (1975), p. 14.

5. Gotthard Fermor, "Das religiöse Erbe in der Popmusik—musik—und religionswissenschaftliche Perspektiven" ("The Religious Heritage in Pop Music—Perspectives from Musicology and Religious Sociology"), in Wolfgang Kabus, ed., *Popularmusik, Jugendkultur und Kirche (Popular Music, Youth Culture and Church)* (Frankfurt, Germany, 2000), p. 44. (Lecture at the Youth Music Workshop in Friedensau, May 8, 1997).

6. See, Jeff Trubey (note 1).

7. See several contributions to the volume on popular music, youth culture, and church, edited by Wolfgang Kabus, an German Adventist church music professor: *Popularmusik, Jugendkultur und Kirche* (Bern, Switzerland, 2000).

8. Michael S. Hamilton, "The Triumph of the Praise Songs," *Christianity Today* (July 12, 1999), pp. 29-30.

9. Josef Hoffmann (a psychoanalyst), "Popmusik, Pubertät, Narzissmus," *Psyche* 11 (1988), pp. 961-980. He sees rock music, but also narcissm (self-centeredness) and merging with the cosmos, as positive tools in becoming an adult. The high tenor voice and the screaming of the rock singers expresses a "grandiose self," the mixing of father, mother, and babe, and the pounding beat would guide the industrialized world into adulthood.

10. Michael Kneissier, "Unser Gehirn baut sich soeben radikal um!" ("Our brain is rebuilding itself radically"), *P.M.* (a weekly journal) 11 (1993), pp. 14-20, relating the research of over 25 years of the *Münchner Gesellschaft für Rationelle Psychologie* (Society for Efficient Psychology, Munich) under the direction of Henner Ertel.

11. Microphones allow the singer to come directly into the intimate zone of the listener. See on eroticism, Frank Garlock and Kurt Woetzel, *Music in the Balance* (Greenville, SC, 1992), pp. 92-97.

12. John Blanchard (note 2), p. 98.

13. Klaus-Ernst Behne, a German musicologist, has conducted an internationally recognized study of 150 adolescents between the ages of 11 to 17, and found an alarming tendency towards a decline of sensitivity towards music. ("The development of 'Musikerleben' ['the perception and experience of music'] in adolescence—How and why young people listen to music," in I. Deliege and J. Sloboda, *Perception and Cognition of Music* (Hove, England, 1997), pp. 143-159.) Musical taste is well established already at 11 years of age and does not change considerably. Concentrated and conscious music listening declines rapidly as time goes on.

14. See, David B. Barrett, ed., *World Christian Encyclopedia: A Comparative Study of Churches and Religions in the Modern World A.D. 1900-2000* (Oxford, England, 1982), p. 3.

15. John Blanchard (note 2), p. 145.

16. Cited by John Styll, "Mylong LeFevre: The Solid Rocker," *CCM Magazine* (March 1986), p. 6.

17. F. Schaeffer, *Addicted to Mediocrity* (New York, 1965), p. 22.

18. John Blanchard (note 2), p. 109.

19. My own measurement of the volume at Christian youth rallies indicates that the levels frequently reach beyond 100 decibels. This is higher than the 90 to 95 decibels the German government commission recommends as the upper limit for discoteques. See, *Zeitschrift für Lärmbekämpfung* [Journal Fighting Noise Pollution] 42 (1995), p. 144.

20. Pierre and Gisela Winandy, "Not All Youth Want Rock," *Adventists Affirm* (Spring 1998), pp. 25-29; John Thurber, "Adventist Youth Prevail with Calm, Dignified Music," *Adventists Affirm* (Spring 1999), pp. 41-47.

21. For the past several years I have examined the literature produced both the by defenders and attackers of "Christian" rock. Some of the significant publications defending the use of "Christian" rock are: Steve Miller, *The Contemporary Christian Music Debate: Worldly Compromise or Agent of Renewal?* (Wheaton,I L, 1993); Dan Peters, Steve Peters, and Cher Merrill, *What About Christian Rock?* (Minneapolis, MN, 1986); John M. Frame, *Contemporary Worship Music: A Biblical Defense*

(Phillipsburg, NJ, 1997); Wolfgang Kabus (Adventist professor of church music, now retired; ed.), *Popularmusik, Jugendkultur und Kirche* (*Popular music, Youth culture and Church*), (Frankfurt, Bern, 2000, "Friedensauer Schriftenreihe" - series of publication from the Adventist University at Friedensau/Germany, Vol. 2). This is a highly sociological approach to the study of rock music.

Chapter 12
ROCK MUSIC
and
CULTURE
by
Eurydice V. Osterman

Eurydice V. Osterman is Professor of Music at Oakwood College, in Huntsville, Alabama. She earned the Doctor of Musical Arts at the University of Alabama in 1988. She has presented numerous music seminars throughout the United States, Europe, Africa, South America, Bahamas, and Bermuda. She serves as organist, choir director, and a Board member of the American Guild of Organists.

Osterman has received awards for her compostions and recordings. She has composed music for the University of Alabama Symphony Orchestra, the General Conference Session of Seventh-day Adventists, and the London Chorale on BBC. Several of her articles have been featured in a textbook on music. She is the author of the book *What God Says About Music*.

The music played at the inauguration of Nelson Mandela as President of South Africa was radically different from the music played at the inauguration of William Clinton as President of the United States. The former was driven by excitement, jubilation, and dance. The latter was characterized by a stately and somewhat somber mood. The two presidential inaugurations were celebrated with two different cultural styles of music. Was the American music better than the South African one? Obviously not! Each music style was appropriate for the culture in which the events took place.

Culture entails the characteristic features and behavior of a group of people and the ideas and values that they espouse. "It is the sum total of their language, dialect, thoughts, actions, and behavior that has been learned and transmitted through the years."[1] Culture is the badge of identity of a people. Consequently, a knowledge and understanding of the language, customs, music, and other elements of culture increases one's level of tolerance, acceptance, and appreciation of a particular culture. What was once unfamiliar can be understood on its own terms—as the people understand it. Today we have greater opportunities for learning about different cultures, due to technology, travel, and media which have made this world smaller—a global village. Instant communication exposes us daily to different cultures in a way that was unthinkable in the past.

Elements of Cultural Music. Each culture defines its music according to its own criteria. These involve value judgments about *aesthetics*—judgments about what is proper and beautiful; *contexts*—the notion of when and how often music is performed as well as the occasion and its association with lifestyles; *social organization*—the age, gender, and racial and ethnic composition of the group; *status of musicians*—that is, their training or lack of it; *stylistic elements*—the characteristic sounds, levels of pitch, meter, timbre, and dynamics that a group understands as its own; *genres*—the standard units of the repertory; *text*—the way language and music are mixed together; *composition*—that is, whether the music is composed by an individual or by a group; *transmission*—that is, whether the music is transmitted by a system of notation, by imitation, or by memory; and *movement*—the physical activity, the dance, and the musical instruments used in the production of the music. These are some of the elements that help define the music of a particular culture.

Ethnic music is generally based upon an oral tradition and originates from or is shaped by its role and function in society. Music in non-Western societies generally has a religious or philosophical context, and musical practices are determined by value systems within that particular framework which seek to preserve the sacred or mystical nature of music. Each group has its own sources of sound, scale system, timbre, selection and arrangement of pitches, intervals, and vocal styles (sometimes hovering around a single tone, speech inflections, timbre changes, sliding tones, shakes of the voice, etc.) which are all a part of the characteristic sonority.

Most often, ethnic music is uncultivated and engenders an emotional response from the listener. Many elements of music are linked to words or text, with pitch variations that are subtle but essential. They are simple in texture and consist of repetition or repetition with change which is fundamental, and have their own characteristic rhythm and harmony. They also have their own characteristic instruments—chorodophones or strings; aerophones or winds, idiophones or percussion; and membranophones or drums.[2]

African Music. In the African culture, music encompasses ceremonial life, work, and leisure activities. Music has been transmitted orally and has served to communicate history and current events. It also has preserved communal values and solidarity, expressed feelings that could not be verbalized, and created a way to maintain a spiritually healthy community.

African music has no theoretical base. It is functional and social in purpose—dance, entertainment, rituals, and ceremonials. By being a tonal language, pitch height is vital to the meaning of words. Therefore, it is easy to make a transition from speech to songs. In some instances, there is a fine line of demarcation between the two.

Some characteristics of the performance are call and response, vocal polyphony, spontaneity, slurs, slides, and glissandos. Because the music is unrehearsed, there is no concern for a right or wrong way of singing. The music is designed to invoke a response from the listener as an acknowledgment of what is being said. The body also can be used to help beat rhythms or to dance.[3]

The cultural diversity of music reminds us that variety is God's gift to humanity. Being a God of variety, He understands that all forms of worship are shaped by culture and environment. Today God is worshiped in a variety of ways according to culture, style, and geographic location—even within the same denomination. With such a cultural diversity, it is no wonder that there is controversy about what is acceptable or unacceptable music for worship.

Objectives of This Chapter. The overall objective of this chapter is to consider whether or not culture really matters to God, especially when it comes to church music. Is there one particular music style that God expects us to adhere to? Are our value judgments about *God's ideal* worship music really His values?

The more specific objective is to discuss whether or not the use of rock music, in its various versions, can be legitimately justified as a cultural expression of the African-American heritage. From a Christian perspective, should music be evaluated in terms of its cultural association or on the basis of the biblical distinction between the sacred and profane, which applies to any culture?

With these questions in mind, this chapter has two parts. The first part looks at rock music in its cultural setting. Specifically, it examines the prevailing assumption that rock music is part of the African-American heritage and, consequently, is a legitimate form of expression. Our study shows that this assumption is inaccurate. There is a substantial difference between the structural components of rock music and those of African-American heritage music.

The second part of the chapter suggests some basic principles to guide Christians in making good musical choices. Consideration is given to six important characteristics of sacred music. The aim is to help the reader define what constitutes sacred music, not on the basis of biblical principles but of cultural concerns.

Part 1
ROCK MUSIC AND ITS CULTURAL ROOTS

The roots of rock music are generally traced back into the West African slave culture, which was eventually taken to the West Indies and finally to the southern part of the United States. Primitive, home-made instruments were gradually replaced by the clarinet, guitar, trumpet, trombone, double-bass, and drums, all of which were used to create a special rhythm.

When African slaves were brought to America, they were stripped of two very important elements of any culture, namely, music and language. They were forced to speak and sing in a vernacular that was totally foreign to them. As time passed, however, they developed a vocabulary, a dialect, and a music that became distinctly their own.

Negro Spirituals. Music played a very important role in the lives of the slaves, because it enabled them to express their emotions according to their own traditional culture rather than of that dictated by their masters. Their music became known as "Negro Spiritual." Their songs were inspired by the hardships experienced by the slaves: whippings, beatings, destruction of the family unit, lynching, and other abuses.

Although Negro Spirituals had a religious or philosophical context, they became the community songs based upon oral traditions emanating from Africa. Their content centered around aspects of everyday life and served as an aid for participants to interact and communicate with each other, to create solidarity, to relieve the monotony of work, and to alleviate fatigue. The Negro Spiritual idiom also gave the community an opportunity to comment on its own situation while providing each member with a sense of belonging in the midst of a confusing and terrifying world. Though rhythmic in music, Negro Spirituals always expressed the hope of God's deliverance of His people.

Because the slaves were denied the right to learn reading or writing, they had to learn a new language by ear. This resulted in the evolution of a new dialect which is reflected in the rhythm of many Spirituals and their arrangements. The Spirituals became the songs sung in a strange land, giving inspiration to a people denied their instrument of communication (drum) and forced to accept the Puritan idea that their dance and former life in Africa was sinful.[4]

The swing of the spiritual is also a part of the religious experience of the African American and is more of a feeling and a nuance than a notation. For this reason, performance is based upon popular entertainment practices.

It is unfortunate that many of the Negro Spirituals are becoming lost or unknown to this younger generation because they are so seldom sung and passed along. The result is that many African Americans do not know their own musical heritage, especially the circumstances under which the Spirituals were born. Instead, the youth of today tend to gravitate toward contemporary Black music, which they claim as their own "heritage" music.

Black Classical Music Heritage. Black youth today ignore the contribution of Black composers who created and performed classical art forms long before and even during slavery days. For example, Ignatius Sancho (1729-1780) wrote the book entitled *Theory in Music*, dedicated to the Princess Royal of England, and composed Twelve Country Dances for harpsichord (1779). Chavalier de Saint Georges (1739 or 45-1799) was a violinist and conductor for the Opera's Academie Royal in Paris and wrote operas, symphonies, string quartets, concertos, and more.

The Rev. Richard Allen (1760-1831) was the author of the first Black church hymnal. George A. Polgreen Bridgetower (1779- 1860) was a good friend of Ludwig van Beethoven and was so highly respected that he was hired by the Prince of Wales to play in the court orchestra.

Francis "Frank" Johnson (1792-1844) was an American Black composer from Philadelphia who became the first to win acclaim in America and in England and take a musical ensemble abroad to perform in Europe. He was also the first to introduce the promenade concert to the America, the first to establish a school of Black musicians, and the first to have his compositions published as sheet music (1818). The list goes on.[5]

This sampling of Black composers and performers suffices to show that Blacks do have a legitimate classical musical heritage and do not need to seek their musical roots in rock music, a music that rejects Christian beliefs and values. Today, over five thousand Black composers and performers have recorded. This information is significant because it shows that Black music and musicians no longer need to be relegated to the rock genre.

Negro Spirituals, beautiful though they may be, represent a sad but significant chapter in the history of Black people. Their contribution to religious music has not been fully recognized. One reason Blacks tend to gravitate toward rock music and claim it as their "heritage" music is because rock does not have the negative association that spirituals have. Black rock musicians and performers are respected for their talent and are portrayed as prosperous individuals who have contributed to the music scene. Hence, they become the icons and role models for those Blacks who seek to rise above the stigma of the past.

Rock Music and African Music Heritage. The prevailing assumption that rock music is a legitimate expression of African-American heritage ignores the significant differences that exist between the two. African-American heritage music is predominantly melodic and is based upon the rhythm of the dialect. Rock music, on the other hand, is based upon and is driven by a beat that overshadows and dominates all other musical elements.

The roots of the rock beat are to be found not in the religious music of the African-American heritage, but in secular and often irreligious music known as "Rhythm and Blues." This music became the expression of those Blacks who strayed away from or rejected the Christian faith.

They wanted to become respected entertainers by playing a secular music. The mood of the Blues is one of sadness, punctuated by a regular, heavy beat. The emphasis is on the pleasures of this world, especially the enjoyment of illicit sex before or outside marriage.

After World War II, White entertainers, fascinated by the beat of the Blues, began to copy this style of music and augmented the instrumentation with electric guitars, bass, and drums. Soon this music was popularized by singers like Bill Haley, Chuck Berry, Buddy Holly, and, especially, Elvis Presley. From this fusion, a new musical style was born—Rock and Roll. The latter differs from the Blues because of its constant drum beat that makes it conducive to dancing.

The distinction that we find in African-American music between the religious Negro Spiritual and the secular, irreligious Rock and Roll reminds us of the simple fact that in all cultures we can expect to find some music which is pro-Christian and some which is anti-Christian in its values. This is the result of the fall of humankind which is present in every age, country, and culture. "All have sinned and fall short of the glory of God" (Rom 3:23).

Rock Versus Heritage Music. A closer look at the characteristics of the African-American heritage music and those of rock music reveals significant differences. While heritage music preserves and fosters unity, rock music creates division and influences rebellious attitudes toward moral values and a disrespect for authority. Perhaps the similarity is due to the fact that the drum, a key instrument in both situations, is involved. The truth is that, other than the use of the drum, neither has anything in common.

In the African tradition, drums are considered to be "society drums" which speak a *language* that could be understood by the people of the culture. They are functionally based and social in purpose. They serve as a means of communication—signaling, dance, entertainment, rituals, and other ceremonies. Even the body was used as a drum to beat rhythms.

In rock music, drums are also a key instrument for they create a static punctuation through incessant pounding that is so characteristic of this type of music. While most people use the terms "rhythm" and "beat" interchangeably, there is a technical difference between the two. The "beat" is vertical in structure, and is, by definition, a regular recurring pulsation, like the heart beat. "Rhythm," on the other hand, is horizontal in structure and results from a combination of long and short note values that create a flowing, forward motion. Scholars have traced the origin of rock music back to the African drum because of the complex rhythms that are also said to call forth supernatural evil beings.

Are Drums Evil? The myth that drums are evil originated from European missionaries who went to Africa and could not relate to the culture. Africa was nicknamed the "Dark Continent" not only because of the skin color of its inhabitants, but "mostly because the outside world knew very little about the geography and the peoples of this vast land mass, particularly in the area south of the Sahara Desert.[6]

Drums were and still are an integral part of African culture. However, because the missionaries did not understand the intricacies of playing them and because they were sometimes used in voodoo and other rites involving spiritualism, they were deemed evil. Failing to deal with African music on its own terms led the missionaries to substitute these traditions for those European standards familiar to them. Consequently, this acculturation attempted to strip Africans of one of the most important elements of their culture.

By observation, one can see that all drums are not created equally and that they do not all have the same function. For example, authentic African drums are constructed from wood and animal skins. "They may be played at religious ceremonies of social gatherings, traditional dances for children's games, for work, and for war."[7]

What the missionaries failed to realize was that, as an instrument, the drum is not sinful per se and the rhythm of the drum is merely a language—a tool of communication that could travel much farther than the human voice, due to the nature of its acoustics. In fact, the drum is to the Africans what the shofar or the trumpet was to the Israelites.

Two Kinds of Drums. Today, drums seem to be the most controversial of all instruments. This is partly due to their traditional association with conjuring up evil spirits, and partly because of the way they are used in rock music to produce its relentless beat.

In Western music, however, drums have two categories— pitched (timpani, steel drums, tom-toms, etc.) and non-pitched (snare, bongos, drum kit often referred to as a trap set, etc.). The "drum kit" (bass, tom-toms, snare, suspended cymbal, hi-hat) descends from the

European military and marching-band instruments and is the source of contention today.

In the 1920s, jazz drummers experimented with one person playing several instruments, using feet as well as hands. As technology and techniques improved over the ensuing years, the drum kit became one of the main components of popular music, rock bands, jazz ensembles, and even gospel music.

It is interesting to note that these drums are played mostly with sticks or mallets, while African drums are played with the hands. In light of this, the ensuing discussion on drums is in reference to the drum kit, and the principles cited also apply to electronic instruments—synthesizers, drum machines, and all others that reproduce the sound of acoustic instruments.

Effects of Rock Music. The birth of rock has impacted upon various cultures around the world. In fact, the widespread popularity of rock is causing the gradual loss of many cultural traditions, and a decline in social mores. Initially, when the "pop music" of the 1950s was called "rock and roll," it still exhibited some characteristics of "good" music. The melody was still the dominant element.

Within a few years, however, the emphasis shifted from the head (melody) to the body (rhythm) both in message, sound, and nuance. Rock music gained popularity when the Beatles came to America in 1964, bringing with them drums, amplified instruments, and "the beat" which became the dominant element, totally displacing melody and harmony. Even the spelling of their name—BEATles—announced the arrival of a new type of music that would soon attract people around the world. Rock is a type of music that was created to be felt and not heard—a music that would anesthetize the senses of people from every culture.

As rock has hardened over the years, its hypnotic beat has inundated all genres of music, including Gregorian Chant, the most monotonous of all sacred music. In addition to its hypnotic beat, another dimension has been added to ensure total mind control—video recordings. While the body is bombarded by the pulsation of the beat, the mind is hypnotized by the rapid fluctuation of light in the video.

For example, when a television is on in a dark room, one can better observe the strobe effect of the light upon a wall. This is due to the frequency with which the scenes change. While the effect is not as noticeable in a room with light, the result is the same because the eyes are focused in one direction—that of the flickering light.

In October of 1999, Dr. Neil Nedley appeared on Three Angels Broadcasting network on the program, "Health for a Lifetime." He delineated from his book, *Proof Positive,* seventeen dangers of watching entertainment shows, such as MTV, with fluctuating lights which he calls "the rapid change of reference scene." The seventeen dangers are:

- Hypnosis
- Reduced interest in reading and learning
- Weakened brain power
- Promotion of poor life-style habits (smoking, drinking, eating, morals, etc.)
- Obesity
- Increased daydreaming
- Weakened creativity
- Reduced power of discrimination—inability to tell right from wrong
- Conditioning to non-reaction response (laugh at rape, and crime)
- Violence lightly regarded
- Irritability
- Increased aggression
- Accelerated sexual activity
- Addictedness
- Reduced time for productivity
- Lessened family time
- Adverse effect upon spiritual pursuits

The effects of the "rapid change of reference scene" are parallel to another phenomenon of rock music called "switching." This causes the body to incur confusion and alarm, perceptual difficulties, a decrease in performance (in school and work output), hyperactivity and restlessness, reduction in decision-making capacity, and a loss of energy for no apparent reason.

There is also a drop in blood sugar (the brain's nutrition source) which, over a period of time, results in structural changes in the brain cells. This subsequently renders the body unable to distinguish between that which is good or that which is harmful, and, in so doing, impairs the capacity to make moral decisions. This mental effect is significant to our ensuing discussion on worship styles.

The Real Origin of Rock Music. While the birth of rock music is traced to the 1950s, the phenomenon of rock music is not new. The Bible suggests that the gripping hypnotic drum beat, which has so adversely affected humankind, originated with Lucifer, the crowning act of creation in heaven. "Thou hast been in Eden the garden of God. . . the workmanship of thy tabrets [drums] and of thy pipes was prepared in thee in the day that thou wast created" (Ezek 28:13. KJV).

Satan desired to "be like the Most High" through rebellion and deception. Ultimately he was expelled from heaven, and from that day he has sought to malign God's character and erase His image in humankind. His aim is to etch his own image upon the character of every individual. This can be seen especially in the rebellious and perverted behavior engendered by rock music.

The influence of the rock beat is not a new phenomenon. Some of the characteristics of rock music already existed at the time of Moses. We read that upon returning to the Israelite camp after receiving the Ten Commandments on Mount Sinai, Joshua said to Moses, "'There is a noise of war in the camp.' But he said, 'It is not the sound of shouting for victory, or the sound of cry of defeat, but the sound of singing that I hear.' And as soon as he came near the camp, and saw the calf and the dancing, Moses' anger burned hot." (Ex 32:17-19).

The Israelites danced around the golden calf at the sound of the beat. Centuries later it was the dance of Herodias's daughter that influenced the demise of John the Baptist. Biblical examples such as these indicate that rhythmic, dancing music has been around for a long time and has played a major role in fostering opposition to God's will and and moral perversion.

By worshipping the golden calf, the Israelites rejected the Creator and Redeemer God, choosing instead to worship an object of their creation. Having just emerged from Egyptian bondage, the Israelites were still in bondage to that cultural influence. They imitated the idolatrous worship that they had witnessed for so long by employing the rhythmic dance they had learned in Egypt.

The "mixed multitude" that joined the Israelites undoubtedly influenced their apostasy. Although their worship around the golden calf was spirited, they were not spiritual. Spirituality manifests itself in attitudes and behavior that coincide with that which is scripturally acceptable to God.

Two Ancient Worship Styles. By way of contrast, visualize another scene, namely, the inauguration of the Temple by Solomon. We are told that all the Levite singers "made themselves heard in unison in praise and thanksgiving to the Lord. . . . The song was raised, with trumpets and cymbals and other musical instruments, in praise to the Lord, 'For he is good, for his steadfast love endures for ever,' the house, the house of the Lord, was filled with a cloud . . . for the glory of the Lord filled the house of God"(2 Chron 5:13-14).

The music of the Levite choir and that of the worshippers of the golden calf was similar in the sense that both involved a loud and emotional response. However, the one obvious difference between the two is that one expressed an authentic worship of God and the other was a counterfeit. It is significant that Joshua initially perceived the music directed to the golden calf as being the noise of a battle. Such a description fits well the blasting noise of rock concerts.

Unlike the singing at the inauguration of the Temple, God was not present at the worship of the golden calf because it was the worship of a man-made idol. God declared, "They made a calf in Horeb and worshipped a molten image. They exchanged the glory of God for the image of an ox that eats grass. They forgot God, their Savior" (Ps 106:19-21).

Their music was an outward expression of an inward condition. The "noise" of their music was a cacophony of sound—discord, clamor, commotion, disharmony, and pandemonium. The same characteristic attitudes—commotion, disharmony, and behavior—are present today in the rock music that counterfeits the worship of God.

Two Worship Styles Today. Two worship styles still exist today. One is known as the *conservative style* and the other the *liberal style*. The church music in the conservative worship style is derived from the European tradition and consists of hymns, anthems, classics, and some contemporary Christian music.

The organ and piano are the main instruments used, although other instruments are employed as well. Contrary to what some people say, the music of this worship style is not dead or dull. On the contrary, some of the most lively, beautiful, and moving music is rendered within this style. A determining factor is a dynamic, competent, and spiritual song leader who can inspire the congregation to sing wholeheartedly.

The liberal style of music, on the other hand, is more Pentecostal and improvisational in nature. Usually it consists of gospel music that fosters a foot-tapping, hand-clapping, and body-swaying response. Instrumentation includes drums, electric guitars, and synthesizers which are coupled with the piano and organ. In most cases, the musicians (and some pastors), although quite talented in other areas, have had little or no musical training; consequently, they perform mainly *by ear*. Because music within this context is erroneously called "heritage" music by some, the quest for cultural preservation is at times taken to the extreme.

"Black music" is more or less a label that has been attached to a style and sonority of music that is generally associated with African-American culture because it bears certain ethnic characteristics—compound meter (sometimes referred to as long meter), rich harmonies, rhythm, syncopation, improvisation, bending and surging of notes, ornamentation, blues notes, and the like.

Some think that contemporary styles are heritage music because of these characteristics and because they are popularized by Black artists. By definition, however, "heritage" music is that which has been passed on to succeeding generations. This is hardly the case with the various versions of contemporary rock music. It is rightly called "contemporary," because it departs from both the African and European music heritages. We have shown that there is a radical difference between the heritage music of the Negro Spirituals and that of rock music.

The tendency today, among various ethnic and religious groups, is to deify their culture through icons, symbols, and the music that best represents them. They deem worship less meaningful if it does not fit into their cultural values and personal tastes. They seem to forget that culture, like anything in this world, is tainted by sin. This means that culture must be tested by the normative authority of Scripture and not vice versa.

The "Language" and "Dialect" of Music. After pondering for some time the ongoing debate over worship styles, I sense that the cause of the problem may not necessarily be the worship style itself, but the musical "language" and "dialect" that are used. *Language* is a communication tool made up of a vocabulary that is *understandable* and *meaningful* to the hearer.

The "dialect" associated with the language is what groups people together and becomes their identification badge of kinship. Anyone who speaks the language with a different dialect is usually called a "foreigner." When Paul listed "tongues" as one of the spiritual gifts, most likely he meant not only the ability to speak different languages but dialects as well.

To further illustrate the point, let us consider the various kinds of "languages" that exist within the same language. For example, there is legal language, street language, professional language, sports language, academic language, musical language, and the list goes on. If the vocabulary of any of the above "languages" is configured in a way that all cannot understand, then it becomes a "foreign language" and is utterly useless to the hearer.

The same is true for music. For example, what is known as "ebonic" or "Black" music has crept into the church and has changed the "language" and "dialect" of music from sacred to *commercial* sounding. The result is that a new musical culture was born, which is resisting and rejecting the European musical tradition, especially when it is elevated to "the standard" to evaluate music.

The psychological scars resulting from this conflict have not yet healed. This conflict has affected the worship experience of many. "Walls of separation have been built up between the whites and the blacks. These walls of prejudice will tumble down of themselves as did the walls of Jericho, when Christians obey the Word of God, which enjoins on them supreme love to their Maker and impartial love to their neighbors."[8]

Edification. In worship, the operative word is *edification*. If the musical "language" is foreign to the congregation, it is irrelevant and meaningless and becomes as "sounding brass, or a tinkling cymbal." The message is lost, and the church is not edified. This is one reason why the Catholic church finally permitted the mass to be conducted in the vernacular of the people.

If the musical language is foreign to the congregation, how can it be edifying? When we offer our music with the Spirit and with understanding, heavenly musicians join in with us. God expects us to cultivate our voices so we can speak and sing in a way that all can understand.

Music in worship must be edifying to the congregation. When it is rendered in a form that is foreign to the hearer, it is meaningless. This does not mean that everything is appropriate for worship as long as it is expressed in the idiom of the culture. As noted earlier, our culture must be tested by Scripture, and not vice versa. Unfortunately, often in an attempt to *emphasize* cultural identity, the latter becomes the object of worship.

The Danger of Ethnic Pride. It is interesting to note that before the civil rights movement, ministers preached the doctrines of the church without being concerned about ethnic differences. But after the civil rights movement, many ministers became caught up in culturalism and began preaching on the attributes of a race, instead of those of Christianity. Thus, were born the concepts of "Black power" and "Black awareness." Christianity was placed in competition with culture. The music began to reflect this philosophy as well.

We must be aware of the captivating influence of ethnic pride which is used by the enemy to divert our attention from God. Christian principles transcend cultural boundaries, because the blood of Jesus Christ was shed for every person in every race, and every culture. What merit do these issues have in light of our salvation? Jesus Christ taught that there are no territorial lines, castes, or ethnic pride in God's kingdom.

In 1969 the Edwin Hawkins' arrangement of "Oh Happy Day" crossed the line. Never before had a "religious" song been aired on secular "Top 40" radio programs, to say nothing of becoming a number-one hit. Since then, many religious-record companies have come into existence. They have provided opportunities for more Black artists to become involved in religious rock.

As various rock groups sprang up after the debut of the Beatles, their music and lifestyle changed for the worse. Drugs, sex, violence, and all sorts of immorality became prevalent among the youth culture and reached its zenith at the Woodstock concert in 1969. At this time, some young people, who had been searching for something better without finding it, decided to "Try Jesus." Thus the "Jesus Movement" came into existence. Youth around the country began to "get high" on Jesus as they sang religious songs to the rock beat that they so dearly loved. This marked the beginning of the Contemporary Christian Music industry or what I call "pop gospel" music.

How Rock Music Entered the Church. How has rock music been able to enter the church? A major reason is the weak spiritual leadership of pastors who have been easily swayed by popular demand. Paul warned that "the time will come when they will not endure sound doctrine; but after their own lusts shall they heap to themselves teachers, having itching ears; and they shall turn away their ears from the truth, and shall be turned unto fables" (2 Tim 4:3-4. KJV). Popular pressure can sway weak leaders, as illustrated by the example of Aaron. He feared for his own safety and thus yielded to the whims of the Israelites. Had Aaron stood for principle, most likely he could have averted the apostasy at Mount Horeb.

"How often in our own day, is the love of pleasure disguised by a 'form of godliness!' A religion that permits men, while observing the rites of worship, to devote themselves to selfish or sensual gratification, is as pleasing to the multitudes now as in the days of Israel. And there are still pliant Aarons, who, while holding positions of authority in the church, will yield to the desires of the unconsecrated, and thus encourage them in sin."[9]

When leaders are weak or afraid to take a stand, they tend to yield to the whims and desires of the parishioners. Instead of leading, they are led, causing their own eternal loss as well as that of the people entrusted to them. Today, as in ancient Israel, the problem is leadership more than membership. When leaders fail to lead the people into paths of righteousness, they allow them to follow the path to self-destruction.

Church leaders need to understand that though certain musical styles reflect "the language" and "the dialect" of a particular people, they do not necessarily represent the principles of God's Word. Often in Contemporary Christian music, the holy is mixed with the profane, because the ultimate concern is to make sales, rather than to save lost sinners.

Music produced for the sake of profit, entertainment, and sensationalism does not foster spiritual growth. Instead, it weakens intellectual and moral powers, dulls our appreciation for that which is sacred, and has an adverse effect upon our prayer life and Bible reading.

In many instances, the spirit and manner in which Contemporary Christian Music is performed reflects the entertainment environment of the secular concert, night club, disco, etc. The music sounds like R & B, Rock, Rap, Jazz, Country Western, or some other pop genre. It is inundated with sensual overtones that dazzle, excite, and induce undulation. When the holy is mixed with the unholy and is incorporated into our worship, it becomes a blemished offering that God cannot accept.

Even during Jesus' day, the system had become so corrupt that the Lord expressed His righteous indignation by expelling the money changers from the Temple because they had commercialized God's House. There exists today the same need to protect the integrity and sanctity of the worship place, including its music. It is imperative for church leaders to teach their congregations how to worship God in the beauty of holiness by explaining to them the basic principles of sacred music.

Part 2
PRINCIPLES OF SACRED MUSIC

Music is God's gift to the human family. It is a powerful tool that can uplift, edify, inspire, elevate, evangelize, reinforce doctrines and beliefs, subdue uncultivated traits of characters, and promote harmony. It can fix words in the memory and impress the heart with spiritual truth. It can serve as a weapon against discouragement and bring heaven's gladness to the soul.

Discerning "good" music that honors God may be easier for some than for others. The following elements of good music should serve as a guide for those who are interested in understanding more fully what constitutes sacred music that honors the Lord.

Unity. A first characteristic of sacred music is found in 2 Chronicles 5:13 where we are told that the Levitical singers were to "make themselves heard *in unison* in praise and thanksgiving to the Lord."[10] There was an unmistakable oneness and harmony in the sound of their music. The voices and the instruments blended together. Unity is vital in Christian music.

A characteristic of much contemporary music is *improvisation.* Often instrumentalists or vocalists improvise, composing and performing simultaneously on the spur of the moment. Hot bands are known for "doing their own thing," blending in but not in any planned manner. Musical renditions are often inundated with or motivated by sensationalism (vocal gymnastics, excessive use of ornamentation, keyboard runs, lavish chords, etc.) in order to dazzle, excite, or induce undulation, hand clapping, swaying, etc. Such music is characterized by polarization and discord, and not by *"unison in praise,"* like in sacred music.

Practice is needed to present our best music to the Lord. Some Christians believe that practicing in order to praise the Lord is unnecessary, because singing should be natural. The attitude that a few minutes of choir practice before the service is sufficient hardly reflects the importance the Bible places upon music.

To achieve unity, musicians must have a knowledge and understanding of the nature and function of their instrument in music making, especially drums. They need to understand that drums should be *orchestrated* to add *"color"* to the music and not be loud and overpowering or distracting from the message of the music. When the instruments overpower the melody, harmony, and lyrics to the point that the message is lost, then the rendition does not edify the listener because there is no "unison in praise."

Word-Centered. A second characteristic of sacred music is its "Word-centeredness." It helps to hear the Word of God more clearly. Sacred music, presented to the Lord and heard by His people, should strengthen the message of the Gospel and not cheapen it. The Bible tells us that "faith cometh by hearing, and hearing by the word of God" (Rom 10:17, KJV). Music should contribute to the hearing of the message of God's Word which builds faith.

This means that the *sound* of the music must harmonize with the *words*. Biblical truths are heard in *words,* and the music must not distort or push into the background "the word of truth" (Col 1:5). If the volume or the dissonance of the music are such that the words cannot be heard clearly, then the whole performance becomes an absurd and disrespectful exercise.

Praise and Thankfulfness. A third characteristic of sacred music is its praise and thanksgiving to God. The Temple choir was "heard in unison in *praise* and *thanksgiving* to God" (2 Chron 5:13).[11] Repeatedly the Scripture summons us to sing praises to the Lord with thanksgiving (Ps 7:17; 47:6-7; 18:49; Jud 5:2; Ez 3:10; Jer 20:13).

Contemporary Christian Music places considerable emphasis on praise, but those songs which express *meaningful* praise are scarce. Some of them are trite, shallow, simplistic, and entertaining. While the hymns of the Bible extol the greatness of God and His mighty works, much of contemporary music uses constantly the first and second person pronouns.

The first recorded song in the Bible has these remarkable words: "The Lord is my strength and my song, and he has become my salvation" (Ex 15:2). Moses refers to God as "my song," because the whole song is consecrated to the honor of God and is intended to praise Him for delivering His people.

Can this be said of the "Christian" rock music characterized by beat, rhythm, loudness, and syncopation? Does such music express the purity, majesty, and holiness of God? Does it celebrate God's marvellous creative and redemptive accomplishments? Music about God should be like God, reflecting Him, and communicating something of the beauty of His character.

Ministry Unto the Lord. A fourth characteristic of sacred music is its goal to minister "unto the Lord," as opposed to entertain the listener. The difference between the two is perceived by both the listener and the performer. Sacred music that ministers to the Lord exalts His holiness and majesty, while entertainment music seeks to bring attention to the musician.

As Jacob Aranza points out, "the musician becomes another music star and the main attraction in place of the Lord. In such cases, Jesus just becomes the platform for the musician to display the flesh. This would be like Jesus riding into Jerusalem on a donkey and the people applauding the donkey. How foolish and sad!"[12]

In his book *A Philosophy of Church Music,* Robert Beglund writes: "If entertainment is a prime goal of church services then music that primarily entertains is appropriate. However, one is hard pressed to develop a biblically based argument that advocates entertainment as a primary (or even secondary) goal in church services."[13]

There is a clear distinction between sacred music that ministers "to the Lord," and so-called "Christian" music that entertains the listener at home or in church. "In the former (ministry) the musician and listener are moved by the music, by the godly character it reflects, and by the clear message of the lyrics. In the latter (entertainment) the musician and audience are moved by the performer's ability to communicate, influence, control, and inspire. In ministry, attention is drawn by the vehicle to the subject of the music. In entertainment, the vehicle causes the focus to be on itself."[14]

Music is either sacred or secular. The holy should not be mixed with the profane. "Teach my people the difference between the holy and profane, and cause them to discern between the unclean and the clean" (Ezek 44:23, KJV). This biblical imperative applies to the music as well.

There is no such thing as "gospel jazz," or "Christian Rap," or "Christian Rock." Such labels are an oxymoron. To assume that music that promotes perversion can be made into a medium that proclaims salvation just by changing its label and lyrics is like believing that the devil can be made into a Savior just by changing his job description.

The gospel is the good news that Jesus suffered inhumane abuse in order to gain our salvation. To trivialize the message of the gospel by mixing it with that which is secular (commercialism) is not only sacrilegious, but is also an affront to the magnitude of Christ's atoning sacrifice.

Rap "music" is rhythmic *speech* which contradicts the biblical directive to "sing" and make a "melody." The enemy does not want us to "sing unto the Lord," so he created a counterfeit singing. Unfortunately, there are those who have deluded themselves into believing that such music can be used to lead others to Christ. God never has nor will He ever use the devil's tools to attract sinners unto Himself.

"There is always danger, when the common is mingled with the sacred, that the common will be allowed to take the place of the sacred. ...When objectionable matter is mingled with sacred matter...[God's] blessing cannot rest upon the work done."[15]

Godly Living. A fifth characteristic of sacred music is its capacity to encourage disciplined, godly living. Discovering God's will for our lives should be the constant concern of every serious-minded Christian. "This is the will of God, your sanctification" (1 Thess 4:3). Sanctification does not come easily. It is not handed over to Christians on a plate.

"The Christian life is a fight, not a festival; a conflict, not a concert. It is a constant battle against the forces of evil and calls for vigilance, discipline, sacrifice, and spiritual determination. Does your music tend to lead you in these directions, or does it tend to be soft, slushy or sentimental? Does it help you focus your mind on things that are 'true . . . noble . . . right . . . pure . . . lovely . . . .admirable . . . praiseworthy'? (Phil 4:8)."[16]

Sacred music helps us to live in the world without becoming part of it (1 John 2:15). This has been the Christian challenge in every age. Today the challenge has become more intense because Christians are pressured from every side to conform to those philosophies, standards, values, and life-styles that are diametrically opposed to those presented in Scripture. Sacred music should inspire us to renew our commitment to the Lord, saying "I would be, dear Savior, wholly Thine; Teach me how, teach me how."[17]

"What voice are you hearing in your music? Does it appeal to the sensual or to the spiritual? Does it seem to have its roots in this world or in heaven? Does it stimulate pure appetites or impure? Does it lead you to want more of the world's values or less? Are godless people comfortable with it or embarrassed by it? Does it help or hinder a desire to break free from the worldly way of doing things? There is no neutrality here—the Bible makes it clear that 'Anyone who chooses to be a friend of the world becomes an enemy of God' (James 4:4.NIV). The question is not essentially one of what you like, but of whom you love."[18]

Music Suitable for Heaven. A sixth characteristic of sacred music is its suitability for heaven—the homeland of music. God revealed to the apostle John that *there will be music in heaven.* In one of the most breath-taking passages in all of Scripture we are told that every creature in heaven and earth joined together in singing: "To him who sits upon the throne and to the Lamb be blessing and honor and glory and might for ever and ever" (Rev 5:13).

Is the music you enjoy suitable to praise God in heaven? Does it give undivided glory to "the Lamb, that was slain"? (Rev 5:12). Can you imagine this music being played or sung by heavenly beings? Can you imagine yourself singing the same song while standing before the indescribable majesty of the triune God? It is important to remember that "Our citizenship is in heaven" (Phil 3:20.NIV) and every aspect of our lives, including our music, should be a preparation for that glorious experience.

CONCLUSION

Cultural diversity began when God confused the languages at the tower of Babel and subsequently "scattered [the people] abroad from thence upon the face of all the earth" (Gen 11:8.KJV). Each people group became relevant in their own uniqueness. Their badge of identity is reflected in their music, language, dialect, behavior, ideas, and values which were learned and transmitted from one generation to the next. It is the *gift of uniqueness* that God gave to humanity.

Music can be classified in four major categories: art music, church music, folk music, and "pop"/commercial music. Each of these is distinctly different. Of these categories, "pop"/commercial music, which is characterized by the rock beat, is the only one that has aggressively infiltrated each of the others and has blurred their distinctive features. By so doing, it makes all music sound similar.

The widespread popularity of rock music around the world is causing the gradual disappearance of some musical traditions, especially among the youth. They have no desire to preserve the classical music which has come down to them, because they find it dull and irrelevant. It does not stimulate them physically like rock music. This sentiment is transferred into religious music. Hymns, which are the didactic aspect of religious beliefs, are being replaced by praise songs which are more lively, but they often lack biblical content and music quality.

A humorous story may serve to illustrate the difference between hymns and praise songs. A farmer attended a city church one weekend. Upon returning home his wife asked him, "How was the service?" "Well," said the farmer, "It was good. They did something different, however. They sang praise choruses instead of hymns." "Praise choruses?" said his wife, "What are those?" "They're sort of like hymns, only different," said the farmer. "Well, what's the difference?" "Well, it's like this. If I were to say to you, 'Martha, the cows are in the corn,' well that would be a hymn. If on the other hand I said to you, 'Martha, Martha, Oh Martha, MARTHA, MARTHA, the cows, the big cows, the brown cows, the black cows, the white cows, the COWS, COWS, COWS, are in the corn, are in the corn, are in the corn, are in the corn,' well, that would be a praise chorus."

Praise songs can be described as one phrase, two chords, three hours. When punctuated by a rock beat, this is the result—mindless repetition that soon becomes hypnotic in its effect. Some seek to glorify this hypnotic type of music by labeling it as a "cultural heritage."

The purpose of worship is to glorify God, not culture. When culture becomes the focus and the foundation upon which worship is based, then the true motive for worship is lost. God accepts the worship of people of all cultures offered to Him in their different languages and music styles, but in each culture a distinction must be made between what is holy and unholy, sacred or profane.

Frequently, the question is asked, "What is wrong with rock music? After all, it is part of my cultural heritage." The Word of God advises us to resolve this question, asking instead, "What is right with rock music?" Does it glorify God (1 Cor 10:31)?

The question for the Christian must be: "What will please the Lord? Is there anything good about rock music that will please the Lord? Does it promote Christian values? Does it give a repentant view of human depravity? Does it build up the Christian faith or does it tear it down? Does it glorify God or extol human perversions?

The answer to these questions is not difficult to find, because the message of the various versions of rock music is loud and clear. Its emphasis is on violence, rebellion, anarchy, sexual promiscuity, drug culture, occultism, homosexuality, and not on peace, faithfulness, temperance, and holiness.

We are serving a God who says: "My thoughts are not your thoughts, neither are your ways my ways" (Is 55:8). The challenge of our Christian life is to "try to learn what is pleasing to the Lord" (Eph 5:10), rather than to follow the dictates of our cultural heritage or societal trends. Let us remember that if God is not pleased with our worship, including our music, then all our efforts becomes idle chatter—"sounding brass and tinkling cymbal" (1 Cor 13:2.KJV).

ENDNOTES

1. Jeff Todd Titon, James T. Koetting, David P. McAllester, David B. Reck, Mark Slobin, *Worlds of Music: An Introduction to the Music of the World's People* (New York, 1984), p. 9.

2. Andrew J. Broekema, *The Music Listener* (Dubuque, IA, 1978), p. 200.

3. Ibid., p. 203.

4. Marvin V. Curtis and Lee V. Cloud, "Traditions and Performance Practices," *Choral Journal* ACDA (November 1991), p. 15.

5. Nevilla Ottley, *Some Famous Black Composers Born Before 1850* (Washington, DC, 1994), pp. 1-12.

6. Jeff Todd Titon (note 1), p. 64.

7. Claire Jones, *Making Music: Musical Instruments in Zimbabwe Past and Present* (Harare, Zimbabwe, 1962), p. 146.

8. Ellen G. White, *The Southern Work* (Washington, DC, 1966), p. 43.

9. Ellen G. White, *The Story of Patriarchs and Prophets* (Mountain View, CA, 1958), p. 317.

10. Emphasis supplied.

11. Emphasis supplied.

12. Jacob Aranza, *More Rock Country & Backward Masking Unmasking* (Shreveport, LA, 1985), p. 44.

13. Robert Berglund, *A Philosophy of Church Music* (Chicago, IL, 1985), p. 20.

14. Frank Garlock and Kurt Woetzel, *Music in the Balance* (Greenville, SC, 1992), p. 178.

15. Ellen G. White, *Testimonies for the Church* (Mountain View, CA, 1962), vol. 8, p. 88.

16. John Blanchard, *Pop Goes the Gospel* (Durham, England, 1991), p. 164.

17. *The Seventh-day Adventist Hymnal* (Washington, DC, 1985), Hymn no. 308.

18. John Blanchard (note 16), p. 165.

Chapter 13
MUSIC AND MORALITY
by
Wolfgang H. M. Stefani

Wolfgang H. M. Stefani is an Australian musician, scholar, pastor. He has earned graduate degrees in music, and a Ph.D. in Religious Education from Andrews University in 1993. His dissertation deals with "The Concept of God and Sacred Music Style."

Stefani has taught church music, hymnology, philosophy of music, and religious education at the graduate and undergraduate levels. He has served for 14 years as a church musician: organist, pianist, minister of music, church music coordinator, and choir director. He has presented over 60 seminars on music in the United States, Mexico, Japan, Australia, France, Britain, Poland, and Scandinavia.

Musician and teacher, Henry Edward Krehbiel, once quipped: "Of all the arts, music is practised most and thought about least."[1] Rather than taking this as a rebuke, in today's postmodern world a significant number would respond with the words, "Bravo, and that's how it ought to be!"

Indeed, many people are convinced that music is to be felt and experienced, not thought about and analyzed. Because feelings are very subjective, the common view is that music means different things to different people, and hence its usage must be considered a matter of culturally conditioned taste and preference. The notion that music is in some way governed by morality or that musical expressions could or ought to be evaluated as right or wrong, appropriate or inappropriate according to external norms, is considered preposterous.

Objectives of This Chapter. This chapter examines the prevailing assumption that music, apart from its lyrics, is morally neutral. The examination of this popular assumption is vitally important because defenders of "Christian" rock strongly appeal to the alleged neutrality of music to justify their adoption of modified versions of rock for worship and evangelistic outreach. If this popular assumption is correct, then the efforts to Christianize rock music must be commended, but if it is mistaken, then Christians ought to be warned about the moral consequences of their efforts.

This chapter is divided into three parts. The first part defines the issues and looks at the morality of music from a historical perspective. The second part considers how the medium of music affects the message it conveys. The last part examines the correlation between music styles and different conceptions of God.

Part 1
AN HISTORICAL PERSPECTIVE

Defenders of Music Neutrality. The alleged music's moral neutrality is defended by people from all walks of life. A few examples will suffice for the purpose of our study. Listen to the almost irate statement of Maurice Zam (former director of the Los Angeles Conservatory of Music) made in a *Chicago Tribune* column to Ann Landers in 1993: "Let us emancipate ourselves from the myth that music has anything to do with morals. Music is as amoral as the sound of the babbling brook or the whistling wind. The tones E, D, and C can be sung to the words, "I love you," "I hate you," or "three blind mice."[2]

On face value, this illustration seems to hold, so people accept the premise as well. In fact, many today would agree with Zam, including a large proportion of Christians.

Whether overwhelmed with the complexity of the issues or simply ambivalent, many Christians question whether or not decisions for Christ need to be made regarding music. A growing number feel that providing lyrics are acceptable, the music itself is not really an issue either for worship or everyday use. For them, music is simply a medium and as such is morally neutral.

This view is forcefully presented in Dana Key's book *Don't Stop the Music*. A Christian rock musician, Key openly states that "*sound* is not the important issue. It's meaning. It's what the song is saying—and the *lyrics* of a song are what gives us that meaning." He goes on to assert: "I believe that music (particularly instrumental music) is absolutely void of moral qualities for either good or evil. This is not to say that there is not good instrumental music or bad instrumental music. Instrumental music can be good or bad, but that isn't a theological issue—it's an artistic one.

"The 'goodness' or 'badness' of instrumental music is based on the performers' competence and skill. If the music is played without skill it is bad. If it is performed skillfully, it is good."[3]

Is the Message Only in the Lyrics? Thomas Dorsey, the famous gospel musician, came to the same conclusion. He said: "The message is not in the music but in the words of the song. It matters not what kind of movement it has, if the words are Jesus, Heaven, Faith, and Life then you have a song with which God is pleased regardless of what critics and some church folk say."[4]

Michael Tomlinson, writing in *Ministry* in September 1996, took a similar stance. He wrote: "I believe music itself is without moral qualities either for good or evil. The question has more to do with what the music is employed to say or do than with the music per se."[5]

Even classically trained Christian musicians go along with these ideas. In his book, *Music Through the Eyes of Faith*, Harold Best (Wheaton College) took the position that "with certain exceptions art and especially music are morally relative."[6] Harold B. Hannum, well-known and respected Seventh-day Adventist musician and scholar, also maintained that "moral matters have to do with human actions and relations to others, not with the notes of a composition."[7] Later in the same work he affirmed that "moral and religious values should be kept separate from purely aesthetic ones."[8]

The evident strength and assurance in these statements seems to suggest a consensus. So, why cannot the issue be laid to rest once and for all? Perhaps the indignant suggestion that conservative religionists and other "self-appointed guardians of morals" (as Zam termed them) keep their interfering noses out of it and let others get on with using and enjoying music according to their tastes and preferences is valid? Or is it? Is there another side to this issue?

Now, it should be said that it is legitimate to affirm that aesthetic values are distinct from moral values. Aesthetic criteria such as "unity,

variety, balance, climax, integrity, logic and a feeling of inevitability
. . ."[9] are rightfully used in evaluating both musical compositions and
performances. However, before dismissing all evaluation as simply a
matter of assessing these parameters according to culturally conditioned taste and preference without reference to any moral dimension,
it is worth considering further.

Morality of Music in Ancient Cultures. In contemporary Western culture, music has come to be viewed almost exclusively as a form of
harmless entertainment intended to provide pleasure and create congenial
atmospheres with individuals consulting their likes and dislikes as the
basis for usage. This was not so, however, in earlier times. For example,
two and a half millennia ago, music was considered to be such a potent and
influential force in society that leading philosophers and politicians
advocated its control by the nation's constitution. This was the case in
Athens and Sparta, city states of ancient Greece.

In Japan in the third century A. D., an imperial office of music (the
Gagaku-ryo) was established to control musical activities.[10] Other ancient cultures, including those of Egypt, India, and China, evidenced
similar concerns. Legislation or governmental censorship of this kind is
considered almost unthinkable today.[11] But, even during the twentieth
century, Communist, Fascist, and Islamic regimes voiced concerns about
and implemented laws within their borders to control music.

Why all the fuss? What was the problem? For the ancients the
problem was clear. They believed music affected the will, which in
turn influenced character and conduct. For example, Aristotle and
Plato taught that "Music . . . directly imitates (that is, represents) the
passions or states of the soul—gentleness, anger, courage, temperance,
and their opposites and other qualities; hence, when one listens to
music that amadous a certain passion, he becomes imbued with the
same passion; and if over a long time he habitually listens to the kind of
music that arouses ignoble passions his whole character will be shaped to
an ignoble form. In short, if one listens to the wrong kind of music he will
become the wrong kind of person; but, conversely if he listens to the right
kind of music he will tend to become the right kind of person."[12]

There is no mistaking the clear relationship of music and morality
in this understanding. Half a world away in China, Confucius expressed
a very similar understanding: "If one should desire to know whether a

kingdom is well-governed, if its morals are good or bad, the quality of its music will furnish the answer. . . . Character is the backbone of our human culture, and music is the flowering of character."[13]

The Greeks and Chinese were not alone in their view. The idea that music has moral influence is evident among early Christian writers,[14] the Roman writer Boethius,[15] and many others. Even the statement of a prominent contemporary cultural anthropologist, Alan P. Merriam, has strong implications for the connection between music and morality. He wrote: "There is probably no other human cultural activity which is so all-pervasive and which reaches into, shapes, and often controls so much of human behaviour."[16]

So what do we make of this? Clearly there is wide historical support apart from recent religious writers[17] that music and morality are intimately connected. Is this notion a relic of ancient superstition, or does it have some validity? One thing is clear, while some think that music is amoral, historically many others believed the very opposite. Obviously, it would be risky to decide the issue by majority vote.

Music and the Fall. Before pursuing this line of investigation further, one theological point deserves consideration. Clyde S. Kilby framed the issue in the form of a question: "A man may tie his shoe laces or brush his teeth amorally, but can he create anything apart from some degree of moral involvement?"[18] A good number of Christians feel somewhat uneasy about the idea that on a sin-infested planet products of human creativity (which originate from deep within) are somehow undefiled and not subject to moral evaluation. As Kilby observed, common tasks may be adjudged as amoral, but can we really make that assessment of a product of human creativity?

There is general consensus that song lyrics need to be evaluated as either compatible or incompatible, right or wrong, in relation to Christian faith and outlook. But what about the music itself? Doesn't it need similar assessment? Unquestionably, if we respond in the affirmative, we enter a difficult arena with another raft of perplexing issues to confront. However, why should that challenge manipulate us into a default acceptance that music is an amoral island?

Why, then, have so few Christians grappled with this problem? Furthermore, why have so many argued for the moral neutrality of music, and the arts as a whole for that matter? Frank E. Gaebelein makes the following perceptive observation which throws considerable light on this: "The bulk of the work being done in the field of Christian aesthetics represents Roman and Anglo-Catholic thought. Its roots go deep into sacramental theology, Thomism, Greek philosophy, and such great writers as Dante."[19]

The dominance of Roman and Anglo-Catholic thought in the field of Christian aesthetics is highly significant. During the Middle Ages of Western culture history, human creativity came to be seen as an aspect of humanity that was not touched by the Fall—an intact remnant of the original *imago dei*. Hence, in evaluating the arts, appeal was made to aesthetic criticism to ensure good quality art, but moral accountability was never an issue because the creative impulse was considered to be essentially pure and innocent. Even the immoral life of an artist was considered of little moment as long as he/she produced aesthetically superior art.[20] Only the best was good enough for God, and the best was equated with aesthetic excellence.

So aesthetic evaluation came into prominence in Christian circles to the point that it eclipsed moral considerations. While the church dominated society, aesthetic excellence tended to be defined in terms of the religiously acceptable. However, as the church lost its hold, society became more secular, multiple worldviews surfaced, and aesthetic pluralism also emerged.[21]

As aesthetic excellence continued to be upheld as the only way to evaluate music, good quality rock, rap, thrash metal, classical, jazz, Country and Western, soul, and a host of other musics, each with their own individual aesthetic standards, have inevitably become acceptable forms of musical expression, even in worship contexts.

Music Vulnerable to Sin. For many Protestants, however, this paradigm does not take into account the "radical distortion" that sin has wrought in every field of human endeavour. Building on a concept of Emil Brunner, Gaebelein suggested that "those areas of thought and activity that are closest to our humanness and our relation to God are most severely twisted by the bentness in us."[22]

Gaebelein goes on to explain how he understood this to work out in life as follows: ". . . in the more objective fields like physics and chemistry they are less affected until in mathematics the distortion approaches zero. By such an estimate, the arts, which speak so subjectively and so very personally regarding who and what we are in relation to our Maker, are very vulnerable to the distortion that sin has brought into the world. This means that Christian artists and all of us for whom the arts are an essential part of life and culture must constantly be keeping our eyes open to the marks of the Fall in them and in us also."[23]

For Gaebelein, this does not mean that humanity is totally worthless, and neither is the image of God utterly wiped out. By the exercise of God's common grace, "humanity has been in the past and can still be today wonderfully creative to His glory."[24] However, we cannot be thoughtlessly *laissez faire* here.

If Gaebelein's logic is correct, then Christians of evangelical Protestant persuasion have no option but to explore meaningful and legitimate ways to evaluate music, not only to determine what is beautiful, but also to establish what is morally compatible with the worldview we espouse. This in no way supports cavalier, simplistic assessments that lack integrity and are spawned through ignorance. What I am suggesting is no easy task, or perhaps many others would have already successfully tackled it. But, here are two suggestions as a beginning. They both highlight the fact that the supposed moral neutrality of music is really untenable.

Part 2
THE MESSAGE IN THE MEDIUM

Speaking at the Second International Symposium on Music in Medicine at Ludenscheid, West Germany, in 1984, Manfred Clynes (a neurophysiologist, researcher, inventor, and acclaimed pianist) made the following statement: "Music in fact is an organization created to dictate feelings to the listener. The composer is an unrelenting dictator and we choose to subject ourselves to him, when we listen to his music."[25]

Music Dictates Feeling. What does this prominent scientist mean when he says music "dictates feelings?" How can music do this? One simple way to understand how this happens is to tune into a movie soundtrack, bypassing the picture for a while. How much can you determine about the film's action simply by listening to the background music? Alternatively, imagine a scene in a sci-fi horror movie in which a lethal monster spider is creeping up on an innocent, unsuspecting child. You can almost "hear" the creepy background music, can't you? But, why do film producers use music to accompany such scenes, especially when some would have us believe that words, not music carry meaning? And how do producers decide what music to dub with the scene? Why isn't "approaching monster music" dubbed onto a movie scene of a birthday party or a baby nursery?

If lyrics such as "sleep baby sleep" were set to "approaching monster music" would it become a lullaby? Or would addition of the text "Jesus loves me this I know" render it suitable for children's worship? In this last example, would we only want to make sure that the "approaching monster music" was composed creatively and performed skillfully, or would we evaluate the music as intrinsically inappropriate, even wrong in that context?

Music Communicates Apart from Words. While this may be an obvious example, several salient points about the nature of music are highlighted here and they must not be lost to our discussion. First, music apart from lyrics communicates a message. Music is not a neutral medium. Words are not required in order for music to have meaning. Film producers make decisions about music, not lyrics, in background music applications.

Second, while some may argue that music means different things to different people and that its affect is really only a matter of conditioned response, this does not account for certain major assumptions made by film producers. For example, incorporating music on a film soundtrack takes for granted that music impacts all people similarly. Indeed, if this were not the case, a music soundtrack would be pointless. Even when a film is released internationally, only language tracks are changed. The musical sound track that "dictates the feelings," as Clynes put it, stays the same. The underlying belief is that background music will communicate the same message to all viewers, even across cultural boundaries.

Third, while it cannot be denied that with the rise of globalized mass media some mass conditioning regarding musical associations may have occurred, it is also clear that music's impact is not only a matter of conditioning. Even before mass conditioning could be said to be a factor, producers seemed to be able to predict very accurately what music fitted with specific scenes or sequences. It has never been a hit-and-miss venture.

Research over the last thirty years or so has verified that the way music is constructed and performed embodies certain inherent characteristics that have long provided intuitive clues to its meaning. That's precisely why the secular industry makes informed decisions about the music it uses quite apart from lyrics that may or may not be present. Sadly, the "children of this world" seem to be wiser than the "children of light"[26] in some of these things.

Music and Human Feelings. In the recently established discipline of *sentics,* there is one example of how a growing body of documentary evidence is deciphering how human emotion is expressed and perceived, and how music is, in fact, a form of emotion communication. Indeed, respected contemporary thinkers about music have continued to affirm the conclusions of the Greeks about music representing the passions or states of the soul.

For example, Susanne Langer: "The tonal structures we call 'music' bear a close logical similarity to the forms of human feeling. . . . The pattern of music is that . . . form worked out in pure, measured sound and silence. Music is a tonal analog of emotive life."[27] In a similar vein, Gordon Epperson maintained: "Music is the expression . . . of the emotions; an aural image of how feelings feel, how they operate."[28]

In the development of sentics, Clynes has begun to show how music does this. Having demonstrated that the expression of emotion occurs through certain predictable forms (which he termed essentic forms),[29] Clynes has gone on to show how musicians can manipulate the pitch and loudness of individual tones to embody essentic forms in a melody line. This is achieved much the same way tone of voice is modulated to make a sentence meaningful. He describes it thus: "In producing a melody, a composer places the notes so that they in effect fit the outline of the appropriate essentic form. . . . Musical tones are placed at suitable points along the path of an essentic form so that internally they can act as markers in the generation of the form. That is to say, the musical tones engender internally the motor pattern of essentic form corresponding also to program points of a touch expression of the same quality."[30]

When composers construct well and performers read and interpret their compositions accurately, powerful communications can take place. Indeed, when an essentic form is expressed well "a melody has direct access to engender the emotional quality in the listener without the need of auxiliary symbolism."[31] As Clynes elaborated: ". . . it can touch the heart as directly as can a physical touch. A caress or an exclamation of joy in music needs not to be consciously translated into a touch caress or a physical 'jump for joy' to be perceived as of such a quality. It does so directly through perception of essentic form."[32]

Besides using the tones of a melody line, further embodiment of emotional communication can be demonstrated in the structure of the rhythmic pulse.[33]

Music Conditioned by Message. Of course, all this brings Zam's illustration quoted earlier into perspective. Actually, I am sure Zam is aware that the tones E, D, and C never exist in clinical isolation in a piece of music. The surrounding harmonies, rhythms, phrasing, accentuation, etc., make those three tones take on a variety of emotional colorations. Any composer setting Zam's three sets of lyrics ("I love you," "I hate you," and "three blind mice") to music would not compose identically in each case.[34]   This is precisely where Zam's point begins to break down.

Without trying to be comprehensive at this point, enough has been provided to substantiate that a body of research now exists that demonstrates that music does communicate meaningfully in a way that can and ought to be evaluated for appropriateness, and even rightness or wrongness in a given context.

From a Christian viewpoint, emotions like anger, hate, fear, love, or joy are not intrinsically good or bad. However, to present the lyric, "Jesus loves me this I know" with an accompanying musical/emotional message of fear and suspense would not simply be a harmless mismatch of cognitive and affective communication. According to Christian belief, it would surely be crass misrepresentation of the Gospel (especially in light of 1 John 4:18) and, hence, morally wrong, not merely aesthetically poor.

The same would be true if lyrics about Jesus' love for humanity were presented accompanied by music portraying anger, violence, and aggression. Such mixed messages provide a confused communication of truth which is morally reprehensible, not just a matter of taste.

Celebration of Violence. This last scenerio is not merely an idle, hypothetical example. In the late 1980s to early 1990s an extension of so-called heavy-metal rock music emerged and became known as Thrash or Speed Metal. The violence and aggression in the music was suitably acted out in the accompanying moshing pit where fans gyrated to the music in frenzied thrashing movements, sometimes even breaking limbs in the process.

This type of music continued to be popular and was much in evidence at the 1999 Woodstock Music Festival. In an essay in *Time*, August 9, 1999, Lance Morrow described the arson, pillaging, and free-lance mayhem that "was much in the spirit of the music" at the festival.[35] A crowd the size of Rochester, New York, in hot conditions and under the influence of drugs and "vehemently moronic music" became a riot. He summed it up in the words: "Garbage in, garbage out."[36]

When this form of music first emerged, however, some churches in Los Angeles sponsored concerts and developed worship services around a Christian form of this music to cater for enthusiasts. Even *Contemporary Christian Music* magazine was divided on whether to support or condemn this new phenomenon.[37] While the older, maturer commentators tried to weigh up the pros and cons of violence in a Christian context, arguing about the end perhaps justifying the means etc., a letter from a young person to the editor of the April issue of the same magazine seemed to cut through the confusion.

Alisa Williams from Chicago wrote: "What's with this 'Moshing for the Master' crap?! [Feb. '89] Some of those thrash people have their heads screwed up. I see absolutely nothing Christian about diving into an audience on top of people or running around like maniacs, risking being trampled to death! This kind of violence has no place in a Christian concert. No violence at all should be involved!

"Now as for their 'thrash' sound—it's a bit too wild. I know we all have different musical tastes, but once you over step a certain point it's just unbearable. I know you mean well—You want to bring those headbanging unbelievers to Christ—but I think you've taken it a bit far. God bless you anyway! By the way, this letter is not from an old granny. I'm 15 years-old!"[38]

What this young person saw so clearly highlights the hypocrisy of allowing the market to dictate music choice. Despite the recognized meaning of this music, some considered it acceptable simply because it was popular. If we have no external moral yardstick by which to evaluate our music, market forces will become the moral rudder by default. Ironically, within a Christian music context, this means that you end up with those knowing least about the Gospel determining most about its expression. No wonder we are left with a plethora of mixed and confused musical messages.

Part 3
THE MATTER OF STYLE

There is an even more pervasive factor that needs to be taken into consideration. It is often said by Christians discussing music that musical style is not an issue.[39] This idea is usually strongly argued by those supporting music's moral neutrality. This view reflects a stance taken in Western musicology over the past several centuries. Since the Enlightenment, when the anti-supernaturalist bias really began to grip Western culture, most disciplines have sought to become independent of metaphysical and religious considerations. Even in the study of the development of musical styles this is evident.

It has become fashionable to explore and emphasize the influence of environmental, sociological, economic, and even biological factors, despite general acknowledgment that religion is intimately intertwined with the development of music in every known culture.[40] However, ethnomusicologists working in non-Western cultures are gradually dragging Western scholars back to some important correctives in their understanding of how a musical style develops.[41]

Music Styles Reflect Theological Views. Before continuing this discussion further, however, we need to define what is meant by "style." Style has been simply described as "a characteristic way of doing something."[42] Style is a term used almost exclusively of human actions or creations. It designates a product of human choices. Clearly, in musical compositions, humans do not create the tones, but the way tones are combined, how they are sounded, how they are organized in time is all a product of human choice. Hence, these factors become known as characteristics of a particular style.

So, what drives the choices behind the development of style? Why compose this way, and not that? Paul Tillich once gave succinct utterance to a sweeping truth which sheds light on these questions. He wrote: "Religion as ultimate concern is the meaning-giving substance of culture, and culture is the totality of forms in which the basic concern of religion expresses itself. In abbreviation: religion is the substance of culture, culture is the form of religion."[43]

It is becoming increasingly evident that fundamental beliefs or worldview factors are one of the major determinants of music style. In other words, that which rules the heart, forms the art.[44] For example, in any culture there is an observable human quest for compatibility between fundamental beliefs and the character of art utilized in a religious setting.

J. H. Kwabena Nketia, describing sacred music in Africa, stated this was a fundamental principle that appears to underlie the use of music in worship: namely, that the selection of music used, the control of musical forms and instruments is in accordance with the conceptualization of the gods or of the individual focus of worship.[45] Similar substantiation could be cited from various other religions and cultures.

Early Christian Music and the Concept of God. How this happens is well illustrated in the Islamic context. Al Faruqi describes how the Islamic sacred music style is moulded by a significant, fundamental belief—the nonphenominal and transcendent aspects of divinity. To worship such a god was to leave the everyday world behind and enter an awe-inspiring realm. Noting this theological emphasis in both Islam and early Christianity, she observed the following of their music: "Religious music . . . avoided the emotive, the frivolous, the unfettered responses either to great joy or great sorrow. The limited range and contiguity of notes in Gregorian and Quranic chant, the prevalence of stepwise progression, the avoidance of large melodic leaps—all these contributed to this demand. The relaxed tempos, the calm and continuous movement, the rejection of strong accents and changes of intensity or volume were likewise conducive to an attitude of contemplation and departure from worldly involvement. The use of regularly repeated metric units would have tended to arouse associations, kinaesthetic movements and emotions incompatible with the notion of religiosity among Muslims and early Christians. These were therefore avoided. . . . Music contributed little or nothing to dramatic/programmatic content or tone painting imitating the objects, events, ideas or feelings of this world. Hence abstract quality has been a marked feature. . . . Formal characteristics accorded with this tendency, making elements of unity and change dependent upon correspondence with poetic units rather than with narrative or descriptive factors."[46]

She continued by demonstrating that not only structure but also performance practice was belief-driven. "Performance practice, relying on the human voice, has avoided the secular associations which instruments might bring, as well as the chordal harmonies which could be suggestive of emotional or dramatic effects. Even the use of the human voice or voices . . . has avoided the sensual and imitative in order to enhance the spiritual effect on the listener."[47]

Music Styles and the Concept of God. Notice the detailed extent to which style is influenced by belief in this case. As one would expect, emphasis on the immanent conceptualization of deity spawns a very different style of music, including a deliberate rejection of the abstract and the contemplative in favor of a strongly psychophysiologically stimulating musical expression. Repetitive rhythm is emphasized over melody and harmony, and percussive instrumental playing (often with a loud performance style) which promotes group participation and instinctive movement is commonplace.

Whereas in the transcendent orientation, meditation, or contemplation of the deity's revelation of himself is worship's goal, in the immanent orientation possession is the ultimate desired outcome. Two very different conceptions of god engender two very different styles of music because that which rules the heart, forms the art.[48]

As one begins to explore the intimate connection between worldview and music style, it becomes clear why Tillich suggested that it may be possible to "read styles" with appropriate discernment to detect which ultimate concerns are driving them.[49]

The demonstrable relationship between style and belief exposes the superficiality behind the claim that musical styles are neutral and incapable of proclaiming worldview.[50] In fact, the very opposite is true. Music styles are value-laden. They are veritable embodiments of beliefs. Stylistic features are brought into existence in a search for fitting aesthetic expression of deeply held truths about the really real. If this is so, then decisions about the appropriateness, even rightness and wrongness of musical styles, especially for worship contexts, are mandatory, not merely a matter of cultural taste and preference.

Indeed, Titus Burckhardt has a point when he writes: "Granted that spirituality in itself is independent of forms, this in no way implies that it can be expressed and transmitted by any and every sort of form."[51] He went on to note that "A spiritual vision necessarily finds its expression in a particular formal language; if that language is lacking, with the result that a so-called sacred arts borrows its form from some kind of profane art, then it can only be because a spiritual vision of things is also lacking."[52]

In other words, Christians have a moral responsibility to seek not only fitting lyrics for their songs but a musical style that legitimately expresses their understanding of God and of life. Further (even if it is not openly recognized), the evidence indicates that the issues surrounding sacred, music-style discussions extend far deeper than petty likes and dislikes.

At the bottom line, the clash over sacred music styles is really a clash of underlying beliefs about the ultimate nature of reality, not just inconsequential aesthetic preferences. Perhaps that's why the discussions just won't go away, because intuitively people sense a deeper substratum even if they can't verbalize it.

CONCLUSION

Three major conclusions emerge from the preceding investigation into the morality of music.

First, to seriously espouse the idea that music is a morally neutral medium may be understandable from a secular viewpoint or if one believes that human creativity is untouched by the Fall. However, if one believes in a moral universe lovingly and purposefully created, but infected by sin to the extent that a terrible distortion has marred (though not totally obliterated) God's image in humankind, one is committed to both appreciating the evidences of good in our world and also recognizing and distinguishing the evidences of evil.

The creative element (so closely tied to the very core of human nature) cannot be considered immune from sin's distortions. The answer is not to espouse moral neutrality in this domain, but to thoughtfully and prayerfully work out ways of facilitating discernment.

Second, while individual letters in an alphabet may be neutral, as they are combined together into words, phrases, and sentences, they take on meaning that can be evaluated as refined and decent versus crude and rude; reverent and respectful versus blasphemous and offensive; appropriate verssus inappropriate; right versus wrong, and so on because of the ideas they encapsulate. In the same way, while individual tones may be neutral in themselves, they never appear in isolation. In music they are always presented in conjunction with other tones, played with certain accents, in certain rhythmic formations, and sounded on certain instruments.

The ability to understand more precisely the vocabulary and syntax of music's emotional communication is beginning to emerge. Hence, evaluations of calm and peaceful versus angry and aggressive, bold and reassuring versus fearful and apprehensive, appropriate versus inappropriate, right versus wrong are increasingly possible. If accurate matching and assessment of music is possible in movie production, it is surprising, even ludicrous, to suggest that it is impossible in the worship setting.

Third, as the evidence mounts that styles of music are artistic embodiments of significant worldview factors in the belief systems of individuals and cultural communities, the implications for moral evaluation are imperative for Christians. Taste and preference cannot be the arbiter of appropriate/inappropriate musical styles. However, evaluations cannot be made simplistically or superficially.

Although a start has been made in my doctoral dissertation, much more study is required to provide increased discernment in "reading" styles of music and making accurate assessments. Clearly, this task is not an optional endeavour. The evidence gathered makes it imperative.

"Thinking about music," although sadly neglected as Krehbiel suggested, is a very important task and one that will be rewarded with great insights into one of God's noblest gifts to humankind. It may also open a way for Christians to develop a unique and more consistent aesthetic witness to the worldview they hold. At present Christians tend to be followers rather than leaders in the arts, especially in music.

Christianity claims that it has a life-enhancing and life-changing message for the spiritual, mental, physical, social, and emotional facets of humanity. But, what distinctive aesthetic witness to a lost world is being given in Christian musical communication? If it exists at all, it is in the lyrics; not in the music. Essentially the message is that in God's kingdom we do music the same as the world does it.

Risieri Frondizi posed a significant and worthwhile challenge when he wrote: "The essence of the moral reformer and of the creator in the field of the arts lies in not adjusting to the predominant norms, or tastes, but unfurling the flag of what 'ought to be' over and above people's preferences."[53] This is the twenty-first century's challenge to all dedicated Christians committed to unfurl the flag of God's Kingdom.

ENDNOTES

1. An aphorism quoted in *Australian Journal of Music Education* 27 (October 1980), p. 12.

2. Maurice Zam in a letter to Ann Landers, *Chicago Tribune,* August 19, 1993.

3. Dana Key and Steve Rabey, *Don't Stop the Music* (Grand Rapids, MI, 1989), p. 69. This is very similar to Oscar Wilde's view about literature: "There is no such thing as a moral or an immoral book. Books are well written or badly written. That is all." (Oscar Wilde quoted in James L. Jarrett, *The Quest for Beauty* [Englewood Cliffs, N.J., 1957], p. 216.)

4. Thomas A. Dorsey quoted in Oral L. Moses, "The Nineteenth-Century Spiritual Text: A Source for Modern Gospel," in *Feel the Spirit: Studies in Nineteenth-Century Afro-American Music,* George R. Keck and Sherrill V. Martin, eds., (New York, 1988), p. 50.

5. Michael Tomlinson, "Contemporary Christian Music Is *Christian* Music," *Ministry* 69 (September 1996), p. 26.

6. Harold M. Best, *Music Through the Eyes of Faith* (San Francisco, CA, 1993), p. 42.

7. Harold Byron Hannum, *Christian Search for Beauty* (Nashville TN, 1975), p. 51.

8. Ibid., p. 112.

9. Ibid., p. 50.

10. Ivan Vandor, "The Role of Music in the Education of Man: Orient and Occident," *The World of Music* 22 (New York, 1980), p.13.

11. An evidence of this is the furor caused in the United States, when, in the mid-1980s, it was suggested that popular music recordings should carry some kind of warning label regarding explicit, pornographic, and violent lyrics—let alone music.

12. Donald Jay Grout, *A History of Western Music,* Rev. ed. (London, England, 1973), p. 7.

13. Confucius in *The Wisdom of Confusius,* ed. Lin Yutang (New York, 1938), 251-272.

14. See, for example, the writings of the early church fathers such as Basil, John Chrysostom, and Jerome in Oliver Strunk, *Source Readings in Music History: Antiquity and the Middle Ages* (New York, 1965), pp. 64-72.

15. Ibid., 79-86.

16. Alan P. Merriam, *The Anthropology of Music* (Chicago, IL, 1964), p. 218.

17. For example, Ellen G. White, *Testimonies for the Church* (Mountain View, CA, 1948), Vol. 4, p. 653.

18. Clyde S. Kilby, *Christianity and Aesthetics* (Chicago, IL., 1961), p. 24.

19. Frank E. Gaebelein, *The Christian, the Arts and Truth: Regaining the Vision of Greatness,* ed. D. Bruce Lockerbie (Portland, OR, 1985), p. 56.

20. This view is still strongly presented in Jacques Maritain, *Creative Intuition in Art and Poetry,* Bollingen Series 35, no. 1 (New York, 1960), pp. 374-376; John W. Dixon, Jr., *Nature and Grace in Art* (Chapel Hill, NC, 1964), pp. 61, 70, 73, 76 and 200; Winfried Kurzschenkel, *Die Theologische Bestimmung der Musik* (Trier, Germany, 1971), pp. 328-334. The subject has been discussed in detail in Wolfgang H. M. Stefani, "Artistic Creativity and the Fall: With Special Reference to Musical Creativity," unpublished paper (Andrews University, Berrien Springs, MI, 1987).

21. Roger Sessions alluded to this general problem at the outset of a chapter on aesthetic criteria in his classic book, *Questions About Music* (New York, 1971), p. 124.

22. Frank E. Gaebelein (note 19), p. 74.

23. Ibid., pp. 74-75.

24. Ibid., p. 75.

25. Manfred Clynes, "On Music and Healing" in *Music in Medicine: Proceedings Second International Symposium on Music in Medicine, Ludenscheid, West Germany,* ed. J. Steffens (R. Spintge and R. Droh, 1985), p. 4.

26. Luke 16:8

27. Susanne K. Langer, *Feeling and Form: A Theory of Art* (New York, 1953), p. 27.

28. Gordon Epperson, *The Musical Symbol: An Exploration in Aesthetics* (New York, 1990), p. 75.

29. Manfred Clynes, *Sentics: The Touch of the Emotions* (New York, 1978), pp. 26-41.

30. Manfred Clynes, "When Time Is Music," *Rhythm in Psychological, Linguistic, and Musical Processes,* ed. James R. Evans and Manfred Clynes (Springfield, IL, 1986), pp. 184-5.

31. Ibid., 185.

32. Ibid. It is unfortunate that in an essay of this nature that all this cannot be practically illustrated. When presented in seminar form with musical examples, it proves very persuasive.

33. See, for example, Manfred Clynes, *Expressive Microstructure in Music, Linked to Living Qualities in Studies of Music Performance,* ed. Johan Sundberg (Royal Swedish Academy of Music, Stockholm, No. 39, 1983), pp. 120-122.

34. Perhaps a comparison could be drawn with the use of the word "no" said in different settings. (For example, in anger, in disbelief, in fear, and in defiance.) Notice that the same word is used, but the colorations of the voice communicate very diverse meanings and emotions.

35. Lance Morrow, "The Madness of Crowds," *Time* (August 9, 1999), p. 64.

36. Ibid.

37. See, Doug van Pelt, "Moshing for the Master," *Contemporary Christian Music* (February 1989), pp. 20-21.

38. *Contemporary Christian Music* (April 1989), 4.

39. See, for example, Gene Edward Veith, Jr., *The Gift of Art: The Place of the Arts in Scripture* (Downers Grove, IL., 1983), pp. 58-59, and Harold M. Best (note 6), p. 26.

40. See, for example, Bruno Nettl, "The Role of Music in Culture: Iran, A Recently Developed Nation," in *Contemporary Music and Music Cultures* by Charles Hamm, Bruno Nettl and Ronald Byrnside (Englewood Cliffs, NJ,1975), pp. 98-99 and Bruno Nettl, *The Study of Ethnomusicology: Twenty-Nine Issues and Concepts* (Urbana, IL, 1983), pp. 159,165.

41. Lois Ibsen Al Faruqi, "*Muwashshah:* A Vocal Form in Islamic Culture," *Ethnomusicology* 19 (January 1975), p. 1; and Donna Marie Wulff, "On Practicing Religiously: Music as Sacred in India," in *Sacred Sound: Music in Religious Thought and Practice,* ed. Joyce Irwin (*Journal of the American Academy of Religion Thematic Studies*, vol. 50, Chico, CA, Scholars Press, 1983), p. 149.

42. Robert L. Scranton, *Aesthetic Aspects of Ancient Art* (Chicago: University of Chicago Press, 1964), p. 28.

43. Paul Tillich, *Theology of Culture,* ed. Robert C. Kimball (New York, 1959), p. 42.

44. This aphorism was developed during the writing of the author's doctoral dissertation. It is not really a new idea. It is simply a rewording of the biblical principle from Proverbs 23:7 "As a man thinketh in his heart, so is he." KJV and Luke 6:45 "Out of the abundance of the heart the mouth speaketh." KJV

45. J. H. Kwabena Nketia, *African Gods and Music* (Legon, Ghana: Institute of African Studies, University of Ghana, 1970), pp. 11-12.

46. Lois Ibsen Al Faruqi, "What Makes 'Religious Music' Religious?" in *Sacred Sound: Music in Religious Thought and Practice,* ed. Joyce Irwin (*Journal of the American Academy of Religion Thematic Studies*, vol. 50, Chico, CA, 1983), 28.

47. Ibid.

48. The implications of this transcendent/immanent contrast are profound for the Christian setting and are discussed in detail in the writer's doctoral dissertation, *The Concept of God and Sacred Music Style: An Intercultural Exploration of Divine Transcendence/Immanence as a Stylistic Determinant for Worship Music with Paradigmatic Implications for the Contemporary Christian Context* (Ph.D. dissertation, Andrews University, Berrien Springs, MI, 1993), pp. 218-270.

49. Paul Tillich, *Systematic Theology* (Chicago, IL, 1951), vol 1, p. 40.

50. See, for example, Harold M. Best (note 6), p. 42; and Nick Mattiske, "What Would Jesus Think of Today's Music?" *The Edge* 16 (*Record* Supplement, March 4, 2000), p. 5.

51. Titus Burckhardt, *Sacred Art in East and West: Its Principles and Methods,* trans. Lord Northbourne (London, England, 1967), p. 7.

52. Ibid.

53. Risieri Frondizi, *What Is Value? An Introduction to Axiology,* 2nd ed. (La Salle, IL, 1971), p. 29.

Chapter 14
FROM ROCK MUSIC
TO
THE ROCK OF AGES
by
Brian Neumann

Brian Neumann is a South African musician who spent 16 years of his life in the Rock-Pop industry before returning to the Seventh-day Adventist church. He worked as a vocalist, guitarist, composer, and performer, both in Europe and South Africa. *Polydor Records*—one of the largest international recording companies in Germany—signed up his band *The Reespect*, and released the popular record, "She's so Mystical."

During this time his band appeared with musicians such as Elton John, Janet Jackson, and the Communards. As a musician Neumann had the opportunity of working in some of the best studios available in the recording industry.

Since his conversion, Neumann has done extensive research into the language of music and its mental, physical, and spiritual effects. At present he performs and conducts music seminars across Africa, Europe, Canada, and the United States.

My spiritual pilgrimage from rock music to the Rock of Ages is a painful story of addiction, self-destruction, and final redemption. Sharing this painful experience is like opening a wound that is healing. Yet it is my hope that this pain can have a healing effect in my life and a redeeming influence on the life of others.

I was born in Malawi, Africa, on March 25, 1961, after Bill Haley and "The Comets" burst onto the scene in the fifties with "Rock Around the Clock." At that time, no one dreamed that rock 'n' roll would, indeed, rock till the hands of the prophetic clock struck midnight. Bible students who look down the prophetic unfolding of the end-time signs can sense more than just the irony behind this statement by Nick Paul: "Perhaps rave truly is the music at the end of the world."[1]

From the early pioneer days of Elvis, Little Richard, and a whole host of other pop-rock celebrities to the present trends of rap, techno, and rave, we can still feel, almost to the very core of our bones, the *"shake, rattle, 'n' roll"* of that driving essence behind nearly all forms of popular music—the beat.

How Rock Music Entered My Life

Born into the home of a Seventh-day Adventist missionary couple, in the heart of Africa, it seems absurd that I, their youngest son, would ever find my way into the world of rock. Yet it happened. By the time I had reached the age of three, we had moved near Cape Town, South Africa, and my mom and dad were divorced. I felt rejected and cheated; and the circumstances of my life were just right for me to begin taking a course that would lead me further and further from the faith of my birth. Let me tell you how it all began.

Until 1976, we did not have television in South Africa. Thus, my early exposure to popular music was through radio and the records that my friends bought and shared with me. I come from a fairly protected environment in my Adventist home, so I was seldom exposed to the sounds of rock music. My introduction to rock music was very gradual. One song led to another, and soft rock led to heavier rock.

In a short time, my natural love for music and art was channeled into the swirling, psychedelic "pipedream" of 70s rock. Instead of the meek and lovely Jesus, my new heroes were pop stars who came and went as pawns in the hands of Satan—Jimi Hendrix, The Rolling Stones, Pink Floyd, Uriah Heep, Led Zeppelin, Carlos Santana, and Deep Purple, to name a few. They became my role models. They took drugs, so I took drugs. They were obsessed with sex in their dark existence, so I made sex a driving force of my life also. Some rock stars dabbled in the occult, so I, too, became fascinated with the Devil. By the time television hit South Africa in the mid 70s, my mind was made up. I would no longer live according to the values my family had taught me.

Rock music soon became my heart and soul, the ultimate language to express my values, goals, and lifestyle. As for countless other young people, rock music became the medium through which I could express my rebellion against the values of my family, the church, and society.

In a relatively short time, I became hooked to the "groove," to the whole idea and philosophy that drove the thundering freight train of rock. My mind and body became completely captivated. I was captured by the power, the clothes, the fame, and the sheer global presence of the rock revolution.

My addiction to rock music became so strong that I desperately sought to satisfy my craving by constantly listening to, feeling, and feeding on the hypnotic beat. Soon I found myself almost bodily severed from the world and religious faith of my parents. A new era, a new culture, had taken center stage in my life—as it has done in the lives of many others.

A Life of Rebellion and Isolation

The rebellion and isolation that rock music brought to my life gave prophetic realism to the words of rock star David Crosby: "I figured the only thing to do was to swipe their kids. By saying this I'm not talking about kidnapping, I'm just talking about changing the value system, which removes them from their parents' world very effectively."[2]

Rock music did remove me effectively from my parent's world. Before I was out of my teens, I had run away from boarding school, run away from home, been arrested by the police for drugs and theft, and fought, sometimes physically, with fellow students and teachers. My mother's heart was broken. At that time, it was hard for her to see any light at the end of the tunnel, yet she persevered in constant prayer and faith, trusting that some day a radical change would occur.

Even if I had understood the mind-bending power of rock music, most likely it wouldn't have made any difference. I still would have chosen against any better judgment to do "my own thing." Doing *"your own thing,"* of course, is an oxymoron, because "doing your own thing" invariably entails following the dictates of popular trends. Most kids who tell their parents, *"I want to do my own thing,"* are saying in reality that they want to do what the other kids are doing. They don't want to be the odd ones out.

In my case, doing my own thing meant expanding my recently discovered musical talents into the psychedelic world of popular music. My dream was to learn to play the guitar, which I was doing with haste, so that I could work my way into the glamorous world of 'sex, drugs, fashion, and rock 'n' roll.' Of course, I knew—or thought I knew—that this was what it was all about. The advertising, the lyrics, the fashion, and the lifestyle of my heroes sent a loud and clear message. The manager of the Rolling Stones once stated unequivocally: "Rock IS sex. You have to hit teenagers in the face with it!"[3] Without question, rock hit me with full force.

It is well known that rock 'n' roll is deeply ingrained in sex and the avenues of the occult. For example, in 1994, two issues of the South African metal magazine, *Ultrakill*, carried a back-page article entitled, "The Truth about the Devil." It stated: "We've got Satan, Beelzebub, Satan, the Serpent, and lord of misrule. There is a musical connection with all of this. Even before heavy metal, the Devil took an interest in rock 'n' roll. The very term rock 'n' roll started life as a Black American expression for sex. And sinful procreation has been the Devil's province for a long, long time."[3]

How Rock Music Rocked My Life

For those who do not understand the mechanisms at work in rock, it is difficult to perceive how something as apparently innocuous as music can have such life-altering effects on those who expose themselves to its influence. Right from the very beginning, I sensed the effects of rock on my mind and body.

Years later, I learned the scientific reasons for the physiological and psychological effects of rock music. Discovering these scientific reasons was no real enlightenment to me. I had already lived and experienced the hypnotic mind-bending power of rock. All that I learned, and am still learning, just serves to corroborate what I painfully experienced during those years I spent listening to and performing rock music.

I was first exposed to heavy rock in the early 1970s. It immediately grabbed my attention and it was impossible for me to break away from it. I religiously was absorbing the relentless, pulsating beat of rock. It caused an incredible adrenaline rush in my body and evoked the feeling of reckless abandon and fearless confidence. I knew, even then, that barring a divine act, I would never be liberated from its grip on my life.

Suddenly, everything became possible, and not only possible, but also acceptable. This was the age of free sex and drugs promoted by the world of rock. I wanted to be a part of this dreamworld. The music had a strange ability to break down the walls of resistance in my mind and opened me up to the idea of drug experimentation and a whole host of other things. The music itself had become a drug to me.

In reality, I didn't need any other mind-altering substances. The music itself created a "high" of its own. Of course, this did not diminish my need for other "real" drugs. Rock only increased my desire to push the adrenaline high to its outer limits. The combination of rock and dangerous narcotics made it possible to reach ecstatic "highs." That which had been wrong suddenly became right; that which was right became either boring or wrong. It is hard to believe how rock and drugs can impair and even destroy one's moral conscience.

From the early days of rock, all of the big stars have known that rock music has the ability to hypnotize and weaken the moral resistance of people. Jimi Hendrix himself explicitly stated: "Atmospheres are going to come through music, because music is a spiritual thing of its own. You can hypnotize people with the music and when you get them at their weakest point, you can preach into the subconscious what you want to say."[5]

Rock music and popular culture preached to my subconscious that nothing was wrong with pre-marital sex. The result became evident in 1980; one year after finishing high school, my girl friend became pregnant and gave birth to a baby girl. Indeed, having children out of wedlock is one of the most common characteristics in rock culture. The very terminology connected with the rock culture has strong sexual or demonic overtones. For example, the terms *jazz, rock 'n' roll, groovy, mojo, funky,* and *boogie* all have sexual or demonic overtones.

Climbing the Rock Ladder

After the birth of our daughter, which we gave up for adoption, I was busy establishing myself on the local music scene in South Africa. "Front Page" was the name of the band I was with, and we were appearing on television. Our music was played on some of the popular radio stations. We were touring and performing, and having radio and newspaper interviews. To all intents and purposes, we were climbing the ladder to the "top of the stack."

Drugs had become a natural part of my life, and my interest in the occult which had begun in my youth was by now a full-blown obsession. Astrology, numerology, and other occult practices became the order of the day. Although I was climbing the ladder to rock success, I was falling fast into the downward spiral of rock 'n' roll outer darkness.

By the age of fourteen, I had had my first encounter with the spirit world. My Seventh-day Adventist background made me forcefully aware of the fact that I was playing with fire, but the desire for the fame, money and high life of the popular rock culture had become so overpowering that I was ready to sell my soul for the opportunity to be a part of it.

This was literally the price I was prepared to pay. One day in my room at Helderberg High School I poured my heart out to my lord—but my lord was no longer Christ. I made a promise to the Devil that if he helped me to fulfill my dream, I would give my life to his service.

Germany: From the Top to the Bottom

In 1980, I was becoming known in the professional field of popular music. For a time I performed with the popular local band Trapeze. Soon I was invited to join the prestigious Front Page, and through the group I established a strong friendship with Manlio Celloti, a leading Italian producer of HI-Z Studios in Cape Town. Cellotti was instrumental in forming a new three-member band which became known as The Reespect. Two members of the band had performed with The Boys—a popular band that had a hit with the song called "Fire."

After a year in the studio recording music for new albums, we were invited to perform in Germany. In February 1986, I found myself on a flight to Europe and to new horizons in my pursuit of musical euphoria. I met there with the other two band members and Manlio, our new producer and our manager.

Within three months of arriving in Germany, our rock band The Reespect signed a contract with *Polydor Records* in Hamburg. (We inserted the extra 'e' in the name of our band in order to give it a luckier numerical value.) This prestigious record company handled record releases for such bands as The Beatles, Level 42, Chris de Burg, and many other rock bands.

In 1986, *Polydor* released our first album "She's so Mystical" and then "Mamma Mia." The release of these albums opened new doors of opportunity for us. We were invited to appear on a German LP compilation of various hits with such artists as Janet Jackson and Elton John.

Our keyboard player, Thomas Bettermann, had come from the famous international jazz ensemble Volger Kriegel, Mild Maniac. He became a regular part of all our composition and studio work. In September 1986, we were flown from Cologne to Hamburg for a major recording convention. At the airport, we were met by a *Polydor*'s representative in an oversized black limousine. It looked like we were on our way to the "big time."

Life became a constant mirage of performances, studio sessions, interviews, women, drugs, and more drugs. By this time, my moral state had deteriorated to such a point that no type of vice was beyond me. The success of our recordings caused dissension among our band members, our egos clashed, and our different musical ideas, which had initially worked to our advantage, now began to pull us apart. Eventually we broke up.

I launched into a solo career that found me in more studios doing session work. Session work is like free-lance performance where one is hired to do recording or live performance for different bands or studios. With this change, my drug intake increased.

As you can imagine, by this time my life had turned into moral wreckage. Paradoxically, in my twisted New Age concept of religion, I thought I had reached a kind of spiritual nirvana. In reality, I was scraping the bottom of spiritual darkness. Faintly, at times, I would glimpse the rays of true light that would flicker in, and I would grasp pathetically at them, only to let them go and then find that the light was getting dimmer and dimmer.

It was at this time in my career that after a marathon studio session and a huge drug binge in Hamburg, I one day found myself face down on a cold bathroom floor in the home of a female vocalist. I was drowning in my own vomit, fighting for my life, and calling out to the God of my youth whom I had long since neglected.

This was the most important life/death struggle of my life. For hours I fought against the clutches of darkness that threatened to engulf me. My body was loaded with four days of hash, speed, cocaine, and heroin. Had it not been for God's compassion and providential help, the battle for my life would have been lost right then. But God heard my cry of desperation and, though I deserved no grace, He snatched me from the edge of the precipice and gave me another chance.

The Return to South Africa: A New Beginning

Something happened that day in Hamburg, Germany. My helpless condition made me realize that there is only one God and only one true way to life and happiness. I sensed that in His mercy, God was willing to forgive my sinful past and accept me back like the Prodigal Son. My spiritual journey had taken an important turn, but this was only the beginning of a tortuous journey. Many times I experienced a relapse into rock music before I gained complete freedom from its addiction.

The first important step I took was to cancel all my previously accepted engagements for recording and performing in Germany. I decided to return to South Africa to start my new life. Unfortunately, my sudden decision disappointed and hurt quite a few people. My Swedish girlfriend, my producer, and my flat mate were all affected by my urge to "just get out."

But the peak of the mountain remained hidden from sight. The seventeen years I had spent performing rock and doing drugs had taken its toll. Looking back, I realize that not only the drugs and decadent lifestyle had consumed my body. The most important factor in the equation was the rock music itself that instigated all sorts of evil in my life.

It is impossible to describe the devastating effects of rock music on my spiritual, moral, and physical life. The rock beat, apart from the lyrics, attacked all the sensibilities of my organism with a relentless demonic force. This has been true not only for me, a relatively unknown individual, but for all the countless numbers of celebrated victims in the massive swimming pool of rock 'n' roll.

The famous rock star David Bowie, with almost prophetic insight, warned: "I believe rock 'n' roll is dangerous, it could very well bring about a very evil feeling in the West . . . it's got to go the other way now, and that's where I see it heading, bringing about the dark era. . . . I feel that we are only heralding something even darker than we are. Rock 'n' roll lets in lower elements and shadows that I don't think are necessary. *Rock has always been the Devil's music, you can't convince me that it isn't.*"[6]

Numerous rock stars have spoken unequivocally about the destructive effects of the rock beat on the human organism. John Lennon himself stated: "Rock 'n' Roll is primitive and has no bull. . . . It gets through to you. Its beat comes from the jungle—they have rhythm."[7]

Punk Rock manager Malcolm McLaren declared: "Rock 'n' Roll is pagan and primitive, and very jungle, and that's how it should be! The moment it stops being those things, it's dead . . . the true meaning of rock is sex, subversion, and style."[8]

From Hard Rock to Christian Rock

The return to my native South African soil left many loose ends untied overseas. These problems did not worry me because I was determined to break away from my sinful past and forge a new life. I decided to follow the example of Contemporary Christian Musicians by using my musical talent and a modified version of rock music as a witnessing tool.

Instead of perverted lyrics, I began writing songs with a strong prophetic, spiritual message that was biblically based. The style of music was a mixture of funk, rock, rap, and commercial pop. Like many other CCM artists, I believed I could reach especially the younger generation by presenting to them the message of the Gospel through the rock medium which they readily recognized and accepted.

Here I liken my musical compromise to a customized car. The interior of my vehicle was done up in the fabric of a Christian message, the body work was graffitied with the dazzling paintwork of rock 'n' roll, and the windows were tinted with the dark shadows of semi-spiritual blindness. No one could really see inside the vehicle I was driving. I never realized, at the time, how inadequate my spiritual vision was.

In spite of my spiritual blindness, I sincerely felt that the Lord was leading me in a new avenue of service for Him. The reasoning and logic behind my choices and the decisions I was making appeared deeply sincere and coherent to me, and the encouragement I received from those who were blessed by my ministry confirmed my convictions.

Like Paul, I wanted to become "all things to all men, that I might by all means save some" (1 Cor 9:22). This logic is used today by Christian artists who create modified versions of rock music to witness to the world. Unfortunately, they fail to understand that to become all things to all men does not mean to compromise the purity and principles of the Gospel.

Nowhere does the Bible suggest that to effectively witness to the world we must use the world's methods. On the contrary, the Bible teaches: "Do not be mismated with unbelievers. For what partnership have righteousness and iniquity?" (2 Cor 6:14). The application of this principle calls for courage to dissociate from the various forms of evil promoted by rock music.

Once one accepts that the road to compromise is always progressive, then one must recognize sin in his or her life for what it really is. And when convicted of sin, the next step is repentance. Once one has repented, all would seem like a load of emptiness if that repentance were not accompanied by true conversion—the putting off of the old and the taking on of the new.

To experience the renewing power of the Holy Spirit, we need to heed His convicting voice and toss out the garbage hidden in our closet in order to make room for purity and holiness. James reminds us that "Friendship with the world is enmity with God. Therefore whoever wishes to be a friend of the world makes himself an enemy of God" (Jam 4:4). It took me time to learn this important lesson. Needless to say, my pilgrimage from rock music to the Rock of Ages was a rocky one.

Changing the Lyrics Is Not Enough

When I left my rock-music career behind to begin composing and performing "Christian Rock," much had changed in my life. However, the very thing that had captured me in the first place still remained. I was addicted to the rhythm of rock music itself. It had chained me down more than all my other vices put together. The lyrics are very important, but the most powerful element of rock music is its beat.

So many Christian artists try to justify the use of rock in Christian services by the futile, illogical attempt of changing the lyrics. That had become my pitfall, too. I failed to realize that I could not legitimately reach the secular world by using a language that has been proven to be disastrous.

Christ mixed with the outcasts in order to reach them, but He never once sacrificed His moral principles to attract those He was ministering to. He did not dress like a prostitute in order to reach one. He never became a drunkard to reach the alcoholics. He did not practice dishonesty to please the tax collectors. He did not sing sensual music in order to excite people physically. In all circumstances, He set an example of pure, refined, and unblemished conduct. It was His life of purity and integrity combined with the convicting power of the Holy Spirit that touched the lives of so many.

Secular Rock and "Christian" Rock

In spite of contrary claims, no significant difference exists between secular rock music and its "Christian" version. Why? Simply because both share the same musical rhythm and are driven by the same relentless beat. Contemporary Christian Music in its rock, rap, rave, jazz, metal, or related forms shares the same accentuated, syncopated, and persistent rhythm of the "rock beat." Other aspects may also be shared, but the beat is the real heart and soul of it.

Irrespective of its lyrics, Contemporary Christian Music that conforms to rock's essential criteria in any sense cannot be legitimately used for church worship. The reason is simple. The impact of rock music, in whatever version, is through its music, and *not through its lyrics.*

Some argue that so-called "Soft Rock" should not be placed in the same category as the other harder forms of rock. This is not true. A lot of soft rock, although slower in nature, still carries a consistent, syncopated beat and often overaccentuates it. Another important point to consider is the expression, atmosphere, and delivery of soft rock.

Lyrics sung in a breathy, over-sentimental tone suggest an atmosphere of love or lust between a man and woman. These hardly provide an appropriate medium to express love to a Holy God. I am not talking only about lyrics here, but also of atmosphere and tone. All words, whether spoken or sung, are delivered in a unique tone to convey a special intent.

Music designed to express love for Jesus should conform to what the Greeks call *agape*–love, which is unselfish—and not to what is termed *eros*–love, which is erotic and self-centered. When choosing our Christian music today, we have to exercise great care and discernment because not everything that comes with a Christian label attached to it is necessarily Christian. This is true even if it does not have a heavy beat.

Music as an Evangelistic Crutch

Contemporary Christian Music is seen by many as an effective medium to convert people to Christ. Surprisingly, however, nothing in the Bible or in the history of the church indicates that music was ever used as an evangelistic tool. The primary function of music is to worship and praise God. It is the lack of faith in the power of the Holy Spirit that has made music for many an essential crutch for evangelizing unbelievers and entertaining believers. *The result is that our worship services are becoming spirited rather than spiritual.*

Some have supplanted the power of the Holy Spirit with the hypnotic spirit of music. They have been so blinded by the magical power of popular music that they now eagerly accept the lie as if it were the truth. I speak frankly on the deceptive power of rock music in all its forms, because I have been deceived by the same lie and know exactly how easy it is to fall into this trap.

Had I retained Contemporary Christian Music as one vital link to the world of rock, it would have been just a matter of time before I would fool myself into "comfortable Christian compromise" or fall right back into the world of secular rock once again. Only a radical break from rock music cured me from this addiction. It took me years to learn that lesson.

From "Christian" Rock Back to Secular Rock

My radical break from rock music was a gradual process, especially since upon returning to South Africa I had embarked on a "Christian" rock ministry. This lingering attachment to rock music proved to be my downfall. Slowly I slipped back into milder drugs. I convinced myself that marijuana was not so bad because it is a natural drug, used ritually by indigenous native tribes as a peace-inducing herb. I began compromising also on the kind of music I was performing. The compromise was easy because all I had to do was change the lyrics. The music style remained the same. In spite of my good intentions, I found myself gradually spiraling back into complete darkness.

It was not long before I reestablished my rock career in Cape Town. By 1989 I became recognized as one of the national top guitarists and was respected as a competent songwriter. I became very active on the local, live-music scene, building up a following of people who enjoyed my technical rock-guitar style and who were looking for something new and original. Weeks turned into months, months became years, and the endless cycle of clubs, drugs, and socializing all but killed the spark of hope that once was ignited in a foreign land.

Paradoxically, spirituality still remained an important aspect of my life. I could spend hours writing about the depths to which I had sunk, while still convincing myself that I was having some deep spiritual experience. One reason was that I had sworn I would never get involved with heavier drugs again, like cocaine and LSD. But somewhere along the line, that promise was broken.

At some parties and during moments of willful weakness, I began sharing a line of cocaine or two, a cap of acid here and there, and a spot of hash if it were available. The compromises became endless and covered almost every aspect of my existence, which in essence was encapsulated in that well worn-out rock 'n' roll slogan, "*Sex and drugs and rock 'n' roll.*"

The Second Turning Point of My Life

In 1992, I experienced the second turning point. The Lord used two persons to influence my life in a tangible and permanent way. One of them was Sue, the young lady who eventually became my wife. The other was the baby girl given up for adoption at birth and who I had dreamed of meeting for many years.

I met Sue for the first time in 1988 in Cape Town, at a live concert in which I was performing. We met again a year later at a restaurant where she was a waitress, not realizing that we were the same two people who had met a year before. Both times we were attracted to each other.

In 1990, almost two years after meeting Sue, I had the opportunity of meeting my daughter who had been adopted almost ten years earlier by an Adventist family, Pastor Tinus Pretorius and his wife Lenie. I immediately fell in love with my daughter Leonie, as her adoptive parents had named her. I could see so much of myself in her, and felt a strange, new emotion that I had never experienced before.

Under normal circumstances, such a meeting would never have taken place. When a child is given up for adoption in South Africa, the biological parents lose their rights to see her or him again. But the kindness and caring attitude of this pastor and his wife cannot be overestimated. Within less than a year of their first visit with me, they moved with my daughter down to Cape Town. Pastor Tinus was assigned to two local Seventh-day Adventist churches. This new relationship had a tremendous impact on my life, causing me to consider once again my destitute spiritual condition.

Right at this time, I received an offer from a lady friend with strong connections to the music industry in Los Angeles to continue my music career in the United States. The potential opportunities were too tempting to turn down, and I made all the necessary arrangements to leave at the earliest opportunity. But God had other plans for my life.

Sue learned about a prophecy seminar being held near our home. We decided to attend the meetings. I was hoping to learn something new that I could use in the music recording that I was working on.

At the prophecy seminar, I learned far more than I bargained for. As a result of those meetings, I canceled my ticket and travel arrangements to the United States. Within two months, Sue and I were baptized into the Seventh-day Adventist church. Everything seemed to be just right. The new-found truths satisfied our deepest convictions. Yet, just three months later, we were out of the church. Rock music was still in my soul. Once again, I was performing on a stage across the country with my electric guitar slung around my neck, churning out the message of rock 'n' roll to captive audiences wherever I went.

No misery is worse than knowing the truth and yet running away from God's sanctifying power. Rebellion, compromise, and sorrow followed the few steps I had taken toward Christ. But I thank God that He never gave up on me. In spite of my timid steps toward Christ, I had not been willing to be broken on the Rock.

The Final Turning Point

It is hard to believe how many times I relapsed into the rock scene before gaining permanent freedom. I had once again compromised myself right back into my previous existence as a rock musician. The only way I knew to survive was to play music. I didn't have the faith in Jesus that I needed to see me through making a radical break with the music scene, even if it meant financial loss for a while. The apparent issue of survival became the mechanism the Devil used to trap me once again.

At this time, I formed my own band called "Project Cain," a fitting name for my spiritual despondency. I was busy recording with Duncan Mckay, the popular keyboard player of the famous band 10 CC, when I received a call to go to Port Elizabeth, a city located about 700 miles north of Cape Town. The contract called for me to perform there for three months. I was hired as a solo rock artist performing six nights a week at one of the top night spots in the city.

Port Elizabeth became the final turning point of my spiritual pilgrimage. I rented a house far out in the country near a beautiful, isolated beach. Since my performances were at night, I had time during the day to wander along the beach and reflect on all that had transpired in my life for the past few years. I believe that this is where God wanted me to be.

Much of my professional life was spent surrounded by admirers and rock musicians. But at last I found myself on an isolated beach where God brought me face to face with my sinful past. During those three months, I sensed the Holy Spirit speaking to me as never before. Many days were spent on that lonely beach, examining the innermost recesses of my confused mind.

At times, the hidden truths of my wounded soul were very hard to face. I would break down in shameful anguish and allow the tears of repentance to flow like rivers of crystal clear water to wash away the stains of my sins. Sometimes I could almost feel the presence of the chiding and consoling Spirit of God bringing spiritual healing to my life.

The door of acceptance stood wide open. Finally, I boldly walked through it and closed behind me the door to my sinful and dark past. Upon my return home, in June 1994, Sue and I made the decision that by God's grace there would be no turning back into the world of rock. I severed all my business relationships with the rock-music scene. On January 15, 1995, we were married and decided to dedicate our lives to a special ministry on behalf of those who seek deliverance from the hypnotic power of rock music.

Helping Others to Find Deliverance from Rock

Today, I see myself as a grateful, living witness to what God can do for those who are willing to allow Him to change their lives and tastes. The goal of our ministry is to help Christians of all faiths to gain victory over their addiction to rock music and to develop appreciation for good Christian music.

During the past few years, I have traveled across Africa, Europe, and North America conducting seminars on "Music and Worship" at churches, schools, universities, hospitals, and many more venues. Whole churches have reconsidered their stand on the use of religious rock after learning *all the facts* about its mental, physical, and spiritual effects.

It has been a most gratifying experience for me to see people who once were fans of my rock music leaving behind forever the discordant atmospheres of rock and committing their lives to the Lord.

My deepest concern is for those who believe that rock music can be rightly used to worship God, as long as the lyrics are religious or speak about Jesus. I have witnessed the fallacy of this assumption time and again in my life and music ministry. Rock music, in whatever version, stimulates people physically rather than elevating them spiritually. I've seen the fruits of "Christian" rock in live concerts. They are essentially no different than those of secular rock. I have heard every possible justification for the use of this music in worshiping a holy God, but none of them is biblical.

Making Good Musical Choices

Experience has taught me that there is a danger in teaching people how to make good musical choices by providing them with a clear-cut classification of what I would consider appropriate listening music, both secular and religious. This does not mean that good musical choices are simply a matter of personal taste. Taste, whether stemming from a cultural or developed personal bias, must be subject to certain musical, psychological, physiological, and spiritual/biblical criteria.

In other words, just because I have developed a taste for heavy metal or listening non-stop to Mozart's requiem does not mean that these are good musical choices for me. Persons who have lost their taste for water because over the years they have conditioned themselves to enjoy whisky on the rocks are not in a position to argue that whisky is healthier than water.

We have all been desensitized through the popular media, and our ability to effectively discern between good and bad music (and a host of other things) has been seriously compromised. Thus, to make good musical choices, one is wise to ask five probative questions:

1. Does the music really have something worthwhile to say? Are real moral truths communicated lyrically and instrumentally in the message of the music? Or is the music bland, repetitious, or coarse?

2. What is the intention behind the music? Is it sending out a positive or negative message? When you listen to the music, do you find that it conforms to the criteria spelled out by Paul in Philippians 4:8 about thinking and listening to whatsoever is pure, lovely, gracious, and worthy of praise? Does the music elevate you spiritually or stimulate you physically? Answering these questions requires honesty and practiced listening.

3. Is the intention of the music being communicated effectively? In other words, is the musician as a communicator good at what he does? Does he or she generate an atmosphere of reverence or frivolity?

4. Are the musical instruments used suitable for communicating the intention of the music? For example, if the music calls for flowing, extended, melodious notes, are the instruments being used those that can produce only short, percussive tones?

5. Are we seeking the guidance of the Holy Spirit in our choice of both secular and religious music? We must remember that spiritual things can only be discerned spiritually. This means that we need the Holy Spirit to guide us in our choice of music. This is especially true today when we have been exposed to so much information, musical and otherwise, that has desensitized us.

We cannot rely solely on our judgment or taste when it comes to making good musical choices. We must allow the Holy Spirit to enlighten us on whether the music we are listening to has a spiritually uplifting effect, or is making a rebellious, depressive impact.

We need to be aware that it is not only heavy, beat-oriented music that can have a negative effect on us. Some other types of music with no beat whatsoever can dump us into the depths of depression. Some of these styles of music can be found in the classics, though they are usually recommended as alternative to modern pop and rock.

It is imperative to let the Holy Spirit guide us in rightly interpreting whether the *atmosphere* of a song is positive or negative. This does not mean that we put aside those guidelines that identify the objectionable aspects of rock music. What it means is that we will exercise our good judgment in tune with the guidance of the Holy Spirit. This process may very well lead us to discard a whole genre of music.

How to Make Radical Decisions Regarding Music

When faced with the challenge of making radical decisions regarding our music, a person may ask: "What then is there left to listen to if all the rock music I like has to go out the window?" Don't let this attitude get in the way. The devil would love to have us believe that rock is the only music worth listening to. The practical way of approaching the issue is first to look at the present situation from a different perspective, and then to consider our future course in a more positive light. Let me share five suggestions that can help you make radical decisions regarding music.

1. Decide to become an individual by making up your own mind regarding good music on the basis of real information and not from peer pressure or personal taste. You won't have to sacrifice your personal taste or special preferences. They will simply have to become sanctified and refined. You won't need to go back into the nineteenth century or the dark ages to please God and to live a life that respects the body temple.

It is simply a matter of getting rid of bad music while retaining good music. In this process, though you may get labeled as square or fanatic, it will show that you had the courage to stand for what you believe to be right and not follow the crowd. Indeed, you will then truly have become unique.

No one likes to be considered a sheep or zombie that follows the crowd without any individuality, yet this is the case with most people. It was true in my case. Nearly everything I did, as far as music, fashion, language, and attitude were concerned, was the direct result of pressure coming from popular trends. I was not an individual in the real sense of the word. I started to like rock because it was the "in" music to listen to. I wore what I did because fashion dictated that it was a "cool" way to look. In fact, *part of the reason why "Christian" Rock exists is that Christians are too scared to be different from the world.*

2. Consider your new musical choices to be an adventure, a process of discovery. Take time to define and refine your taste, to search out the musical gems in the pit of musical rot. Suddenly, you will discover that what you considered the only option in music was but a small fraction of the good music available. It may take some searching and prayerful listening, but in the end it will be worth it all.

3. Consider the five probative questions given above for making good musical choices and put them into practice when you listen to music. Search out and retain that which conforms to these basic rules. In that framework you will have room to exercise your own taste in music. Bear in mind that after years of exposure to negative types of music, your taste may have been perverted. Ask the Lord to help you recognize where your taste is defective. Once you feel sure that this has been revealed, do not hesitate to take the necessary step forward.

4. Listen carefully to lyrics to determine whether or not they are theologically sound. This is a very important exercise for it would be contradictory to have a lovely melody with lyrics that are totally unbiblical and insinuate an erroneous message. Ellen White correctly points out that a "song is one of the most effective means of impressing *spiritual truth* upon the heart," and can be effectively used to "proclaim the gospel message for this time."[9]

This means that the message of a song—words and atmosphere—must be tested by the teaching of Scripture. After all, a song can preach a sermon. It would be downright shameful if we allowed singing evangelists to get away with unsound doctrines in their lyrics, all in the name of freedom of expression and artistic license. Evangelism provides an ideal opportunity to combine the choosing of music with serious Bible study. What a great combination!

5. Choose songs with lyrics that concentrate on pure and ennobling aspects of life. Although a distinction remains between the music we use for worship and that for personal relaxation, the underlying principle of choosing that which is pure and ennobling remains the same. Consider Paul's admonition when making musical choices: "Finally, brethren, whatever is true, whatever is honorable, whatever is just, whatever is pure, whatever things are lovely, whatever is gracious, if there is any excellence, if there is anything worthy of praise, think about these things" (Phil 4:8).

CONCLUSION

My spiritual pilgrimage from rock music to the Rock of Ages gives me reason to believe that many sincere people are seeking for divine deliverance from the addiction of rock music. The good news is that the God who delivered me from the bondage of rock music is able to liberate anyone who turns to Him for help.

The many years I spent as a performer, first of secular rock and then of "Christian" rock, have fully convinced me that, in whatever version, rock music embodies a spirit of rebellion against God and the moral principles He has revealed. The defining characteristic of the various forms of rock music is and remains the driving, pulsating beat which can alter the human mind and stimulate the physical, sensual aspect of human nature.

Our challenge today is to follow the example of the three Hebrew worthies on the plain of Dura. They refused to bow down before the golden image at the sound of Babylonian music. May God grant us wisdom and courage to reject the music of Babylon and to worship with music that honors Him and ennobles our character.

ENDNOTES

1. Nick Paul, *Cosmopolitan Magazine* (March 1997), p. 76.

2. Peter Herbst, *The Rolling Stone Interviews*, Rolling Stones Press, 1981.

3. Manager of the Rolling Stones, *Time* (April 28, 1967), p. 53

4. *Ultrakill Magazine*, vol. 2 (1994), back page.

5. Jimi Hendrix, *Life* (October 3, 1969).

6. David Bowie, *Rolling Stone Magazine* (February 12, 1976), p. 83. Italics supplied.

7. John Lennon, *Rolling Stone Magazine* (January 7, 1971).

8. *Rock Magazine* (August 1983), p. 60.

9. Ellen G. White, "Freely Ye Have Received, Freely Give," *Review and Herald* (June 6, 1912), p. 253. Emphasis supplied.